CITIES OF GOD

Beginning with an account of how Christian theology is called upon to read the signs of the time, *Cities of God* traces the shift in urban culture in North America and Western Europe that took place in the 1970s. The modern sites of eternal aspiration and hope became the postmodern cities of eternal desires. The old, modern theological responses to the city become unbelievable and inadequate, necessitating a new theological approach to urban living. Such an approach would have to engage with and respond to the insurgent social atomism and the celebration of virtual realities evident in late-capitalist, postmodern civic living. The book seeks to develop that approach, emphasising the analogical relations which exist between physical, ecclesial, sacramental, social and political bodies. It argues for a profound participation of all these bodies in the Body of Christ. Working through analyses of contemporary film, architecture and literature, and drawing upon traditional theological resources in Augustine and Gregory of Nyssa, the book lays out a systematic theology which has the preparation and building of cities of God as its focus.

In the mid-sixties Harvey Cox published his famous theological response to urban living. Since then Christian theology has lacked a detailed theology of the city. The need for such a theology became highly evident with the publication of the 1985 Archbishop's Commission, *Faith in the City*, as theologians sympathetic to the project made clear. But the city was undergoing dramatic changes at the time. The shape and extent of those changes are now becoming evident; a theological response becomes possible. *Cities of God* offers the first detailed theological response to the city for thirty-five years.

Graham Ward is Professor of Contextual Theology and Ethics at the University of Manchester and executive editor of *The Journal of Literature and Theology* (OUP). He is the author of a number of books, including *Theology and Contemporary Critical Theory* (Macmillan), and the editor of *The Postmodern God* (Blackwell) and *The Certeau Reader* (Blackwell). He is the co-editor, with John Milbank and Catherine Pickstock of Routledge's *Radical Orthodoxy* series.

RADICAL ORTHODOXY
Edited by John Milbank, Catherine Pickstock
and Graham Ward

CITIES OF GOD
Graham Ward

DIVINE ECONOMY
D. Stephen Long

RADICAL ORTHODOXY
edited by John Milbank, Catherine Pickstock and Graham Ward

TRUTH IN AQUINAS
John Milbank and Catherine Pickstock

CITIES OF GOD

Graham Ward

London and New York

First published 2000 by Routledge
11 New Fetter Lane, London EC4P 4EE

Simultaneously published in the USA and Canada
by Routledge
29 West 35th Street, New York, NY 10001

Routledge is an imprint of the Taylor & Francis Group

© 2000 Graham Ward

Typeset in Baskerville by Taylor & Francis Books Ltd
Printed and bound in Great Britain by Clays Ltd, St Ives PLC

British Library Cataloguing in Publication Data
A catalogue record for this book is available from the British Library

Library of Congress Cataloging in Publication Data
A catalog record has been requested for this title

ISBN 0–415–20255–8 (hbk)
ISBN 0–415–20256–6 (pbk)

TO NEIL AND STEWART TO WHOM I
OWE SO MUCH AND ONLY NOW BEGIN
TO RECOGNISE, AND TO ALL THOSE
WHO WORKED ON *FAITH IN THE CITY*

CONTENTS

Preface   ix
Acknowledgements   x

Introduction: the signs of the times   1

PART I
Cultural atomism   **25**

1 Cities of eternal aspiration   27
2 Cities of endless desire   52

PART II
The analogical world-view   **79**

3 Transcorporeality: the ontological scandal   81
4 The displaced body of Jesus Christ   97
5 Communities of desire   117
6 The Church as the erotic community   152
7 The erotics of redemption   182

CONTENTS

PART III
Theology and the practices of contemporary living   **203**

  8 Cities of angels   205

  9 Cities of the good: the redemption of cyberspace   225

    Notes   261
    Bibliography   280
    Index   303

PREFACE

This book is an attempt, in the face of unprecedented social atomism and the deepening of virtual reality, to construct a new analogical world-view. It is a world-view which issues from, and continually returns to, the consideration of gendered embodiment in an urban context. An analogical world-view is, necessarily, a theological world-view. For the analogical cannot pertain to values and meanings which are only immanent. The analogical, to be *ana*-logical, requires a transcendent horizon. Analogical operations which appear to bear relationships between immanent meanings and values either require a univocity of being (and analogy dissolves when univocity is announced) or establish what Wittgenstein termed 'family resemblances'. These resemblances, like Derrida's principle of iteration, simply repeat the sign in another context. The relationship established is semiotic and pragmatic. Analogy establishes something more than this. The relationships it establishes are also semantic and tremulous with the intimation of a world-order. Analogy as *ana*-logical is theologically freighted. It bears the weight of a profound cosmological significance. It is profound because creation is related to an uncreated creator, who not only inaugurates but maintains a world-order within which analogy is an index of participation. The world as such is not brutally given; it is an artefact resonant through all its parts with intelligibility. It is cosmological because analogy traces an order that is dependent upon a creating God, an active God. Another way of saying what the concern of this book is, would be to suggest it is an attempt to construct a theological cosmology which does not ape or long to return to the analogical worlds of past times. This theological cosmology is composed here in the contemporary world. It is narrated out of the fragments of this contemporary world with its technological advances, its traumas, and its enchantments; its fears, its fantasies and its fetishisms. It is a Christian theological cosmology founded upon dwelling in analogical relation, in complex communities which constitute cities of God.

ACKNOWLEDGEMENTS

This has been a long project and several earlier versions of material have appeared in various journals and collections of essays: Grace Jantzen (ed.) *The Bulletin of the John Rylands Library* (1998); John Milbank, Catherine Pickstock and Graham Ward (eds) *Radical Orthodoxy*; Andrew Ballantyne (ed.) *Architecture and Sacrifice*; *Cultural Values*; and *New Blackfriars*. Over the years it has taken to research and write the book many friends, colleagues, students and critics have shaped my questions, honed my perceptions, directed my reading and enabled me to see connections. I would like to thank particularly Conor Cunningham, Robert Gibbs, Elaine Graham, Laurence Hemming, Grace Jantzen, Walter Lowe, John Milbank, Catherine Pickstock, Janet Soskice and Edith Wyschogrod (who asked me what I dared to risk). Throughout, my three teachers, whose presence I have internalised, stand like sentinels at the beginning and end of every sentence: Fergus Kerr, Nicholas Lash and Rowan Williams. They continue to inspire and provoke. As always Mary, Rachel and David provide the context out of which all my work emerges, but we are a family within a much wider family and I dedicate this book to my brothers Neil and Stewart and all those affected by Huntingdon's Chorea.

INTRODUCTION

The signs of the times

> Cities have reemerged not only as objects of study but also as strategic sites for the theorisation of a broad array of social, economic, and political processes central to the current era.
>
> (Sassen: 1994, 7)

This book was conceived in New Orleans and brought to birth in Manchester. In between there were flirtations with Sydney, Bonn, Amsterdam, Cape Town, San Francisco, and Jerusalem.[1] If it is only movie legend that the German film-maker Fritz Lang was inspired by the New York skyline, seen from an ocean liner, to direct *Metropolis*, it is recordable fact that my first glance of New Orleans, coming over the freeway from the airport, opened my eyes to the excitement of the city. Rising from the plain, as so many American cities do, its towers of polished glass and steel shimmering with the associations of jazz, voodoo and the New Jerusalem, New Orleans posed a question I could not at that time articulate. Returning to Manchester, a city in which I grew up and which I then rejected in a teenage flight to Oxbridge, the question began to take on form: what kind of theological statement does the city make today? This book is an attempt to answer that question.[2]

In the Jewish tradition, adopted by the later Christians, the first city was built by Cain as a monument to his first born son, Enoch. Much, theologically, can be read into that founding by a murderer as we will see when we examine some theological responses to the city (in Chapter 1). The first cities, archaeologists inform us, were founded by the Sumerians on that great stretch of fertile land between the Tigris and Euphrates. The earliest example of what can be termed urbanism is traced in the excavations of the fourth millennium BCE which tell of Warka, in the Near East, later known as Uruk and possibly Abram's Ur of the Chaldees (see Redman: 1978; Adams: 1981; and Maisels: 1993). And from here onwards cities have flourished, vanished beneath sands and floods, fallen into uninhabited ruins, or complexified to the point where they become holographs of time: Athens, Luxor, Rome, London, Berlin. They are the symbols of civilisation, the products of human aspiration and cultural endeavour, the

1

expression of the energies and fragilities of our existence. The city is human-kind's most sophisticated image of order: social order promoting personal order, and both concomitant with cosmic order. In the collocation of the city there are so many histories – of founders and buildings, of families and highways; histories personal, spiritual and material. Cities are both planned and lived, developed and experienced. Like the church described in a poem by Philip Larkin – and this is no insignificant comparison – the city is that place 'In whose blent air all our compulsions meet, / Are recognised, and robed as destinies'.[3] To examine the city theologically, therefore, is to examine at its most profound the question of being human, of being made 'in the image of God' (Genesis 1.26). As such this book writes another chapter in the history of Christian anthropology, starting not like Augustine (in his *Confessions*) with an examination of the individual,[4] but with the collective – the social and political bodies in which each individual body is implicated. To examine the city theologically is also to ask the question about orderings and correspondences between bodies, about what maintains and constitutes those orderings, those analogies. But exactly how do we do this? How do we examine what kind of a theological statement cities make?

The concerns of this book lie with the contemporary city. Insofar as that city inherits a geographical mapping and a monumentality from its past; insofar as that city has been shaped by past theological understandings and imaginings of what the significance of cities has been and is; insofar as walking through the present city is a passing through the time-frames, spacings and ideologies of the city that constitute the conceptual oxygen we breath whilst walking – then this book reviews that past. But the dominant concerns of the book lie with living in the contemporary city, and what that means theologically. How do the various bodies – physical, social, political, theological – relate and interpenetrate today in what I will call and define later as our current post-pluralism? And, methodologically, how do we approach answering that question?

The question of time

By way of answering *those* questions, let me suggest that the most difficult question Christian theology addresses is not the question about the nature of God. As Aquinas reminds us: God is not a proper name (*Summa theologiae* Q. 13, Art. 1, Pt. 1). Theology does not handle what God is; only what God is in relation to the world. The most difficult question theology addresses concerns that relation and that world. For traditional Western faiths – Judaism, Christian-ity and Islam – the question of that relation is a question about history and salvation. For these faiths the question becomes very specific; it becomes the question concerning 'What time it is?' There is a time to laugh and a time to cry, there is a time to love and a time to cease from loving. Time is the unfolding of God's grace, of God's gift of God's self in and through creation and our being created. Those involved with the living out of those faiths stand consciously enfolded in that unfolding. They stand not as self-grounded beings, nodes of

2

individual agency. They stand rather as those who come to stand within *this* time, rather than *that*, in *this* space rather than *that* space, moving and moved in *this* direction rather than *that* direction: constantly working out a salvation personal, national, ecclesial and global. For Christianity, and it is the Christian perspective that this book explores, that time (*kairos*) and that space are opened up by and in Christ. Christians live *for* the time they have been given to, to serve and to prosper, to redeem and be redeemed.

And so Christians must constantly ask 'What time is this in which we stand?' For this question in inseparable from 'What am I called to be and do?' and 'What is the will of God?' In turn these questions veer off into the larger theological fields of dogmatic inquiry – the doctrines of salvation, election and ecclesiology, the eschatological coming of the Kingdom, the work of the Spirit of Christ in creation, the nature of being made in the image of God, Christology etc.

To ask what time it is is to engage in analysis and assessment of a specific cultural situation; it is to observe the various phenomena and the significance given to them in a particular context and from a particular standpoint; it is to learn from those who study and interpret these phenomena from other standpoints. To ask what time it is is to work with social and critical theorists, grasping and evaluating their methods, assumptions, conclusions and observations about living in various parts of the globe today. To ask what time it is requires taking cultural studies seriously. But, to ask the question of time as a Christian theologian is not to treat time arbitrarily: asking about *this* time rather than *that* because this time is more interesting, or more useful, from one perspective among myriad time-zones, periods, epochs and eras. To ask about time as a Christian theologian is to accept that no time (nor any perspective) is arbitrary, that all time is time of and for redemption, all time is grace. And so the cultural analyses of a particular time have to be read in terms of past examinations of the mission and purpose of the Church, its teachings on the operation of salvation, its continual grappling with a faith seeking understanding. To ask what time it is is to begin to rewrite the teaching of the faith (and begin a teaching of the faith) for the contemporary cultural context; to reinscribe the cultural context within the Christian faith and so bear the Christian tradition into the future. This is the task of this book.

Determining the time

So what time is it? Who or what can tell us? For assistance, we might turn to one of the several cultural gurus on offer. Jean-François Lyotard characterises the time as postmodern (Lyotard: 1984); for Fredric Jameson the time is late-capitalist (Jameson:1991); Charles Jencks wishes to emphasise persisting aspects of what he terms 'late-modern' and 'high-modern' (Jencks: 1991); Gianni Vattimo speaks more generally of 'the end of modernity' (Vattimo: 1988). Attempting to delineate the cultural *Zeitgeist*, even provide a typology for it, inevitably involves simplifying; and sometimes the reduction involved leaves the dominant category-term itself (postmodern, late-capitalism etc.) suffocating in its own vacuity. While having, then, in previous books (Ward: 1996, 1998), worked within the schemas provided by these various analyses, drawn up maps of my own and suffered the intellectual guilt of knowing all the spaces cordoned betray the complexity of any singularity, this book attempts to work from analyses of specific cultural tropes.

What is meant by a trope with respect to contemporary culture, and more specifically urban culture? Broadly, I wish to examine contemporary culture (and cities within that culture) as composed of various kinds of writing through which worlds are produced. To explain further: There is an ancient connection between urbanism and writing.[5] The city as an administered and architectured organisation is only possible because of communication. Records needed to be kept, agreements and promises noted, contracts drawn up – memories scripted. The city's complexity is bound to the complexities of script and scribbling (or chiselling). In the accumulated debris of that early Sumeran city of Uruk was found the earliest known form of writing: tablets inscribed with a proto-cuneiform. As far as we can calculate, on the evidence available, the Sumerians invented writing around 3000 BC (Renfrew: 1989, 43). And the relevance of these tablets for the beginnings of urbanism are emphasised by archaeologists: 'their appearance is commonly believed to have been not merely coincidental with the rise of city life but, in conjunction with other factors, productive of city life' (Sweet: 1997, 37). Literature and literacy are urban phenomena. With the collapse of the classical city in the Late Roman Empire, when people in Western Europe began to leave the cities for rural conclaves, schools closed and literary culture declined (Liebeschuetz: 1992, 22). The symbiotic relationship between the city and writing would give rise to the writing of imaginary cities, ideal cities, cities of desire, literary cities. The city became a dominant symbol in literature – from Plato's *Republic* to Tom Wolfe's New York (1987), from Christianity's New Jerusalem to Marcel Proust's Paris (1981), from Judaism's Babel to Thomas Pynchon's San Narciso (1966). But it could do so because the city was already a living figure for the activities and economies of representation. The city produces and promotes itself through symbols and symbolic action – the building of this bridge, the election of this woman, the labour of this man, the schooling of this child. Urban culture issues from this symbolic production. As such, it is writing *par excellence*: the public inscription of several million upon its pavements and upon the lives of each other. The city itself is a writing within which all other writings are circumscribed. As such the city is a trope.[6] It is a text written by all those who walk down its streets, drive down its boulevards, plan its future, build its reputation and, more generally, impact upon its mapped out body.

But then how do we examine the dense complexity of this world of symbolic interconnectedness? I suggest we approach it through viewing certain aspects of its character as cultural metaphors. The analysis of these metaphors will be fundamental to this project. The metaphors themselves compose the very substance of the analogical world-view I wish to argue for and their analysis provides me with an account of the times we live in. They are the signs of the times which I wish to read from a Christian standpoint. In what follows, then, in this introduction I will, first, provide two accounts of such signs: (1) an examination of a Christian theology of signification, and (2) a narrative of the development towards a psycho-social semiotics through Freud and structural linguistics to Žižek. There are approaches to social semiotics which do not depend upon a psychoanalytical background, but I map this approach because of its fruitful correspondences, explored later in the book, with respect to Christians as subjects of desire (Butler: 1987). Then, secondly, I will sketch a methodology for the reading or interpretation of such signs. The analogical world-view I am proposing issues, methodologically, from reinscribing the urban symbolic production and exchange (as it is examined by various cultural theorists) within a Christian theology of signification. That is, reading the signs of the times through the grammar of the Christian faith.

Cultural metaphors I: a Christian theology of signification

Christians are called upon by Christ Himself to read the signs of the times. He rebukes the Pharisees and Sadducees who desired that he would show them a sign from heaven, saying 'O ye hypocrites, ye can discern the face of the sky; but can ye not discern the signs of the times?' (Matthew 16.3). Consistently Jesus refuses to give a sign (Matthew 12.39; Mark 8.12; Luke 11.29) for he is the sign of God's redemptive activity in the world. And the secret spring of faith lies not in demonstration but operation: being able to read the signs that are available correctly and work with them. To read them correctly, in fact, to recognise that a sign has been given, is to read objects and actions in the world analogically and eschatologically. Christ's own teaching, preaching and healing were the signs for those with ears. Being born of a Virgin, creating sight in a man born blind, riding into Jerusalem on a donkey, the parables themselves – these were all the giving and exchanging of signs for those able to read them. Furthermore, 'Take ye heed, watch and pray: for ye know not' (Mark 13.33), we are told; know not the time for the coming of the Kingdom. 'What sign will there be when these things shall come to pass?' the disciples request (Luke 21.7), speaking of the end of all signs in the final understanding of all things. Reading signs is a fundamental Gospel teaching. Learning what it means to be a disciple, participating in the way of salvation, recognising the advent question in the quotidian – these are all aspects of the theology of signs presented by the Gospels (see Ward: 1991, 1999). In John's Gospel the miracles outline a theology of the semiotic which follows the arrival of the Word itself as the tent of the *shekina* presence pitched among us (John 1.14). The miracles are manifestations of his glory – theophanies. They are theophanies communicated in, through and by signifying gestures; in, through and by a specific cultural idiom (water into wine at a wedding, the healing of a man born blind through the application of mud upon his eyes, the raising of Lazarus etc.). In these miracles Christ practises a social discourse – performs a set of signifying acts comprehensible to (and readable by) a specific social context which shared what Charles Taylor terms 'common and inter-subjective meanings'.[7]

With the increasing middle Platonic influence – which emphasised mediation and the movement beyond it, in contemplation, to the One – that theology of the semiotic became more pronounced. Augustine and Pseudo-Dionysius offer different perspectives on it. Augustine, the teacher of rhetoric, understands, as a poet, the weight of words. There are discussions on the relationship between signs and knowledge in several of his major works, notably *De dialectica* (AD 387) *De magisto* (AD 389), *De doctrina christiana* (AD 396), *Confessiones* (AD 398), *De trinitate* (AD 400–17). (For commentary, interpretation and critique see Jackson: 1969; Markus: 1975; Baratin: 1981; Louth: 1989; Williams: 1989; and Ferretter: 1998.) *De magisto*, though an early work much given to the portrayal of a gifted son (Adeodatus) who had died not long before the dialogue was composed, gives something of the breadth of Augustine's theological vision with respect to signs. Early in the dialogue Augustine tells his son, 'by speaking, we merely call something to mind since, in turning over the words stored therein, memory brings to mind the realities themselves which have words for signs' (Augustine: 1968, 9). Augustine's concept of memory is not Plato's teaching on recollection in *Meno*: God is ultimately the teacher, He gives us to know all things (the realities themselves) through an enlightening action from within which memory recalls. This knowledge is of two kinds – sensible knowledge and intellectual knowledge. The first is mediated and the second is innate, but with either form of knowledge it is the triune Godhead who gives us what we know and, with sensible knowledge 'our words do not refer to the things themselves, but to the images impressed by them upon the senses and stored away in memory' (Augustine: 1968, 53). These senses are the 'interpreters', for the mind alone is the proper cause of sensation (Augustine: 1968, 52). And we cannot engage in dialogue at all, we cannot communicate, unless the mind is directed by the sounds of the words, by signs (Augustine: 1968, 35). We live, then, in a world mediated to us, interpreted to us with respect to what Augustine, in *De trinitate*, will term the 'inner word' (Augustine: 1963, IX, vii, 12). This inner word stands in analogical relation to the Word of Christ, such that 'We may compare the manner in which our own word is made as it were a bodily utterance ... with that in which the Word of God was made flesh' (Augustine: 1963, XV, xi, 20). All signification, in order to become knowledge, has to be governed by an understanding of the eucharist, which itself is governed by the doctrine of the incarnation of Christ (Williams: 1989). We will return to this in chapters 3, 4 and 6. Christians have to learn to read the world, and can only communicate about it truly, by being enlightened as to the realities of things by the inner operation of God. This world is mediated through signs: 'there are signs which signify themselves; signs that signify each other mutually; signs that have the same extension; signs that differ only in the sound' (Augustine: 1968, 29). But the signs themselves are what Saussure will later term 'arbitrary'. They have no natural connection with the signified (the idea of the tree, for example, or the table). For words in and of themselves Augustine emphasises, in a lecture which concludes *De magisto*, give us nothing but themselves. We learn nothing from them *qua* signs. They operate as a self-referential and deferential matrix, 'they merely intimate that we should look for the realities' (Augustine: 1968, 49) – realities which have to be revealed to us by the operation of God within creation and the human soul. Governed by the Word of God the signs become sacramental – dense with mystery. Since, for Augustine, even a 'thing' is a sign, both in the sense that it is a word – *'rem, verbum est'* (Augustine: 1975, V) – and in the sense that the world is God's book – then all things only exist as they participate in the divine being, sustained in their contingency. What is only is *as* presented as sign. So our knowledge, of and through the reading of these signs, is partial and time-bound.

Pseudo-Dionysius speaks similarly of the Light which 'by way of representative symbols, makes known us to' all things. Creation is a gift and 'gifts are granted to us in a symbolic mode' he writes, so that we move 'through the perceptual to the conceptual, from the sacred shapes and symbols to the simple peaks of the hierarchies of heaven' (Pseudo-Dionysius: 1987, 146–7). Our perceptions are constituted in, as and by signs. Creation is itself a network of signifiers which compose a hymn of praise continually being offered up.

I could go on to detail how this theology of the sign, this theology of reading God's two Books – the Holy Scriptures and the Book of Creation (reading the latter through the former) – is prominent in the twelfth century with Hugh of St Victor[8] and in the thirteenth century with Aquinas.[9] The Jesuit theologians Henri de Lubac and Hans Urs von Balthasar, and the Jesuit historian and critical theorist Michel de Certeau, concur that in the late Middle Ages there was an opacification of the sign – associated with the rise of nominalism and the linguistics of William of Ockham. The sign is gradually secularised and understood as, at best, functional or, at worst, irrelevant to communication. It is this opacification, and secularity of the sign which is evident when we turn to more recent attempts to read the signs of the times theologically.

Since Schleiermacher's *On Religion: Speeches to its Cultured Despisers* (1799), Protestantism has sought to come to terms with the culture of modernity. In 1921, the German theologian Emil Fuchs gave expression to one of the dominant positions: 'God himself, is the supporting strength of culture, which is "culture" only so long as it is related to God, whether it is aware of it or not' (Fuchs: 1968, 310). A certain assimilation between the theological and the cultural is evident which renders the reading of the signs of the times difficult – for there is no critical distance. Furthermore, the recognition by Fuchs that this is 'a time when we are so oppressed by the full seriousness of all the questions of life and death' (Fuchs: 1968, 306) fails to be substantiated. It is self-evident, but Fuchs does not realise that given the identification of theology and culture this observation announces a failure not just in the cultural situation, but in theology itself.

7

Friedrich Gogarten *does* realise this implication and it is he, more that Bultmann or Barth, who makes a serious attempt to tackle the relation between contemporary culture and theology. His dialectical method, which radically distinguishes the theological from the cultural, enables him to speak of the crisis in culture and theology's obligation with respect to it. He, more than Bultmann and Barth, wrestled with reading the signs of the times. Speaking to the liberal Protestants, he testifies to 'the demise of your world' (Gogarten: 1968, 278). He inveighs against their over-investments in romantic historicism (with its beliefs in progress and evolution), the *Bildung* tradition, the liberal humanism that such investments fostered, and its cultural opportunism. Dialectics facilitate the critical distance: Gogarten speaks of the purity of Christianity, of the No which comes from a position beyond the things of this world 'and brings them and their worth completely into question' (Gogarten: 1968, 289). He speaks of a transcendence in utter judgement of cultural immanence, of an opposition between God and human beings. But if Fuchs' positions errs with respect to collapsing the distance needed for reading the signs of the times theologically, Gogarten errs in a similar, albeit, antinomous, direction. In a Weimar culture rich in expressive violence and rhetorical extravagance, a culture which in many ways, offers us a glimpse of a postmodern world that was forestalled by the Second World War (Toulmin: 1990), Gogarten can say very little about the signs that contextualise his thinking. At one point he speaks of his jubilation at reading Oswald Spengler's *Decline of the West* but, on the whole, there is no analysis of cultural phenomena, just a blanket condemnation of the cultural *per se* and the theological need to 'fulfill the crisis in our culture' (Gogarten: 1968, 287) by perpetuating 'the deepest skepticism, the darkest pessimism' (Gogarten: 1968, 289).

What is lacking in these early-twentieth-century attempts to read the signs of the times with respect to the grammar of the Christian faith is an analysis of culture itself. Schleiermacher is much more subtle here. What is absent is a theology of the sign itself. There is either, with Fuchs, an implicit symbolic philosophy (neo-Kantian in the sense developed by Wilhelm Humboldt), in which some divine reality is pointed to in and through the particular historically located symbols of any culture (the symbols themselves pointing but not participating in that divine reality). Or, with Gogarten, the signs are so divorced from Christian truth that, on the one hand, they blind and delude those without that truth while, on the other, they are rendered utterly worthless by those who speak from the position of the truth. The opacification and secularisation of the sign is evident in both positions.

I will refer to this again in later chapters when we revisit the premodern theologies of signification with respect to modern correspondence theories of the relationship between words and the world. For the moment what is significant is the tradition of Christian teaching on the nature of signs and how to read them, and the occlusion of that tradition in modern theology. But it is important to recognise that the recovery of what might be termed 'theological textuality' is not simply a nostalgic return to a neo-platonic view of the world.

Theological textuality is evident in the Bible. It is there inchoately in the words of Christ to the Pharisees on his entry into Jerusalem: 'I tell you, if these (the crowds) should hold their peace, the stones would immediately cry out' (Luke 19.40). Creation voices. It has never been silent. From the beginning creation announced to God its goodness. Neo-Platonism provided this voicing, this communication through the giving and receiving of signs, with a metaphysics. In the contemporary linguistic turn, the attention to signification, Christianity is again given an opportunity for continuing, for mapping out for today, for making intelligible for today, a theology of signification so fundamental to Scripture and in the traditional teaching of the Church. Such a theology makes possible a new analogical world-view.

The recent revival of interest in semiotics and grammatology not only recalls Christian theologians to the Church's traditional teachings on these things, it can assist Christian theologians in their most important task: reading the signs of the times. For cultures are, again, being read as symbolic systems; forms of behaviour are being interpreted in terms of symbolic fields; attention has increasingly turned, since Herder and Humboldt (Ward: 1995) to the develop-ment of a social semiotics. With roots in nineteenth-century anthropology – Feuerbach and Fraser, among others – we take up the story with respect to a line of thought concerning metaphor, cultural interpretation and what Noam Chomsky called 'deep-structures'. Christian theologians can learn from these social anthropologists and critical theorists not only what they themselves read into the signs of the times, but the ways in which they set about producing their readings.

Cultural metaphors II: the development of social semiotics

In 1900 Freud published his explorations into the structure of dreams. Influential in many ways, the book inspired a new movement in psycholinguis-tics. In particular, Freud (who frequently uses metaphors culled from speaking and writing to describe processes in the unconscious) wrote three methodological sections in *The Interpretations of Dreams* which outlined the 'characters and syntactic laws' of dreams (Freud: 1953, 217). He began by distinguishing between a dream's manifest and latent content. The first of these he called 'dream-content' and the second 'dream-thoughts'. His interest was in the latent content where the meanings of the dream lay. To approach this latent content he would work through the multiple strings of disparate thought which went into the formation of the dream, and discover one string which, out of them all, represented the content and was indispensable for the dream's interpretation (Freud: 1953, 280–1). In the representation of the content what struck the dreamer as most vivid constituted a nodal point in which the dream's meaning was concentrated. This point of psychic intensity (identifiable by the overdeter-mination of its figuration) was, for Freud, the knot of psychic value that had to

9

be untied. From his analysis of these figurations he proposed that the formation of any dream was governed by two main principles: condensation (*Verdichtung*) and displacement (*Verschiebung*). The focal figuration in a dream either synthesised a multiplicity of connections (condensation) or, because of the operation of an inner censorship concerning this dream content, substituted another figure in its place (displacement). In turn these two laws were related to the processes of identification (where the dreamer identifies with a person in the dream) and reversal (where the dreamer resists identification with any object, person or action). Freud commented that dream-formation highly favours 'the relation of similarity, consonance or approximation – the relation of the "just-as" ' (Freud: 1953, 319–20). In doing so he was drawing a parallel between the deep structures of consciousness and tropology or figures of speech.

The French psychoanalyst and theorist, Jacques Lacan claimed he was simply developing this analogy in Freud's work when he stated that the unconscious is structured like a language.[10] He was developing Freud's suggestions on the basis of the work by the Russian linguist Roman Jakobson. In 1956 Jakobson published his seminal essay 'Two Aspects of Language and Two Types of Aphasic Disturbance'. His attention to aphasia was symptomatic of his interest in psychology and neurolinguistics; symptomatic also of the scientism that had always dominated his work (as it did the work of all the Russian formalists). The formation (and interpretation as the elucidation of that formation) of meaning (which had been Freud's concern) was translated into the modes of arrangement whereby a linguistic sign signifies or communication between an addressor and an addressee becomes possible. Jakobson had had some acquaintance with Saussurean linguistics in 1917 and had read the *Course in General Linguistics* in 1920. Like Saussure, Jakobson divided the operation of language into two axes: signs signified by selection and combination.[11] By 'selection' he meant the way in which, on the basis of similarity, we select one word over another or substitute one word for another; by 'combination' Jakobson meant the way we combine one word syntagmatically with another, contiguously linking differences. In an oft quoted passage from his essay 'Two Aspects of Language' he sums up his position: 'The development of a discourse may take place along two different semantic lines: one topic may lead to another either through their similarity or through their contiguity. The metaphoric way would be the most appropriate term for the first case and the metonymic way for the second, since they find their most condensed expression in metaphor and metonymy respectively' (Jakobson: 1987, 109–10).

These modes of operation are continually manifest in our verbal and written behaviour, though there can be a predominance of one over the other. Much earlier, in an essay published in 1935 entitled 'Marginal Notes on the Prose of the Poet Pasternak', Jakobson had pointed out how the poetry of Majkovskij emphasised the metaphoric, whereas the work of Pasternak gave preference to the metonymic. The metaphoric axis was associated with poetry, particularly lyric poetry, whilst the metonymic axis was associated with epic and prosaic realism. But, for the development of this thesis, what is important about Jakobson's work is threefold.

First, in the later essay the operation of the metaphoric and the metonymic, selection and combination, similarity and contiguity is given a broad cultural application. By it Jakobson interprets literary history from the nineteenth to the twentieth century – for the romantic preference for the metaphoric gives way to the metonymic preference of the Realists which, in turn, is counteracted by the return of the metaphoric preference with the Symbolists. As such Jakobson sets up a materialist dialectic of history whose dynamic is the economics of the sign. Furthermore, he points out that these processes are 'by no means confined to verbal art. The same oscillation occurs in sign systems other than language' (Jakobson: 1987, 111). His own work examined painting and film, but he suggests that personal lifestyle, habits and current fashions might also be suitable subjects for examination. In fact, the analysis of the competition between the metaphoric and metonymic is appropriate for 'all verbal behaviour and for human behaviour in general' (Jakobson: 1987, 112).

Secondly, Jakobson directly relates his work to Freud's metonymic 'displacement' and synecdochic 'condensation' (Jakobson: 1987, 113) – although he views 'condensation' in terms of contiguity and relates his similarity axis to Freud's account of identification and symbolism. This is not a good reading of Freud, and it is exactly at this point that Lacan alters Jakobson's proposal.

Thirdly, Jakobson draws attention to the metaphysics, the world-views, manifest in giving preference to one axis over the other. Metonymy expresses dislocation, atomisation, and the exaltation of the random: 'the fascination of autonomous meaning' takes on prominence, whilst 'material connectedness is subdued ... A connection once created becomes an object in its own right' (Jakobson: 1987, 312). Alternatively, metaphor expresses participation and interdependence. These two metaphysics (one the reverse side of the other) will be revisited throughout this book; they are double-bound aspects of modernity's project: radical individualism and community. Furthermore, the metaphysics of tropes will be fundamental to the analogical world-view I am proposing. For the emphasis upon cultural tropes is a methodological tactic to move us away from the atomistic and facilitate a new account of analogical relations, participation, community.

With Jakobson's structuralism we have the establishment of a dualistic grammar operating within a social semiotics. It is Lacan who cements the relationship between this grammar and Freud's account of latent meaning and, more recently, Slavoj Žižek who demonstrates how Lacanian accounts of the real, the imaginary, the symbolic and the self-perpetuating desire of the unobtainable *objet petit a* can be used to interpret cultural phenomena as disparate as the current fascination with the sinking of the *Titanic*, the cult appeal of cybersex, and the films of Alfred Hitchcock. We will deal with this briefly, for there will follow further analyses of Lacan's work and Žižek's later in the book.

It is probable that Lacan's introduction to linguistic theory first came via Jakobson rather than Saussure.[12] Also influenced by Jakobson, Lévi-Strauss had demonstrated how the insights of structural linguistics might be applied to other sign systems and 'the Prague version of structuralism worked out by Jakobson and Troubetzkoy allowed Lacan to arrive at a logic of the signifier' (Roudinesco: 1990, 277). This logic superimposed a Freudian schema of condensation and displacement upon Saussure's axes of synchrony and diachrony[13] and related both to Jakobson's 'polar figures of speech' (Lacan: 1977, 105), metaphor and metonymy.[14] Lacan announced this new logic in his 1957 paper 'The Agency of the Letter in the Unconscious or Reason since Freud'. Metonymy reflects the 'word-to-word connection' (Lacan: 1977, 156) or combination of one signifier with another to constitute the endless flow of signifiers, the chain of signs producing and expressing the object of desire which is forever missing from that chain. Metaphor reflects the substitution of one signifier for another: 'It flashes between two signifiers one of which has taken the place of the other in the signifying chain' (Lacan: 1977, 157). With irony and verbal play (rather than formal etymological analysis), Lacan writes:

> *Verdichtung*, or 'condensation', is the structure of the superimposition of the signifiers, which metaphor takes as its field, and whose name, condensing in itself the word *Dichtung*, shows how the mechanism is connatural with poetry …
>
> In the case of *Verschiebung*, 'displacement', the German term is closer to the idea of that veering off of signification that we see in metonymy, and which from its first appearance in Freud is represented as the most appropriate means used by the unconscious to foil censorship.
>
> (Lacan: 1977, 160)

It is characteristic of Lacan to mask his own views as Freud's. Displacement is associated with distortion and reversal by Freud, but not explicitly with metonymy. Nevertheless, with Lacan, the economy of desire and its representation is given a structure. Metonymy charts the course of libidinal desire and metaphor manifests the symptom (Lacan: 1977, 175). These tropes characterise 'mechanisms of the unconscious' (Lacan: 1977, 169). They stand synecdochically for a list of stylistic figures which Lacan discerns in the analysand's representation of his or her self: 'Periphrasis, hyperbaton, ellipsis, suspension, anticipation, retraction, negation, digression, irony, these are the figures of style (Quintilian's *figurae sententiarum*); as catachresis, litotes, antonmasia, hyptoasis are the tropes, whose terms suggest themselves as the most proper for the labelling of these (unconscious) mechanisms. Can one really see these as mere figures of speech when it is the figures themselves that are the active principle of the rhetoric of the discourse that the analysand in fact utters?' (Lacan: 1977, 169).

Lacan mainly employed this structure to define the relationship between subjectivity and signification, but in the continual appeal his work makes to myths, literary anecdotes and texts (most famously Poe's short story, 'The Purloined Letter') the structure is universalised: it becomes the basis for a cultural logic. The work of Slavoij Žižek most clearly and consistently parses this logic as we will see in Chapters 5 and 6. For the moment it is important, for this methodological introduction, to show in what way I wish to exploit this logic of the cultural signifier to fulfil the Christian injunction to 'read the signs of the times'. But let me do this by returning us explicitly to a theological construal of semiotics.

In one of Lacan's early seminars, in mid-June 1954, having listened to an account of Saussure's and Benveniste's work on signification, a Jesuit priest and teacher of theology, R.P. Beirnaert, interjects to say all he had so far heard was already detailed 'in the *Disputatio de locutionis significatione*, which constitutes the first part of *De magisto*' by Augustine (Lacan: 1975, 273). The seminar then proceeds, under Beirnaert's direction, to examine Augustine's text only to conclude that it has taken linguists fifteen centuries to rediscover the ideas outlined by Augustine (Lacan: 1975, 285; see also Barzilai: 1997, 200–21).

What I have attempted to trace in the last two sections of this introduction is (1) a Christian theology of signification, and (2) the development towards a social semiotics that emphasises process and movement in terms of a correlation between time and desire. What emerges as a consequence of this dual examination is a twofold insight. First, that Christian theology until the late Middles Ages read the world and its times analogically (Gurevich: 1985; Huizinga: 1996). It developed a theological account of what today we would call textuality – the interrelationship of signs, their production and exchange. Secondly, that for some time now critical theorists and cultural analysts have been returning us to an understanding of our psycho-social realities as composed of the interleafing of various symbolic worlds. They have been endeavouring to teach all of us how to read the various cultural signs – evident in dreams, in literature, in ideologies, in institutions and social transformations. It is the contemporary concern with symbolic production and its interpretation that gives Christian theology an opportunity to develop an analogical world-view and constitute, for today, a theological cosmology. But this development requires that we not only historically situate social semiotics. It is also necessary to understand exactly *how* various theorists working in this field read these signs they have drawn our attention to and *what* is achieved by their doing so. By exploring these two directions of thought Christian theologians might learn how to read in-depth the cultural metaphors of their times and their social, political and economic implications. Furthermore, it is necessary to examine the metaphysics of this turn to semiotics in cultural studies, for this will enable the theologian to grasp the extent to which these metaphysics are supportive of, or running contrary to, an analogical world-view constructed from a Christian perspective. It will also, and significantly, point up the fact that the discourse of Christian theology is itself a cultural product, standing not over and against the times in which certain signs signify, but is itself a sign of the times and part of the market of their exchange. There is no pure theological discourse; and there is no room for naïveté. The space culturally opened today calls for continual self-reflexivity and analysis.

Reading cultural metaphors

Social and symbolic anthropologists have been concerned with the interpretation of metaphors as culturally specific material artefacts or ritualised actions, since the 1960s. The work of Mary Douglas (1966), James W. Fernandez (1972, 1974), Victor Turner (1967, 1974), and Sherry Ortner (1973) attempted to define master metaphors, root metaphors, key metaphors or organising metaphors within particular cultural settings. The attention paid to metaphor was only partly a response to Lévi-Strauss' work. Franz Boas (1914) and Paul Radin (1945) were influential as also the work on rhetoric and symbolic action by Kenneth Burke (1941, 1950, 1966). Christopher Tilley suggests something of the reason why this examination was viewed as so fruitful:

> The objectification of fundamental cultural values is not conveyed in words but in performances in which material forms are metaphorically put to work to effect the social transformations required. Memory and meaning are linked to the performance and become attached to the artefact. The power of the artefact to create meaning resides in its very materiality, a materiality that is recontextualised in ceremonial per-formance ... Things create people as much as people make them.
>
> (Tilley: 1999, 75–6)

As such, material bodies, culture and metaphor constitute each other.

Several recent cultural and/or social theorists have attempted to establish bases for the reading of cultural metaphors. Each has, in his or her own way, a grammatical understanding of culture which is applied to a specific phenomenon, thus translating metaphor out of linguistics and the philosophy of language into material forms and social actions. Lévi-Strauss employs the structural model of linguistics in an analyses of kinship groups and myths in *Elementary Structures of Kinship*. Charles Taylor employs a more hermeneutical model with respect to discussions of the breakdown of intersubjective and common meanings in North American politics and ethics. Clifford Geertz adopts more of a Wittgensteinian approach to the relationship between language and social practices in order to develop his 'thick descriptions' of cultural events and his analyses of religion and ideology within cultural contexts. Michel de Certeau develops the analysis of action and symbolic fields of production in the work of Pierre Bourdieu to investigate the cries of the possessed in seventeenth-century Loudon. Foucault looks to Nietzsche's genealogies – offering non-foundational accounts of the real and rejecting the 'metahistorical deployment of ideal significations' (Foucault, 1984, 77) – to examine prisons and hospitals, taxonomy, madness, punishment and sexuality. Stephen Greenblatt often works from an anecdote to unravel the 'shared code, a set of interlocking tropes and similitudes that function not only as the objects but as the conditions of representation' (Greenblatt: 1988, 86) and describe a web of social energies which both produce and are produced through a play by Shakespeare or Marlowe, the work of Thomas More or Francis Bacon. Potent cultural events and artefacts generate interpretation, reflexive thinking and participation in the excesses of their meaning. They produce a transferential process that fosters the dissemination of their meaning, energising their recontextualisation, and the continual commutation of their values.

Often, for these thinkers concerned with artefacts and practices which are excessive to the theories which might lend them the familiarity of being meaningful, a specific site is taken, their philosophies or approaches emerging from specific analyses. It is their rejection of the abstract, the essential, and the conceptual which leads them to renounce deductive for inductive thinking, thinking which issues from the unique materiality of the object that concerns them and organises their examination. The anecdote, for Greenblatt, gives the effect of the real because of the sheer contingency that gives the curio narrated a freshness. The striking brio of an event is evident. After the Introduction, Michel de Certeau opens *The Mystic Fable* with several stories (one about an idiot woman saint in the fourth century, the second and third about mad male saints in the sixth century) and a detailed reading of Hieronymous Bosch's painting *The Garden of Delights*. The stories and the reading serve to orientate the analysis of the science of 'mystics' which follows. Geertz, in his *The Interpretation of Cultures* moves towards the practical application of his 'thick description' in the last part of the book with respect to his famous interpretation of the Balinese cock fight. Foucault, though, is the master of this approach with his championing of 'effective history': ' "Effective" history ... deals with events in terms of their most unique characteristics, their most acute manifestations' (Foucault: 1984, 88).

Frequently Foucault's books open with a particularly dramatic occurrence – Damiens' horrific punishment for regicide or Charcot's methods for investigating women's sexuality in Salpetrière – which constitutes the catalyst for his subsequent analysis. That which follows is an attempt to understand the singularity of what has been 'eventualised' (in his terminology). In *The Order of Things* a detailed reading of Velázquez's painting *Las Meninas* acts as a prism through which the various themes of the book – representation in the seventeenth and eighteenth centuries and how it constructed an order of things – are both focused and dispersed. He concentrates his reading on the way the picture is organised by the theme of the gaze and the representation established in and through gazing. He points to how the picture has two foci: a mirror which is brightly illuminated in the otherwise dark background and the stare of the young Infanta in the foreground. It is that which is absent and outside the frame we are observing, and the frame in the painting itself, which provides the final centre generating the spectacle in the painting and so the entire process of representation. What is absent can be recognised under three headings: the artist who

15

conceives and paints the scene; the sovereign, Philip IV and his wife who are the subjects being painted by the artist in the painting (and who are reflected in the mirror at the back of the painting); and the observer, Foucault or ourselves. This absent but generative centre is the ideal point in relation to what is being represented, the sovereign view from no where which makes representation (and its self-consciousness) possible. From this Foucault goes on to conclude:

> It may be that, in this picture, as in all the representations of which it is, as it were, the manifest essence, the profound invisibility of what one sees is inseparable from the invisibility of the person seeing – despite all the mirrors, reflections, imitations, and portraits. Around the scene are arranged all the signs and successive forms of representation ...
>
> Perhaps there exists, in this painting by Velázquez, the representation as it were, of Classical representation, and the definition of the space it opens up to us ... And representation, finally freed from the relation that was impeding it, can offer itself as representation in its pure form.
>
> (Foucault: 1970, 16).

Despite the hesitancy of 'may be', 'perhaps', and 'as it were' what Foucault is doing here is laying bear a set of preconceptions – those unexamined elements which make a position, a knowledge, possible or credible. Certeau would ask a similar question about the production of the believable; what makes some thing acceptable, believable – for example, the realism of Velázquez's world, crossed as it is by a conflict of gazes? The preconceptions are not passive, for Foucault, but evidence of a staging of certain cultural forces. Part of the function of the archaeologies which will follow this reading of *Las Meninas* is to foreground the play of interpretations, the confrontations and entanglement of events – to 'reveal the heterogeneous systems which, masked by the self, inhibit the formulation of any form of identity' (Foucault: 1970, 95). For someone who is highly critical of substantial notions of the subject and psychoanalysis in any form, nevertheless, Foucault writes (in a way that will return us to Lacan), that in his genealogies: 'What I would like to do ... is to reveal a *positive unconscious* of knowledge' (Foucault: 1970, xi).

Cultural metaphors are sites where a certain cultural isomorphism, linking disparate fields, condenses. They are the creation of a community. For the condensing of iconic meaning takes place because of a collective, public attraction. They are generated out of, furnish and foster a public participation.[15] In approaching and opening up these sites we come to understand the constitution of a certain knowledge; that which makes such knowledge possible. It is not what has caused them that is of central significance, but rather how they came to be, and what they allow to be, believed by the society producing and produced by them. It is in this way, then, that we might speak of analyses of these metaphors as disclosing the 'unconscious of knowledge'. The analyses are the cultural equivalents of biopsies; an examination of the tissue of the social body at a given point in time and space.

What the examination of cultural metaphors by so many different social theorists (employing a number of different approaches) share, and which will guide my own theological readings of such metaphors, is six characteristics. These characteristics betray some of the metaphysics inherent in the contemporary turn to semiotics. As I said earlier, any theological approach would have to assess these in order to understand how correlated a new analogical world-view could be with today's examination of symbolic production and exchange.

The shared characteristics

1. They accept that there is no immediate knowledge of brute data or the given. All our knowledge is mediated by the cultural and linguistic codes within which we are situated. That position entails that all our knowledge is partial or from a particular perspective. There is no God's eye view of things, no access to a reality 'out there' beyond or behind our systems of communication which enable us to conceive of a reality to start with. Judgements, therefore – which are inevitable because as we experience so we have to evaluate or interpret that experience – are always 'prejudiced' (to use Gadamer's term). No appeal can be made to an objectivity or to neutral 'facts' which can verify a judgement. Geertz insists that despite the desire for verification, no verification is possible for his anthropological narratives. All he provides is description and the value of that description lies in its 'thickness' – that is, the way the event or act or object described is related to the culture's symbolic nexus within which it is embedded. It is important to recognise that this position does not lead either to perspectivalism or linguistic idealism.

It does not lead to perspectivalism because this position refutes the notion of a self-grounding Cartesian ego. Foucault makes plain the change of emphasis: knowledge is not governed by 'a theory of the knowing subject, but rather (by) a theory of discursive practice' (Foucault: 1970, xiv). All subject positions (and some of the theorists, like Foucault, for example, would have very loose construals of subjectivity and others a much stronger sense of agency, Taylor and Certeau, for example) possess three safeguards against perspectivalism: (1) Subjects are unstable, because the self does not have immediate consciousness of itself and therefore has no immediate knowledge of itself or its own identity. This instability thwarts a phenomenological approach; since in phenomenology the subject is the origin of meaning. (2) Subjects are in process, because the time and spacing within which any subject position is orientated and active is constantly changing. (3) Subjects are in relation to other subjects which help constitute the very sense of the self and its identity. While universal knowledge is rejected, involvement in a discursive practice requires shared knowledges; these are, culturally specific models of explanation constituted through metaphor. There is a high regard among these social theorists for the interpenetration of subjects and the intersubjectivity of meanings such that knowledge is not simply relative to the individual, a property owned by that individual. It cannot be because the language framing and producing that knowledge is shared with so many other individuals. There is no private language. What I know I already share.

Neither does the acceptance that all knowledge is mediated and constituted by the cultural and linguistic codes within which we are situated lead to linguistic idealism – I name it so and therefore it is. For there is no denial of the given, of a material world which we inhabit, a physical and experiential substrate. It is simply that all our understandings and accounts of the given are predetermined by our cultural location and its symbolic resources for thinking and communicating. We see and hear 'as', we do not simply see and hear (taste, touch and smell). Therefore we *make* sense. In a strong sense of 'make'. Again there would be difference here between various theorists concerning the degree of our constructedness of the real. Foucault would seem to hold to an 'out there' which is simply flux; malleable to all forms of power and production. We make what we will. In line with more recent accounts, such as Judith Butler's (Butler: 1993), Taylor endorses a more circumscribed understanding of our constructiveness. For Taylor, there are limits to our discursivity and what it produces, and those limits are a matter of matter itself. A difference remains for Taylor, albeit hard to cash in, between 'meaning and substrate' (Taylor: 1985, 25). Our understandings and accounts of the given are not so predetermined that we cannot ever think things anew. We have linguistic means of making new connections – figurally in metaphors, for example, syntactically in conjunction. But what we come to know will always be part of the trajectory of what we once knew. The chain of signifiers admits no breakage or rupture. It moves diachronically, filtering the past into the present and both into the future.

2. From this axiom of the mediation of the given, it follows that in the various readings of cultural metaphors no simple move can be made from description to explanation. All explanations of an act or an object and all descriptions of an act and an object are interpretations. There is no stepping out of (or stepping into) the hermeneutic circle. This has fundamental implications for the status of the work accomplished and calls forth certain paradoxes and circularities of thought. For example, Geertz calls his own work 'interpretative anthropology'. In his account of the Balinese cock fight, he gives the impression of moving from the event to its meaning. The cock fight becomes, in his description, a mirror of Balinese culture itself – its masculine orientation, its ritualised violence, its rigid class structure and kinship responsibilities. As such, the practice of 'thick description' fosters a concern for the local and microscopic, while nevertheless wishing to draw more general conclusions. Geertz tackled the various objections to this tension in his methodology by emphasising that, given the complex overlay of symbolic systems, 'Cultural analysis is intrinsically incomplete' (Geertz: 1973, 29) and necessarily contestable. But one analysis builds on, develops and extends the thickness of another. So that, given the

symbolic nature of social actions, analysis of micro-practices will inevitably speak to larger issues, possessing, intrinsically, wider implications for social discourse and the politics of meaning. But it is evident that a certain circularity appertains to Geertz's method. For Geertz reveals the manifold and complicit layers of social semiotics that he assumes to be there to start with. His model of culture is both the lens through which he views the particular situation and the object he finds presented for his view. In other words, Geertz's 'thick descriptions' elide a difference between what is out there and his description of what is out there; the object under study and his interpretation of the object. The same might be said of Foucault, only Foucault did characterise his 'descriptions' as '*récits*', as fictionalised histories that tell us more about our present cultural context than the past (Foucault: 1979). Similarly Certeau defined his own analyses of seventeenth-century mysticism as '*fables*' (Certeau: 1992) and Michel Serres, discussing angels past and present, employs the term '*légende*' (Serres: 1993). Foucault, Certeau and Serres make no ontological claims for their work. They are and remain interpretative descriptions – although it remains impossible to believe their various accounts have no explanatory value. Certainly those working with Foucault's genealogies, or Certeau's historiographies have used them *as if* they constituted explanations of past phenomena.

3. What perhaps we can say is characteristic of those investigating cultural metaphors, is that the line between description and explanation, the object of study and its meaning, is traced in water. There is no end to the process of interpretation and reinterpretation; and so no final judgement can be made as to the status of the descriptions. They are acts of persuasion, they are narratives useful for the production of other interpretations; they are rhetorical strategies. Their value lies in their productivity – how stimulating they are for other academics in the field; their productivity is intrinsic to their power to persuade. The meaning of the object under their examination is open-ended. For the number of contexts from within which this object or action or event can be viewed is potentially infinite. Limits to recontextualisation arise because of a certain politics, forgetting, and ignorance intrinsic to the present cultural scene with respect to its past. For what is culturally significant in any given time issues from a certain cultural politics that facilitates the credibility of believing, or the acceptance of one set of values while discrediting, being ignorant of or repressing others.

4. The recognition of a cultural politics, that which operates in any culture to make a belief believable, introduces a further characteristic of those concerned to evaluate cultural metaphors: the recognition that there is no ideology-free zone. Critical genealogies, examinations of cultural metaphors, and the construction of a new Christian dogmatics – the three critical engagements in this present volume – are not politically innocent. All acts of representation – acts of critique, interpretation and construction – are acts of persuasion seeking adherence, seeking to find cultural space. All such acts are part of larger systems of beliefs and assumptions. As his critics have pointed out, Geertz's 'thick descriptions' are not only caught up in a certain colonial politics,

but they endorse those politics insofar as the description sets down and reaffirms the *status quo*: this is how things are in Balinese culture and this is the way they will remain (Pecora: 1989, 243–76). The fact that I chose *this* metaphor rather than *that* to examine, that I regard *this* thinker rather than *that* as more productive for my line of argument, that I have available *this* resource rather than *that* resource to develop my thinking, that I value *this* in this way rather than *that* in that way – is all part of a cultural matrix which is producing this work as well as enabling this work to produce something about the matrix itself. No act exists *in vacuo*. The circulations of its meaning draw in and upon both other contextual meanings and the situation in which it is being refigured or figured as at all significant. But the implication of this is that the object's meaning always transcends or escapes, by the very excess of its signification, the circularities of interpretation. Geertz's analysis of the Balinese cock fight, Foucault's (or Asad's) analysis of medieval confession (Foucault: 1981; Asad: 1993), each prove the respective cases for their author's argument, and are, therefore, reduced to a thesis, a politics, an ideology. But the richness of the cultural metaphor itself transcends all its interpretations, leaving room for more, requiring more, like a character in a medieval allegory who is too lively, too well-conceived, merely to be reduced to, though named as, Indolence, Mercy, Love, Estrangement or Despair.

5.   A certain view not only of the world, but of human beings with respect to that world, emerges with these various analyses of cultural metaphors; a certain anthropology. Human beings are *homo symbolicus, homo faciens*. Charles Taylor will speak of 'man (a)s a self-interpreting animal' (Taylor: 1985, 26); 'man (a)s a self-defining animal. With changes in his self-definition go changes in what man is' (Taylor: 1985, 56). In the work of Michel de Certeau and Emmanuel Levinas the human condition is one of journeying into continual exile like Abraham, producing and being produced. The human being is characterised by desire and movement, a *homo economicus*. And the desire is installed before consciousness, before culture, prior to memory. The steles, temples, coliseums, mounds and memorials left behind are the mouldings of a desire which passes by and passes on; monuments to a collective reflection that represents the cultural imaginary at a certain time and place.

6.   Finally, the work of those concerned with evaluating cultural metaphors espouses what Gianni Vattimo would term a weak or a hermeneutical ontology, as opposed to the strong ontology of Being as true identity. Weak ontology takes 'leave of metaphysical Being and its strong traits ... That which truly is (the *ontos on*) is not the centre which is opposed to the periphery, nor is it the essence which is opposed to appearance, nor is it what endures as opposed to the accidental and the mutable, nor is it the certainty of the *obiectum* given to the subject as opposed to the vagueness and the imprecision of the horizon of the world. The occurrence of Being is rather ... an unnoticed and marginal background event' (Vattimo: 1988, 86 and 1997).

These six shared characteristics – that knowledge is mediated, that descriptions are acts of persuasion more than acts of explanation, that the meaning of anything is excessive to all interpretation, that all acts of representation have ideological investments, that this semiotic world-view fosters a specific anthropology and a weak, hermeneutical ontology or metaphysical non-foundationalism – will be taken up, in the chapters that follow, and developed theologically. Just as Christian theology already has a theology of the sign and a theology of grammar, so reading the signs of the times in the way these other social theorists have read the signs of the times will involve theological accounts of shared knowledge, mediation, desire, acts of persuasion, models of what it is to be human and a hermeneutical ontology.

Which signs are significant?

Accepting then this semiotic world-view, the question must arise as to which signs, in a world feverish with significance, are the ones to be read by the Christian theologian. Žižek makes much of a relation between lavatory types in Germany, France and Britain and German conservativism, French revolutionary radicalism and English moderate liberalism. For 'one of the features which distinguishes man from the animals is precisely that with humans the disposal of shit becomes a problem' (Žižek: 1997, 5). Jean Baudrillard and Roland Barthes both saw fashion as a prime cultural indicator: 'fashion is at the core of modernity ... The very appearance of fashion bears the closest resemblance to ritual – fashion as spectacle, as festival, as squandering' (Baudrillard: 1993, 90; Barthes: 1985). In one essay, Certeau examines railway travel and the ships and submarines in the fiction of Jules Verne to develop his thesis that in modernity 'The machine is the *primum mobile*, the solitary god from which all the action proceeds' (Certeau: 1984, 113). As I pointed out earlier, in the work of the new historicist, Stephen Greenblatt, the sheer contingency of an anecdote – a police report on the atheism of Christopher Marlowe – is translated into the paradigmatic. Sometimes the choice of metaphor can seem arbitrary.

Furthermore, the role of the analysis of the cultural metaphor can become ambiguous. It moves between providing an illustration of a cultural trend, theme or dominant social value and being the forensic means of accessing the 'unconscious of knowledge', those networks of assumptions, connections, analogies and isomorphisms which give value or significance to *this* object rather than *that*, *this* event rather than *that*. In both procedures, the illustrative and the forensic, the danger is circularity: that what one discovers is what one already presupposes to be there. Of course, circularity is the essence of reflexivity and part of my argument lies in demonstrating how theology not only produces a space for belief within particular cultures, but is itself a cultural product. Furthermore, circularity does not just pertain to critical method, but does itself have theological import: the structure of the faith believed in is reaffirmed. Christian theologians do not reinvent the Christian faith, but work within the unfolding of the revelation of God. So it is not circularity as such, but the self-enclosing circularity, the dogmatic circularity, that has to be guarded against – so that there is a movement beyond the affirmation of what was already presupposed and the teachings of the Church are recognised as being conducted within the traditions of orthodoxy.[16] This calls for a critical practice and an interdisciplinary practice. That is, to narrate the theological reading of the world from within the grammar of the Christian faith *and* to be critically aware that it *is* a narration, and as such subject to all the cultural vicissitudes of narrations. If fundamental to this project is the denial of the sacred/secular dualism such that the theological has an important critical perspective to offer the world, then theology too cannot conceive itself as separated out, as distilled and objective truth. The discourses which comprise theological study are not unequivocal – they are subject themselves to interpretation, analysis and critique. Theological knowledge, like theological subjects, must pass on to follow after – must engage in pilgrimage in order to practise discipleship.

Still the question emerges: how do we determine which signs to examine? The question has been tackled, to some extent, by social and symbolic anthropologists. As I observed earlier, there has been much discussion in anthropology concerning master metaphors, root metaphors, key symbols or organising metaphors. Drawing on the vaguely defined term 'root metaphor' in Stephen C. Pepper's book *World Hypotheses* (1942), Victor Turner attempted to clarify foundation metaphors or major conceptual archetypes which yielded access to forms of cultural organisation, 'each susceptible of many meanings, but with core meanings linked analogically to basic human problems of the epoch' (Turner: 1974, 28; see also Fernandez: 1972, 39–60 and 1974, 119–45). I do not wish to specifically treat 'human problems' in any epoch (Turner is concerned with conflictual events like the circumstances which led to the death of Thomas à Beckett), but the central concern of this book is a theological account of analogy and analogical relations – which root metaphors, for Turner, provided an access to. Turner related these metaphors to what he termed 'root paradigms' in any culture. These paradigms are the cultural equivalents of genetic codes – matrices which give rise to complex cultural organisations. Root paradigms 'have reference not only to the current state of social relationships existing or developing between actors, but also to the cultural goals, means, ideas, outlooks, currents of thought, patterns of belief, and such, which enter into those relationships, interpret them, and incline them to alliance or divisiveness' (Turner: 1974, 64). As such they are closely connected to communal identities and in developing a Christian model of analogical relations, this book is concerned, sociologically, with *communitas*, communion (eucharistic), communication and *ecclesia*.

If Turner's work provides some justification for (and examples of) choosing one sign over another – understanding some metaphors as more fundamental than others in terms of their organisational roles within a culture – Sherry Ortner, in a seminal essay, 'On Key Symbols', helps with the identification of these foundational tropes. She lists five indicators for a key symbol: (1) the investigator is told of its cultural importance; (2) people are 'positively or negatively aroused by X, rather than indifferent'; (3) X occurs in many different contexts, actions, situation, interactions and symbolic domains like art, ritual and myth; (4) there is 'a greater cultural elaboration surrounding X'; and (5) there are 'greater cultural restrictions surrounding X, either in the sheer number of rules, or severity of sanctions regarding misuse' (Ortner: 1973, 1,339). Having prescribed these indicators of key symbols, she then draws a distinction between summarising symbols which dominate and densely focus significance across cultures and times – like the Cross – and elaborating symbols which facilitate the ordering of experience and action and the weaving of different realms of experience through a logic of analogy. In a way that is similar to Turner's distinction between root metaphor and root paradigms, she distinguishes key symbols from key scenarios. Key scenarios function culturally to motivate and give shape to various forms of behaviour: 'Root metaphors, by establishing a certain view of the world, implicitly suggest certain valid and effective ways of acting upon it; key scenarios, by prescribing certain culturally effective courses of action, embody and rest upon certain assumptions about the nature of reality' (Ortner: 1973, 1,342).

Ortner not only provides a schema for the identification of fundamental metaphors – indicators of which signs of the times are functioning more significantly in any given culture – she also draws attention to the practices (and the narratives which inform and produce these practices) that are implicit in these signs. Recognising and examining the manner in which knowledge is produced is an important part of this book, an important aspect of the claims being made, and the Christian theological model being offered. For this book too is implicated in the very cultural forces it is examining theologically. It is producing a certain body of sense; it is a literary *corpus*. It needs therefore to examine how *its* body is woven into not only the eucharistic and the ecclesial body of Christ, but the multiple social and political bodies which constitute various cultural agencies.

The gendered body is the key organisational metaphor throughout this work.[17] It is towards an analogical conception of embodiment – physical, social, political, ecclesial and theological – that it proceeds. Hence the cultural metaphors examined – urban planning, civic architecture, concepts of community, the sex shop, cyberspace, the cult of angels and aliens, globalism, the eucharistic liturgy – are examined with respect to their construals and productions of these various bodies. The city acts as the focus and forum for these examinations. For these bodies are not isolatable givens (the critique of the atomism – scientific, social, logical and metaphysical – which yields 'isolatable givens' is one of the main aims of this book). These bodies are only available in and through what Michel de Certeau termed the practices of everyday life in specific locations. Insightfully, Baudrillard has written: 'The city was the first and foremost site for the production and realisation of commodities, a site of industrial concentration and exploitation. Today the city is foremost the site of the sign's execution' (Baudrillard: 1993, 77). It is with the city, then, that we will begin and towards a recognition of that Christian other city, that heteropolis operating in, under and through the civic and the civil, that we move. In reading the signs of the times we render perceptible the watermark of Christ within creation.

A holographic[18] presence of St Augustine permeates these pages whispering of the 'two loves' (*amores*) of which only one is holy, the other impure (*immundus*); the one sociable (*socialis*) and the other self-centred (*privatus*) (Augustine: 1972, XI, 20). He whispers also of places in which these two amorous desires operate 'the mortal course of the two cities, the heavenly and the earthly, which are mingled together (*permixtarum*) from the beginning down to the end. Of these, the earthly one has made to herself ... false gods whom she might serve by sacrifice; but she which is heavenly and is a pilgrim on the earth does not make false gods, but is herself made by the true God of whom she herself must be the true sacrifice (*cuius verum sacrificium ipsa fit*). Yet both alike either enjoy temporal good things, or are afflicted with temporal evils, but with diverse faith, diverse hope, and diverse love, until they must be separated by the last judgement, and each must receive her own end, of which there is no end. About these ends of both we must now treat' (Augustine: 1972, XVIII, 54).

Part I

CULTURAL ATOMISM

1

CITIES OF ETERNAL
ASPIRATION

If you see a philosopher determining all things by means of right reason,
him you shall reverence: he is a heavenly being and not of this world. If
you see a pure contemplator, he unaware of the body and confined to the
inner reaches of the mind, he is neither an earthly nor a heavenly being:
he is more a reverend divinity vested with human flesh ... we can become what we will.

(Pico della Mirandola [1487]: 1948, 226–7)

Introduction

Faith in the City, the report of the Archbishop of Canterbury's Commission on
Urban Priority Areas, was first published in 1985. The report, without going into
many theological details, announced a Christian commitment to the city. In this
it was following the footsteps of Christian socialists of the previous century like
F.D. Maurice, and R.H. Tawney. In the nineteenth century the famous Scottish
preacher, Henry Drummond, spelt out the nature of that Christian commitment. 'Christianity', he said, 'is the religion of cities. It moves among real things.
Its sphere is the street, the marketplace, the working life of the world ... Take
away people, houses, streets, character and it ceases to be.' He concluded: 'the
perfect saint is the perfect citizen' (Drummond: 1988, 11–12). The Archbishop's
report concurred (Church of England: 1985, 70), outlining the need for a
theology in a picture of a disintegrating cityscape. But it did not provide the
theology it called for – and its critics made this plain.[1] Anthony Harvey sought to
clarify and redress the omission with a collection of essays which theologically
reflected upon the findings of the Archbishop's Commission, entitled *Theology in
the City*. One of those essays by Professor, now Lord, Plant commented incisively
that the Commission was simply misreading the signs of the times – in particular
the nature of conservative capitalism and, we are in the eighties here, New Right
Thinking. For all its detailed awareness of the poverty and destitution of UPAs
(Urban Priority Areas), for all its compassion and sense of outraged shock, and
for all its recognition that there is a serious situation in major cities of this
country – *Faith in the City*, and its call to affirm the belief that our cities are still

flourishing centres of social, economic and political life, misunderstood that cities as they believed in them were rapidly changing. While understanding that 'the modern consumer economy, depending as it does on the continual stimulation of all attainable desires ... come[s] perilously close to encouraging the sin of covetousness' (Church of England: 1985, 55), the Commission still wished to employ the language of 'collaboration', 'liberation', 'community', 'development', 'locality', 'fellow citizens', 'contribution', 'solidarity' and 'participation'. It never asked whether the social atomism of city-life had moved beyond being able to collaborate; it never asked who contributed and why, and who couldn't or wouldn't contribute; it never asked about the growing numbers who have already opted out – who have already opted for a virtual reality (in drugs, in drink, in interactive computer games, in play-station fantasies, in film, in televiewing). It appealed for state intervention when the state was in the process of dismantling its welfare concerns. It referred continually to the concept of nation (and implicitly to a nationalism) that flew in the face of increasing globalisation. It expressed its belief in its own unique position to be 'responsible for, the whole of the society, and proclaim [s] its care for the weak, its solidarity with all' (Church of England: 1985, 59), with little regard to the fact that the Church of England no longer had the resources nor the social standing to carry out such paternalism. The Church, albeit in a different way, is as marginal as so many of the poor it portrayed, and all the indications are that cities are turning into something else: radically eclectic places where each pursues his or her own consumer interests under the ever-watchful eye of surveillance cameras ready to pinpoint when radical difference flares up into riot. How then do we begin to think about today's city theologically?

Metropolis: Berlin 1927

On a freezing January evening in 1927, the city of Berlin buzzed with an excitement that had been building for almost two years. On this night would be premiered the longest, most expensive and most technically sophisticated silent film made to date. The film was called *Metropolis*. It opened at Berlin's largest movie theatre, Ufa Palast, the front of which had been mounted with billboards portraying monumental skyscrapers. The film's director was Fritz Lang – a man obsessed in his early years by architecture – and its subject was social life in a futuristic city. It was being premiered in a Western European city second only to London in size. A city which the pioneering German city developer, Werner Hegemann, depicted at the forefront of an international battle in urban development 'in the struggle for the beneficial arrangement of [a] completely new world in which we have been living since modern techniques in industry and transport first came into effect' (Sutcliffe: 1981, 45). Berlin had already established itself as a prototype city, for Germany; staging, in 1910, the first town-planning exhibition to promote the regional planning that had gone on in the city since the publication in 1862 of James Hobrecht's huge *Bebauungsplan*

(Sutcliffe: 1981, 35). According to Lang – who already had an eye on American film-production, whose studios he would later grace – it was inspired by viewing the New York skyline from an ocean liner.[2] But the film had been financially made possible by the newly stabilised Mark, and produced by Berlin's Ufa (*Universum Film Aktiengesellschaft*), in a Germany widely recognised, at the time, as a world leader in urban planning (McGilligan: 1997, 8). The film's production reflected a growing interest in the discipline that would come to be known as urban studies. It illustrated the 'very real contemporary fears and ambiguous attitudes about cities' (Neumann: 1996, 35) and their design – particularly the debates between the conservative and younger architects about cities composed of skyscrapers rather than cities centred around one huge building that might act as a modern version of the mediaeval Cathedral. Luis Buñuel, who saw the film when it opened in Madrid wrote: 'Now and forever the architect is going to replace the set designer. The movies will be the faithful translator of the architect's boldest dreams' (quoted in Neumann: 1996, 9). We will return to this observation in the next chapter. A number of earlier German films had also reflected the debates among the architects and urban planners – Hans Werckmeister's *Algol* (1920) and Murnau's *Der letzte Mann* (1925) – but it was *Metropolis*, and the set designs of Erich Kettelhut, in particular, which presented the symbiotic relationship between cinema and the city: the glamour and scintillations of the former reflecting the energetic buzz of the latter.

Urban studies, theorising about the city and cinematography all emerge around the same period. It was the early 1900s when *Stadtebau*, *Stadtbaurat* and *Stadtebauer* were organising town planning as a distinct profession in Germany (Sutcliffe: 1981, 34); it was 1904 when Ebenezer Howard's dreams for the new garden city became a fully-fledged plan for Letchworth and the president of the Manchester and Salford Citizen's Association, Thomas Horsfall, published his groundbreaking book *The Improvement of the Dwellings and Surroundings of the People: The Example of Germany*; and it was 1907 when the United States set up its first commission for city planning. In France, urban planning came much later; the first town-planning law not being passed until it was deemed necessary, in 1919, following the devastation of the First World War. Urban studies emerges as, by 1900, thirteen cities around the world were estimated to be occupied by over one million inhabitants (Chandler and Fox: 1974, 19).[3]

We begin then with *Metropolis*, a film set in the modern city, at a time when the city was being seen as a field requiring separate study and analysis; with a film about the conflicting desire, politics and psychology of civic living. We begin also with a film, not a novel or a theological account of the city because of the relationship we have acknowledged between them, and the commitment of this study to working from a Christian analysis of cultural metaphors towards a theology of the times. Film owes its appeal and possibility to city life. As Wim Wenders, the German filmmaker who is frequently invited to take part in discussions on the urban landscape, observes: 'there are links between the cities, the urban landscapes and the cinema. Film is a city art. It has come into existence and it has blossomed together with the great cities of the world. ... The cinema is the mirror of the twentieth century city and twentieth century art' (Wenders: 1997, 93).[4] The content – what the film is about – and the form – cinematography – correlate in *Metropolis*. Just as the city is preoccupied with the structure and control of what can be seen – Joh Fredersen (the Master) watches the city from a glass-fronted tower – so the silent film, as a medium, communicates through the organised textures of what is screened. Both the city and the film organise what and how people will see. Each are metaphors of modern life – metaphors which express a profound ambivalence. As Buñuel noted, they express dreams and aspirations and so reflect a certain utopianism, while at the same time, their imposing visibilities threaten to overwhelm, to dominate. Fritz Lang's *Metropolis* creatively plays with this ambivalence – the futuristic city rehearsing feudal power in an epic film.

The plot of the film and the way the camera frames its shots, both play with the hidden and the visible. And what is outside the frame (and concealed) frequently dictates the activity in the frame (and revealed). As one film critic writes: 'This is the atmosphere of Lang's world, with an intangible threat existing nowhere but felt everywhere' (Jensen: 1989, 13). The camerawork plays with the hidden and the visible, evoking the presence of a power that is unlocatable. This expresses itself in terms of the plot: beneath the visible city, for example, the citizens go about their work in labyrinthine underground caverns and corridors. The camera's silent and panoramic eye has access both to this hidden city as well as to the visible city of towers above it. Joh Fredersen's surveillance is itself surveyed.

The film is set in the year 2000. Under the surveillance of Fredersen, the workers toil, oppressed and exploited. They are encouraged, inspirited, and consoled by a female prophet called Maria who speaks to them of their future salvation. One day a mediator will come from the world above to deliver them. Freder, the only son of Fredersen, becomes that saviour (by self-appointment).[5] He has crept down from the city and listens, unseen, to Maria. Fired by what he hears he accepts the mission as his. Only elsewhere ... his father, who has heard about Maria's political activism, has had a mad scientist create a robotic simulacrum of Maria. This 'Maria' is seductive and sexually aggressive and evil; whereas the real Maria is virginal and pure. Fredersen sends down the robotic Maria to stir the workers into anarchy, so they will destroy their world. In the unleashed anarchy the workers turn on the robot itself and burn it before the doors of the Cathedral. In the meantime the real Maria escapes from her imprisonment. In a final effacement of the feminine, it is then Freder who affects a reconciliation between his father and the workers, once more before the Cathedral doors.

The topological planning of the film reflects a powerful Germanic folk-myth of dwarves and trolls inhabiting underground caverns, working invisibly to perform the labours that make daily life in the world above pleasurable, leisured; the myth that Wagner dramatises in *Das Reingeld*, where the *Niebelungen* work away hidden from the world and ruled over by the tyrannical dwarf, Alberich.[6] Lang's previous two films were adaptations of these Germanic myths – *Siegfried* and *Kriemheld's Revenge* (both 1924). Utopian civic structures are crossed by a medieval politics of oppression, the future technopolis by the nationalism and imperialism of the past. The twenty-hour day is divided into two working shifts of ten hours; the clock and the great rotating cogs of industrialism dictate production. Power, paranoia, hysteria, madness – are viewed as the other, repressed side of the sharp-edged city with its geometric surfaces and its 'rationalisation and commodification of space and time' (Kasinitz: 1995, 1).

But the plot and characterisation of the film rehearse several theological concerns and resonate with Christian and biblical allusion. 'Maria … acts as a Christian priest to the workers', one critic observes. Certainly the scenes in which Maria teaches the workers about the one who is to come and save them take place in a catacomb-like chapel – replete with cross and altar. Another critic writes about Maria that 'She is Christ the Redeemer and Madonna the Virgin rolled into one' (McGilligan: 1997, 110). This is blind to the gender roles being played out here. Maria is the virgin prophet in John the Baptist mode, Joh is the father God Jehovah, but the Christic the mediating role is male and the father's only son.

The biblical allusions are self-consciously present. Thea von Harbou, who was Lang's second wife and with whom he worked on the screenplay, said the structure in the metropolis was known as 'The New Tower of Babel'. The city's hierarchical socio-political power structure is mirrored in a vertical mapping, with the pleasure gardens of Eden at the highest point and, at the lowest, the underground city ruled over by fire and built upon vast reservoirs of water.

When Erich Kettelhut first drew up plans for downtown Metropolis and made the Cathedral (a very Köln-like Cathedral) the focal point of the city, Lang carefully crossed out the Cathedral twice adding 'Away with the church: Tower of Babel itself'. Nevertheless, in a film in which the city is seen as both potential champion of a new social order and potential exploitative monster (again reflecting the two views of city-living current at the time), it is the Cathedral which is the final locus for reconciliation.

The question I wish to ask is what does this film tell us about the modern city and Christian theology's relationship to it? This will involve (1) saying something about the biblical view of the city and (2) the history of civic development with respect to theological concerns. Examinations of both of these will enable us to provide some answer to that question which then must be related to prominent aspects of the film itself. I suggest there are four such aspects.

First, the film is structured around dualisms: the human versus the machine;[7] the darkly erotic and self-interested versus the saintly and altruistic; the male opposed to, and fearful of, the female; the conscious world of control and organisation against the unconscious, silenced but volatile world of the emotions; the city above ground and workplace underground; the individual opposed to the masses; good against evil; and several others – all filmed in black and white.

Secondly, what characterises this city is industrial labour, on behalf of a few technocrats, by strongly bonded, quasi-religious fraternities – what, in Germany, after the pioneering sociologist, Ferdinand Tönnies, would be termed *Gemeinschaft* as distinct from communities based upon location and impersonal, self-interested relationships, *Gesellschaft*.[8] *Gemeinschaft* social bonds are natural, organic and intellectual and function unconsciously (beneath the civic surface). *Gesellschaft* social bonds are rational, mechanistic, means-to-ends and function consciously.[9] The film visually spatialises Tönnies' conceptual schema. When they rebel, the workers' anger irrupts impulsively, breaking through the rational, geometric planes which compose the film sets which frame them. Nevertheless, the workers move forward as one, in a disciplined if mute co-operation mirroring the way they had lived together in their destitution and oppression. They march towards the Tower in a great triangular wedge. They are the producers and their working alongside each other fosters a sense of community – a corporate identity.

Thirdly, it is a city of towers and high density residence, rather akin to the Gotham city of Batman fame. It is a city made possible by advanced technology, migration of the populace towards places of high employment and wages, the production/consumption rhythms of developing capitalism. It is attractive because it suggests wealth – as potential if not possessed – and it is electric with the excitement of the new, the latest, the most efficient, the most antiseptic. The skyscraper is the symbol of human aspiration and potential; the proud phallus of masculine-led power.

Fourthly, the city's problems are believed to be resolvable with the establishment of reciprocal responsibilities. The final scene of the film establishes a social contract between patrician-capitalist and worker-citizen allowing for a new consensus politics to arise. Modernity's metaphysical aspiration to synthesis is evident here: the move beyond Cartesian splits between the mind and the body, the intellectual and the physical, and Marx's dialectics between labour and capital.[10] The liberal dream of respectful tolerance and co-operation, founded in the common denominator of the human condition, makes city life possible. Urbanism fosters, in fact requires, liberalism or, when the tide turns and we all become more sceptical about humanism, pragmatism. The class divisions in *Metropolis* can be extended towards gender divisions and racial divisions – all these distinctive sections of the urban populace can only co-exist within such a concentrated space if a liberal *laissez faire* mentality (which may take an implicit or an explicit social contractual form) operates.

Cities and secularity

The Bible is ambivalent towards cities. The first cities were built by men of demonstrable power and ambition. Cain, having murdered his brother Abel and, being informed by God that he would be a vagabond all his life, 'built a city, and called the name of the city after the name of his son, Enoch' (Genesis 4.17). The

32

origins of the city, for the Bible, seem to lie in masculine expressions of defiance, insecurity, the need to find substitutions and consolations for the loss of God, and the desire perhaps to take the place of that God, to become a dynasty. In the second wave of city-building, following the flood, it was Nimrod, son of Cush, a warrior, who established Babel and Nineveh (Genesis 10. 9–11).

If Abraham represents the righteous Jew, the ideal is a wanderer, a nomad, not a city-dweller – city-dwelling, like the need for a king, was later sanctioned by God, but ambivalently so. Cities like Babel, Sodom and Gomorrah in Genesis are places one abides in at risk. Jerusalem, following the amalgamation of Israel, Judah and Caanan under David and Solomon, begins to take on a mythic, utopian quality as Zion, the seat of God, but nevertheless it is counterpoised by the city of Babylon, the pagan, hostile, city of destruction, exile and subjugation. It has been argued recently that the myth-making of the great Jerusalem was part of a political move to 'write up' what was, in fact, a small provincial centre (Zvi: 1997, 194–209). In the New Testament, these two cities meet again in an apocalyptic battle – Babylon now figuring Rome under the Emperor Domitian. And though Jerusalem is the site for the great unfolding of Christian salvation, Jerusalem by Christ's own predictions will be levelled to the ground. It is a place of intrigue, hypocrisy and corruption. The only city sanctioned is the heavenly Jerusalem; the city of the resurrected and redeemed.[11] This is the other city, what might be called, after the postmodern architect and architectural historian Charles Jencks, heteropolis (Jencks: 1993) – the Greek for other city – in contrast to metropolis – the Greek for mother-city, capital city. The Letter to the Hebrews takes up the theme of the righteous nomad and speaks of Abraham looking for a city whose builder and maker is God Himself. Christians, as either rural or urban dwellers move towards a final role as citizens, but in a city not to be found among the cities of this world. For God 'hath prepared for them another city', a *heteropolis* (Hebrews 11.16).

In the Bible, then, a complex weave of myth, fact, fear, hope and history circulates about cities. The utopian dreams of city-builders wishing to construct paradise within their boundaries, is crossed by a dark sense of judgement by God on 'all the lofty towers and all the sheer walls' (Isaiah 2:12), and both these strains are filtered through stories of a heavenly archetypal city, the eschatological city of divine manufacture and perfection.

Outside the Bible, history teaches us that the rise of the city makes possible the advancement of a civilisation. With city-dwelling – at Athens, at Rome, at Alexandria, at Memphis, at Jerusalem – comes culture. Cultural productivity is only made possible by trade routes and the development of a merchant class and financial organisation. These cities, like the later mediaeval cities, remained small, defensive, interrelated communities. The sense of community seems to have been palpable, as opposed to imaginary, in Benedict Anderson's understanding of that term for modern societies (Anderson: 1983). But cities have changed, in size and in importance, through three major epochs.

The first was in the early Renaissance period, though Lefebvre dates it from the Middle Ages: the time 'was animated and dominated by merchants and bankers, this city was their *oeuvre*' (Lefebvre: 1991; see also Wallerstein: 1974, 1980). Cities like Venice became fabulously wealthy and demonstrated this wealth (and the power it brought them) in numerous civic buildings. Cities now begin to have an autonomy. The rest of the countryside gravitates around and takes its significance from the mother-city, the metropolis (van der Wee: 1990, 15–27). This gendering of the geographical is not innocent, but part of what Michel Foucault called biopower and biopolitics (Foucault: 1981 and 1997). Motherhood is viewed in terms of productivity. The rise of the city is, then, like the rise of the nation state, linked with developing economies – capitalism that is no longer kept in check by the Church's laws on and against usury (Anderson: 1983, 37; Noonan: 1957). The collapse of these laws against loaning capital as speculative capital in chase of rich returns; the Reformers' break from Rome and Catholic canon law; the opening of the New World and the mass of new mineral wealth – silver and gold – that poured into Western Europe through Spain and Portugal: all gave rise to the cult of worldly goods (Jardine: 1996). The cost of an item was no longer in accord with the labour it took to produce it. Its value became divorced from its worth.[12] And everyone is now a merchant, as Adam Smith understood. The cost of an item was fixed by how much someone else would pay for it – what the market could sustain. Cities grew up in, through and because of the accelerated secularism of the sixteenth and seventeenth centuries (Tawney: 1984, 75–89 and 227–51; Sommerville: 1992). As Tönnies pointed out: the social relationships that organised and characterised city-living found their prototype in 'barter or exchange, including the more highly developed form of exchange, the sale or purchase of things or services' (Tönnies: 1955, 20). Relationships are contractual.

This type of city has been called the mercantile city and is characterised as 'set in a context of petty commodity production, international trade, and limited industrialisation' (Soja: 1989, 175). But as the age of revolution became the age of capital, in the nineteenth century, this kind of city (and the practices of living that both produced and were produced by it) changed. With the second major epoch, the Industrial Revolution – whose legacy most of our cities still live with – we move towards the Competitive Industrial Capitalist City.

International trade expanded at an unprecedented rate and new kinds of cities were born. These, like the older cities, were 'hierarchical city-systems', but '[n]ever before was production so geographically concentrated, so locationally centralised, so densely agglomerated' (Soja: 1989, 177). In the intensification of land use, zoning emerges largely in terms of class. The city featured in Lang's *Metropolis* is heir to the sociological and technological changes heralded by the Industrial Revolution and the development of the Competitive Industrial Capitalist City. Those impressive skyscrapers are only possible because of the advances in engineering and the development of new materials fostered by the Industrial Revolution. New, larger markets, new demands for production, new expectancies from consumers all followed in the wake of the rise of a powerful class of industrialists and entrepreneurs.

In Britain, the Great Exhibition was the staging of an imperial pre-eminence and the new, advanced capitalism that facilitated and maintained it. Under the great glass domes and iron scaffolding of the Crystal Palace, objects from all over the world were on show. A global economy was on the horizon. Two facts about the 1851 showhouse bear symbolic weight. First, the building itself was conceived in terms of a church, with nave and transept. Its architectural aspirations were informed by the mediaeval gothic cathedral, which itself aspired to constructing walls of transparency. It furnished the first examples of techno-gothic – a style revisited in postmodernity. This palace, the largest greenhouse ever built, constituted a secular paradise of glass, to enter which was to experience the sublime and transcendent. Secondly, in this international market all the goods on show were unpriced. For the value of them depended entirely upon how many other people wanted them. The object takes on a value independent of its function or its need: it is reified. A gap opens between the labour going to produce these reified goods and the rewards offered for them by those who consumed them. Marx and Engels spoke much about this reification and the alienation of the worker from the work. Engels, in particular, came to understand these activities from firsthand observation of cities like Manchester and Salford (Engels: [1845] 1987). But the struggles against reification, and the rhetorical resistances to alienation, like the tendencies towards reification and alienation, are conditions for the function of capitalism. For capitalism functions by continually drawing upon the genuinely human activity of those subject to it. It continues to operate through an inability by all involved to fully realise the nature of reification and alienation (Castoriadis: 1997, 16). For example, the opening shots from *Metropolis* – of workers changing shifts and mechanically coming up from or descending back to their world below ground – illustrates this alienation of the worker; the labourer drugged with labour. They appear to be suffering from the effects of the metropolis documented in George Simmel's influential essay of 1903, 'The Metropolis and Mental Life': indifference, self-preservation and social atomism (Simmel: 1995, 30–45). Nevertheless the film offers a way of healing that gap by bringing the worker and the industrialist back together again – saving themselves by saving their livelihoods. The fraternities of workers (Tönnies' *Gemeinschaft*) embrace the alienated *Gesellschaft* of industrial *realpolitik*. Capitalism thus achieves a new level of stability for its continuing productivity. The city is, and will always remain, the face of capitalism.

Another stage in the development of the industrial city was evident by the 1920s and again *Metropolis* reflects this to some extent. There arose the Corporate-Monopoly Capitalist City in which 'industrial production became less concentrated around the city centre, as factories spread into formerly residential inner rings. ... As a result, the old urban cores became increasingly tertiarised, replacing lost industries with an expanding number of corporate headquarters, government offices, financial institutions, and supportive and surveillance activities' (Soja: 1989, 179). Lang's focus is the urban core, but Fredersen's dominance of that core, from the executive suite he occupies overlooking the city, makes visible the Corporate-Monopoly capitalism which galvanises the social system and constructs the Tower of Babel which dwarfs the gothic Cathedral.

The main point, theologically, is that with the rise of market-driven consumerism, cities become increasingly secular places – given over to the production of goods for consumption. As a consequence, in such cities, faith becomes privatised. Like women, religious sentiment becomes a matter of domestic interest. If God-talk went on it went on privately, for it was the concern of privately held feelings and convictions. God-talk had little currency on the open (open, that is, to men) and public market. Churches were the places for religious consolation and quiet prayer, and their spaces and iconography were feminised.[13] In *Metropolis*, there are many shots of chases and struggles on the roof of the great Cathedral, and along its buttressed walls. Important scenes are staged outside its doors, but we are never led inside. Inside is a private and secret domain. Religious sentiment takes place underground. No connection is ever made between Maria's catacomb-chapel, which fostered the prophetic vision of deliverance to the captive workers, and the activities of the Cathedral. The Cathedral is a gothic anachronism in the futuristic city. It has no function. It is a shell, a theatrical backdrop against which civic action can be staged. Like Maria, its role is effaced in the male power-plays of the plot. Privately in these cities there could be devotion, even spiritual ecstasy, but publicly the world presented itself as a great opportunity to be taken, mastered, and made successful by. Creation was there to be excavated and utilised for the service of man.

One notes how the opposition here of public and private – civic office, on the one hand, religious devotion, on the other – forms one of a series of extended oppositions: soul dominating body, male dominating female, the technical over against the imaginative, the conscious mind over against the unconscious. These are the kinds of oppositions I emphasised in the black and white film. And the end of the film, where the workers are united behind the great director, does not dissolve these oppositions, it just confirms and keeps them all in place. Modernity's great synthesis is not effected: it is mimicked, it is aesthetic, it is virtual. Keeping all the dichotomies in place, reifying them, while portraying a harmony between the oppositions, the happy resolution to the film, is viewed as salvation for humankind, the establishment of a perfect society of consensual co-operation.[14] But it is perfection at a price. First, there is the price of those halves of the dualities subjugated and made to suffer. Secondly, there is the price of what Coleridge termed 'the willful suspension of disbelief' that facilitates acts of the imagination.

It was this social harmony – built upon corporate responsibility and co-operation – this organic and integrated view of civic life, that cities were meant to symbolise. This ideal of human beings sitting down in peace together had been the dream and aspiration of modernity (that period in history from the seventeenth to the twentieth century). The city was the great hope for that integration of various energies and talents and skills. The first fingers of modernity's dawn compose texts about utopian places, places where social harmony reigns – with Thomas More's *Utopia*, published in Latin in 1516 and Francis Bacon's *New Atlantis*, published in 1627. These utopian projections usurped the place which notions such as the Kingdom of God and the community of the saints held in the imaginations of the people. In brief, they brought about an emphasis upon what theologians call realised eschatology (Becker: 1932; Blumenberg: 1983, 37–51, 103–21; Marin: 1984). They were part of the new concern with the *nunc* and the now that characterises modernity's ambitions, and of which I will say more in Chapters 3, 6 and 9.

Secularity comes from the Latin word for the age or generation – *saecularum* – which, in the mediaeval period came to mean the realm of human affairs as distinct from ecclesial affairs. Christ governed the universe (*mundus*) and the Pope as Christ's vicar governed the earth (*orbis terratum*), but the world of the affairs and politics of the laity (which the Church wished to have as much control and influence over as possible) was the secular world. When the secular world begins to dominate, the Christian world-view begins to collapse. This happens dramatically in the seventeenth and eighteenth centuries when a mechanical view of the world begins to take hold of the imagination. The world is no longer sustained in its orders by the triune God (as in the mediaeval period and given expression in both Aquinas' *Summa theologiae* and Dante's *Commedia*). The world is maintained and sustained by a series of forces that operate according to certain laws that may be investigated and determined. God – now a great Father-figure, alone in the sky – simply kick-started the process and watches from some cool distance. The secular world runs itself according to its own laws and the moral and political task of human beings is to bring about peaceful co-existence so that each can fulfil their own potential and satisfy their own desires. Utopias pictured this peaceful coexistence – in fact life within such a state (to be brought about now and here below, not up above and after death) was deemed to be paradisial: the return to the garden of Eden. In 1793, Kant could write: 'In men's striving towards the ethical commonwealth, ecclesial faith thus naturally precedes pure religious faith' (Kant: 1960, 97). So that at first we required temples, church buildings and priests. But pure religious faith can do without these things and become the means and vehicle for 'the public union of men'. In the ideal city, then, there is the public union or the commonwealth of human beings, but without a church or temple. Kant believed the one thing necessary was the Bible and that this showed human beings their duties towards one another and had to be interpreted according to the laws of universal human reasoning. But other thinkers, like the French philosopher Jean-Jacques Rousseau, writing earlier than Kant, in the middle of the eighteenth century, had already dispensed with the Bible as a special site for revealed truth. All that was necessary was a social contract established by the people for the well-being of the people, and education – the civilising education that would make good citizens, men and women of reason, of us all. Kant kept the Bible because he was a little more pessimistic about human beings fulfilling their duties outside being told to do so by a God who transcended them. He talked about a principle of radical evil that stood outside and yet made necessary the moral reasoning he advocated. The principle stands as an unresolved aporia at the very roots of his later thinking (Derrida: 1998, 1–78). But the liberal humanists of the eighteenth and nineteenth centuries were much more optimistic – scientific progress, the advancement of learning, the movement towards greater degrees of moral and political perfection: these were the key ideas of the age.

It was in this age that today's cities took shape, cities of eternal aspiration which reflected the new confidence in human beings being able to 'become what we will' (Mirandola: 1948, 227). Advancing capitalism, humanism, secularism divorced now from any need for God (for the sciences social and natural could explain it all) and galloping technological know-how make the city of *Metropolis* possible: the proud erections of glass, concrete and iron that make up the skylines of New York and Chicago; the massive rebuilding programmes of Frederick III for Berlin in the nineteenth century and Georges-Eugène Haussmann, who masterminded the urban development of Paris, also in the nineteenth century. In England, where there were only 15 cities or towns with populations over 20,000 in 1800, by 1890 there were 185. As one urban developer observes; 'If God is dethroned and man is ascendant, then the great city – the largest and most complex of man's creations – is the embodiment of human genius' (Kasinitz: 1995, 3). The city, which demanded high degrees of recognised dependency and human co-operation, and was a symbol of 'mutual help and friendly co-operation' (LeGates and Stout: 1996, 348), structured the possibility for a utopia – an ideal commonwealth. It was a godless commonwealth and a city ideally without a church because salvation was endemic to living in it. It was a city where the new monumental buildings were not cathedrals, but town halls, libraries, public squares, museums and art galleries.[15] It was a city or commonwealth (the meaning of the Latin *civitas*) within which religion was one option on offer for private and leisure-time activity.

Urban planning and the parodies of the eschaton

Urban planners and visionary architects became the new priests of a religion without religion. If one examines Ebenezer Howard's plan, for example, at the centre of a city conceived in terms of concentric rings, stands a paradisial garden, ringed by cultural, educational and administrative foci (a library, a theatre, the town hall, an art gallery etc.). This Eden of knowledge and leisure is further ringed by central parks and a glass arcade called a crystal palace (deliberately echoing the building at the centre of the 1851 World Fair) where shopping can take place in light and openness. Churches stand between the centre and the periphery. They are plural in number and expressions of human responses to the divine: 'of such denominations as the religious beliefs of the people may determine' (Howard in LeGates and Stout: 1996, 251–2). The religious is important for Howard; he hopes his new city 'will pour a flood of light' on current social problems and 'even the relationship of man to the Supreme Power' (Howard in LeGates and Stout: 1996, 346). But the creation of Eden is a task for town-planners. The outstanding contemporary historian of the city, Peter Hall, observes that issuing from the appalling Victorian cities of the night in which middle-class people feared rebellion and revolt, the reaction of urban planners like Howard (and others like Unwin and Parker and Louis de Soissons) 'took the form of a secular Last Judgement: the virtuous poor would be assisted to go directly via the settlement house or the municiple housing project to the garden-city heaven' (Hall: 1996, 364). But, significantly, it has also been observed how 'The garden city is the physical paradigm that presages Disney space' (Sorkin: 1996, 397). We will examine this in the next chapter.

Nurtured on the Christian socialism of F.D. Maurice, the more recent Fabianism, the older traditions of critiquing industrialism by the likes of William Blake and John Ruskin and the Arts and Crafts Movement, by 1904 British architects, inspired by the American City Beautiful movement, began developing 'visionary schemes for civic centres, boulevards and parks' (Sutcliffe: 1981, 75). Howard's was one of the first, but Patrick Geddes published his *City Development: A Study of Parks, Gardens and Culture Institutes* in Edinburgh in 1904, followed by *Cities in Evolution* in 1915. Raymond Unwin published his *Town Planning in Practice* in 1909 in which a Pre-Raphaelite medievalism emerges as a strong figure for *communitas*. 'The order [in feudal times] may have been primitive in its nature, unduly despotic in character, and detrimental to development of the full powers and liberties of the individual, but at least it was an order. Hitherto the growth of democracy, which has destroyed the old feudal structure of society, has but left the individual in the helpless isolation of his freedom', Unwin eloquently writes (Unwin in LeGates and Stout: 1996, 355). Unwin strikes a note that is common and enduring in urban planning: mediaeval communities have remained the nostalgic ideal of historians of the city (like Max Weber: 1960), sociologists of the city (like Ferdinand Tönnies: 1955) and theorists of the city (Lefebvre: 1996, 68–9; Lefebvre: 1991). What is missed by each is the order within these cities, the corporate life, the shared sense of life's good things. What is forgotten is the theological framework, the analogical world-view, that facilitated and produced the mediaeval *communitas*. A theologically informed cosmology is replaced by the surveyor's theodolite, the architect's elevations and the constructor's reinforced concrete.

Elsewhere it was not medievalism that inspired the secular Edens filling the notebooks and essays of architects, nevertheless the same sense of shaping an environmental order to simulate a cosmological order is evident. As gardens, parks and opens vistas functioned in the writing and planning of Howard and Unwin as lungs for new forms of healthy living, so from the 1920s to the 1950s, the American architect, Frank Lloyd Wright, was advocating an architecture that *is* landscape and a landscape that *is* architectured. In his essay 'Broadacre City: A New Community Plan', published in 1935 he wrote: 'the best architect is he who will devise forms nearest organic as features of human growth' (Wright: 1935). From this principle he dreamed up his own ideal community of Broadacres. Broadacres is an ordered city – 'all symmetrical' – but its order is conceived as organic and therefore individualistic both locally, on each homestead, and nationally (for more than one city was conceived). As with Howard's garden city, Broadacres configures a social harmony allied to a natural harmony, fostered by a political egalitarianism. A natural theology informs this project as with all the projects we will look at. Wright's elementalism is proto-New Age: human beings have a right to the ground as they have a right to the sun and the air, he wrote (Wright: 1935). And yet, in a way that augurs a contemporary tension between New Age naturalism and advanced electronic information services, Wright's techno-dependence (self-sufficient homesteads are linked to each other via telecommunication and advanced transportation) foreshadows the advent of the virtual communities in cyberspace that we will examine in Chapters 5 and 9. The pattern and rhythm of living that unfolds from within the developing city will erase social ills, eradicate sin: 'To build Broadacres as conceived would automatically end unemployment and all the evils forever', he confidently tells us (Wright: 1935). 'Unwholesome life would get no encouragement and the ghastly heritage left by overcrowding in overdone ultra-capitalistic centers would be likely to disappear in three or four generations. The old success ideals having no chance at all, new ones more natural to the best in man [*sic*] would be given a fresh opportunity to develop naturally' (Wright: 1935). Architecturally, this led to the advocacy of the extensive use of glass and 'roofless rooms'.

Wright shares this appeal to light with the Swiss architect, Le Corbusier, who was planning, at the same time, what became known as his Radiant City. The language of light, conceptions of openness and constructions imaging transparency – found in Howard's work and Wright's – dominate his own visionary project. The language of light has, since at least the speculations of Brunelleschi on Euclid's *Optics* in the early part of the fifteen century (Burgin: 1988), conflated the inner light of reason (Cicero's and Descartes' 'natural light') with the divine light in Plato and the Neo-Platonists, and investigations into the physics of light which Newton claimed was in unity with matter (Blumenberg: 1993; Koyre: 1957). The light of revelation, the light of the eschatologically realised, is confounded with the light of the *Aufklärung* and the light of what Derrida has termed 'photographic instantaneity', the light of self-presence (Derrida: 1998, 40). Le Corbusier's architectural conceptions stand, then, in an unfolding language of light which appealed to a transcendent horizon in the form of the sublime (see Milbank: 1998, 258–84 and Ward: 2000c). For him, glass towers were to reach up into the arc of the sky and become the centre-pieces of his city of perfection, expressive of aspirations for transcendence. But before we examine these conceptions more closely, it is important to return to that ideal governing the modern city: a place where all a human being's desires might be met and potentially realised, a city without a church because the moral perfection of each human being has been fulfilled. For the ideal is informed by, and parodies, the Christian heteropolis itself – the city made and built by God Himself towards which we, like Abraham, move (see Cavanaugh: 1998: 182–200). For the paradise we regain, in biblical terms, is no longer a garden to which we are allowed access once more, but a city without a church. As the Book of Revelation describes it: our civic destination is a city in which 'the twelve gates were twelve pearls; and every several gate was one of pearl: and the street of the city was pure gold, as it were transparent glass. And I saw no temple therein: for the Lord Almighty and the Lamb are the Temple of it' (Rev. 21.21–22). This is the eschatological realisation, the kingdom at the end of time. The logic of the twelve gates and one street announces the heavenly city to be an open light-filled, transparent and eternal cube, whose walls, foundations, measurements and materiality are all symbolic. 'And the city lieth foursquare, and the length is as large as the breadth: and he measured the city with the [golden] reed, twelve thousand furlongs. The length and the breath and the height of it are equal. And he measured the wall thereof, an hundred and forty-four cubits, according to the measure of a man, that is, of the angel. And the building of the wall of it was jasper; and the city was of pure gold, like onto clear glass' (Rev. 21.16–18).

It is the creation of this now godless, but nevertheless light-filled, spatially harmonious, timeless city of which the architect Le Corbusier dreamed. His work set the pace and tone which dominated architecture from the 1920s to the 1970s. His work, like Howard's, announces that perfection is possible in this world through human efforts alone. Buildings and cities can be designed and built which will satisfy our deepest religious desires. Architecture, he once wrote, 'is the skilful, correct and magnificent play of volumes assembled in light' (Le Corbusier: 1965, 32). Light, form and harmony are the essential hallmarks of Le Corbusier's designs, as they were of Wright's. But unlike Wright, it is mathematics rather than biology that provides the central figure for Le Corbusier's conceptions. In 1923 he published his ground breaking collection of essays *Towards a New Architecture* in which he wrote:

> Such forms, which may be elementary or subtle, smooth or rough, work physiologically upon our senses (sphere, cube, cylinder, horizontal, vertical, oblique etc.) and stimulate them. When thus affected, we are able to see beyond bare sensations; certain relationships are born that, acting upon our consciousness lift us into a state of delight (or harmony with the universal laws that govern us and all our actions) in which we can use our full powers of recollection, reason and creation.
>
> (Le Corbusier: 1965, 20–1)

Note the natural theology expressed – both in these words and the buildings that are inspired by them – 'universal laws that govern us and all our actions'.[16] The inspiration for the dramatic roof of his chapel at Ronchamp was the harmonious proportions of a shell found on a beach in Long Island. There is a belief here in mathematical truths, a universal and spiritual geometry that human beings can align themselves with and reach their full powers by means of the right kind of buildings and, in a larger context for these buildings, the right kind of city. Resurrection life is to be lived now. Again the end times, the total presence of the eschaton, is realised or realisable now. Today is salvation – through the city; a city which has no need of a Temple because it is the Temple.

Le Corbusier, in a series of books spanning the 1920s and 1930s, developed his theory of the city. 'The layout of a city', he wrote, in 1925 (the year work on *Metropolis* began), 'determines the physical and mental condition of its residents' (quoted in Guiton: 1981, 94). He advocated the need for a contemporary city which would be built vertically. High density blocks of residence among planted areas arranged upon a grid system would, he advocated, create a tranquil atmosphere that would offset the strain produced by the accelerated tempo of modern business. Social problems – violence and vandalism – are resolved here by the belief that people living in beautifully proportioned spaces will align themselves with the moral and spiritual geometries of the universe. 'It is a question of building which is at the root of the social unrest today', he wrote (Le Corbusier: 1965, 14). Light and spacing creates a sense of freedom within which human beings can flourish and realise their greatest potential. He called the skyscrapers of Manhattan as 'new white cathedrals' (Le Corbusier in Kasinitz: 1995, 108). He defined his 'radiant city' (his term which is again reminiscent of the heavenly city which has no need of lighting for the lighting comes from the presence of God within the city itself) as 'inspired by physical and human laws ... to bring machine age man *essential pleasures*' (quoted in Fishman: 1977). Sports ground provision would stimulate and increase the sense of participation and co-operation between residents.

The Christian heteropolis, its cosmology and its metaxis, becomes, with Le Corbusier, the kingdom of this world. The city comes of age – men and women can have resurrection life and have it now in 'the radiant city', the metropolis, those lofty erections which scrape the skies. This city has no need of God (or religion), for its values (aesthetic, moral and spiritual) lie all at hand. The cities of aspiration can embody transcendence in the sublime heights of their towers. They can engineer the euphoria of the sublime through panoramic vistas offered from these towers. As two recent academics in urban planning have observed in a survey of the tensions between the dreams of the architect/planner and the pragmatism of the engineer, 'planning theory is in any case not so much an attempt to explain the world as it *is* but as it *ought* to be. Planning theory sets itself the task of rationalising the irrationalities, and seeks to materialise itself in social and historical reality (like Hegel's World Spirit) by bringing to bear upon the world a set of abstract, independent, and transcendent norms' (Scott and Roweis: 1977, 1,116). Cities like Le Corbusier's radiant city are transcendent, sublime and atheistic cities – cities where light, space, freedom and harmony can penetrate into the very heart of buildings and bodies. They are virtual cities, cities of the imagination, cities of light. They express a secular dream that will reach its apotheosis in cyberspace and its electronic communities (see Chapter 9).

Human beings aspire in their cities to replace the God who Hegel and Nietzsche, in their different ways, proclaimed dead: they aspire to imitate and embody the properties of this object-God fashioned by various deisms: the control of His omnipotence, the knowledge of His omniscience, the command and realisation of the moment, the now, of His omnipresence, the municifience of His grace and goodness and the sublimity of His beauty. The centre-piece of *Metropolis* is the Tower of Babel, not now in ruins but rising magnificently towards total knowledge and fully immersing pleasures.

Theological responses

The discipline of Christian theology has four possible responses in such a city. All four possibilities find expression in the various schools of twentieth-century theology.

1.   Theology can simply retreat, and see itself as irrelevant, part of the past which must vanish in the preoccupation with the present, the up-to-date, the modern, the new. It can embrace the 'truth' that there is nothing transcending or outside this world. It can accept that all values are at hand – there is no world beyond, no truth higher, no ultimate good, no truly real, God is dead. The production and marketing of this kind of response is found in the work of Don Cupitt, in Britain, and the purveyors, in the States, of what is called atheology (Taylor: 1984) or Christian atheism (Altizer: 1966).

2.   Christian theology can advocate a natural theology. That is, see the orders of human reason (those mathematical truths) reflected in the created orders of the world and trace the names of the creator in creation. Despite David Hume's savage attack upon such theology in the eighteenth century, natural theology and a mathematical basis for understanding God's relation to the world have remained popular, as the theological approach of Richard Swinburne, at Oxford, demonstrates (Swinburne: 1977). Natural theology is also frequently the basis for those attempting to make connections between theology and science: the work of Arthur Peacocke and John Polkinghorne in Britain.

3.   Christian theology can correlate the cultural and the sacred, examining religions as symbolic systems expressing not only the unity of being human, but also a divine, overriding reality, a transcendental ground. Religion here is not divorced from culture but is itself a cultural expression. And so the specifics of the Christian faith – incarnation, crucifixion, resurrection – can be understood as metaphors or symbols, as buildings, music, painting, literature are composed of metaphors and symbols, all expressing this one transcendental ground of Being. This is the fundamental position of liberal theologians who dissolve the distinctiveness of any faith and, in doing so, can put the symbols of that faith into dialogue with the symbols of other faiths, beliefs and cultural forms. Liberal theology, then, can be seen as a theology enabling conversation and integration between a multitude of different neighbours in any residential quarter of the city. Peter Hall explicitly relates the utopianism and socialism of the garden-city

43

planners and the designers of city towers to liberal theology – particularly in Britain: 'in the welfare state era of the 1950s and 1960s came the triumph of liberal theology: now, all – even the urban underclass – were instantly perfectible; all might gain immediate access by the strait gate to the Corbusian city of towers' (Hall: 1996, 364). The work of theologians like John Robinson, John MacQuarrie, Maurice Wiles, John Hick and, more recently Keith Ward, are, in their different ways, examples of this theological response.

4.   Christian theology can emphatically reject this earthly, secular city; denounce its atheism, repudiate its values, and appeal to a radically other city, a heteropolis, yet to be revealed. Throughout the 1920s, while Lang was filming *Metropolis* and Le Corbusier was dreaming of his contemporary city, Karl Barth was issuing the various editions of his *Commentary on the Epistle to the Romans* which spoke out against the pride of man and culture as a substitute for faith. He wrote, in a vein reminiscent of Luther's two kingdoms and an acceptance of modernity's opposition between secular and sacred, that 'Grace is and remains always the Power of God, the promise of a new man, of a new nature, of a new world: it is the promise of the Kingdom of God. Grace is and remains always in this world negative, invisible, and hidden; the mark of its operation is the declaration of the passing of this world and of the end of all things' (Barth: 1933, 103).

The range of options for a theology of the city are evident in the key studies published between the mid 1960s and the late 1970s, prior to the designation in Britain of Urban Priority Areas and the constitution by the Archbishop of Canterbury of his Commission on Urban Priority Areas. Surprisingly, none of them are actually referred to in *Faith in the City* as possible sources for the development of its own theological statement.

The two earliest – John S. Dunne's *The City of the Gods: A Study in Myth and Mortality* and Harvey's Cox's *The Secular City* – were both published in 1965, and demonstrate various liberal approaches.

John S. Dunne

While making an appeal to aspects of the Christian faith, Dunne views all religious teachings as mythological. Christ stands in a long line of saviour kings, ruling over an eternal city, a symbol among many symbols for the desire to live forever (Dunne: 1965, 226). The theological dissolves into the anthropological; the fundamental human concern with being-towards-death wrestles with an equally fundamental desire to prolong life upon earth. Rooted in a none too precise account of Heideggerian existentialism, the book proceeds to explore the myths and symbols whereby human beings have expressed their attempt to circumvent their mortality. The city is part of the quest for life everlasting. It is a symbol of timeless, static utopian possibilities. Once a place made sacred by the king, a place in which human beings consorted with the gods, it became increasingly secularised. In the ancient world it is bound up with a concept of

44

the past that never dies, an immortal past. With Plato it became a transhistorical place sought after by immortal souls, then later (Dunne believes with Augustine) it became bound up with a *post-mortem* future in a heavenly city (see Chapter 9 for an alternative account of Augustine's two cities). In more recent times it has become an actual project: the Christian critique of cities (like Rome) attempting to divinise themselves has become 'a constructive plan for an earthly society in which man, by renouncing every attempt to divinize and immortalize society, can achieve a freedom never attained in any previous society' (Dunne: 1965, 158–9).

All these manifestations of the city are solutions to the problem of death. A profound necrophilia permeates Dunne's project, a necrophilia which is ultimately articulating a metaphysics of nihilism. In this, he is, without making reference to them, at one with the Death-of-God theologians, who were, at that time in the States, announcing their own programme of Christian atheism (Altizer: 1966, 1967; Altizer and Hamilton: 1968). Like Altizer, Dunne is aware of the striking analogy between the ancient myths of the death of the god and dialectical idealism in which 'the personal God and his individual incarnation are abolished in a Calvary from which there emerges the autonomous human spirit, the "absolute" spirit' (Dunne: 1965, 19). The community is founded upon, and eternally lives out, the death of God; the city as place is fundamentally a mausoleum, the city as community (*civitas*) is composed of individuals existentially in crisis because bound to die. While recognising that this Hegelianism has led to two other myths of evading death – personal sovereignty with its right to life (Dunne: 1965, 204, 227) and totalitarianism with its Nietzschean embrace of death in order to be strong and available for an immortal future (Dunne: 1965, 211) – the thesis concludes with the sovereignty of death. It offers its own solution (myth?): 'it would be more reasonable simply to recognise that if he must someday die there is nothing he can do that will satisfy his desire to live' (Dunne: 1965, 228). Human beings have to lay down their will to live for themselves, accept death and (in an abrupt retrieval of Christian symbolics) hope in the resurrection. In words that echo Tillich's book *Courage To Be* (Tillich: 1952), this courage would be freedom, and then 'the city of man will have become in truth the city of God' (Dunne: 1965, 231).

The conclusion is ambivalent, as ambivalent as the use of the word 'truth' in this final sentence. In a world of mediated representations of an existential conflict governed by the evolutionary process of history what is 'truth'? If the thesis, while recognising the emergence of a new mysticism of death and the absence of meaning, does not accept that as a solution, it has no argument against those that *will* accept such a solution other than an unanalysed appeal to being 'reasonable'. The atheologians, post-Christians and Christian atheists are all ready to graduate and rise on the next crest of this liberalism. All positions within this post-Kantian account of myth and symbol, are equally valuable and equally arbitrary. They are equal insofar as they are attempts to solve a problem. They are arbitrary insofar as they pragmatically function as necessary explanations, as culturally and historically specific representations of the human condition. We are back with Socrates in Plato's *Phaedo* practising how to die, quietly, among the civic reliquies to our aspirations to be otherwise.

Harvey Cox

In his book, *The Secular City*, Cox is far more actively content with this situation. But then the evolving secularism and the negative atheologies of God *as* death, traced by Dunne, are to some extent offset in Cox by the conviction that the evolving secularism has its origins in the Bible, was mediated first by the Christian Church, and that, as such, is a good to be welcomed. Like Dunne, he accepts an historical determinism (which is vaguely theologised in terms of Providence): a process of secularisation (which he distinguishes, briefly and unconvincingly, from secularism as an ideology). What secularity has produced is openness and freedom, with a desacralisation of politics, values and the cosmos. Cox is far more confident also that the individualism this has fostered is salvific. It is not the usurpation of a self-grounding sovereignty that previously only pertained to the notion of God. Standpoints are now relative because no one's account of things is ultimate, and this is not nihilistic because, for him, the nihilist is one who revels in the things the dead God once forbade: worshipping, in effect, a negative shadow of that God.

The city is conceived as a technopolis akin, on a larger scale, to the switch-board linking everyone through telecommunications. Its anonymity and mobility are positive goods that foster biblical faith. The scope for the freedom of choice is immensely broadened, for relationships can now be chosen, rather than imposed by a more constricted environment. Theologically, this new cultural context, like the 'God of the Gospel ... wills freedom and responsibility' (Cox: 1965, 47), encourages the development of an I–Thou theology, and supports the ongoing creativity of human beings in the making and naming of their world. Though critical of pragmatism as a new ontology, pragmatism as a style of living is endorsed as theologically good and in accordance with biblical principles. The Christian faith, instead of supplying a ruling ethos, will provide one of the living options in a genuinely pluralistic culture (Cox: 1965, 92). And in this way secularisation puts an end to cultural hegemony.

It is a city without the need for a church, for 'Secular man [*sic*] relies on himself and his colleagues for answers. He does not ask the church, the priest, or God' (Cox: 1965, 81). The Church is criticised for its small-town mindedness and its inability to face the new urban reality of rapid social change. Cox addresses it with a call to repentance, since the secular city is the symbol of the coming of God's Kingdom (Cox: 1965, 116–23). It is the call to adult accountability. Therefore the Church should be prophetic and *avant-garde* in proclaiming this new world, help people to grow up and 'stop blaming economic forces or psychological pressures for social injustice and family strife' (Cox: 1965, 130). Employing the language and style of the dialectical theologians, he calls the Church to the crisis of choice.

Not all in the secular city is bright, light and promising. There are structural inequalities and a new kind of poverty, for example. But the Church can and must act as a cultural exorcist. It must cast out the mythical meanings that obscure the realities of life and hinder human action (Cox: 1965, 162). Given the constructed nature of our world, which Cox accepts, it is difficult to appreciate what this existential appeal to the realities of life might mean, but a typical Bultmannian pronouncement is made: we are to be delivered from mythology into history, to speak in a secular fashion of God.

Despite Cox's appeal to Barth above Tillich, the liberal correlationalism is evident, likewise the values and the metaphysics of modernity. The biblical language is redeployed in new desacralised, demythologised ways. The values embraced – freedom, autonomy, choice, accountability – have been at the centre of social and political ethics since Hobbes and Locke. They are perceived as universal, transcultural values – the values necessary for a pluralist world in which Christianity is one option among many. One can see, to retain any credibility for the Christian discourse at all, why Cox needs to insist on the distinction between secularisation and pragmatism as an historical movement and a style of living, respectively, rather than as, respectively, an ideology and ontology. It is much more difficult to see how he can maintain this distinction unless he believes that the processes of secularisation bear no implicit values or metaphysics. Where does the historical movement of secularisation end, for example? His secular Christian values are indistinguishable from the values of consumer capitalism (Taylor: 1999, 140–67). Twenty-seven years later Francis Fukuyama could inform him: the culmination is *The End of History and the Last Man* (Fukuyama: 1992).

The optimism in the marriage Cox proposes between Christian theology and the secular technopolis is palpable. It reflects the optimism of the film made forty years before in Berlin. It somehow manages to disregard the growing tide of urban violence evident in American cities before, during and immediately following the publication of *The Secular City*. Between 1963, when civil riots broke out in Birmingham, Alabama and 1967, when they flared up in Detroit, American urban planners came to realise that their work had done nothing to ameliorate the dismemberment of inner-city communities (Hall: 1996, 332; Soja: 1989, 182). The year 1968–9 saw similar riots in France and Italy. Six years before the publication of *The Secular City*, in a book Cox makes passing reference to, Lewis Mumford, employing the electric-grid as an image for the new invisible cities of telecommunications that were emerging (which he termed megalopoli) ends his history of the city on a profoundly pessimistic note: 'Our civilization is faced with the relentless extension and aggrandizement of a highly centralized, super-organic system, that lacks autonomous component centres capable of exercising selection, exerting control, above all, making autonomous decisions and answering back' (Mumford: 1973, 644–5). Cox's theology is not possible in Mumford's technopolis. For Mumford, the new cities are akin to Ridley Scott's 'aliens', in the film by that name, or the forms of artificial intelligence imagined by the Wachelski brothers in the film *The Matrix*: highly intelligent, highly adaptable, mechanised organisms that will exploit and then destroy humanity. While certain theologians of the city, then, were calling upon the urban church to get real the urban geographers and historians were already warning of great changes on the way.

The response of the natural theologians

As far as I can discover no Christian theologian developed the natural theologies implicit in Le Corbusier and Wright as a Christian response to the city. Those who might have been inclined were occupied on other fronts: philosophy of religion (with analytical approaches to the natural theology they believed evident in Thomas)[17] and the relationship between science and religion. But architects and visionary urban planners did still continue to stress the correlation between the natural, the spiritual and the technological. Of the more sobre and academic of them, Constantinos Doxiadis developed his science of human settlements, named Ekistics, which was based upon the relationship between the dynamic growth of settlements and what 'we in Nature and in the evolution taking place in many organisms' experience (Doxiadis: 1968, 376). He spoke about how the large urban developments would, over time, become a Dynamegalopolis and this would then become an ecumenopolis, a universal city characterised by happiness, safety, and a balance between the organic and the mechanical.

This was city-planning for the age of Aquarius. It was taken much further by Paolo Soleri who designed cities based on geometric shapes. He developed his concept of Arcology (architecture plus ecology) explicitly on the basis of the spiritual writings of the Jesuit Pierre Teilhard de Chardin. Conceiving himself as a prophet from the desert, come to teach ecological salvation, his Mesa city was an urban landscape for 'purified man'. It would be a city resonant with 'symbolic and mystical inferences',[18] a city of cosmic beauty for the development of that sentient and reflective life Teilhard de Chardin termed the Noosphere.[19]

These natural theology approaches share Cox's optimisms: about the human and about the relationship between the technological and the natural. Theology of any organised, ecclesial form dissolves into spirituality, which itself cannot be divorced from aesthetics, an aesthetics of the sublime. Soleri's vision was to transform everything into the aesthetically useful. But this is and has always been the danger of natural theology. With God as an architect any disharmony or perceived fault in the design reflects badly upon the manufacturer. Soleri stands in a long line of architects who saw their own mission as divine: men who have taken upon themselves the office of God-as-designer.

Jacques Ellul

Alongside these liberal and natural theologies of the city is the conservative one. In the sixties, more directly under the influence of Karl Barth than Harvey Cox,

Jacques Ellul, who had already published a monumental critique of the technological society (*La technique ou l'enjeu du siècle*, 1954, translated as *The Technological Society* in 1965) wrote his *Meaning of the City* (translated into English in 1970). Ellul, Professor of the History and Sociology of Institutions at the University of Bordeaux, sketches a picture radically opposed to Cox's and illustrates the fourth of our theological options in modernity: separation or Christian apartheid. Like Cox, he begins with the Bible, but unlike Cox, reads there a profound divine judgement against cities and all they symbolise. Israel was seduced by them; the prophets condemned them; Jesus refused to spend a night in them. For what cities express, for Ellul, is human murderous aspiration in the face of God. Cities are founded on Cain's refusal of God and, in agreement with Dunne's thinking, Ellul views them as expressions of the human desire to design our own eternity. The city is a substitute for God and an act of *ressentiment*; the embodiment of human power and revolt. The city is Moloch, its archetype is Babylon – reminding us of the city's dark side in *Metropolis* – and 'Urban civilization is a warring civilization' (Ellul: 1970, 13). Cities are founded on what Augustine would call the *libido dominandi*, the desire to conquer time, space and power and to mark that conquest. As such they are places given over to the expression of this desire in terms of sin and idolatry. The chosen of God are held captive here, Ellul states; the Church 'is a prisoner in the world, in the city, the absolute synthesis of all that is worldly, all that is noncommunication, all that makes the Gospel impossible to share' (Ellul: 1970, 20). The city – like technology, for Ellul – stands in utter opposition to the divine nature of creation and so it cannot become even an instrument for goodness and salvation (Ellul: 1970, 36). So the sociologists, lawmakers, urban specialists, politicians, architects and economists may all search for a moral and legal solution to the inhuman problems brought up by the city, but there is nothing to be done. For the city is cursed and condemned (Ellul: 1970, 44–84).

Separation becomes the only godly response; separation on the basis of repentance. This does not mean leaving the city. The leaving will come only when the city is fallen and destroyed (which is coming about). The separation means defending God's counter-creation within the city and living out the eschatological promise of reconciliation. The archetypal city here, with all its ambiguities, is Jerusalem. The urban dwelling advocated must continually announce the disappearance of cities, the dehumanisation of technology, and the establishment of God's own building, the living body of Christ. In line with Mumford's own thoughts (and Scott's 'aliens'), though employing a different image, Ellul concludes that the city's nature is parasitic: 'Like a vampire, it preys on the true living creation, alive in its connection with the Creator. The city is dead, made of dead things for dead people. She can herself neither produce nor maintain anything whatever ... the city devours men' (Ellul: 1970, 150–1).

There is a disturbing gendering of the city here, the metropolis is a barren mother, a techno-gothic *la belle dame sans merci*. This is the other side of the Crystal Palaces, those modern cathedrals with their walls of light. There is no space here for Cox's Enlightenment freedom, but then there is no place here for the central value of living theologically: incarnational embodiment. The polarisation of the two kingdoms, the earthly and the heavenly city, is central to this theology of the city. There is no dialogue between them. The crowning act of God is a break with history (Ellul: 1970, 163); the new city is a transcendent one with no part in the cities built by human beings. An inheritor of Calvinist biblicalism and Barthian dialectics, Ellul's Protestant 'active pessimism' (Ellul: 1970, 181) finds no other function for theology in the city than prophesying its ruination.

The first three of these responses can be read as attempts by theological discourse, facing its own marginality in modernity, to be included. The atheological and the liberal responses most evidently do this, but natural theology also is an appeal to be sheltered under the wings of a soaring, and socially acceptable, scientism. The fourth response, in a manner similar to the various religious fundamentalisms of the twentieth century, is profoundly antimodern. This response is significant, as Harvey Cox has recently pointed out in his own attempt to describe an adequate theological response to the postmodern city (Cox: 1984).[20] It is counter-cultural and ultimately nihilistic with respect to creation and human beings formed in the image of God.

All of the responses fail to take account of *gendered* corporeality: of sexual differences and the performance of these differences in civic culture. Maria is effaced in *Metropolis*, and that effacement is not incidental. She continues to be effaced – with consequences also, among many other things, for what it means to be masculine – in accounts and configurations of the cities of aspiration. No one asks whether this is her aspiration. And, in a way, this failure to think through who is oppressed so that the city might become eternal, salvific, and sublime was already an indication that the city would not attain the glories imagined by Lang, Howard, Wright and Le Corbusier. Cities have not seen human beings joining peacefully together in a civic labour to develop the freedom and creative capacities of all. Cities have not seen human beings joining together at all.

As one recent urban planner notes: 'For many Americans [and I think we can include Brits as well] the city has come to symbolise chaos, social breakdown and the lack of civilisation ... a symbol of lawlessness, danger and marginality' (Kasinitz: 1995, 387). The human hopes and aspirations summed up in those cities of the 1920s with their ambitious skylines (and the theologies which responded to them) were built upon industrial potential, a notion of public utility and regulated capitalism. We have moved elsewhere.

We have moved into a fourth epoch in the development of cities. We have moved into a post-industrial culture in which service economies flourish as manufacturing commercialism declines, creating ghettos of deprivation and IT illiteracy. We have moved into what David Harvey calls 'flexible accumulation capitalism' (Harvey: 1990), a late-capitalism where consumption outstrips production, credit or virtual money outstrips real reserves, and the market is becoming increasingly deregularised so that in certain parts of this world anything can be bought: frozen sperm, ballistic missiles, stolen organ parts, a boy, a girl, the life of an enemy. Cities have gone into what is technically termed 'overurbanisation' or 'overshoot' – that is, cities can no longer provide sufficient job opportunities, education, welfare or basic public services for their increasing populations. One researcher writes: 'In an overshoot condition, the population members frantically grasp for any resources that will keep them alive' (Milbrath: 1985, 7) – whether legal or illegal. By the 1960s the American translator of Max Weber's seminal sociological study, *The City* (published in 1927, the year Lang's *Metropolis* was showing in Berlin), could end his introduction by saying: 'The modern city is losing its external and formal structure. Internally it is in a state of decay ... The age of the city seems to be at an end' (Martindale: 1960, 62). Mumford's history of the city ends with concerns for its future and Peter Hall, in many ways Mumford's successor, concludes his account of urban planning in the twentieth century darkly prophesying a circular return to the Victorian cities of night (the cities out of which the utopianism of urban planning emerged). By 1985 when the Archbishop's Report was published, the secular city built to be without a Temple seemed to lie in ruins. The 1980s and 1990s saw the imaginations of film directors haunted by post-apocalyptic cities: Ridley Scott in *Blade Runner*, Luc Besson in *The Fifth Element* – alongside the *Mad Max* series, *Escape from L.A.*, *The Dark City*, *Waterworld* and *City of the Lost Children*. The monumental buildings of Gotham, with its strong patrician order, is always under threat from the Jokers and the Penguins, always requiring either the supernatural deliverance and protection of a Batman, a Spiderman, a Superman or the extraordinary intelligence of a private dectective.

A new city-form is emerging – has been emerging since the late 1970s. *Faith in the City* was caught between what Michel Serres has recently termed the Old City and the New City (see Chapter 8). The best critics of *Faith in the City* were able to see that: 'it is our belief that a failure to take free market claims sufficiently seriously may undermine the credibility of a theological response to the issue', Raymond Plant and others said (Harvey: 1989, 70). Elaine Graham speaks of the Commission's incarnational theology as a perfect expression of 'the Church of England's position in a settled, harmonious social order' (Graham: 1996, 184). Haddon Wilmer, observing how the story of modern British town planning told of a quest to build the New Jerusalem (see Stevenson: 1988, 53–70), pointed out that '*Faith in the City* was written in this tradition at a time when it was already falling into disarray and was widely as well as wilfully discredited' (Harvey: 1989, 38). We have now to ask what has become of the cities of eternal aspiration and what an adequate theological response to these present cities might be – since the other responses are for cities no longer credible and articulate theologies no longer acceptable.[21]

2

CITIES OF ENDLESS DESIRE

Disneyland exists in order to hide that it is the 'real' country, all of 'real' America *is* Disneyland ... Disneyland is presented as imaginary in order to make us believe that the rest is real, whereas all of Los Angeles and the America that surrounds it are no longer real, but belong to the hyperreal order and to the order of simulation.

(Baudrillard: 1995)

Dorthea, Anastasia, Despina, Fedora, Zobeide – all feminine names, all cities of desire constructed by Italo Calvino in his collection of fantasies, *Invisible Cities*. All but one of the descriptions (fictionally 'transcribed' from Marco Polo's reminiscences of his expeditions to Kublai Khan), feature women in erotic tableaux. These cities are gendered: they structure and institutionalise sexual desire. They are texts produced by and producing a certain longing. Each of Calvino's (or Polo's) cities is a city of signs. In an essay entitled 'The City as Protagonist in Balzac', Calvino observes how the French novelist followed 'his first intuition of the city as language, as ideology, as the conditioning factor of every thought and word and gesture' (Calvino: 1989, 184–5). Calvino performs this intuition. The reader wanders down Calvino's streets in the same way, at the same time, as he/she negotiates the words composing each written line.

Desire builds different cities. Despina 'displays one face to the traveller arriving overland and a different one to him who arrives by sea' and 'Each city receives its form from the desert it opposes' (Calvino: 1989, 17–8). The signs issue from and return back to the silent margins of a textual world. 'In every age, someone, looking at Fedora as it was, imagined a way of making it an ideal city, but while he constructed his miniature model, Fedora was already no longer the same as before, and what had been until yesterday a possible future became only a toy in a glass globe' (Calvino: 1989, 32). Time star-crosses desires: so that the space within which the city operates can never be colonised, frozen, subject to the politics and mania of any single utopic desire. Fedora is always other, it exists as a heterotopia. All Calvino's cities destabilise their institutional forms. 'There are two ways of describing the city of Dorothea' (Calvino: 1989, 9), we are told, and Polo's description of an idyllic polis of order, youthfulness and sexual innocence is crossed by another voice and an account of Dorothea from one who contemplates the desert expanses and recognises, as a result of seeing Dorothea, that his 'path is only one of many' (Calvino: 1989, 9). The unity of the ideal collectivity is always fractured; there always remains the desert, that expansive space out of which the city-form was carved, that space which haunts and displaces utopias with the other, the outside. The city of Zobeide, the white city, was founded upon the common dream of several men from various nations. They saw a woman running at night through an unknown city and they dreamed that they pursued her. In unison they decide to build Zobeide, like the city in their dream, though 'they arranged spaces and walls differently from the dream, so she would be unable to escape again' (Calvino: 1989, 45). But outsiders could not understand what drew people to Zobeide 'this ugly city, this trap' (Calvino: 1989, 46).

A certain economy is evident in Calvino's cities of desire. Desire, which is always drawn to the desert (as if only there is it given the space for the infinity of its longing), is constrained in order that the city can be founded. There is a labour installed by desire, which founds and forms, constructs and organises, and which dreams the ideal. The ideal is the final consummation of that desire. But it is a labouring that the restlessness and endlessly desiring also thwarts. Even so, in that labouring, desire itself undergoes a transformation. In the structuralist language of Roman Jakobson and Jacques Lacan, Calvino's cities are metaphors continually crossed by the trope of exile and sojourning, metonymy (Jakobson: 1987; Lacan: 1977; Ward: 1991).

To enter into Calvino's cities is to glimpse some of the libidinal dynamics of contemporary urban life, primed with fantasy, hyped with ecstasy, dazzling in the allure of promised, sybaritic pleasures. These are imaginary communities, and we will say more about such imaginary (and virtual) communities in Chapters 5 and 9. For the moment we need to examine the nature of the changes which have helped to bring about the new urban lifestyles and geographies, the cities of endless desire.

The development of the postmodern city

Various accounts have been rendered for the transformation of urban culture through the 1970s to 1980s. Many of these accounts are also accounts of the onset of the postmodern condition (see Harvey, Jencks, Jameson, Soja, Bauman among others). Having discussed the various philosophical (Lyotard), cultural (Jencks), historical (Toulmin) and political (Certeau) narratives for the general origins of postmodernism and postmodernity elsewhere (Ward: 2000a), I wish to draw attention here to three significant factors which have impacted most specifically upon the city and have been responsible, among others, for the changes which have occurred there. These factors are: the introduction of flexible accumulative or late-capitalism or the onset of post-Fordism; the demise of urban planning in the wake of the sudden mobility of land-use and the dis-

and relocation of production in a post-industrial context; and the new order of simulation in which the proximity of production to reproduction becomes so pronounced the real vanishes behind the sign of or the designer label or the logo for the actual goods. In Chapter 9 two more factors for urban change will be examined: globalism and the rise of what Manuel Castells calls the network society (1996). I postpone detailed discussion of those factors here because we will see more clearly by the last chapter the theological vision that both informs and is perverted by globalism and cyberspace. All these factors are profoundly interrelated, and what they have produced is a new space for cultural activity and theological productivity. For the increasing deregularisation of the market necessitates transformations in spatial movements – of commodities, of labour, of production sites. This affects not only the tempo of urban living, but the shape and internal organisation of cities – urban planning, redevelopment, the rerouting of traffic and the reconsideration of zoning. In turn, to the effects of these two factors are added the production of what Jean Baudrillard terms a hyperreality: where in the process of the reproducibility of goods, the real is not only that which can be endlessly reproduced, but that which is always and already reproduced. Baudrillard observes that the result of the new processes of consumer reproduction is 'Travelling signs, media, fashion and models, the blind but brilliant ambience of simulacra' (Baudrillard: 1993, 77). In the cities of eternal aspiration Culture attempted to imitate or translate Nature. In the cities of endless desire Culture imitates Culture. We have already seen, in the Introduction, how, for Baudrillard the city is first and foremost the site of the sign's execution.

We need now to explore the logic relating these three factors and their implications for urban transformation. If we begin with the economic reorganisation this is not to suggest it is the fundamental dynamic for urban transformation. The work of Michael Peter Smith (Smith and Feagin: 1987), Manuel Castells (1983) and Anthony Giddens (1984) draws attention to the fluidity of social structures, the multiplicity of forces which construct and reconstruct both the social and the economic. '[F]ar from being mere epiphenomena of capitalism's structural logic, consciousness, politics and culture are essential' (Smith and Feagin: 1987, 89). This is an important reminder. Urban and economic geographers, like David Harvey, who do make capitalism the substructure for social change, suggest a determinism which leaves little room for resistance.[1] It will be crucial to the argument of this book that change is possible, that there is no deterministic link between economic and cultural productivity. The Christian community can and will make a difference, and it will become evident how that difference can take place as we discover the levels of interdependence in the analogical world-view.

Economic reorganisation

Having qualified the attention post-Marxists pay to the role of capital in social transformation, we cannot minimise the global economic restructuring that arose as a consequence of the post-World-War-Two boom, and the rapid development of new financial systems that took place in the 1970s when the United States went off the gold standard. Two urban events which make visible the changes taking place, subsequently take on symbolic weight: the 1972 dynamiting in St Louis of the Pruitt-Igoe Housing Development (exemplifying Le Corbusier's dream for social engineering by architectural design) as unfit for human habitation and the technical bankruptcy of New York City in 1975.[2] In the wake of historical developments, we discern the undercurrents which shape our contemporary condition: the demise of the old industrial locations with the abandonment of fixed capital investments in plant, warehouses, and offices as manufacturing decentralises; the erosion of Keynesian welfare systems and historically developed social contracts between governments, corporations and organised labour; the growth of multinational corporations (several with more economic power than nation states) searching for what Ernst Mandel (who coined the term 'late-capitalism') called 'superprofits' (Mandel:1978); the development of flexible and migratory labour pools, the short-term contract, and the reskilling programmes to take advantage of and become adaptable to market trends. Each of these are unavoidable contemporary phenomena and the result of no one agent, policy or ideology (whether Reagan's Republicanism or Thatcher's New Right thinking).

The effect of the move 'From Fordism to Flexible Accumulation' (Harvey: 1990)[3] is registered most graphically in the two juxtaposed views of Sheffield which open the film *The Full Monty*. The first view of the city, which unfolds as the credits and titles roll, takes the form of a promotional exercise on behalf of the city in the 1960s. The newsreel effect creates the sense of a documentary. And what is being documented is Sheffield, the home of steel manufacture, as a city of industrial and commercial plenty. The second view, which follows the credits, is an interior shot of one of the steel sheds in the 1990s, now abandoned, gutted, derelict. The camera looks down impassively on the scene from the ceiling and into the corner of the frame walk two of the former workers-turned-petty-thieves bearing an old girder (symbol of that erstwhile plenty). The surplus of unemployed male labour as contrasted with the pool of lowly paid female labour, and the constant interweaving of consumer and sexual desire, around which the plot revolves, again reflects the effects of economic restructuring on urban social life and its gendered implications.

The effect of the economic restructuring has been a dramatic dismember-ment of the social and industrial body as the top 50–100 multinational corporations have established, since the 1970s, a world-wide network of production, exchange, finance and corporate services arranged in a complex hierarchical system of cities (Castells: 1996, 151–200). We will treat these global cities in the final chapter. What is significant here is the manner in which the world can be scanned by these corporations for optimal labour costs (cheap, reliable pools of disciplined or compliant workers) and control factors, resource costs, markets and state subsidies (Smith and Feagin: 1987, 5). The older liberal notions of moral autonomy, personal integrity and knowledge of self as constitutive of democratic freedom and consensus is erased. The market turns us all into consumers who produce only to afford to be more powerful consumers. Cities become variants on the theme-park, reorganised as sites for consumption, sites for the satisfaction of endless desire. The *libido dominandi* is implicitly both economic and sexual:

> In the Thatcherist view there is nothing else, beyond the satisfaction of desires. There is not even identity: government does not express it and individuals do not possess it ... The assumption behind the demand for flexibility in the workers – which denies them the continuity of a fixed identity – is that as consumers too they will have no fixed or limited de-sires, not give themselves an identity by voluntarily renouncing any of those desires (e.g., to buy furniture on Sundays or to receive forty chan-nels on their TV set) for some more general – and therefore non-marketable – good. In the Thatcherist society we each become a Faust, whose endless and innumerable desires can all be satisfied provided only that he gives up his identity, his soul.
>
> (Boyle: 1998, 27–8)[4]

There is one important omission in this account: the desire is gendered. The agency of this desire is phallic. Its logic is the fear of castration (of being excluded or thwarted), the intensification of erectile pleasure, the penetration and conquest of the new and the novel. The contemporary erotification of culture – about which more will be said in Chapter 5 – is only a foregrounding, and reductive literalising of the libidinal monads hatched and fostered by the changing matrix of global and national economic forces. But these monads are either male or masculinised in order to conform to phallic desire.[5] Where urban planning is driven by economic interests and employed men still earn more than women, where the massive development in jobs for women arises because their labour is cheap and flexible (because used to fitting around domestic arrange-ments) and their salaries still deemed 'second incomes', nothing disrupts the 'accepted framework of analysis [which] has inherent biases that isolate and denigrate women' (Ritzdorf: 1996, 457. See also Liggett: 1996, 451–55; Rose: 1993). Space reflects and constructs gender relations (as well as racial and class relations). The economic restructuring has exacerbated polarisations in these relations forcing a vivisection of the civic body.[6]

Changes in urban geographies

The forces shaping the contemporary city have not been simply economic, though economic factors have played an important part in, for example, deregularising urban planning at local and national levels (King: 1987). Utopian city developments began to lose credibility in the 1960s (Soja: 1989, 182), partly as a consequence of the urban riots in the United States, France and Italy, the declining urban populations and all-too-evident urban degeneration. '[B]y the mid-1970s planning had reached the stage of a "paradigm crisis" ' (Hall: 1996, 334).[7]

Planning of all types – principally economic and social – had been the centre-piece of Friedrich Hayek's critique of the repression of market forces and competitiveness in his 1944 book *The Road to Serfdom*. His work was being read widely in the 1970s by right-wing thinkers. Hayek, fully aware of the myths and metaphysics implicit in his thinking, wished to deconstruct Enlightenment rationalism (the father of planning) while avoiding the Nietzschean fatalism of atomistic competition. His synthesis – 'planning and competition can be combined only by planning for competition, but not by planning against competition' (Hayek: 1944: 42) – is reminiscent of the solemnised partnership between patrician capitalist and organised labour in the concluding scene of *Metropolis*. But read in the 1970s, Hayek's philosophy argued powerfully for the dismantling of public planning in favour of private speculation and market values.

During the late 1970s and throughout the 1980s (before, in Britain, the collapse of the property boom in the early 1990s), urban transformation was in the hands of the private developer backed by the state. The regeneration of waterfront areas in cities like Baltimore, London, San Francisco, Liverpool and Cape Town are expressions of what Hall calls the Cities of Enterprise. Hall, should know. He spawned the idea in 1977, taking his inspiration from the city of Hong Kong, and Sir Geoffery Howe introduced it into public debate in 1978. Committed to the play of market forces, the first important state intervention in urban planning, in Britain, came (instigated by the Labour Party) in the 1978 Inner Urban Area Act which linked local to central government with respect to trying to attract private capital interests and investment. Then, in 1980, under the Conservatives, Enterprise Zone schemes were established (eleven were designated to begin with), and the regional-planning system, that had experi-enced a golden age from 1950 to 1970, was dismembered (Hall: 1996, 359; Timberlake: 1987, 38; Soja: 1989, 168: Weaver: 1984). Enterprise Zones were mainly located in previously derelict areas. Private investment was attracted by the exemption, in Britain, from land tax and property tax, with allowances against corporation and income tax. Planning procedures for development were kept to a minimum, thus avoiding the normal delays where permission to build or modify existing buildings required lengthy consideration (Butler: 1981, 95–163). The States took up the idea in 1979, although there had already been some discussion about what was termed 'incentive zoning' where 'market forces are allowed to determine what is built, where it is built and when it is built' as early as 1974 (Wolf: 1974, 167). Furthermore, the word enterprise was gaining cult significance throughout North America in the mid-seventies with the new *Star*

Trek series. As Zones were being designated in the States, the SS *Enterprise* hit the big screen in *Star Trek: The Motion Picture* (1979).[8]

The effect of the *quid pro quo* arrangements between private investment and public land-use, which Enterprise Zones spearheaded and the entrepreneurial culture fostered, was to focus consumer energies and economic wealth in certain areas of the city, draining it (and isolating it) from the rest of the urban context. This deepened inter-urban tensions by creating inter-urban competition and derailing the processes of community construction (Harvey: 1984, chapter 8). Furthermore, resources and energies were drained from the wider regional context, so that urban development was uneven at the county level. Urban policy now revolved around business rather than, say, housing or public utilities. It was state initiated and state supervised (Harloe and Fainstein: 1992, 248–50). The effect was social atomism, a certain disenfranchisement,[9] the replication of the global decentralisation of manufacturing industry at the civic level, and the polarisation of earnings – for these areas were serviced by pools of cheap labour in low-skilled, low-paid jobs.

The atomism and polarisation were not just economic, they were political and cultural. Just as on the global level the neat compartmentalisation of First, Second and Third Worlds was buckling under the new international division of labour (Soja: 1989, 162; Sassen: 1991, 197–319; Castells: 1996), so cities were becoming locations in which First, Second and Third World orders might be traced and the tensions between the orders intensified by the collapse of geographical distance (Sassen: 1991, 323–38 and 1994; Mollenkopf and Castells: 1991, 402; Harloe and Fainstein: 1992, 253–64). Inner-city revivals were zoned (and policed manually and, with CCTVs, technologically). Safe, consumer sites were created for the marketing of customised, designer items (sought after by the new influx of very highly paid corporate managers) and for a developing leisure and tourist culture.

Since the late 1960s there has been increasing awareness of what Pierre Bourdieu terms symbolic capital (Bourdieu: 1991; 1993). Cities have become aware of their heritage as so much cultural capital to be marketed. Peter Halley writes, insightfully, that cities today 'exist only as nostalgic references to the idea of city and to the ideas of communication and social intercourse. These simulated cities are placed around the globe more or less exactly where the old cities were, but they no longer fulfil the function of the old cities. They are no longer centres; they only serve to simulate the phenomenon of the centre' (Halley: 1995, 20). The sense of ephemerality in these centres is palpable and the commercial turnover of property is ferocious. 'The process of creating successful places is only incidentally about property development [and therefore about urban development]. It is much more like running a theatre, with continually changing attractions to draw people in and keep them entertained' (Falk in Hall: 1996, 350).

A certain Disneyland-effect begins to dominant civic culture. In fact, Disney World in Orlando is in many ways the prototype for Enterprise Zoning. The

Disney Corporation extracted extraordinary and unprecedented concessions from the government of Florida to develop the site; tantamount to complete sovereignty. The area has its own police force, taxation, administration and freedom from environmental control. Time and space, conceived by modernity according to measurable dimensions, collapses. In Epcot (Experimental Prototype Community of Tomorrow) the international tourist visits sites from around the globe reproduced to scale. 'In this new city, the idea of distinct places is dispersed into a sea of universal placelessness ... leading always to a single, human subject, the monadic consumer' (Sorkin: 1996, 401). Time is reduced to the euphoria of present consumption which the experience of the 'rides' intensifies and focuses. Community and social participation are telescoped into these shared emotional moments. The present consumption, or consumption of the present, is there at every level of enterprise culture, for fundamental to the capitalisation of potential benefits (comforts, pleasures, thrills or the money to obtain these things) is seizing the present opportunity: *carpe diem*. And one can always have it the second time around because nostalgia commodifies in the present the missed or the passed opportunity, the past perfect. This omnivorous consumption of the present takes place in a world rendered safe and clean (morally as well as environmentally) by the Mouse. Paradise has been regained – and in this Disney World is only a continuation of the Enlightenment dreams for civic order. An international peace, harmony and pleasure reigns, where work is rendered invisible by placing all the servicing evidence that makes the Disney World possible beneath the ground. Built upon the equally invisible flows of electronic money (credit or debit), the Disney corporation (and the Disney-effect in other urban revivals) creates virtual cities: cities which traffic in simulacra. They trade in reproduction: Epcot's Eiffel Tower,[10] the Magic Kingdom's cartoon castle, the 3-D replication of movie scenes at Disney-MGM. Simulacra are just like the real thing, only better because when they date they can be identically replaced. The effects of time are overcome. The real itself is commodified and the commodification becomes the new benchmark for what is real. '[T]he goods at Disneyland represent the degree zero of commodity signification' (Sorkin: 1996, 400).

The staging of public spectacle (festivals for this and that, open-air concerts in central parks etc.), the exaltation of the kitsch, the glorification of the superficial, the enormous investment in sports and leisure centres, the new commodification of the city's past (manufacturing a nostalgia that substitutes for continuity and tradition), the inflationary suggestions of its state-of-the-art future, its 'under-construction' technicolour present (China towns, heritage centres, gay villages, theme bars etc.) – these are the characteristics of the new city-myth, the postmodern city-myth which has come to replace modernity's city-myth so powerfully evoked in *Metropolis*. The natural, the normal and the real are all simulations technologically produced. The possible panic in which the human disappears and technology becomes auto-referential and autogenetic surfaces in many science fiction narratives. It is at the heart of the horror in the novels of

William Gibson and films such as David Cronenberg's *EXistenZ* and the Wachelski brothers' *The Matrix*. But even this panic is commodified; the horror is made fascinating, a scene for diversion and entertainment. In the order of simulation even our fears are produced and exorcised through signs that can be exchanged so that capital can be made.

The order of simulacra

Cities are cities of the sign, concerned with image and culturally self-conscious. '[I] n the post-modern city we have moved beyond individualism with a sense of communal feeling being generated, to a new "aesthetic paradigm" in which masses of people come together in temporary emotional communities. These are to be regarded as fluid "post-modern tribes" in which intense moments of ecstasy, empathy and affectual immediacy are experienced' (Featherstone: 1994, 394; Maffesoli: 1991, 7–20).[11] We have moved into the order of simulacra – and that order has theological repercussions, as Jean Baudrillard has shown: namely, the extermination of the name of God in a hyperlogic of death and destruction.

A certain social Darwinism pervades Baudrillard's work – a story of an evolution from production to reproduction. The riots in Paris of May 1968 expressed, for Baudrillard, a coming to terms with the fact that production is an illusion. No one produces any more. The structural inflation of the signs of production, the proliferation of signs (particularly monetary signs) means that the use-value of products (and signs of products) increasingly declines. 'In the immense polymorphous machine of contemporary capital, the symbolic ... no longer counts for anything' (Baudrillard: 1993, 35). We have moved to what he describes as the third order of simulacra, a post-symbolic condition in which there is a zero degree of significance. Here the metaphysics implied by symbolism (and the hierarchy of values established by metaphysics) comes to an end, and hyperreality begins. For simulacra have been with us since the Baroque when things began to disappear beneath their representations (Ward: 2000c). But, according to Baudrillard, the real has now been erased entirely so that only the representations (no longer re-presentational) remain. Nominalism, which divorced things from their names, has become textual or semiotic idealism: things are as they are named. All social substance as such vanishes (Baudrillard: 1993, 66). Hyperreality is the pure form of representation, the overcoming of the reality principle by the pleasure principle. For enjoyment now belongs to the symbolic order, the symbolic exchange in which we invest all our hopes for the fulfilment of our desires (Baudrillard: 1993, 241). A euphoria follows from the new lightness of being. Aesthetics, rather than ethics or even physics, provides the sole criterion for judgement. Because the economy of representation, of symbolic exchange, issues from the libidinal and death-drives (here Baudrillard's thinking is indebted to Freud and Lacan), the age of simulacra announces the culture of death.

Baudrillard sees no way out of this culture other than pushing it to its most extreme – 'Things must be pushed to the limit, where quite naturally they collapse and are inverted' (Baudrillard: 1993, 4) and, meanwhile, experiencing the ecstasy of the desert.[12] The 'naturally' in that quotation alerts us again to the latent Darwinism. Nevertheless, despite his strong teleology, even essentialism (which amounts to a grand narrative of explanation and prediction), his analysis and observations of the contemporary city have a certain credibility.

Throughout his work there is a curious interlacing of the aesthetics of the sublime and the kitsch with the Catholic imaginary. He employs the language of transubstantiation, speaks about grace and the gift, the death and the omnipresence of God, the Church, angels, transcendence and Jesuits. He is not a Christian believer and he is a poor theologian. What his work does is to disperse the discourse of God, using the names and terms of Christian belief in a way which disseminates them across the networks of deferral and difference which constitutes meaning in language. He speaks of those 'who no longer have a god, but for whom language has become a God (the full phallic value of the name of God is diffused for us throughout the extent of the discourse)' (Baudrillard: 1993, 210). This gesture fuses Hegel's death-of-God (where the transcendent Father gives Himself over to the immanence of history and community), with Nietzsche's death-of-God (where the body of God is torn apart in a Dionysian frenzy), with Lacan's death-of-God (where our enjoyment only issues from the putting to death of the transcendentally signified).

As we have noted, Baudrillard concludes that 'Today the city is first and foremost the site of the sign's execution' (Baudrillard: 1993, 77). Under the third order of simulacra we enter a city of profound godlessness; a city wedded to the ruthless pursuit of the present, the seizing of the moment, the experience of degree zero. It is a city upon which an urban *speragmos* has taken place, a dismemberment that fosters an atomism rendering the language of community (or even responsibility) toothless. The endless appeal to and demand for transparency and accountability, by the state and local organs for state ideology, is a rhetorical opiate. It is an attempt to inject a moralism into a situation which is profoundly indifferent to ethics. It is calling us to be responsible for a society that is simply imaginary – a representation being peddled in the market-place. The social *is* now the cultural. Beyond liberalism, beyond humanism, beyond realism, beyond naturalism, beyond ecumenism (which requires a strong sense of corporate identity), beyond pluralism (pluralism, that is, as the belief in distinct symbolic practices sharing some ontological and/or sociological basis), the space is shrinking for 'strengthen[ing] the Church's presence and promot[ing] the Christian witness' (Church of England: 1985, 165). Henri Lefebvre advises us that any ' "social existence" aspiring or claiming to be "real", but failing to produce its own space, would be a strange entity, a very peculiar kind of abstraction unable to escape from the ideological or even the "cultural" realm. It would fall to the level of folklore and sooner or later disappear altogether, thereby immediately losing its identity, its denomination and its feeble degree of reality' (Lefebvre: 1991, 53). We are entering a different world-order, another kind of city; we require another kind of theological response.

Heteropolis: Las Vegas 1995

We need to enquire about the character of living in this new form of the city with its new understandings of space and time and materiality.[13] For it is a Christian theology of space, time and materiality and the analogical imaginary that theology establishes which is the dominant concern of this book. The Marxist social theorist Poulantzas observes: 'transformations of the spatio-temporal matrices refer to the materiality of the social division of labour, of the structures of the state, and of the practices and techniques of capitalist economic, political and ideological power; they are the *real substratum* of mythical, religious, philosophical or "experiential" representations of space-time' (Poulantzas: 1978, 26). While not wishing to reduce cultural transformations to economic ones, then, we need to recognise a contemporary theological response has first to come to terms with the changes that have taken place, and the new cities which have arisen.

Before we proceed with that response, though, we need to give an account of how we are able to recognise and, more significantly, interpret the change. Charles Taylor has made the following observation, in attempting to interpret radical transformation in another sphere:

> My principal claim is that we can only come to grips with this phe-
> nomenon of breakdown by trying to understand more clearly and pro-
> foundly the common and intersubjective meanings of the society in
> which we have been living. For it is these which no longer hold us, and
> to understand this change we have to have an adequate grasp of these
> meanings. But this we cannot do as long as we remain within the ambit
> of mainstream social sciences, for it will not recognise intersubjective
> meaning, and is forced to look at the central meanings of our society as
> though they were the inescapable background of all political action.
> Breakdown is thus inexplicable in political terms; it is an outbreak of ir-
> rationality which must ultimately be explained by some form of psy-
> chological illness.
>
> (Taylor: 1985, 51)

I would add here that if the breakdown is explained as a form of socio-psychological illness then the old therapies come into play. This is how we might charitably understand *Faith in the City* – as the application of an old therapy by the Church of England to the crisis in British urbanism. Taylor goes on to say, 'After a big change has happened, and the trauma has been resorbed, it is possible to try to understand it, because one now has available a new language, the transformed meaning of the world' (Taylor: 1985, 56–7). Whether we are sufficiently post the trauma, whether the trauma of change has been sufficiently resorbed, I am not sure. We return to that primordial theological question with which we opened this book 'What time is it?' But that we are in a better position than the Archbishop's 1985 Commission, set up to examine Christianity in the collapse of the city, is possible. We have now entered a recognition of cultural change that has given us that 'new language, the transformed meaning of the world'.

In 1995, Mike Figgis directed Nicholas Cage and Elizabeth Shue in a re-markable film about two lives caught up in the dynamics of a new economic, urban and symbolic order. It is cities on the East coast which have mostly influenced the American literary imaginary in which the urban landscape has been a dominant metaphor: New York, Boston, Philadelphia most specifically. (See Weimar: 1966 for an analysis of these verbal cities.) But it is the cities on the West coast which have mostly influenced the cinematic imagination[14] and in which the city has been a dominant metaphor: Los Angeles and Las Vegas, most specifically. Figgis' film is entitled *Leaving Las Vegas*.

Las Vegas is a city which has become something of a symbol for the post-modern *polis*. It is employed as a metaphor for our present cultural situation in films like *Conair*, Terry Gilligan's, *Fear and Loathing in Las Vegas* and Martin Scorsese's *Casino*; in Jean Baudrillard's sociological journey through America; in the architectural history of Robert Venturi; and in the theological meditations of Mark C. Taylor.[15] Las Vegas offers a three-dimensional VDU on the character of living in our postmodern cities. For Las Vegas self-consciously announces that its concern is material greed (for money and all money can purchase). It advertises both its superficiality and its access for escape into capitalism's glitterdomes, both its ruthless, endless consumption and also its unbounded capacity to seduce the public, draw them in, milk them dry.

The city grew up in the middle of the dessert as a gaming capital, where certain laws did not apply. Money was pumped into lavish buildings, often by American mafia groups looking for big investments with a legal appearance. In the 1950s and 1960s fabulous gambling palaces developed along what is now famously known as the Strip. This is the main gambling thoroughfare: a space given over to financial speculation (the secularised mode of what was once a metaphysical project). The casinos are built on either side of the Strip and behind their spangled, fantasy frontages there is only desert, only wasteland. To the American architects Robert Venturi, Denise Scott Brown and Steven Izenour, Las Vegas epitomises the power games, the adrenaline rushes, and the offers of unimaginable satisfaction through fabulous wealth. The dreams of successful urban living where each of us has everything we want is considerably and self-consciously hyped. In their acclaimed book *Learning From Las Vegas*, they draw attention to how, following the functionalist and utopian buildings of Bauhaus, Mies van der Rohe and Le Corbusier, casino structures in Las Vegas like Caesar's Palace, Dunes, Alladin, Stardust, Tropicana etc. were announcing a whole new idiom – fantasy – and a parodying hyperbole that exalted the kitsch. These buildings created domains of transitory illusion. Mimicry was taken to such an extent that Caesar's Palace employed a cohort of muscular men dressed as Roman soldiers to stand guard around its porticoes and patrol its oasis. What Venturi *et al.* admired was the flamboyant self-creation of these escapist expressions on the Strip. They were unashamedly superficial and glossy productions in the middle of no where. They were like film sets or the façades of film locations; virtual realities (Venturi *et al.*: 1978).

In *Leaving Las Vegas*, Mike Figgis captures something of what it means to be a citizen in this seductive space. Sacked from his job as a script writer (the film reflects upon film-making on several occasions), Ben Sanderson sells up and moves to Las Vegas with the intention of killing himself with drink. There he meets Sera, a prostitute who recognises Ben as a soul-mate. The film tracks the impossibility of their relationship. For although there is attraction, Ben is impotent through the alcoholic addiction he is not prepared to kick, and Sera's desire has always been to please rather than be pleased, to give out of an inability to receive. Like the characters in Sartre's *Huis Clos*, the reciprocation of desire is rendered impossible.

Theirs is neither love nor lust. Walking under the cascades of Las Vagas' neon lights, they represent the bankruptcy of urban desire, the stage beyond the illusions of satisfaction when the death-drive seeks the ultimate castration. One leaves Las Vegas from within Las Vegas, having been stripped and pumped. Fixed irredeemably in the self-destructive cycles established by past damage and present social need, in their fragility and the means they employ to protect themselves from that fragility, they are both beyond helping each other. In fact, Sera is caught fast in the phallocentrism of the desire which subjugates her to Ben, who has no real need of her in order to kill himself. Both are still fundamentally consumers – but the consuming now is pointless, it can of itself offer nothing. In fact, consumption (going on all around them) is dominant in Ben's addiction to drink and Sera's consumption of Ben's presence (even though Ben is only present in a profoundly withdrawn inebriation). Sera admits she is using him as he her; her consumption is dramatised in her shopping for presents to offer him. The consumption is narcissistic, valueless (material objects – particularly clothes – mean nothing to either of them) and viewed ultimately as suicidal. They play with non-consummating sex, with the language of 'home' and 'we', lover' and 'wife', with the gentle cusps of romance (which the sound-track by Sting commercialises). But the relationship is strictly bound by contract: that Ben will never stop his alcoholic suicide and Sera will never stop turning tricks through the Las Vegas night.

In the final scene, Sera arrives at a motel room where Ben is dying. Still drinking, he has his only erection in the film. She inserts him into her and the alcoholic racking of a body on the edge of total collapse becomes indistinguishable from the thrusts of love-making. Love, need, consumption and death. Ben dies. Sera survives, but only to continue again. For the cycle is not broken. Her final words are: 'He needed me. I loved him.' The title of film is the closing shot before the credits: *Leaving Las Vegas*. As one film reviewer observed: 'this is, after all, a story of excess'.[16]

The theological is not absent from the film. Two nuns (in full habit) distribute tracts in the background while Ben and Sera strike a bargain about their future. And the camera frequently focuses on the black jewelled crucifix around Sera's neck when she is getting ready to pick up on the streets. The theological is cynically pointed to as inadequate to save the situation: as anachronistic and socially invisible (like the nuns in habits) or as a commodity which has lost its magic powers since, unlike in vampire movies, it fails to ward away danger. The bright lights and seductions of Las Vegas remain – the city-as-spectacle, the city-as-endless-desire, in the desert.

Figgis' account of the city is taken from the point of view of the losers: the average, educated man or woman caught up in a matrix of virtual productions from which there is no escape. Scorsese's *Casino* views the city from the perspective of the winners, the casino bosses and the mobster backing organising the main financial economy that operates there. Scorsese takes up Las Vegas where Robert Venturi left off – in the mid-seventies. The closing shots of the film reveal the old modernist-styled casinos being blown up and great Lion King and Pyramid theme-park buildings being raised in their place. In *Casino* the city itself acts, and the third order of simulacra is announced in the self-conscious Disneyfication of the landscape.

Heteropolis: Los Angeles 1992

Charles Jencks, the architectural historian of high- and postmodernism, has been observing similar trends in Los Angeles. Like Las Vegas, Los Angeles shares the fact that there was a relative absence of older industrial and mercantile urbanisation. Those cities with such histories become collages, in which a modernist past is refigured by postmodern urbanisation (Rykwert: 1988, 118–49). Los Angeles, on the other hand, can be viewed as 'the quintessential postmodern metropolis' (Soja: 1989; 1995, 128; Sorkin in Smith and Feagin: 1987, 178–98). Los Angeles has seen the development of new 'technopoles', entrepreneurial zones of high technology electronics and telecommunications, alongside the vast design and fashion sensitive media industry. Experiencing severe deindustrialisation in the 1960s and 1970s, the city has been restructured and transformed by the setting up of Free Enterprise Zones by the Reagan administration. Los Angeles has experienced rapid internationalisation which has brought 'into the global city pools of capital and labour from nearly every world culture' (Soja: 1995, 130). The labour from Third World migration and undocumented homeworkers is cheap and easily disciplined. In 1960 the population was 80 per cent 'Anglo' or white and non-hispanic, now there are significant enclaves of Mexican, Guatemalan, Filipino, Japanese, Korean, Vietnamese, Cambodian, Hmong, Armenian, Iranian, Samoan and African-Americans.

At the opposite end of the social scale, Los Angeles has emerged as a centre for global banking and finance with a high proportion of prime downtown properties owned by foreign corporations or by partnerships with foreign companies. This, plus the access to large sources of venture finance, has created 'a massive urban "shopping spree" by international capital' (Soja: 1987, 193). New patterns of social fragmentation, segregation, and polarisation have generated inter-ethnic conflict, crime and violence. In turn, there has been an acceleration in 'armed response', in the private ownership of guns, in the employment of security guards, in the creation of vigilante groups, and the use of surveillance. LA has become, in the words of Mike Davis, a fortress citadel (Davis: 1990). The emphasis is upon establishing controlled environments. The policing is less public in two senses. First, in the sense that it is being done by private security companies or collections of private householders. Secondly, it is less visible, because it employs unobtrusive techniques like video surveillance posts on the corners of city thoroughfares. Soja observes: 'The postmodern City, with its kaleidoscopic complexities, has become increasingly ungovernable, at least within the confines of its traditional local government structures' (Soja: 1995,133).

Into this civic maelstrom must then be added the manufacture of hyperrealities: from the cyberspace marketeers (more is grossed from computer games than the box-office film industry) and the Hollywood studios (which gross more from pornography than block-buster movies) to Disneyland. 'Everything imaginable appears to be available in this micro-urb but real places are difficult to find. ... With exquisite irony, contemporary Los Angeles has come to resemble more than ever before a gigantic agglomeration of theme-parks, a lifespace comprised of Disneyworlds' (Soja: 1989, 243–6).

Charles Jencks draws attention to two dominant forms of civic architecture in this context, beginning with the new Chiat/Day/Mojo offices – home of one of the most powerful advertising agencies. Outside, the entrance is constructed to resemble a huge pair of binoculars: announcing a self-conscious concern with spectacle and visibility. Inside, the workplace is an urban village, turned inside out. The fantasy shell conceals a series of streets and work areas arranged to create an artificial sense of the workplace as a village and the work-force as a community. These buildings are not meant to stand for centuries. They are here only to be replaced in twenty years or so when a new façade is necessary, a new image. Frank Gehry's Walt Disney Concert Hall stands like a number of cardboard boxes ready to be thrown away and something else put in its place in another generation. Monumentality is ironised by ephemerality, temporality, fashion and the hype of consumer logos. This kind of architecture parades the built-in obsolescence of all manufactured things.[17]

Frederic Jameson made famous his own observations of John Portman's Westin Bonaventure Hotel, the centrepiece of the LA downtown area. Composed of four symmetrical cylindrical towers of reflective glass around a central atrium, the building resembles the fuel-base of a rocket (money from military defence and NASA is an important contributor to the LA economy). For Jameson, it injects a utopian, high-tech language into 'the tawdry and commercial sign system of the surrounding city' (Jameson: 1991, 39–44). The atrium is an experience of hyperspatiality, with its rising balconies capped by a conservatory-effect roof and its central column surrounded by a miniature lake. Surfaces and spaces on the inside refer back to themselves. Outside, the building stands powerfully and aggressively, a techno-gothic castle, over against the city. Its polished glass reflects back the city's downtown face and so achieves 'a peculiar and placeless disassociation from its neighbourhood' (Jameson: 1991, 44). The architectural historian, Heinrich Klotz, examining other postmodern buildings such as Charles Moore's Piazza Italia in New Orleans, speaks of the fictionalisation of architecture (Klotz: 1988, 128–42).

A second form of architectural response, which Jencks praises as authentic to urban living in the 1990s, is what is called 'the Dead Tec' design. These buildings resemble small fortresses. They are security obsessed buildings. The film star Dennis Hooper's Hollywood home is designed to look like a warehouse in disguise. The exposed sides have no windows, only walls of corrugated steel into which one door in set. The roof is glass and all the light comes from above. Frank Gehry's own home is itself a pink shingled 1920s home wrapped in a shell of corrugated metal (Jameson: 1991, 97–126). Jencks notes that these buildings 'suggest a complex civilisation that has been dug up after it has been destroyed by a neutron bomb' (Jencks: 1993, 78). They are cyberpunk buildings from *Mad Max*, *The Crow* and *Johnny Mnemonic*. They are not futuristic, but rather buildings protecting themselves from the future.

Talking about the riots in Los Angeles in 1992, Jencks draws attention to the fact that 68 per cent of the damage done to property was to retail stores. Behind this figure lies the greed and opportunism of shoppers turned looters. With some licence, he calls the riot 'the first consumerist conflagration in history' (Jencks: 1993, 63). Soja – who reminds us that the 1965 Watts rebellion, in the same region, was one of the first explosive indications that the Fordist-led boom had peaked – views the 1992 riot as the first shock wave of a crisis of and in postmodernity (Soja: 1995, 136). 'The American dream', Jencks writes, 'presumes neighbourliness and a tacit understanding of boundaries', but the new city 'presumes conflict, difference and [a] contradiction. ... [A]t a certain moment this self-definition by difference reaches a fracturing point, and the population defines itself by what it is against' (Jencks: 1993, 62). Difference, defining one's place or role in opposition to someone else's, ceaseless competition, concern with personal satisfaction and the maintenance of external image – these are the characteristics of contemporary living in Los Angeles, the postmodern city. The urban theorist Susan Christopherson discloses that since the riots 'dozens of neighbourhoods in Los Angeles have demanded the right to fence themselves off from the rest of the city, to become gated communities. The reason is not primarily personal safety but the protection of equity' (Christopherson: 1994, 420; Wolf: 1974, 166–7). The value of property so protected can rise by 40 per cent over ten years, according to Mike Davis (Davis: 1993). In the collapse of the modern city what takes over is imagined communities which you belong to by buying into what's on offer for you. They are communities of fear; exclusive because the members fear being excluded themselves and sense exclusion everywhere. Such communities undermine the very conception of the common good, of public policy, social rationality, and human rights (to education, health-care and protection from violation): those necessary concepts which make effective political involvement and commitment significant. In fact, politics too, with its emphases upon citizen charters, is viewing urban dwellers as so many customers.

In the collapse of the modern city, Disneyland simulacra take over. The new industries are the leisure industries thriving in and fostering a culture of seduction, a culture of a euphoric grasping of the present in order to forget the present, submerge it in a wet dream or a massive surge of adrenalin. It is this culture of seduction which Christian theology has to respond to.

The Christian response

These are the new cityscapes of endless desire as they are being constructed and filmed in Las Vegas and Los Angeles. Mike Davis sums up what they symbolise in his acclaimed *City of Quartz: Excavating the Future in Los Angeles*:

> The old liberal paradigm of social control, attempting to balance repression with reform, has long been superseded by a rhetoric of social welfare that calculates the interests of the urban poor and the middle-class as a zero-sum game. In cities like Los Angeles, on the bad edge of postmodernity, one observes an unprecedented tendency to merge urban design, architecture and the police apparatus into a single, comprehensive security effort.
>
> (Davis: 1990, 115)[18]

The culture of seduction, simulacra and death, which we see played out in the contemporary heteropolis, is both godless and fearful, self-possessed and self-destructive, embattled and belligerent. So, if this is our civic culture, and in these descriptions we can discern the contours of our own cities, what might be an adequate Christian theological response?[19]

Rather surprisingly, Davis, in a chapter in his book entitled 'New Confessions' (Davis: 1990, 323–72) points to two Christian phenomena in postmodern Los Angeles: first (and his chapter is devoted to sketching a genealogy for this phenomenon), there has been a renaissance of conservative Roman Catholicism; secondly, this renaissance, a by-product of Latino immigration, is doing battle with the rising force of Spanish-language evangelicalism. In his more recent work, Harvey Cox has also draw attention to the relationship between the postmodern re-enchantment of the technological and the prodigious rise of

American fundamentalism. He provides a detailed account of the enormous appeal of the high-pitched emotionalism of Pentecostalism evident in postmodern cities like Los Angeles, Sao Paulo, Singapore and Cape Town (Cox: 1984; see also Castells: 1997, 21–7 for another account of the growth of American fundamentalism).

Charles Jencks concludes his *The Postmodern Reader* with a section on postmodern religion which is characterised by the work of David Ray Griffin (Jencks: 1992, 373–82; Griffin: 1989). Griffin accepts the radical atomism, the reduction of all things to cells and subatomic particles which constitute numerous levels of complexity and individuality. What is is composed of actualities which are responses to and subsequently produce other actualities. Highly indebted to the process thinking of Whitehead, creativity becomes the ultimate reality. But this is not pantheism, Ray argues, since God is not the same as natural creativity; He exemplifies it and surges through it, persuading things towards order, value and higher forms of existence. This is a postmodern neo-Darwinian theism. A variant on the 'natural' theologies discussed in the last chapter: Teilhard de Chardin meets John B. Cobb Jr.

These are explicit theological responses to the postmodern city; though Griffin's is not a Christian response. Of the four theological options outlined for the modern city, Griffin's draws together natural theology and the post-Christian atheism or atheologies of Cupitt and Taylor which exalt in the Hereclitean flux. Cupitt too, in his more recent work, has embraced the metaphysics of a protean *Lebensphilosophie* (Cupitt: 1995, 74–98). But, as a response, the commitment to the optimisms of process and the appeal to the natural order sit uneasily alongside the orders of simulacra. Our understandings of the world, even the natural world, are coloured by the way we represent that world. The postmodern city exalts that power to represent. The natural, as with the miniature lake in the Westin Bonaventura Hotel, is part of a radically constructed and encultured world; part too of a commercial world. The other two theological responses – conservative Catholicism and evangelicalism are both contemporary equivalents of the two kingdoms theology. They are, despite their investment in telecommunications and advanced reprographics, antimodern counter-cultures. But Christian theology cannot renounce the secular world on two counts. First, it cannot do so theologically: its teachings on creation and incarnation stand opposed to such Manicheanism. Secondly, it cannot do so sociologically: Christians are part of the secular world, they work in it, with it, and buy the goods. They too are taken in by and foster the demands of the global market. Furthermore, the retreats to fundamentalism and neo-conservativism do not redeem the secular. They do not therefore bring healing, salvation, and the conviction of what is sinful and what is good. They just leave the secular to rot, retreating into privatised communities. They are other forms of neo-tribalism (Bauman: 1992; Maffesoli: 1991).

Christianity cannot renounce the secular world. That condemns society to playing out its nihilistic and self-destructive drive to consume. On the other hand, neither can Christian theology continue to develop the liberal, humanist approach. We have become more suspicious of hidden ideologies, masked idealisms, imperialisms and constructions of 'religion'. We want to know who is speaking for this universal human nature, who is describing what it consists of, for what reason, from what perspective and what or who has to be marginalised in order for the ideal to be established. Nor can theology dissolve Christian events like incarnation and resurrection into myths and metaphors, as the liberal theologians do in their exaltation of religious experience over the representation of that experience. Dissolving the singularities of the given into empty signs, collapsing the distinction between facts and values, events and meanings, is exactly what happens within Las Vegas and Los Angeles cultures. Like the earlier theological responses to the city of F.D. Maurice (Maurice: [1842] 1996), R.H. Tawney (Tawney: 1984) and William Temple (Temple: 1928; 1942), this response fails to grasp how profoundly developed is today's social atomism, founded upon the rampant individualism of the I am, I want, and I will.[20] Concomitantly, they failed to grasp, in their liberal optimism, how deep the roots of secularism penetrate nihilism; the secular city is a radically unfoundational, virtual city.

Let me clarify what I propose to suggest. It is not that these theological responses are impossible. They manifestly are possible. But they are not adequate. Each of them are responses *within* postmodernism: atomistic, individualistic, neo-tribal fortress faiths, generating virtual realities of their own. They are not responses from *within and beyond* postmodernism; responses which relate positively *and also* critically to the postmodern city. It is in this sense that they are not adequate to the contemporary situation. They do not weave today's urban culture into the fabric of the Christian tradition, a tradition that can offer a critical perspective, can situate today with respect to yesterday and tomorrow.[21] An adequate Christian response is one which listens to the many voices, the many claims for attention in the postmodern city. It risks encounter, knowing that its own voice is never pure, never innocent. It also, speaks: announcing to the postmodern city its own vision of universal justice, peace and beauty, and it criticises the structural injustices, violences and uglinesses which resist and hinder the reception of that vision.

So how does Christian theology facilitate the communication of that vision? I suggest, as those situated within postmodernity, we take one step back into self-reflection, and several steps forward in a constructive theological project which maps our physical bodies on to our social and civic bodies, on to our eucharistic and ecclesial bodies, on to the Body of Christ. To render such a mapping we need to rethink the analogical world-view.

The step back: the politics of believing

Theological discourse, as all other discourses, is caught up in a cultural politics of meaning. One of the characteristics of the new changes which have come about, not only in our cityscapes and in our economics, but in our very thinking, is the move from talk about a response being more truthful or more authentic (for example, *this* theological response is more truthful, more authentic to Christian teaching than *that* one), to talk about whether it is more believable, acceptable and adequate with respect to the situation we inhabit. This would mean developing a much softer Christian ontology; a hermeneutic ontology – to use Gianni Vattimo's phrase (Vattimo: 1988).

If Wittgenstein is right, reasoning gives way to persuasion (Wittgenstein:1974), since its possibility always lies upon unproven assumptions. So what persuades us? Belief arises, is called forth, when the evidence for what is true, the evidence for knowledge, is held on credit. Hence the link between credit, *credo* and credibility that implicates all believing in economics. Where the truth, value or meaning of something is not self-evident, we take on trust, or we entrust our judgement to accredited authorities who stand as guarantors for the truth, value or meaning of that which I have come to believe in. Believing opens up a space, then, of or for a certain kind of activity. It suspends the certainties of present possession with respect to a future fulfilment. So when British Telecom shouts to us from billboards and TV screens up and down the country that a thousand customers are returning to them every week, if I am to accept their claim then I must trust that someone somewhere does have immediate access to those statistics and will guarantee not only their existence but that, as statistics, they present real not forged or manufactured data. I have to trust also the laws governing advertising and such bodies as the Advertising Standards Authority – who have been deputised by an act of parliament to vouchsafe that no advert can blatantly lie to or mislead the public.

What I am sketching here is a politics of believing that must not only be understood, but integrated into a Christian hermeneutical ontology. To enable that integration we need to recognise the metaphysics of this politics. For the examination of what makes a belief believable, whether that belief is a Christian doctrine or a claim by BT, involves certain presuppositions about the way things are.[22] Three of these are paramount.

1. Believing requires accepting the hard-core reality of some forms of legitimation. As such believing is implicated in structures of authority: whether that authority is the expert, or the judge or the policeman or the government official or the ecclesial official or the Scriptures. But even when we come to accept that legitimation, that authority in whom is deposited the true knowledge, we have to believe again in the legitimate operation of that legitimation. That the Advertising Standards Authority *can* vouchsafe, because they have a superior knowledge to the general public's, that we are not being mislead; that the collector of statistics at BT *can* verify that these figures accurately portray 1,000 people who, each week, turn back from Orange or Ionica. So that what we are

given to believe, in that down payment upon which we have to trust, can become representative of the fully realised truth, value or meaning with which we are accrediting it.

2.   Believing involves presupposing the world is a certain shape; that there is a stable reality, a given open to being digitally measured and digitally manipulated. If you like, believing, in our modern world, necessitates ontological foundations. Hence Christian theology since at least the sixteenth century has been attempting to establish such ontological foundations such that God can be treated substantively. Witness Descartes' sixth meditation that the God with whom we have to do will not deceive us (Descartes: [1637] 1984). Believing, in the modern world, involves processes of objectification, commodification. It involves not only the commodification of knowledge – '*this* is true, *that* is false' – according to categories of identification, but an acceptance that such atomistic handling of reality is *the* way to understand and grasp the truth of what is. This implicates the need for legitimation and authority in certain intellectual power structures. Possessing knowledge, becoming the expert, is acquiring the power necessary to take up a position, begin a colonisation, start the process of domination.

3.   Believing involves presupposing that we can not only know what is, but that we can communicate what is. That is, represent the world to ourselves and others transparently. This comes back to a distinction I drew earlier with respect to legitimate agencies of knowledge: to believe in their pronouncements involves accepting that they *can* represent the truth about what is. 'Representation' takes two forms here, both related to the facility to 'stand in for' that which is not immediately available to the rest of us. On the one hand, it signifies the way certain institutions conduct themselves as representatives such that they are able to be firsthand knowers of the truth and therefore efficient mediums for the communication of that truth. On the other, representation concerns the means these people who stand in for the rest of us have for that communication; the nature of communication itself. To believe, in our modern world, involves accepting that we can represent that world as it is: that the modes of communicating what is are transparent. That is, to believe in the modern world involves accepting some construal of what was once deemed angelic knowledge. For the good angel is a messenger who seeks not to glorify himself or herself, seeks not to draw any attention away from the message he or she bears. The good angel is utterly consumed in the message; *is* the communication without remainder. Marshall McLuhan's famous dictum about late-twentieth-century communication – the medium is the message (McLuhan: 1964) – is a secularisation of the knowledge possessed and communicated, possessed *as* communicated, by angels. Believing involves accepting the transparency and the innocency of narratives; performances of persuasion in which the medium melts into air in the process of announcing itself. Only in this way can things be as they are said to be.

These are the three presuppositions, then, for modern believing: the belief in authority; the belief in foundational, demonstrable surety than can be atomistically accounted for; the belief in the transparency of representation. Believing of any kind (secular or otherwise) is implicated in a politics and metaphysics which organise the space opened up by the suspension of possessing the truth. It follows that, if the politics and the metaphysics cannot organise such a space, then that which is offered as something to be believed in *cannot* be believed in – for the cultural space is not available. We will remain unpersuaded, or have to adapt what we are being offered to believe in to the spaces available for such a belief. This is why the theological responses to the modern city, the city of human aspirations, are no longer adequate to the postmodern city, the city of endless desire. But we have to go further.

Contemporary believing is caught up in a double-bind. While it requires that we accept these three things, we are continually reminded, by the very mechanisms for gathering and evaluating evidence to substantiate belief, that authorities are ephemeral and open to challenge, that institutions distort, seeking and finding what they need to keep themselves afloat, that facts and the brutally given are plastic and malleable, and that representation (of whatever kind) involves betrayal. Digits can only speak when decoded, and so statistics can never be absolved from casuistry sanctioned by one body, and policed by others. In other words, the critical reflection which facilitates contemporary believing also calls us to recognise crises of legitimation, crises of ontological foundationalism, and crises of representation. A gap opens up, and continues to open up exponentially, between *what* we are asked to trust in and *the means by which* we are being asked to trust in it. Credibility is being stretched towards incredulity. Alert to this gap, Michel de Certeau writes that what is constant in modern believing *is* the gap between 'what authorities *articulate* and what is *understood* by them, between the communication they allow and the legitimacy they presuppose, between what they make possible and what makes them credible' (Certeau: 1997, 15). What ultimate authorities are there to guarantee the truth, value or meaning of the things we believe? The social scientists, the natural scientists, the government in power, the Pope, the archbishops? And is their authority such that they can possess the certain knowledge of that which we hold on trust? Are they too not reading the newspapers, watching the television, listening to the debates of advisers and, generally, caught up the processes of coming to a belief about something themselves? Belief, it seems, demands a form of legitimation and a process of legitimation which is external to the immanent transactions and exchanges of believing. Belief demands surety. But there is only the endless circulations of information and interpretation. Our very believing rests upon a prior believing; reason gives way to persuasion.

Certeau characterises the current ethos as a 'recited society'. 'Our society has become a recited society, in three senses; it is defined by *stories* (*récits*, the fables constituted by our advertising and informational media), by *citations* of stories, and by the interminable *recitation* of stories' (Certeau: 1984, 186). In a recited society people believe what they see and what they see is produced for them, hence simulacra-created belief. '[T]he spectator-observer *knows* that they are merely "semblances" ... *but all the same* he assumes that these simulations are real' (Certeau: 1984, 187–8). This 'objectless credibility' is based upon citing the authority of others. Thus the production of simulacrum involves making people believe that others believe in it, but without providing any believable object. In a recited society there is a 'multiplication of pseudo-believers' (Certeau: 1984, 202) promoted by a culture of deferral and credit.

In his account of our contemporary believing, Certeau emphasises an aesthetics of absence. We are brought to believe in that which in itself is a representation of an object, not the object of belief itself. We defer the truth about the object to other experts, whom we have never met nor can substantiate. These hidden experts in whom we put our trust enable us to accept as credible that which *we are told* is true. The space we as believers inhabit then is a space of 'consumable fictions' (Certeau: 1997, 25). Caught up in the endless traffic and exchange of signs – from billboards, through television, in newspapers, on film – we construct from this seductive public rhetoric versions of 'reality' to which we give allegiance or in which we place our faith. These productions and exchanges organise what we take as our social reality. But since the flow of signs is constantly changing in the practices which make up everyday living, since ideas are constantly being modified, disseminated, re-experienced, re-expressed and transplanted, what is believable changes also. A continuous writing and rewriting of the stories of the true installs an aesthetics of absence.

In tackling the need for a more adequate, that is believable, theological response to the contemporary city, then, we also have to examine the cultural politics that such a response is implicated within. A certain story is being told, a certain act of persuasion is underway, employing the grammar of the Christian faith, expounding the theologic which relates anthropology to the body of Christ, the eucharistic body to the civic and social bodies. A reflexivity is required, and an account has to be offered why such reflexivity does not render the whole discourse circular. Or why the circularity does not render the thinking invalid, though it necessarily renders it always open to question, to being fractured (see Chapter 7). But these twin requirements of reflexivity and accountability are themselves contemporary cultural preoccupations which have their analogues not simply in the politics issuing from market-based economics. They have analogues also in the ironising discourses of postmodern architecture, film, prose fiction and philosophy. Theological discourse here is in no worse a predicament than any other cultural activity. In fact, what theological discourse is able to do is construct a *theological* argument for why this must be so; why it necessarily must be a discourse always having to re-examine itself afresh, question its own rhetoric, allow its own blindnesses to be exposed. It is in this way that the Christian ontology that informs *this* theological project is herme-neutical and offers itself always for other and for further interpretations. It is in this way that Christian theological discourse is not seeking to colonise the other, but engage it *on the basis of a tradition which is open to its future transformations.*

74

The steps forward: sketched briefly

What follows will be the burden for the rest of the book. It is given *in nuce* here as a map for the direction we will be taking over the next seven chapters.

First, any Christian response has to undermine the social atomism which contemporary cyberspace, global cities, and new forms of mobile, short-term 'employment' (which erodes notions of society, family, and even nation) develop. We are fostering what the French political philosopher, Jean-Luc Nancy, calls an 'inoperative (*desoeuvrée*) community' in which:

> singular beings are themselves constituted by sharing, they are distrib-
> uted and placed, or rather *spaced*, by the sharing that makes them *others*:
> other for one another, and other, infinitely other for the Subject of their
> fusion, which is engulfed in the sharing, in the ecstasy of the sharing:
> 'communicating' by not 'communing'. These 'places of communica-
> tion' are no longer places of fusion, even though in them one *passes*
> from one to the other; they are defined and exposed by their disloca-
> tion. Thus, the communication of sharing would be this very dis-
> location.
>
> (Nancy: 1991, 25)

Christian theology has to respond with a strong doctrine of participation to counter this advanced atomism, but it also needs to locate this divine participation in the particular and the social. For this it requires a doctrine of analogical relations networking the several bodies – physical, social, political, ecclesial, eucharistic, Christic, and divine. The analogical imagination was eclipsed with increasing digitality; a digitality which promised the full understanding and explanation of phenomena. The digital, which atomises, needs to renegotiate or be renegotiated by the analogical.

Secondly, and related to this, in the contemporary city, the body (rather than the Enlightenment mind or consciousness) has become the principal site for the operation of power (Baudrillard: 1993, 101–24). Theologically, there is a need to understand, then, how embodied desire operates, how it constructs objects, things, which we are then meant to desire (even though we might not need them). There is a need to understand how certain forms of desire are promoted and patrolled: the goods in the shop windows get more and more enticing and the surveillance cameras film every moment of our longing to own them. And woe betide if our credit levels do not equal our pumped up consumer desires. There is a need to understand how these things operate in the city and what they produce, and then Christianity has to present its own, alternative accounts of desire and the body. And it is important to draw upon the Christian theological tradition here – for Christianity has profoundly been concerned in the past with what it is for a human being to desire and what it is for God to desire, and how this desiring differs from the lust to consume, own and accumulate. Before the privatisation of Christian faith, Christianity was profoundly concerned with the body, with incarnation, with living as gendered human beings in physical bodies while simultaneously relating to the social and civic bodies and participating in the ecclesial and sacramental body of Christ. Christian theology will have to retell these traditional accounts – in Augustine, in Gregory of Nyssa among others, and learn from them – and retrieve them not out of some nostalgic fantasy; that would simply be to follow the secular Pastimes obsession. Christians cannot live the life these theologians portrayed and practised in the fourth and fifth centuries. Our society is different. It makes different demands. As I said in the Introduction with respect to Augustine, the retellings and retrievals will present certain holographs of the past. But Christian theology can learn from this fruitful past in the same way as other disciplines are culling insights from this past to reformulate their own new positions. The French feminist and philosopher, Julia Kristeva, writes concerning libidinal economies of desire: 'The Christian trinity, for its part, reconciles the seducer and the legislator by inventing another form of love' (Kristeva: 1986, 261).

In order to begin to frame a different account of desire, a different account of seduction, Christian theology first needs to undo something. That is, the denigration of the word eros that begins with the invention of pornography and the development of what Foucault calls the *scientia sexualis* in the seventeenth century (Hunt: 1993, 9–45, 157–202; Foucault: 1981, 53–73 – especially 63). Augustine, Gregory of Nyssa, Bernard of Clairvaux, St Bonaventure all used *eros* or the Latin equivalent *amor*, to speak of a desire for God and God's desire for us. Augustine: 'When a man's resolve is to love God, and to love his neighbour as himself, not according to man's standards but according to God's, he is undoubtedly said to be a man of good will (or desire), because of this love. This attitude is more commonly called "charity" (*caritas*) in holy Scripture; but it appears in the same sacred writings under the appellation "love" (*amor*)' (Augustine: 1972, XIV.7). Divine eros, the love of God, and human eros, the love of human beings for God possess far greater dynamics, operating across far greater domains, than just sexuality. But since the nineteenth century, the development of medicine, and the increasing erotification of our culture post-Freud, eros and sexuality have come to mean the same thing.

Having undone the knot that tied eros to sexuality, and hopefully rescued the idea that Christians are also governed by desire, that desire is fundamental to our nature as human beings as God created us, theology will have to show how Christian desire operates in a way that does not accord with the operation of desire in secular culture, the culture of seduction. Desire in secular culture can never be satisfied – that is fundamental. In its very crudest form – desire for sexual gratification – however many orgasms I have I'll want more. This has other social analogues. However much I earn I can always spend it and beyond it. Whatever I achieve there is more to achieve. Desire within the postmodern city can never come to an end – or the market would cease. Desire here operates because we always sense, or are made to sense privation; and we are always attempting to fill that lack or find compensations for unfulfilment. Now, in the

Christian tradition, desire in God and for God does not operate according to a logic of privation. God does not love us because God needs us to complete God's own desire. And although Christians love God first out of their recognised need, Christian mysticism has long since come to see that pure love for God is abandonment onto God for who God is in God's loving triune self. There is a profound difference between participating in God and a need for God. In the Christian tradition God is not there to fulfil human demands. For that is to treat God as we might treat any other commodity in the market-place. Traditional accounts of *imitatio Christi*, and doctrines of creation and eschatology, teach that the purpose of human beings is to be sanctified, and the function of the Church as those who are in the process of sanctification, is to draw all creation back into participation in God – to co-operate with God in the redemption of the world. Christian desire moves beyond the fulfilment of its own needs; Christian desire is always excessive, generous beyond what is asked. It is a desire not to consume the other, but to let the other be in the perfection they are called to grow into. It is a desire ultimately founded upon God as triune and, as triune, a community of love fore-given and given lavishly.

The desire that operates in the culture of seduction is cannibalistic. In the final scene of Scorsese's *Casino*, Robert de Niro, having narrowly escaped an assassination attempt, talks about the new Disneyfication of Las Vegas gambling. Embraced within the techicolour special effects of the film world, all the family can now participate. So while the kids are entertained with Peter Pan galleons and monumental sphinxes, the parents are stripped of their savings, their mortgages, their endowments, their assets, their hospital and schooling insurances. This secular desire feeds; it preys on others for its own satisfaction. Killer viruses, parasitic creatures that adapt quickly and intelligently to new environments, vampires – are all key motifs in contemporary popular fiction and film expressing the subconscious horror of endless desire. A theological account of desire will describe alternative erotic communities; communities analogically related through desire. These erotic communities will form ecclesial bodies functioning first locally[23] and then expanding ever outward to embrace the civic and social bodies within which they dwell. What we need today is a theology of the city that recalls us to the cosmological. The Christian theology outlined here starts from what it is to be called by God as an embodied soul to participate in Christ's body.

Let us then proceed to enflesh and gender these bones.

Part II

THE ANALOGICAL
WORLD-VIEW

3

TRANSCORPOREALITY

The ontological scandal

The floating signifier relates to the body, this crucible of energy muta-
tions. But what goes on there remains unknown – and will remain so until an adequate semiology (one that can take account of transsemiotic
fields) is established. In particular, it would be important to make a large
part of this deal, not only with the capacity of the body to send and receive signs and to inscribe them on itself, but also with the capacity to
serve as a base for all communicative activity.

(Gil: 1998, 107)

Corpus

In Michigan, a man named David wanted his union of twelve years with Jon
blessed by a representative of God before he died. David lay on the couch while
Jim, a gay Presbyterian minister who also has AIDS, moved his hands to the
silent sounds of peace. He spoke nourishing words of blessing on these two lives
bound by God's grace: 'Those whom God hath joined together, let no one put
asunder. ... ' And then, as the minister began to celebrate the Communion for
those who were present, he spoke the familiar words: 'This is my body, broken
for you ... ' and that was the point at which David died. 'Do this in remembrance of me' (Brantley: 1996, 217). These are not my words. They belong to
another voice, an American voice; the voice of a Christian journalist himself
dying of AIDS. I ventriloquise his voice, because I want to begin by outlining a
Christian construal of the body with respect to the brokenness of bodies in
postmodernity. The brokenness of these bodies is a continuation of the logic
(and, ironically, humanism) of modernity. Postmodernity does not transcend but
deepen, and bring to a certain terminus, the hidden agendas of modernity
(Toulmin: 1990). And so the corpses and carnage of Ypres and the genocides of
Belsen, are repeated, variously, at Pol Pot and Bosnia. The bodies, modern and
postmodern, are concrete and also symptomatic. Where culture can be
understood as a language, as an open field of shifting symbols, these pilings up
of the dead are metaphors of cultural disintegration.

In this chapter I want to examine the racked and viral-ridden bodies of the sick, the engineered bodies of the beautiful, the power-hungry and disenfranchised bodies of the polis, the torn and bleeding body of the Church, the poisoned and raped body of the world and the abused body of Christ. What Christian theology has to offer any discussion of corporeality is not simply in terms of the way its discourses have informed our past understanding (and neglect) of the experience of embodiment. Christian theology also offers a profound thinking about the nature of bodies through the relationship it weaves between creation, incarnation, ecclesiology and eucharist. As Elizabeth Castelli observes, 'From the very earliest Christian texts and practices, the human body functioned as both a site of religious activities and a source of religious meanings' (Castelli: 1991).The work on epistemology by feminist philosophers such as Sandra Harding and Bat-Ami Bar On emphasises that subjects construct 'knowledges' or make claims about the way things are from specific situations and these subjects need to acknowledge their standpoint if, together, we are to move towards what Harding terms 'maximizing objectivities' (Harding: 1993, 49–82, On: 1993, 83–100, Longino: 1993, 101–20). Standpoint epistemology is not perspectivalism (Anderson: 1998, 73–87), but moves out from a position in the margins, with a certain knowledge learnt as marginal, towards new negotiations with non-marginal knowledges. I begin then from a tradition-bound knowledge.

I want to examine the broken bodies of postmodernity through the discourses which access them for us. As Judith Butler reminds us, ' "To matter" means at once "to materialize" and "to mean" ' and, elsewhere, 'the materiality of the signifier (a "materiality" that comprises both signs and their significatory efficacy) implies that there can be no reference to a pure materiality except via materiality' (Butler: 1993, 32, 68). We have no knowledge, and no acknowledged experience of, the material world outside of the way we represent that world to ourselves. Furthermore, that recording of what is physical, that representation, is going to be saturated with cultural meaning. For we have been taught how to represent the world to ourselves – our descriptions are culturally and historically embedded. But through these representations we inhabit the broken fragments of these contemporary bodies; they are mapped on to our bodies through their 'signs and significatory efficacy'. The narratives of their tearing and violation, as we read them, involve themselves in the narratives of our own embodiment. Through these narratives these bodies, and our bodies also, scream and rage for resurrection.

'Take, eat, this is my body.' The shock-wave in these words emerges from the depths of an ontological scandal; the scandal of that 'is'.[1] The literary nature of this demonstrative identification cannot be accurately catalogued. There is no avowed element of similitude or comparison: it is not a simile, it is not a metaphor. There is no element of substitution or proportion to indicate synecdoche or metonymy: it is not a symbol. A piece of bread is held up for view and renamed: this is my body. A is not A in a logic of identification. A is B and, possibly (for there is no stated reason why this should not be the implication) A could be renamed again as C or D or E: this bread is my ... whatever; or this ... whatever is my body. What is being perceived and what we are being told is the nature of what is being perceived are out of joint. The phrase has the literary structure of allegory or irony: something which seems to be the case is so, but otherwise.

The scandal of that 'is', what I call the ontological scandal, raises a question to do with the naming, nature and identification of bodies. The question runs somewhat parallel to a question raised in the title of an (in)famous essay by the critical theorist Stanley Fish. Fish asked 'Is There a Text in This Class?' in order to demonstrate that the stable identification of a text is contingent upon the context. '[B]ecause it is set not for all places or all times but for wherever and however long a particular way of reading is in force, it is a text that can change' (Fish: 1980, 274). Similarly, I am asking 'Is there a body in this room?', the upper room, that is, the room in which the Last Supper of Christ was eaten. This is not to deny embodiment. I am not performing some postmodern act of prestidigitation in which what is disappears in clouds of philosophical obscurity. But I am asking, like Fish, about the stability of the identity and identification of bodies. Is it that bodies are beyond our ability to grasp them and that we deal only with imaginary and symbolised bodies – our own and other people's? What does that ontological scandal in that upper room announce about bodies? What kind of bodies occupy what kind of spaces and in what kind of relationships to other such bodies? This is the constellation of questions being orbited here. If, from the specific standpoint of Christian theology, orderings and accounts of the world proceed from that which has been revealed; and if, therefore, this eucharistic and Christic body informs all other understandings of 'body' for Christian teaching: then what kind of bodies is Christianity concerned with?

The shock-wave of the eucharistic phrase has to be calibrated according to our conceptualisations of the body. Our conceptualisations of the body depend, in turn, upon the way the word is used; upon the discursive practices in which 'body' has been and is now employed. If we take Mark's Gospel as a certain delineated context, then 'body' (soma) occurs four times – three of those occasions in the last, Passion section. On three of those occasions 'body' is used to designate the physical and biological organism – of the woman whose haemorrhage of blood is healed (5.29), of Jesus when he is anointed with the precious ointment (14.8), of Jesus when Joseph of Arimathaea requests the corpse from Pilate for burial (15.43). Only the eucharistic 'This is my body' of 14.22 differs, fissuring the consistent employment of 'body' throughout Mark's text. But the dissonance that it registers in the context of that one text may not reflect the dissonance registered in the wider Greco-Roman culture of Paul's use of soma in his letters to the Church at Corinth or the wider context of the New Testament (Robinson: 1952; Martin:1995). The dissonance registered in Mark will not be the same as that even four hundred years later when a new concept of the body was emerging governed by the ideals of fasting and penance (Brown: 1998). The dissonance will differ further from the manner in which bodies were imaged in the Middle Ages with its notion of the *corpus mysticum* or the dissonance registered today when the meaning of 'body' is so governed by medical materialism and scientific discourses (Sawday: 1995; Laquer: 1990). Perhaps the ontological scandal is greater today, following a long period in which bodies have become discrete, self-defining, biological organisms. A change is certainly evident in the use of the word, for 'body' comes from an Old English word, *bodig*, meaning corpse, inert thing. Today it is used much more in the sense of a living, active form of life. Bodies are measured and identified according to strict, scientific criteria. And so to the logical positivist the demonstrative identification 'this is my body' with reference to an observable piece of bread is simply nonsense, a misidentification.

The ontological scandal of 'This is my body' today lies particularly in the confidence with which the misidentification is made. The grammar (whether English or Greek) announces an unequivocal logic – pronomial object (this) related to possessive subject (my body) through the cupola (is) – but the isomorphism of bread = body defeats the logic. Furthermore the logic of A = A expresses no knowledge; it has the sense only of a tautology. This phrase seems to express a knowledge of bread as body, but it is not a knowledge that can be read off from the sense-data of bread and body. The phrase, then, presents the same structure as, in the context of holding a wedge of Edam aloft, an authoritative subject-position pronounces: 'Here is the moon.' It is an act of madness. But why and was it always?

Corpuscularity

It is an act of madness today because demonstrative identification is linked to perception. That is, philosophically, the way words (and mental conceptions) hook up to the world. As one leading analytical philosopher has remarked, 'Most of us are inclined to suppose that there are close connections between demonstration and perception; and some of these could be brought out by principles of the form "If conditions are C, then if a person makes a statement which demonstrates an object, the person perceives that object." ' But even he then goes on to say, 'But I do not know how to spell out the conditions' (Wallace: 1979, 319). For example, the person making the statement could be blind or the object at a considerable distance. But it is not only the conditions which make the association between demonstration and perception difficult, it is the act of naming and the nature of perception itself. Naming relies upon social consensus and memory of past, confirming, acts of identification. People, generally and contemporaneously, call this a church and that a frog. They have learnt it. Social consensus does not call 'bread' 'body'. To call 'bread' 'body', to rename the world, requires an Adamic act, an act at the origins of the world: 'And out of the ground the Lord God formed every beast of the field and every fowl of the air;

and brought them unto Adam to see what he would call them: and whatsoever Adam called every living creature, that was the name thereof' (Genesis 2.19). Despite modernity's several attempts to think back to and then from beginnings – witness Descartes, Locke, Kant and Hegel, to name a few – with language we always begin after the beginning. Margaret Thatcher may have attempted to rename 'community' those people who are allowed to vote and live in dwellings they have paid a tax on; but older views of community persisted and successfully resisted such distortions. Furthermore, as Gareth Evans points out with reference to Strawson's belief that a subject can identify an object demonstratively if he [sic] can pick it out by sight, hearing or touch, 'the ordinary concept of perception is vague' (Evans: 1982, 144). Perception involves a certain ego-centred orientation and evaluation of objects in a specific spatiality. Each subject position perceives, and in perceiving evaluates (hot/cold, dry/damp, dark/light), differently. I am, at first, alone in what it is that I perceive. Perception is always mediated – we see something *as* something (a chair *as* a chair, the garden *as* a garden), we do not simply see. Sometimes we are blind to what we see. Most of us have experienced what is common to dyslexics, or children learning to write who reverse letters/numbers – that something looks right, when in fact it is not: we are blind to an error we cannot perceive while staring at it. Authors make bad proof-readers of their own work. Only when something is pointed out do we see what it is we are perceiving. More generally, critical assessment – of a painting or a building, a poem or a state of mind – is illuminating to the extent that it brings to light things we have not considered before or things we intuited but did not articulate. Demonstrative identification is, as Gareth Evans emphasises 'an information-based thought' (Evans: 1982, 145), it is not a form of description. But if naming is taught and perception is both relative and mediated, then what the statement 'This is my body' effects when the person saying it is holding a loaf of bread is a scepticism. Do I see aright? Do I orientate myself correctly insofar as 'this' implies a 'here', implies a certain spacing, a certain understanding of place such that I can identify *this* place? Have I learnt to use 'body' and 'this' aright? The I, in its self-certainty, is undermined and has to seek confirmation for what it sees and has learnt from the responses of others.

The scepticism is the product of the metaphysical framework within which we today assess a demonstrative statement. It is evident from Gareth Evans' analytical approach in his essay 'Demonstrative Identification' that what is presupposed in this analysis is the following: first, an independent ego (in order to create the 'egocentric space' from which one perceives); secondly, concepts of space and representation such that a distinction can be drawn between the internal spacing of objects and the external or public spacing of those same objects (so that the latter makes possible the former); thirdly, concepts of relations between objects filling and creating that public space such that a subject 'has an idea of himself as one object among others' (Evans: 1982, 163); fourthly, concepts of materiality or what Russell called 'the ultimate constituents of matter' (Russell: [1917] 1994, 121–39) and, fifthly, a notion of the faculties of the mind and their operation to account for memory (of previous encounters with the object) and perception (such that object *x* can be deemed to be *x* because it constantly has the properties of *x* as seen over a period of time). Overall, what is privileged throughout (whether by logical positivists, empiricists or materialists) is the experience of what Ayer called sense-data as they access the objective properties of the particular object being indicated (Ayer: 1959, 66–104, 125–66; 1963, 58–133, 229–74). This privileging has certain consequences. It assumes that the full presence of the object, all that the object is, was and will be, is available for observation. The 'is' of demonstrative identification dissolves as a word, suggesting direct access to the presence of the object through the assertion. 'This is a table', 'This is a chair'. A commodity is born – the possessable reification of a certain individual's perceptual labour. The name sticks so close to the object named – and it is the sticking close which enables 'identification' and 'verification' – that they become indistinguishable. It is only as such that the communication can be understood as information- (or misinformation-) based.

Read from a Christian theological standpoint, one could say that the metaphysical framework here is a secularised doctrine of realised eschatology – the condition of resurrected and permanent dwelling within the fully illuminating presence of the divine. Even Wittgenstein himself seems to make this very same emphasis in insisting in *Philosophical Investigations* that 'everything lies open to view', that what is called for is 'complete clarity' and that 'nothing is hidden' (Wittgenstein: 1953, nos 126, 133, 435; Cunningham: 1998). As Wittgenstein stated: 'The truth of the matter is that we have already got everything and we have got it actually present, we need not wait for anything' (Wittgenstein: 1979, 138) Putnam has recently pointed out that: 'Materialists think the whole universe as a "closed" system, described as God might describe it if he were allowed to know about it clairvoyantly, but not allowed to interfere' (Putnam: 1990, 49). We will return to the monism of this 'closed' system in a moment. For now what is important is to recognise that with this emphasis upon the world as fully given, fully present, mediation, the act of representation itself, the performance of referring itself, is downplayed at best, but certainly on the road to being forgotten. For what is paramount is the relation of the concept to what John McDowell calls 'the myth of the given' (McDowell: 1994, 21). It is not the statement which acts to bring the object into being as a certain object; it is the object which acts, provoking the assertion. The world asserts its own reality; it is self-grounded. Behind such a view lies an atomism: ultimate reality is found in the independence of each atom asserting its own self-enclosed being. Bodies, as such, dissolve into their distinct properties or sense qualia. A form of dissection is performed as the list of distinctive predicates lengthens. A form of death is performed; death as also the dissolution of the body into its composite elements. So that the care to identify an object through perception and perception's correlation with naming, in fact collapses upon itself – the object is torn up into its various compounds, *Speragmos*.[2] The body is a collection of organs, a binding of chemicals, a grouping of molecular structures etc. Jean-Luc Nancy observes the strong connection between atomism, individualism and claims to unqualified veracity: 'the individual is merely the residue of the experience of the dissolution of community. By its nature – as its name indicates, it is the atom, the indivisible – the individual reveals that it is the abstract result of a decomposition. It is another, and symmetrical, figure of immanence: the absolutely detached for-itself, taken as origin and as certainty' (Nancy: 1991, 3; see also Freudenthal: 1986). With certain ancients, like Leucippus and Democritus, this soulless materialism – materialism without mystery – announced a void, a nihilism. With positivists and radical empiricists, it announces a fluorescent world of fully presenced certainties – indifferent to time, agency and mediation: the eternity of matter, like the ancient *hyle*. To the post-Einsteinian scientist, since matter and energy at root are interchangeable, matter is defined as the contingent but specific focusing of energy. And this is, as McDowell points out in his description of the teaching of modernity, 'devoid of meaning [since] its constituent elements are not linked to one another by the relationships that constitute the space of reasons' (McDowell: 1994, 97).

Corporeality

Within such a metaphysical construal 'This is my body' makes three responses possible: observational self-doubt; a judgement about the mental abilities of the one who has made the misidentification; an ontological scandal (a 'miracle' as certain rational approaches to the philosophy of religion would understand it). Within such a metaphysical construal, because of the independence of the object from the assertion and the one who asserts, the second of these responses would be privileged. The first would be ruled out by appeal to the experience and memory of objects having normative predicates; an appeal to normativity extended through calling upon the experience of other people. The third would be ruled out on Hume's ground that a 'miracle' can only be demonstrated to have occurred when it occurred with a regularity that would make its occurrence normative and, therefore, no longer a miracle (Hume: [1777] 1975, 109–31).

If then we can understand the demonstrative identification involved in 'This is my body' as suggestive of madness (within the current metaphysical construal and its priorities), can we say that this was always so or need be so? What if self, space (place), representation, perception and materiality are conceived otherwise such that 'I', 'here' and 'body' are only contingently stable and identifiable? What if transmutation is written into the fabric of the way things are? What if we take 'becoming',[3] take contingency, seriously such that the *nunc* as the 'is' of Jesus' demonstrative identification constitutes a different kind of ontological scandal?

Take, for example, the theological construal for the interpretation of 'I', 'here' and 'body' in the work of Gregory of Nyssa, a fourth-century bishop living in the province of Cappadocea – and the implications of this construal for understanding self, space (place), representation, perception and materiality. It might seem from the following that Gregory would concur with our contemporary analysis of the ontological scandal of 'This is my body':

> if one were to show us true bread, we say that he properly applies the name to the subject: but if one were to show us instead that which had been made of stone to resemble the natural bread, which had the same shape, and equal size, and similarity of colour, so as in most points to be the same with the prototype, but which yet lacks the power of being food, on this account we say that the stone receives the name of 'bread', not properly, but by a misnomer.
>
> (Nyssa: 1979, 403)

But such a reading would be mistaken. The clues to the Christian metaphysics framing this passage are there in phrases like 'the same with the prototype' and 'lacks the power of being'. The emphasis is not upon the object as such but upon the failure of the object to be part of a power-economy which nourishes, and upon the act of naming. Later in the same treatise, he can write:

> I, however, when I hear the Holy Scripture, do not understand only bodily meat, or the pleasure of the flesh; but I recognise another kind of food also, having a certain analogy to that of the body, the enjoyment of which extends to the soul alone: 'Eat of my bread', is the bidding of Wisdom to the hungry; and the Lord declares those blessed who hunger for such food as this, and say, 'If any man thirst, let him come unto Me, and drink' … 'famine' is not the lack of bread and water, but the failure of the word.
>
> (Nyssa: 1979, 409)

What is is governed here by the operation of the Word, not the perceived predicates of objects existing in and of themselves in a world consisting also in and of itself. The divine, the spiritual, principle prioritises. Nature exists in and through this prioritisation such that even within the human being the intellectual as spiritual is the animating principle that enables nature to prosper 'according to its own order' (Nyssa: 1979, 404). The 'stone' imitating bread in the first passage cannot nourish (and so become a form of bread) because 'it lacks the power of being food'. It is inanimate. But in and of itself as matter it could be animated and therefore become a source for food. The turning of stones into bread is a distinct possibility for the Messiah as Satan points out in the temptation of Christ in the wilderness. This potential is not contained within the material but 'in and around it'. Nature cannot be natural without the spiritual informing it at every point. The perceptually sensed can give knowledge, but Gregory distinguishes between 'knowledge' – which is mixed because its source is the tree of knowledge of good and evil in Paradise – and 'discernment' – which skilfully separates the good from the evil and 'is a mark of a more perfect condition of the "exercised senses" ' (Nyssa: 1979, 410). Without the exercise of discernment human beings cannot understand or see correctly. Building upon the Old Testament story of the fall of Adam and Eve into sinfulness (Genesis 3), Gregory reasons that the progenitors of humankind, having eaten the fruit of the tree of mixed knowledge, incline all subsequent generations towards a dependence upon the material order. This condition of being fallen expresses itself in the reification (and idolatry) of the objects perceived; a forgetting that they are continually in a state of being gifted to us, animated for us, by God himself. Materiality, for Gregory, is a manifestation of divine *energia*, a mode of trinitarian *dunamis*.[4] The danger of the fallen condition, whose disposition is not towards that which is blessed and divinely good, is self-gratification – a certain aestheticisation of the senses such that one can be gratified through them. We will meet this again when examining Augustine on time and presence in Chapter 7. A certain solipsism ensues, a self-subsistence which is not merely illusory but destructive: the material orders are used and exploited for self-gratification, they are reduced to atoms of potential pleasure or pain, their form (which theologically is in harmony with the form of the good) is dissolved.

Corporeality has to be read spiritually, that is, allegorically (Ward: 1999). Creation, as the manifestation of God through His Word, is a text which it is the vocation of the human being, made in the image of that God, to read and understand. Allegorical reading takes representation seriously, it has to; takes agency seriously for the point of reading and understanding is the perfection of the good life (blessedness). Allegorical reading disciplines the naming and therefore the identification of the material world – deception is the structure of evil, where a name and an appearance coalesce. Positivism is therefore evil. The world has to be read with discernment. Even bodies have to be read: 'thou wilt read, as in a book, the history of the works of the soul; for nature itself expounds to thee' (Nyssa: 1979, 422).

Matter is not eternal, it is brought into being by God, *ex nihilo* (Genesis 1.2) and *ex libertate* (through God's sovereign free will). Matter is temporal and transmutation is structured within its very possibility – it came from nothing. Bodies will change until they attain their perfect, impassible state, post-resurrection. It is this transmutational potential that makes miracles possible – turning water into wine, the healing of the sick, the raising of the dead etc. Within this theological construal of corporeality 'This is my body' is another such miracle. The ontological scandal here concerns God's uncreated power to call something into being from nothing, bring flesh from bread. The scandal is the giftedness of being itself – that something should be rather than not be – which the transformative Word of God announces. The very assertiveness of the statement is a practice of authority – authority to rename, refigure – the performance of the transaction. What is involved in this transaction? Gregory writes that 'our nature is twofold, according to apostolic teaching, made up of the visible man and the hidden man' (Nyssa: 1979, 421). So which body is being pointed to, transposed, re-presented in that statement 'This is my body'? For

Gregory, who takes a grain of wheat as an example of his understanding of a body, in which the whole potential of the plant lies still hidden, the 'body' of the wheat is its totality of transformations, the totality of its becoming. Not the object of one moment, but the *skopos*,[5] the whole of the work that it performs, the unfolding of its natural order, defines the nature of a body. By 'natural' here is meant that which is in accordance with the telos of divine blessedness which animates, maintains and perfects creation.

The observation of the outward qualities of an object, what Gregory termed *poiotes*,[6] is not an end itself. The end is the underlying reality of a thing, what Gregory termed *upokeimenon*.[7] This is approached when we see things in relation to God, *epinoia*,[8] when we view what is through our desire towards God. Because we are, and all created things are, subject to time, then this process can never come to a conclusion. Hence, we can never know the *upokeimenon* itself. And so, as one of Gregory's more recent commentators has stated, 'Gregory draws the conclusion that we cannot know the essences of things, even our own soul and body, or the elements of creation' (Harrison: 1992, 38). What we occupy is a certain intellectual processing that operates within a generative semiosis. Since the essence of things cannot be known, the displacement of their identity is endless. The *poiotes* become signs to be read by the intellect and yet their meaning is endlessly not deferred but protracted, extended out of the material order of this world and into what Gregory termed the *aion*.[9] 'Now that which is always in motion, if its progress be to good, will never cease moving onwards to what lies before it ... it will not find any limit of its object such that when it has apprehended it, it will at last cease its motion' (Nyssa: 1979: 410–11). All created things push on towards their final dissolution (in death) and recomposition (in resurrection).

This multiplicity, this fragmentation and dissemination of identities differs from modernity's atomism, insofar as all proceeds from and participates in God, the Lord as the one simple *upokeimenon*, the one *ousia* which is not the same as our *ousia*.[10] 'For according to the diversity of his activities (energies) and of his relations to the objects of his gracious activity, he also gives himself different names' (Nyssa quoted in Harrison: 1992, 40). An object's identity, its intelligibility, only consists in its being an object of God's activity. It has no autonomous identity outside of these divine energies. Gregory writes in his book *The Life of Moses*:

> none of those things which are apprehended by sense perception and contemplated by the understanding really subsists, but only the transcendent cause of the universe, on which everything depends. For even if the understanding looks upon any other existing things (*ousin*), reason observes in absolutely none of them the self-sufficiency by which they could exist without the participation in true being (*metousias tou ontos*).
>
> (Nyssa: 1978, 60)

To experience the world in this way is to experience a profound vertigo. 'For here there is nothing to take hold of, neither place nor time, neither measure nor anything else; it does not allow our minds to approach. And thus the soul, slipping at every point from what cannot be grasped, becomes dizzy and perplexed and returns once again to what is connatural to it' (Nyssa: 1979: 127–8). Since we live in and through metaphors of the real, which are never stable as the nature of the objects they name are never stable, from one moment to the next; since, for Gregory, allegoriesis is the character of creation: we can name this vertigo, semiosis. Semiosis here is the opening up of words to their infinite possibilities to mean. But *this semiosis*, unlike the semiosis argued for by Philippe Lacoue Labarthe where 'madness is a matter of mimesis' (Labarthe: 1989, 138; see also Ward: 1995, 131–58) is not the nihilism of soulless materialism, but a divine not-knowing working within what is seen and disciplining a discernment that sees beyond what it is given to who it has been given by and for what purpose. God is not substance here; God is distinct from substance as created matter is distinct from uncreated, creation from creator. God is transcendent and materiality is suspended.

It has caused some surprise among scholars that Gregory has little explicit discussion on the eucharist, and yet might this not be because, within his doctrines of creation and incarnation, the world *is* a eucharistic offering? The world is maintained and sustained as a giving of thanks for its very givenness. In a way which drives a stake through the heart of the contemporary vampirisms and viruses discussed in the last chapter, all things feed each other – that is the nature of their participation in God. Christ as the bread of life feeds our rational beings that we might continue to discern and desire God in all things.

Bodies here are frangible, permeable; not autonomous and self-defining, but sharing and being shared. When I give I give myself, even though what I give is flowers, a smile, a sweet word, an academic account such as this one. The body itself serves 'as a base for communicative activity' (Gil: 1998, 107). It is the transducer of signs. Communication is embodied giving, and what I give is consumed by the others to whom I give. I touch upon their bodies by the presence of my own body heard and seen, smelt and sometimes tasted by them. The fluidity of time itself is the fluidity of identity. 'This is my body. Take eat. This is my blood. Drink.' The body is always in transit, it is always being transferred. It is never there, as a commodity I can lay claim to or possess as mine. This is the ontological scandal announced by the eucharistic phrase – bodies are never simply there (or here).

Corpus mysticum

It is the scandal of Mark's Gospel – taking the ending that most New Testament scholars advise (16.8) – that the resurrected body makes no appearance. And even though in the other gospels, as in the second century appendix to Mark's, the resurrected Christ makes an appearance, it is neither a stable body nor a permanent one. The body takes on different properties – the propensity to appear and disappear at will, a transformation of its appearance such that even disciples do not immediately recognise who it is who is with them. Finally, the body disappears back to heaven in the ascension. The body of Christ – the archetypal incarnate being, the body given over totally in its witness to God, in its manifestation of God – is a body which constantly exceeds itself, figured forth in signs (the sacraments and liturgies, the scriptures and lives of the saints). As Ephesians puts it, 'The Church is Christ's body, the completion of him who himself completes all things everywhere.' We will say more about this in the next chapter. Here, as we lay the foundations for a Christian metaphysics of the body, it is sufficient to delineate how the body, any body, disseminates itself through a myriad other bodies, which are themselves other signs where tissue is also text. As such, each of us can affect, for good or ill, the world around us. As belonging to other, larger corporations, we necessarily impact upon the world we live in, for good or ill. Similarly, that which I exclude from my body, or that which is excluded in my name from the corporations to which I belong, will affect me, for good or ill. The ghettoisations and the segregations of racism, sexism, class, and ageism done in my name, condoned by my silence, injure me. 'To matter' is 'to materialise' and 'to mean', to return to Judith Butler's comment.

We can call this view of the body transcorporeality. It is a feature of in-tratextuality, and *vice versa*. The body is fractured endlessly, by the Spirit, and yet also, simultaneously, gathered into the unity of the Word and the unity of the Word with the triune God (see Chapter 7). The eucharistic 'This is my body' performs that first act of dissemination, that first transcorporealism. Michel de Certeau notes that this was the understanding of *'corpus mysticum'* until the middle of the twelfth century when 'the expression no longer designated the Eucharist ... but the Church'. He adds, significantly, that 'The Church, the social "body" of Christ, is henceforth the (hidden) signifier of a sacramental "body" held to be a visible signifier, because it is the showing of a presence beneath the "species" (or appearances) of the consecrated bread and wine' (Certeau: 1992, 82). The meaning and scandal of the eucharistic 'This is my body' begins now to make its increasing move towards an emphasis on what is visible (rather than what is hidden). The trajectory of modernity begins, which will culminate, as we saw, in the positivism (and nihilism) of the statement's scandal today. The move can be paralleled with the need in the Lacanian subject to enter the law of the Father, the law of the symbolic as a substitute for the lost real body of the mother, the ineffable and irrecoverable *réel* as Lacan defines it. Certeau points out what is forgotten here, or what (taking the Lacanian picture) is being repressed – the loss of the body as the very possibility for its dissemination. 'Christianity was founded upon the *loss of a body* – the loss of the body of Jesus Christ, compounded with the loss of the "body" of Israel, of a "nation" and its genealogy. A founding disappearance indeed' (Certeau: 1992, 81). It is the loss which prepares the way for the mystical; the kenosis which prepares the way for a semantic diffusion of naming gathered together under him who will be given the Name above all Names.[11] Rather than loss, I wish to speak of 'displacement' – the kind of displacement which accompanies expansion. The displacement of the one, archetypal body, which engenders a transcorporeality in which the body of Christ, is mapped onto and shot like a watermark through the physical bodies, social bodies institutional bodies, ecclesial bodies, sacramental bodies. All these bodies are available only in and through textual bodies (discourses, gestures to be interpreted, social semiotics). But bodies cannot be reduced to signs, they are always excessive to signs, resistant, insistent upon a presence which eludes and discharges signs. The symbolic issues from the demands of the real and the desires of the imaginary. In the logic of demonstrative identification the impenetrability and discreet autonomy of the physical body provides the concrete means whereby these other bodies can be deemed metaphorical. But in the analogical account of bodies, within an account of incarnation and creation, only the body of Christ (hidden, displaced and yet always pervasive for always disseminated) is the true body and all these other bodies become true only in their participation within Christ's body. Christ's body as the true body is the pure sign – the only sign which is self-defining. I recall one of the controversial hymns of the tenth century Syrian monk, Symeon the New Theologian: 'I move my hand, and my hand is the whole of Christ / since, do not forget it, God is indivisible in His divinity ... / ... all our members individually / will become members of Christ and Christ our members' (Maloney: 1976, 54).

We need to go one step further – a highly important clarifying step. For there have been recent attempts to figure transcorporeality as a description of *what is* 'removed from any mystery' (Nancy: 1994, 31). This attempt, frequently owning its indebtedness to a Christian doctrine of incarnation – 'The *spirit* of Christianity is incorporated here in full. *Hoc est enim corpus meum*' (Nancy: 1994, 22) – is more fundamentally indebted to Spinoza's and Hegel's secularisation of this doctrine. (See Chapter 6.) 'There was a spirituality of Christ's wounds. But since then, a wound is just a wound' (Nancy: 1994, 22). Jean-Luc Nancy's justly acclaimed essay 'Corpus' presents such a picture. Here, in a way which seems to push beyond the soulless materialism evident in the logic of demonstrative identification, Nancy writes: '*The body has the same structure as spirit*, but it has that structure *without presupposing itself as the reason for the structure*. Consequently, it is not self-concentration, but rather the ex-concentration of existence' (Nancy: 1994, 26). Bodies are no longer discrete entities, they are disseminated. Body is always and only a community of bodies – textual, social and institutional – touching each other 'separated but shared [*partage*]' (Nancy: 1994, 29). 'This body has no longer any members, if members are the functional parts of the whole. Here, each part is the whole, and there is never any whole. Nothing ever becomes the sum or the system of the corpus' (Nancy: 1994: 28). In Spinoza, there is only one body or substance and everything else is a modification of that One, a part within the whole. Here the body is fractured and disseminated endlessly through the spirit and thus allows for a place of 'ab-solution' (Nancy: 1994, 29), a deepening absence. 'We should lead community towards this disappearance of the gods ... community inscribes the absence of communion' (Nancy: 1991, 143). 'Thus, the body has been turned into nothing but a wound', Nancy concludes (Nancy: 1994, 30).

As Nancy realises the wound here has lost its mystery. It is the final expression of soulless materialism.[12] The piles of corpses at Ypres, Belsen and Cambodia will not go away. This is a fatal wound that bleeds eternally. There is no life here. There may be room for a liberal notion of tolerance – we belong to one another, so bring out the social contract that all may sign. But there is no *telos* for this tolerance, no good life to which it tends, no commonality which subtends its possibility. In fact, Spivak criticised the essay for its adoption of a position which 'is not yet articulated into the ethical, and calculated into the moral and the political' (Spivak: 1994, 36). But what ethics or politics can this position support? Like Levinas, Nancy moves to another, a meta-level. He offers a politics of politics, an ethics of ethics in a transcendental freedom of being (Nancy: 1993; Ward: 2000). Furthermore, human bodies are gendered and there is no account of what that gendering practises or how that gendering is produced in Nancy's 'communities of bodies'. Spivak asks if Nancy is 'performing an Augustine who cannot himself undo the metalepsis of the Eucharist' (Spivak: 1994, 47).[13] Slavoj Žižek also takes Nancy to task for 'the whiff of the incarnation' that lingers about the essay (Žižek: 1994, 52). But this essay announces endless crucifixion, Hegel's endless death of God.[14] There is nothing here to stop the eternal haemorrhaging. The all too real wound will only endlessly replicate itself in other all too real wounds. As I pointed out earlier, this nihilistic monism stands within the trajectory of secularism, the logic of modernity, where all objects are seen as present to themselves. This announces the postmodern brokenness of bodies as much as the paintings of Francis Bacon or the sculptures of Ron Mueck or the fibreglass creations of Jake and Dinos Chapman.[15] This is the fracture of atomism, not of the *corpus mysticum*.

To understand this is fundamental for this project. The postmodern move can only be made from the other side of modernity, as a critique of modernity. There is only one radical critique of modernity – the critique that denies the existence of the secular as self-subsisting, that immanent self-ordering of the world which ultimately had no need for God.[16] The secular to be secular requires a theological warrant. Otherwise the secular implodes; its values collapse in upon themselves. We will discuss the implosion of secularism in Chapter 9 when we take Nancy's dematerialisation of the body one step further – into cyberspace. The Christian doctrines of incarnation and creation stand opposed to closed, immanentalist systems. They stand opposed to positivism's simulation of realised eschatology. They stand opposed also to the endless deferral and unquenchable grief for a lost body. The body is absent yet present, that is what *mysticum* announces. In Christ's ascension his body is expanded to become a space in which the Church will grow. Paul's *en Christo* is a locative use of the dative. Eschatology is both not yet and is being realised in our midst, through our labourings. Christ is both broken and given so that we become partakers in him and yet Christ also gathers us together, calls us to each other as fellow members of his multi-sexual body. Our transcorporeality is towards resurrection, not endless 'ab-solution' (or dissolution). Nancy states how, in transcorporeality, his 'community of bodies', 'Bodies call again for their creation' (Nancy: 1994, 23). But there can be no account of either such a creation or such a re-creation; only, to use Simone Weil's term, de-creation (Weil: 1952). All creation is seen to groan in Nancy's notion of embodiment, but no salvation or redemption can be offered it. The Slovenian philosopher Žižek comments, with reference to Nancy's notion of the body (which he develops in terms of the Lacanian *objet petit a* – an immanent antagonism of the psyche whereby the subject rejects the Real) that the self-positing itself as an object 'appears as an antagonism of God's prehistory, which is resolved when God speaks out of his Word' (Žižek: 1994, 77). In other words, Nancy's body exists on a plane of endless dispersal, the Real, figured as the *nihilo* out which creation will emerge. But this creation is only possible when conceived theologically, as an act of God's Word. Without this the body will dissolve into what Nancy describes as 'millions of scattered places' (Nancy: 1991, 137).

We cannot afford the disappearance of the body. Too many bodies have disappeared already. Ultimately, Nancy announces a metaphysical genocide. While refusing the full, self-realised presence of the body, we must also refuse its endless dissemination.[17] With transcorporeality, as I am conceiving it theologically, the body does not dissolve or ab-solve, it expands *en Christo*. While always located within specific sociological and historical contexts, it nevertheless is continually being opened up, allowing itself to open up, in acts of following which affect the transferral, the transduction. Transcorporeality is an effect of following in the wake of the eternal creative Word. Discipleship becomes transfiguring. The body accepts its own metaphorical nature – insofar as it is received and understood only in and through language. Only God sees and understands creation literally. We who are created deal only with the seeing and understanding appropriate to our creatureliness. We only negotiate the world metaphorically. The body, as metaphor, moves within and along the intratextual nature of creation. As such *metaphor* becomes inextricably involved with participation within a divine economy – *metousia, metexein, metalambanein* and *metanoia*.[18] Continually called to move beyond itself, the transcorporeal body itself becomes eucharistic, because endlessly fractured and fed to others. It becomes the body of Christ broken, given, resurrected and ascended. The body does not disappear. In fact, it realises its own uniqueness, its own vocation, its own irreplaceability, as offering a space for the meeting and mapping of other specified bodies, a sacred site. The transcorporeal body expands in its fracturing, it pluralises as it opens itself towards an eternal growth. Only, as such, can the wounding, can the differences, be redemptive – constitutive of the endless desire to know (where both knowledge and desire correlate with love). Only as such can the wounding, can the differences, image the intradivine wounding, the intradivine differences, of the Godhead. Through the brokenness of the transcorporeal body God's grace operates through his creation. As such 'This is my body' announces, for the Christian, the scandal of both crucifixion and resurrection, both a dying-to-self-positing and an incorporation into the city of God.

Here is announced a theology for the disabled, the sick, the racked, the torn, the diseased, the pained. Only in the context of the Presbyterian minister, the liturgies of marriage and communion, the sanctification of practised love as worship, does the brokenness of David's AIDS and Jon's bereavement become redemptive; redemptive for those of us who bear something of their body weight (with something of its pain) within our imaginaries. For these broken bodies too, perhaps especially, are transcorporeal. Especially, because the body that lives out such a brokenness understands more clearly a living in and through others, a dependency. It is a dependency that the (always relatively) able-bodied need to accept as a gift, as a spiritual food they cannot live without. This Christian theology of the body bespeaks the need to bear the weight of the body's uniqueness. For the Christian, the giving and receiving of our bodies constitutes human beings in Christ; the transcorporeality of all flesh makes possible its transfiguration. We need now to explore the Christology implicit here.

Of course, as I said at the beginning of this chapter, all this is from the standpoint of Christianity. Other standpoints – even within Christianity – are inevitable. Those occupying these other standpoints will read (and write) the experience of embodiment (and the brokenness of so many bodies) differently. What we know, or what we believe we know (and its representations) is always situated – historically, culturally, economically – and sexed. But if we are to make moves towards a 'maximizing objectivity' we need to begin by surveying the scene from where we are, while being open to the resonance and resistance of other voices. For me, something of that standpoint is composed of the fact that I am a male, Christian theologian who openly advocates same-sex unions, who has friends dying or living with the fear of AIDS, and a family who lives the shadows, embarrassments and sufferings of a genetic disorder. But each of us moves out from where we are placed and place ourselves, and in doing so understands that we are also elsewhere.

4

THE DISPLACED BODY OF
JESUS CHRIST

[W]hat I see as a manifestation of sexual liberation is God made a couple: Man and women and not simply God made man. Might Christ be
the harbinger of this living reality? Why is his sexual incarnation denied
or else treated on a human plane alone? … It is for this reason that I've
suggested that the divine incarnation of Jesus Christ is a partial one; a
view which … is consistent with his own: 'If I am not gone, the Paraclete
cannot come.' Why not? What coming of the Paraclete can be involved
here, since Jesus is already the result of his work?

(Irigaray: 1998, 207–9)

Karl Barth announced that theology is always a post-resurrection phenomenon
working within an eschatological horizon. Theology reads Scripture, the
traditions of the Church and the world in the light of the glory of the Risen
Christ in the space opened between that resurrection and our own. While not
wishing to contradict that, I want to argue for the place of the ascension in
Christianity, its practices, its Scriptures and its theological task. This nascent
theology of the ascension is inseparable from a Christology which emphasises
both the gendered body of that Jewish man, Jesus the Christ, and the way that
body is represented in the Scriptures, and the tradition's reflections upon the
Scriptures, as continually being displaced. It will begin, therefore, not with the
concepts philosophically and theologically honed by the ante-and post-Nicene
fathers. It will attempt to demonstrate, through this approach, how questions
such as 'Can a male saviour save women?'[1] and modern investigations into the
sexuality of Jesus,[2] which simply continue the nineteenth-century rational search
for the historical Jesus, fail to discern the nature of transcorporeality in Christ.
For these approaches take the human to be a measure of the Christic. What
happens at the ascension, theologically, constitutes a critical moment in a series
of displacements or assumptions[3] of the male body of Jesus Christ such that the
body of Christ, and the salvation it both seeks and works out (Paul's *katergomai*)
becomes multi-gendered. I wish to argue that, since none of us has access to
bodies *as* such, only bodies that are mediated through the giving and receiving of
signs, the series of displacements or assumptions of Jesus' body continually

refigures a masculine symbolics until the particularities of one sex gives way to the particularities of sexual differences. To that end, this chapter examines the presentation of the male Jesus in the Gospels and its representation in the life of the Church. It examines both the performance of Jesus the gendered Jew and the way that performance has been scripted, reperformed and ventriloquised by the community he brought to birth. It traces the economy of the deferred identity of the body of the Messiah;[4] an economy which becomes visible in a series of displacements. The ascension marks a final stage in the destabilised identity of the body of the Messiah.

Incarnation and circumcision

In a recent book on the sexed body of Jesus, Leo Steinberg writes, 'from Hilary and Augustine to Michelangelo, the humanity of the Incarnate is perceived as volitional condescension' and in this condescension Christ straddles 'humanness in pre- and in postlapsarian modality' (Steinberg: 1996, 296). In what follows, then, I am not denying the credal statement that Christ is both fully God and fully man, but pointing up this pre- and postlapsarian corporeal ambiguity. Tertullian, writing one of the earliest treatises on the body of Jesus Christ, *De Carne Christi*, situates the very ambiguity of Christ's flesh (as opposed to a variety of other forms of flesh, including spiritual flesh and the flesh assumed by angels) in the fact that it is flesh like ours and yet 'As, then, the first Adam is thus introduced to us, it is a just inference that the second Adam likewise … was formed by God into a quickening spirit out of the ground – in other words, out of the flesh which was unstained as yet by any human generation.'[5] This is 'the flesh which was made of a virgin' – a flesh of complex theological designation.[6] It is interesting that later theological figures like Augustine and Athanasius who also embraced the full humanity of Christ found, when describing that full humanity that Christ possessed, prelapsarian faculties beyond those available to human creatures in the postlapsarian world.[7]

From the moment of the incarnation, this body then is physically human and subject to all the affirmities of being such, and yet also a body looking backward to the perfect Adamic corporeality and forwards to the corporeality of resurrection. The materiality of this human body is eschatologically informed. We will be examining such materiality in more detail later. For the moment, it is sufficient to emphasise how the specificity of Jesus' male body is made unstable from the beginning. This is made manifest by the absence of a male progenitor in Matthew and Luke, by the way, in Mark, Jesus issues without a past into the emptiness of the wilderness (like John before him), and by the manner in which John's Gospel is related. The paternity of God is formal, rather than material. But this formality informs substance, such that our notions of 'materiality' itself become unstable. The nature of paternity is redefined – Ephesians 3.14–5[8] – in a way which points out the inseparability of what Butler's 'bodies that matter' from a doctrine of creation.[9] The XY chromosomal maleness of Jesus Christ issues from the XX chromosomal femaleness of his mother as miracle, and so this male body is unlike any other male body to date. Its materiality is, from its conception, unstable; though, with the circumcision, its specifically sexed nature is affirmed.

Patristic theologies of both the incarnation and the circumcision emphasise the instability of Jesus' gendered corporeality. Augustine's description of the baby Jesus – 'His appearance as an Infant Spouse, from his bridal chamber, that is, from the womb of a virgin' (Augustine: 1993, IX.7) – demonstrates this. The baby boy is husband and bridegroom, spouse and prefigured lover of the mother who gives him birth, whose own body swells to contain the future Church. The bridal chamber is the womb the bridegroom will impregnate with His seed while also being the womb from which he emerges. The material orders are inseparable from the symbolic and transcendent orders, the orders of mystery. The material orders are caught up and become significant only within the analogical orders. And so here Jesus' body is caught up within a complex network of sexualised symbolic relations that confound incest and the sacred. Augustine further makes plain that the infant Jesus was not born helpless and ignorant like other children: 'that such entire ignorance existed in the infant in whom the Word was made flesh, I cannot suppose … nor can I imagine that such weakness of mental faculty ever existed in the infant Christ which we see in infants generally' (Augustine: 1956 63–64). Again, the logic here is *theological* – Augustine makes these suggestions on the basis of a doctrine of creation revealed through the incarnation in which materiality participates in the Godhead. Matter itself is rendered metaphorical within the construal of such a logic. Since creation issued from the Word of God, then, seen from the perspective of God's glory, all creation bears the watermark of Christ.[10] The material orders participate in theological orders such that they are rendered both physical and symbolic. In Chapter 7 we will see how this affects an understanding of sexual differences.

One finds the theology of circumcision – developed from the early fathers through to the sermons preached in Rome on the Feast of the Circumcision (January 1st) in the fifteenth century – interpreted this one action upon the body of Jesus as prefiguring the final action in the crucifixion: the first bloodletting becoming the down payment on the redemption to come. The circumcision takes place on the eighth day, and so it is linked also to resurrection, the perfection of creation and corporeality. The body of Jesus is, once more, stretched temporally, the baby body prefiguring the adult body, the adult body figuring the ecclesial body in a march to its resurrection. The physicality of the body, its significance as a body, and the acts with which it is involved, are figured within an allegorical displacement.

Transfiguration

Throughout the Gospel narratives, Jesus the man is viewed to be not a man like other men (or women). This man can walk on water. This man can sweat blood.

This man can bring to life. This man can multiply material so that five thousand are fed from a few loaves and fish. This man can heal by touch; and not just heal but create – wine from water, the eyes of the man born blind, the ear of the Temple guard. But it is the explicit displacements of his own physical body which interest me, the various assumptions or transfigurations that occur in which the divine is manifested in the sexed and corporeal, and the implications of these transfigurations. In these assumptions Jesus is not alone. Tertullian, besides remarking that human flesh is made from the earth and the earth is made *ex nihilo*, points out that angels frequently 'changed into human form' and the Holy Spirit 'descended in the body of a dove'.[11] The displacements of Jesus' body simply gives Christological significance to the nature of embodiment. John's Gospel is particularly emphatic about these assumptions with its repetitions of ontological scandal – I am the way, the life, the truth, the Temple, the bread, the light, the vine and the gate into the sheepfold. But in the Gospels generally, in those stories of the body of Jesus, there are five scenes where these displacements are dramatically performed: the transfiguration itself; the eucharistic supper; the crucifixion; the resurrection; and, finally, the ascension. Each of these scenes, in an ever-deepening way, problematise the sexed nature of Jesus' body and point towards an erotics far more comprehensive, and yet informing, the sexed and the sexual.

The prelapsarian body of Adam is erotically charged – perfect in its form, its goodness and its beauty, and naked. Fashions in the figuration of that form change. Today's cult of the firm, hard, male physique, like the various cultural pursuits it has fostered (body-building and dieting), is the result of certain conventions of masculinity which arose in Germany in the late eighteenth century – a masculinisation modelled on classical sculpture (Mosse: 1996,17–39).[12] But whatever the fashion of our representations something Promethean, powerful and vulnerable sticks close to the image of Adam in Paradise. What is glimpsed in and through his magnificence is the image of God – the trace of the uncreated in the created. In so far as in Christ human beings are restored to their pre-fallen splendour, the transfiguration scene on the Mount of Olives presents us with Jesus as the second Adam. Not naked in any obvious sense, but nevertheless bathed in a certain translucence. What I am describing here as erotically charged is the way these manifestations of humankind glorified by God are attractive. They are incarnations of divine beauty and goodness and, as such, they possess the power to attract, to invoke a desire which draws us towards an embrace, a promise of grace. These disclosures establish economies of desire within which we are invited, if not incited, to participate. The transfiguration does not simply portray a resurrection hope, it performs it, it solicits it. Mark's account of it (9.2–8) bears witness to the event's power to attract and engage. The Greek is simple, but subtle. It employs assonance and alliteration, the repetition of *kai* sets up a paratactic rhythm within which other verbal echoes resound (*leuka ... leukanai; mian ... mian; egenonto ... egeneto ... egegeneto; nephele ... nepheles*). The prose is as liturgical as the event and the details of its setting (tents, a prophet, the lawgiver, the *shekinah* presence). The physical body of Jesus is displaced – for it is not the physical body as such which is the source of the attraction, but the glorification of the physical body made possible by viewing it through God as God. We are attracted to the man and beyond him, so that the erotic economy does not flounder on questions of sexuality (i.e. is my attraction to this man as a man homoerotic, is my attraction to this man as a woman heterosexual). The erotic economy propels our desire towards what lies beyond and yet in and through this man's particular body. This economy of desire does not deny the possibility of a sexual element, it does not prevent or stand in critical judgement of a sexual element; it simply overflows the sexual such that we cannot, without creating a false and idolatrous picture of Christ, turn this man into an object for our sexual gratification. This man cannot be fetishised, because he exceeds appropriation. Desire is not caught up here in a endless game of producing substitutes for a demand that can never be satisfied. Such is the model of both Freudian and Lacanian desire; desire founded upon and furthering the aporetics of lack in attempting to attain that which cannot be attained. This is a desire founded upon a gendering of that desire (the libido is only and always masculine), a gendering of that lack (which is always feminine and maternal) and a gendering of the object never-to-be-attained (the primal scene of the mother, for Freud, the phallus of the father, for Lacan). The transfiguration sets Jesus outside any economy of exchange, any economy where the value of an object can be known and its exchange negotiated. The transfiguration sets up an economy of desire which the three witnesses (who proxy for us all) cannot accommodate. This transfigurability, and its subsequent beauty and goodness, is not something they lack and will now strive to attain. Jesus cannot now become an ego-ideal. In fact, the manner in which Jesus is figured alongside Moses and Elijah, and spoken of transcendentally, suggests he is there to call to mind something forgotten, an image of human plenitude lost. Moses is the past locating the disciples *in* their past; Elijah is the past-as-future translating the disciples into the time of Messianic promise. Jesus does not figure what the disciples lack (Lacan's *objet petit a*). He is transfigured as the realisation of something they remember; that which crosses time and recalls them to a very rooted identity as those who are recipients of the Jewish tradition. The act of naming ('This is my beloved Son'), parallels Jesus' own act of naming at the last supper ('This is my body'). It is a naming outside their expectations; an ontological scandal. They stumble upon this figure as upon one situated within another order, in an economy of loving and being beloved. The transfiguration is, by participation, partly their own, as this experience breaks upon them as a gift they know not how to receive. But by the very fact that this enactment of divine love reaches out to draw them in, receive they will. In fact, they are already receiving. One notes how, in both Matthew's account (17.1–13) and Luke's (9.28–36), we focus upon the face of Christ. It is a face full of light and energy, and no doubt alludes to the shining face of Moses coming down the mountain from having spoken with God. But Matthew's description exceeds any allusion to the lawgiver. He writes of Jesus' face 'shining like the sun'. We are drawn to love the beautiful and the good in Him. His corporeality becomes iconic.[13] We are silenced, like James and John, before this Christic sublime, quite different from the (post)modern sublime.[14] In the presence (where 'in' is strongly locational) of the holy, we listen, we receive, we worship, we give thanks.

The eucharist

The displacement of the physical body becomes more abrupt in the eucharistic supper. The scandal of what is enacted at this supper we have already looked at, but in this chapter I wish to point out how the body of the historical man begins its withdrawal from the narrative, from direct representation. With the eucharist, transfiguration turns into transposition. 'He took bread, and blessed and broke it, and gave it to them, and said "Take; this is my body." ' Matthew adds 'eat'. Neither Luke nor Mark mentions the consumption, only the giving and receiving of the bread-as-his-body. It is the handing-over of himself that is paramount. He places himself into the hands of the disciples who then hand him over to the authorities. It is the surrendering that is important. It is effected by that demonstrative indicative – 'this' is my body. These words perform the transposition. As I have argued, they set up a logic of radical reidentification. What had throughout the gospel story been an unstable body is now to be understood as an extendible body. For it is not that Jesus, at this point, stops being a physical presence. It is more as if this physical presence can expand itself to incorporate other bodies, like bread, and make them extensions of his own.[15] A certain metonymic substitution is enacted, re-situating Jesus' male physique within the neuter materiality of bread (*to arton*). The 'body' now is both sexed and not sexed.

The narrative logic for this transposition is the mutability of the body throughout; the theo-logic for this transposition is Christ's lordship over creation (such that the wind and waves obey him) and yet his identification with and participation within it: Jesus as God's Word informing creation.

With the eucharistic displacement of the physical body a new understanding of embodiment is announced. Bodies in Greco-Roman culture, according to Dale Martin, were not viewed as discreet, auto-defining entities. They were malleable, and because they are made of the same stuff as the world around them 'the differentiation between the inner and outer body was fluid and permeable' (Martin: 1995, 20). Physical bodies were mapped onto other bodies – social, political, cosmic. Hence 'for most people of Greco-Roman culture the human body was of a piece with its environment. The self was a precarious, temporary state of affairs, constituted by forces surrounding and pervading the body, like the radio waves that bounce around and through the bodies of modern urbanities … the body is perceived as a location in a continuum of cosmic movement' (Martin: 1995, 25; Sennett: 1994, 31–148). Even so, the displacement of Jesus' body at this point is somewhat different, more radical. It begins with a breaking. It is not just blurring the boundaries between one person and another – though it effects that through the handing over and the eating of the 'body'. The bread here mediates the crossing of frontiers. But more is involved in what Jesus does and says in that upper room. For 'This is my body' is not a symbolic utterance. The bread is not the vehicle for significance, for anthropomorphic projections. The bread *is* also the body of Jesus. That ontological scandal is the epicentre for the shock-waves which follow. For it is actually the translocationality that is surprising – as if place and space itself is being redefined such that one can be a body here and also there, one can be this kind of body here and that kind of body there. Just as with the transfiguration, the translucency of one body makes visible another hidden body, so too with the eucharist, although in a different way, a hidden nature of being embodied is made manifest. Bodies are not only transfigurable, they are transposable. In being transposable, while always being singularities and specificities, the body of Christ can cross boundaries, ethnic boundaries, gender boundaries, socio-economic boundaries, for example. Christ's body as bread is no longer Jesus as simply and biologically male.

The crucifixion

The crucifixion develops the radical form of displacement announced in the eucharistic supper. The breaking of the bread is now relocated in the breaking of the physical body of Jesus. The handing over is taken one step further. The male body of Christ is handed over to death. The passivity of Jesus before Jewish and Roman authorities and the two scenes of his nakedness (stripped by the Roman guards according to Matthew and implied in Luke, then reclothed to be stripped again for his crucifixion), set this vulnerable body to play in a field of violent power games. The sexual charge is evident in the delight taken by the soldiers in abusing his body and in the palpable sense of power created through the contrast between Pilate's towering authority and Jesus' submissiveness.[16] But the sexual is only one aspect of the circling dynamics of what Greenblatt refers to as the 'social energies' (Greenblatt: 1988). The quickening pace of the narrative, the breathless surge of activity which propels the body of Christ towards the resting-place of the cross, bear witness both to the force-field within which this body is placed and to its own power to become a focus, to affect and draw in. The violence in which bodies touch other bodies – beginning with the kiss by Judas, moving through the slapping 'with the palm of his hand' by the Temple guard in the house of Caiaphas, to the scourging by the Roman soldiers and the nailing on the cross, to, finally, the piercing of the side by the lance – are all manifestations of various desires in conflict, sexually charged. The whipped-up hysteria of the crowd shouting 'crucify' reveals the generative power of such violence, what Girard has analysed as the 'mimetic nature of desire' which seeks out a surrogate victim and marks the approach of sacrificial crisis (Girard: 1977, 169; for the libidinal nature of this desire see chapters 5 to 7, pp. 119–92). It climaxes with the strung-up nakedness of Christ on the cross. The body hangs as neither woman or man, but meat; as that spent form left behind when the other has been gratified: as the body raped. Death degenders.

Throughout the play of these erotic and political power games the actual maleness of the body of Jesus is forgotten. This is a man among men; no sexual differentiation is taken account of. It is no longer 'this' body or 'my' body, but 'that' undifferentiated body. The body becomes an object acted upon at the point when the dynamic for the narrative is wrenched from Jesus' grasp and put into the hands of the Jewish and the Roman authorities. The displacement of Jesus' body is accentuated through the displacement in the direction of the storytelling, the displacement in the responsibility for the unfolding of events. The body as object is already being treated as a dead, unwanted, discardable thing before Jesus breathes his last.

There is a hiatus at this point. The orgiastic frenzy abates and there is the shaping of a new desire. Each Gospel writer shapes this new desire by relocating Christian witness within a scene that, since Peter's betrayal, has lacked it.[17] Matthew reintroduces the women who had followed Jesus from Galilee; Luke, who also frames this scene with the women, first affects the shaping of a new desire through the thief on the cross; Mark introduces his famous centurion; and John inserts a conversation between Jesus and John concerning Mary into the Passion narrative. Perhaps the very variety of different narratives at this point in what is now a salvation history, suggests an awkwardness; a self-conscious difficulty on the part of the four writers with respect to this reorientation of desire following the crucifixion. John's Gospel testifies, proleptically, to the nature of this reorientation, when he has Jesus state: 'And I, if I be lifted up from the earth, will draw all men unto me' (12.32). The desire is no longer libidinal, but issues from a certain pathos.

The iconic status of the body of Jesus re-emerges. But the manner in which it draws now is configured through an identification with the suffering of the body. Earlier, at the eucharist, the identification was effected through the feeding, the sharing, and the being nurtured. In the crucifixion this identification is lost as the focus of the participation shifts towards the violent excitements of the Dionysian sacrifice. The displacement of the body at the eucharist effects a sharing, a participation. We belong to Jesus and Jesus to others through partaking of his given body. We exist in and through relation. The crucifixion effects a detachment, a distance. The displacement of the body here breaks the former relations. Displacement is becoming loss, and with the loss a new space opens for an economy of desire experienced as mourning. The affectivity of one displacement can only come about through the other – without the sharing and participation there cannot arise the sense of a coming separation and loss. With the sense of loss comes also, paradoxically, the recognition of the nature and depth of the former identification. What is being mourned here is not simply the suffering body of Christ, but our own nature as those capable of handing that body over, and therefore handing our own bodies over to some other social corpus (the Jews, the Romans, whoever). The space of this pathos heightens the iconicity of the crucified one. It emotionally colours a certain liminality within which the affectivity of this object is offered to us – the *inter alia* between dying and death, presence and departure; and between death and burial, departure and removal of the departed one. The liminality reinforces the sacredness of the space. Through it the crucifixion is already ritualised.

The transitional nature of Jesus' body at this point is dramatised further by the silence of Holy Saturday which deepens the hiatus affected here; a hiatus made profoundly theological because it is interpreted as the Trinity at its most extended; a moment when the Father is most separated from the Son and the distance between them embraces the lowest regions of hell.[18] The displacement here is mapped onto the eternal displacements of the trinitarian processions; the trinitarian differences: between Father and Son and then between Father–Son and Spirit. Displacement of identity itself, the expansion of the identified Word to embrace all that is other, becomes the mark of God within creation.

Iconicity transcends physicality; but physically subtends iconicity. The physical is not erased, rather it is overwhelmed, drenched with significance. This is quite different from the suspension of the material in the transfiguration, and not simply because we are offered not the glorified but the tortured body of Christ. The suspension is different because of what we have come to understand about ourselves through participation in the events between the transfiguration and the crucifixion, and through the complex psychosomatic identifications and denials which have been staged. The maleness of Christ is made complex and ambivalent, as all things are made ambivalent when their symbolic possibilities are opened up by the liminality. Victor Turner remarks about liminal persona that they become 'structurally, if not physically, "invisible" … They are at once no longer classified and not yet classified' (Turner: 1967: 95–6).[19] The symbols used to represent bodies which are not outside established categories cross or conflate distinctions – social, racial, or sexual (Turner: 1967, 98). In what Turner calls their 'sacred poverty' of all rights and identifications, such bodies become floating signifiers. The mediaeval Church bears witness to this ambivalence in finding it appropriate to gender Jesus as a mother at this point, with the wounded side as both a lactating breast and a womb from which the Church is removed.[20] The pain and suffering of crucifixion itself is gendered in terms of the labour pains of birthing. The mothering symbolism has a logic with the economy of desire itself as set up by the withdrawing of the body; if all withdrawal and subsequent mourning is, even partly, a reminder of the primary break from, and the libidinal desire to return to, self-unity established in and through that primary separation from the body of the mother. The symbolic template of Jesus' crucified body, and the empathy with human suffering it invokes, draws forth deeper awarenesses of our human condition, and of the primary levels of desire which constitute it. His body becomes the symbolic focus for all bodies loved and now departed: real, imaginary and symbolic mothers; real, imaginary and symbolic fathers.[21] His body calls forth all the cathected objects of our past desires which have been abjected in order to facilitate our illusory self-unity

(Kristeva: 1982 and, specifically on the relation of abjection to Christ's death and resurrection, Kristeva: 1988).

The allure of the abject, and the mourning which now will always accompany Christian desire, manifests an internalisation of displacement itself. We are the ones displaced; that is what the crucified body of Christ recalls us to – a primary relationship to God from which we are estranged. The internalisation of the displacement will now foster an eternal longing, and structure the Christian desire for God. The economy of Christian salvation is triggered by this event, for, as Augustine understood, we reach 'our bliss in the contemplation of the immaterial light through participation in his changeless immortality, which we long to attain, with burning desire' (Augustine: 1972, XII.21). It is not simply that the physical body of Jesus is displaced in the Christian story, our bodies too participate in that displacement in and through the crucifixion. At the eucharist we receive and we are acted upon; now, having been brought into relation and facing the acknowledgement of the breaking of that relation readers recognise displacement of the body as part of Christian living. Our bodies too, sexually specific, will perform in ways which transgress the gendered boundaries of established codes. In the Christian tradition which follows, men will become mothers – witness the writings of Bernard of Clairvaux and Aelred of Rievaulx (Bynum: 1992, 158–60); women will become virile – witness the writings of Mechthild of Magdeburg and Hadewijch (Newman: 1995; Castelli: 1991, 49–69).[22] The eucharistic fracture, repeating differently the crucifixion, disseminates the body – of Christ and the Church as the body of Christ. The dissemination sets each body free to follow (and both be transposed and transfigured) within the plenitude of the Word which has passed by and passes on. What initiates the following after is the awareness of being involved, of having been drawn into the ongoing divine activity of Christ. Christian involvement is a tasting of that which Christians now long for; they drink of eternal life in that participation.

Again, the reorientation of Christian desiring, differs from the structural function of lack in the economies of desire in Hegel, Freud and Lacan. The economies of desire in the work of these people, which parody the Christian as subject-of-desire, are circular. A moment of integration and wholeness is posited at the beginning which is followed by the event of a break or a fall into what is other. This event constitutes the recognition of lack. In Hegel this is the fall into self-consciousness which moves out and towards itself in a dialectical sublation of what is other. In his demythologised reading of Adam's eating of the fruit of the tree of knowledge of good and evil, Hegel writes: 'What it really means is that humanity has elevated itself to the knowledge of good and evil; and this cognition, this distinction, is the source of evil, is evil itself. ... For cognition or consciousness means in general a judging or dividing, a self-distinguishing within oneself' (Hegel: 1988: 443). This is following a line of thinking opened up by Kant.[23] In Freud and Lacan, the break comes with the separation from the body of the mother. For Freud, the recognition of exile from 'the mother's womb, the first lodging, for which in all likelihood man still longs' (Freud: 1961, 91) and the loss of the mother's breast, propel the libidinal drive towards finding substitute pleasures and consolations. Eventually this drive then enters the Oedipal triangle which stages sexual development. Lacan is far more metaphysical. The desire of the mother is the origin. Her desire founds the economy of desire itself (Lacan: 1992, 283). Her desire is for the phallus, and the child comes to recognise her as Other through the event of the father which splices the symbiosis of mother–child. The mirror stage spatially performs the alienation. But the desire of the mother is itself a desire structured around lack – the lack of the phallus. The origin, then, itself is a hole which nurtures a nostalgia for presence. The search for identity and presence is therefore a search for the nothing into which all that is folds.

In none of these foundational origins which bring about separations or alienations (which, in turn, set up the endless circulation of desire), do we ever consciously participate. They are events belonging to pre-self, pre-linguistic-consciousness. They are speculative moments which provide the conditions for the possibility of what is and yet lie outside it, as Freud (who attempted to map the morphology of the infant psyche onto primal man and the development of civilisation itself) understood. They provide undemonstrable 'intuitions' of a wholeness and immediacy both irrecoverable and unremembered. They are moments belonging to the metaphysics of idealism – aprioricity. The experience they provide the condition for is loss, bereavement and the necessity of finding consolations. 'Lack' here characterises a kenotic economy of self-emptying *en abîme*, a *via negativa* – the endless search for the beginning which culminates in death. For Freud, the death instinct is inseparable from the libidinal drive and what characterises both is the desire to return to the primal condition (Freud: 1961, 118–22). The 'lack' is a figure of death haunting the whole economy and the immanence of its libidinal logic. Lacan writes: 'This lack is real because it relates to something real, namely, that the living being, by being subject to sex, has fallen under the blow of individual death' (Lacan: 1979, 208).[24] The libidinal logic has no exterior, no memory of that founding wholeness (or nothingness) which governs desire's subsequent teleology. And since it has no conclusion either, for its desires can never be satisfied – 'The programme of becoming happy ... cannot be fulfilled' (Freud: 1961, 83), 'man cannot aim at being whole' (Lacan: 1977, 287) – these economies of desire announce the vicious logic of Narcissus: pursuing one's own shadow until either one's energies are exhausted or one kisses oneself in some act of suicide. Lacan again: 'The subject says "No!" to this intersubjective game of hunt-the-slipper in which desire makes itself recognised for a moment, only to become lost in the will that is the will of the other' (Lacan: 1977, 104–5).

This is not the structure of the economy of Christian desire. The structure of Christian desire is, significantly, twofold – not only my desire, but God's desire for me. It is this twofoldedness which characterises participation. The self is fissured in such participation, and fissured endlessly. It never had the unity of the Hegelian and Freudian ego living in and for itself;[25] it never will. Its completion lies outside, before and after it. This fissuring, and the historical events which make it possible, are performed and reperformed in the eucharist, in the kenosis which constructs the Christian self in every practice of the faith. I will develop this further in Chapter 6. The mourning, which issues from the radical displacement of the body of Christ in the crucifixion feeds a positive regeneration. It bears the charge of resurrection, for in the pain of its present it bears the seed of its future, glorious body. It bears the charge also of a past (the prelapsarian state), and a past promise (of messianic redemption), both of which are recalled. Not-having the body of Christ is not a lack, not a negative: because Christ's withdrawal of his body makes possible a greater identification with that body. In fact, the Church in its identification becomes the body of Christ. This identification does not belong to the Aristotelian logics of identification and non-contradiction. The logic of A = A is, ultimately, the vicious logic of Narcissus. The identification here, in Christ, is analogical – a participation in and through difference that enables a co-creativity. The displacement does not operate within an economy of death-bound subjectivity (Lingis: 1989), but within eternal, trinitarian life.

The theological implication of this is that the displacement of the body in the crucifixion is not cancelled out by the resurrection, as if the tragic moment of the broken is swept into a comic finale of triumphant reconciliation. The resurrection only expands the kenotic movement of displacement effected through the crucifixion. It does not reverse it and neither does it constitute, by its equiprimordiality, the paradox of crucifixion–resurrection. Paradox freezes time; denies history; is the trauma of history, fetishised and rendered aesthetic as tragedy. Time is God's gift for/of redemption. The death of the physical body is not the end of, but rather the opening for further, displacements – the eucharistic fracturing promoted through the Church. It makes brokenness, and love as not-having (Cixous: 1990), a *sine qua non* of redemption. This redemption is not an emptying of oneself into nothingness (*à la* Lacan); but a recognition of the lack of foundations within oneself which requires and enables the reception of divine plenitude. Lacan returns the subject to the *nihilo* and denies that God made anything out of it. The Christian awareness of the absent body of Christ, and of death itself, returns us to our createdness – to the giftedness of creation out of nothing.

The resurrection

The resurrected body of Jesus sums up all the modes of displacement that were seen in evidence before his death. The life of Christ continues, playing out the unstable physicality of the body which walked on water, the glorified body of the transfiguration, the broken body of the eucharist and the degendered anonymity of dead flesh. The ability to disappear, walk through walls, occupy other bodies (which causes so many misidentifications of who he is), is countered by a corporeality which is tangible and able to eat. Displacement opens up a spiritual topos within the physical, historical and geographical orders. Displacement is figured in the narrative first through the empty tomb. This emptiness is emphasised in John's Gospel by the presence of two angels at either end of where the body lay (20.12). It is not emptiness as such, rather it is akin to the space opened by the two angels on either side of the ark of the covenant in the Holy of Holies: the emptiness announces the plenitude of God's presence.[26]

The displacement is figured, secondly, in the actual body of Christ. It is no longer recognisable. The two on the road to Emmaus talk to him for hours, but it is only when he breaks the bread they will eat for supper that they recognise him. John records Mary at the tomb turning from the angels, seeing Jesus and not knowing that it was Jesus, supposing him to be a gardener even when he had spoken to her. She only recognises him when he calls her by her name. Later in the same Gospel the disciples, out fishing, see Jesus walking on the shore and they did not know it was Jesus, even though he spoke to them. It was only after they had obeyed the instruction to fish on the other side of the boat and the nets were drawing in the heavy load that Peter says 'It is the Lord'. Acts of naming are involved in these two last scenes; naming which engenders recognition. These narrative details cannot be taken, as they have been by some, as evidence of disfigurations which follow the atomic-like power of the resurrection. Such an explanation assumes what Mary Douglas calls a medical materialism. The misidentifications are part of the unfolding logic of displacing bodies, bodies which defer or conceal their final identity; bodies which maintain their mystery. In each case, from the hiddenness comes the revelation, the realisation which has the structure of an initiation – the move from what is familiar, to what is strange, to what is once again familiar albeit in another guise. These bodies of Jesus bear analogical resemblance to each other, not Aristotelian identification. The body is analogical by nature – it moves through time and constantly changes and yet all these changes are analogically related to each other.[27] With these new identifications ('It is the Lord', 'Their eyes were opened', 'Mary', 'Rabboni') a new relationship and understanding is opened up. The logic of the displacement and deferral of the Word is a pedagogical logic.

The third figuration of displacement, opening a spiritual topos, is the structure of the narrative itself. The Gospel narrative had previously followed Jesus Christ wherever he went until his disappearance into the tomb, now can no longer follow him. A series of appearances, visitations, or epiphanies occur. The body of Christ keeps absenting itself from the text. Where does it go to? What the body is replaced by is the witness of the Church. First, the angels pass on the news that he is risen (just as they were the first to testify to his birth). Then Mary of Magdala bears witness; alone in John's Gospel, with another Mary in Mark's, and with Mary the mother of James and Salome (in Matthew) or Joanne (in Luke). This gendering of the first human witness is significant. Of course women were related closely with death or the preparations and aftercare of the dead, in the ancient world. But these women are associated here with the beginning of new life. Mary Magdala's witness parallels the Virgin Mary's own recognition of the truth brought forth (though John makes no explicit mention of the birth narrative). Is it that those gendered feminine more easily recognise the analogical nature of embodiment than those living within and practising the patriarchal logics (patriarchalism is not one) of Aristotelian identification? Finally, several other disciples narrate their experiences (those on the road to Emmaus, the disciples in the upper room to Thomas). Jesus' presence is mediated now mainly through the discourses of those who will comprise the early Church.

Patristic and mediaeval theology announced this creation of a new body, through the displacement of Christ's physical body, in gendered language: through the wound in Jesus' side the Church is brought to birth. Jesus makes manifest the motherhood of the divine. Carolyn Walker Bynum has exhaustively researched this material. In her *Speculum of the Other Women*, Irigaray too alludes to the wounding of Christ that marks a femininity within him (Irigaray: 1985, 199–200). There is much more material, and much less explored material, in the writings of the Syrian fathers like Ephraim. Material which speaks profoundly of the wombs through which creation and the Church issue. The water and the blood which flow from the side of Christ are the sacramental foods which nurture and nourish his child-bride, the Church. What I wish to emphasise is the textuality of all these bodies. Certeau has, himself, noted:

> Thus, through community practice and Trinitarian theology, the death of Jesus becomes the condition for the new Church to arise and for new languages of the Gospel to develop. The true relation of Jesus to the Father (who gives him his authority) and to the Church (he 'permits') is verified (i.e. manifested) by his death. The Jesus event is extended (verified) in the manner of a disappearance in the *difference* which that event renders possible. Our relation to the origin is in function of its increasing absence. The beginning is more and more hidden by the multiple creations which reveal its significance.
>
> (Certeau: 1992, 79–90)

The body of Christ is disseminated in 'new languages of the Gospel'. The body of Christ crucified and risen, gives birth to the ecclesial *corpus*, to the history and transformations of that ecclesial body, and each of these bodies can only materialise in, through and with language. The continual displacement of these bodies, the continual displacement of their identities, is not only *produced* through economies of signification, it *is a reflection* (a *mimesis* or repetition) of an aporetics intrinsic to textuality itself. To adopt a Derridean term, the logic of Christ as Logos is the logic of *différance*[28] – the deferral of identity and the non-identical repetition which institutes and perpetuates alterity: this is not that, or, more accurately, this is not only that. Thus, the absenting body of Christ gives place to (is supplemented by) a body of confessional and doxological discourse in which the Church announces, in a past tense which can never make its presence felt immediately, 'We have seen him. He is risen.' The concerns with time here we

110

will explore further in Chapter 6. For the moment it is sufficient to understand how the testimonials cited in the Gospels provide a self-conscious trope for the writing of the Gospel narratives themselves. For we only had the mediated body of Jesus Christ throughout. We have been reading and absorbing and performing an ecclesial testimony in the fact we have the Gospel narratives (and Pauline epistles) at all. The confessions and doxologies staged within the narratives are self-reflexive moments when the narratives examine that which makes the Gospels possible at all: the giving and receiving of signs.

The appearance/disappearance structure of Christ's resurrected body serves to emphasise the mediation of that body – its inability to be fully present, to be an object to be grasped, catalogued, atomised, comprehended. The appearance/disappearance serves as a focus for what has been evident throughout – the body as a mystery, as a materiality which can never fully reveal, must always conceal, something of the profundity of its existence. In Mark's Gospel a young man sits astride the head of the empty tomb and tells the women 'He is risen. He is not here. He goes before you to Galilee'. Galilee was where the story began – and will begin, when the story is retold (at least by Mark). The young man points them back to the beginning of their discipleship. The beginning is doubled. In Matthew's Gospel the young man is an angel (*angelos*, a messenger *par excellence*). In Luke's Gospel there are two angels, and the story proceeds to narrate the testimonies of the disciples who saw the risen Christ appear on the road to Emmaus, noting also the testimony of Simon Peter (whose story of Christ's visitation does not appear in the text). In John's Gospel it is Mary of Magdala who communicates the news, who becomes an angel (and envoy); Jesus subsequently appearing to confirm the news. Meditation, the dissemination of messages, the narration of stories, the communication in one context being transposed and reported in another – these constitute the poetics of the New Testament itself, the letteral Word of God which, borne and born by the Spirit, supplements the incarnate Word of God. The practices of Christian living parse the divine grammar: in our words and our worlding we are adverbial in the sense Eckhart gives that part of speech when he prays: 'may the Father, the Verbum, and the Holy Spirit help us to remain adverbs of this Verbum' (quoted in Derrida: 1987, 578).

Communication confers communion and creates community.[29] From the dispersal of the disciples on the point of Christ's crucifixion, a new collectivity of relations begins to form following the resurrection. People are sent to each other – by the young man, by the angels, and by Jesus. The resurrection play of appearances and disappearances triggers a series of relational relays. These are performed across various geographic, gendered and socially symbolic spaces: across the city of Jerusalem, from Emmaus to Jerusalem, from Jerusalem to Galilee, across the sea of Galilee; across the divide between women and men, believers and doubters, Jews and Gentiles (maybe rich and poor, the skilled and the unskilled, the labourer and the academic, the Temple and the people of the land, slave and freeborn, for all we know about the contexts within which these narratives were composed). Relationality and spatiality, the new collectivity borne within and across the distensive absenting, a new collectivity issuing from the divinely driven imperative to bear witness to the appearance and disappearance of Jesus Christ – all come to an apex in the scene of the ascension.

The ascension

The Ascension is the final displacement of the body of the gendered Jew. Again, let me emphasise, that displacement is not the erasure but the expansion of the body. The interpretation of the ascension is not in accord with Origen's 'ascension of the mind rather than of the body' (Origen: 1954, 23.2). The ascension is 'in the flesh', as Irenaeus argued (Irenaeus: 1910, 1.10.1). The final displacement rehearses the logic of the eucharist: the body itself is transposed. A verse from Colossians elucidates this. 'the Church is his body, the fullness of him who fills all in all'. I will avoid entering into the ambiguities of both the Greek syntax and the authorship of this letter. Scholars have long debated these things. It is sufficient to point out that the Church is now the body of Christ, the distended body of Jesus of Nazareth. The Church is broken like the bread, to be food dispersed throughout the world. The final displacement of the gendered body of Jesus Christ, always aporetic and transgressing boundaries, is the multi-gendered body of the Church. A new spatial distance opens up with the ascension – a vertical, transcending spatiality such as divides the uncreated God from creation. There will be no more resurrection appearances. The withdrawal of the body is graphically described by Luke not as myth – the Acts passage refers several time, to what the disciples saw – but as historical event. The emptiness remaining (to be filled by the Spirit at Pentecost) is emphasised by the angels: 'why stand ye gazing up into heaven?' It is a moment of both exaltation and bereavement.

Michel de Certeau, following Hegel, views the loss of the body of Jesus as the beginning of the community of faith.[30] The Church is founded upon and proceeds on the basis of lack (Certeau: 1992, 79–90). Certainly, with Christ's departing words concerning the Holy Ghost to come and the angels' pro-nouncement that Jesus himself will return, a desire is installed as they who 'continued with one accord' are now orientated towards the future, towards a deferred *eschaton*. Certainly, the gap which now opens up between the Ascension and Pentecost has a similar structure to the gap between Good Friday and Easter Sunday: as if something important is going on behind the scenes which entails a certain suspension of judgement here and now. The disciples are caught between memory and anticipation; a past and a future. But the absenting is not a decisive break. It is not a rupture that is never to be healed. The final absenting is contiguous. I have argued throughout that the body of Jesus Christ is continually being displaced so that the figuration of the body is always transposing its identity. That logic of displacement is now taken up in the limbs and tissue of his body as the Church. Poised between memory and anticipation, driven by a desire which enfolds it and which it cannot master, the history of the Church's body is a history of transposed and deferred identities: it incarnates a humanity aspiring to Christ's own humanity. As one commentator, still employing a language blind to its own gendering, has concluded with respect to Irenaeus' doctrine of the acsension: 'Man is still in the making' (Farrow: 1998, 37). The ascension re-establishes a new anthropology, a new way of being human as being *en Christo* as the Church. Furthermore, the absenting does not culminate in bereavement. The new body of Christ will not promulgate and live out endless simulacra for fulfilment. The loss of the body of Jesus Christ cannot be read that way. The logic of the Ascension is the logic of birthing, not dying, or a continuation of the logic of opening-up. The withdrawal of the body of Jesus must be understood in terms of the Logos creating a space within himself, a womb, within which (*en Christoi*) the Church will expand and creation be recreated. As Gregory of Nyssa observes about resurrection life: 'Participation in the divine good is such that, where it occurs, it makes the participant ever greater and more spacious than before, brings to it an increase in size and strength, in such wise that the participant, nourished in this way, never stops growing and keeps getting larger and larger' (Nyssa: 1978) In this way, the body of the Church and the body of the world are enfolded through resurrection within the Godhead. The body of Jesus Christ is not lost, nor does it reside now in heaven as a discrete object for veneration (as Calvin thought and certain gnostics before him) in and by the Spirit.[31] The body of Jesus Christ, the body of God, is permeable, transcorporeal, transpositional. Within it all other bodies are situated and given their significance. We are all permeable, transcorporeal and transpositional. 'There is neither Jew nor Greek, there is neither bond nor free, there is neither male or female, for ye are all one in Christ (*eis este en Christoi*)' (Phil. 2.12). This theo-logic makes possible, as I mentioned at the beginning of this chapter, an understanding of the omnipresence or ubiquity of God.[32]

We have no access to the body of the gendered Jew. So all those attempts to determine the sexuality of Jesus are simply more recent symptoms of the search for the historical Christ – which Schweitzer demonstrated was pointless at the beginning of this century (Schweitzer: 1954). It is pointless not only because it is a human attempt to give Christianity an empirically verifiable foundation and the metaphysics implied in believing that project to be possible are profoundly anti-Christian (atomism, positivism, atemporality, immanentalism, access to the immediate and subjectivism). It is pointless because the Church is now the body of Christ, so to understand the body of Jesus we can only examine what the Church is and what it has to say concerning the nature of that body as scripture attests to it. The Church dwells in Christ and in Christ works out its salvation and the salvation of the world. The body of Christ is a multigendered body. Its relation to the body of the gendered Jew does not have the logic of cause and effect. This is the logic which lies behind those questions 'Can a male saviour save women?' This is the logic of Hegel's description of the relationship between God and the Church. God in Christ dies and the Church is born. One gives way to the other, without remainder. The relationship between Jesus and the Church is processional, as the relationship between the trinitarian persons is processional. One abides in and through the other. The body of the gendered Jew expands to embrace the whole of creation. That body continues to expand by our continual giving and receiving of signs. This is the textuality of Christian time made up, as it is, of doxological words and liturgical practices. The expansive bloom of the flower is not the effect of the bud, but its fulfilment.

Christology

The criticism, no doubt, of this interpretative strategy will be levelled at its high Christology. The emphasis upon all things being *en Christoi*, of Christ opening a space in the fallen world in which resurrection life expands, might be seen to take us further and further from the historical specificity of Jesus of Nazareth, and closer and closer towards the docetism that the appeal to embodiment is attempting to undermine. Several issues need to be tackled here. First, the concern with 'high' and 'low' Christology is an academic invention of nineteenth-century biblical criticism. High Christology described the cosmic Christology of Paul's (?) *Letter to the Ephesians* and his *Letter to the Colossians*, and later Logos Christologies. The construction of this dualism is concomitant with the dualisms around which Christology of the nineteenth and twentieth centuries continually were figured in their attempt to reconcile or, at least render, theologically coherent, the man-God (see Ward: 1996). Whether Christ was viewed as the synthesis of human and divine (Schleiermacher), or the paradox of the human and divine (Kierkegaard and Barth), or the mode of God the Father's givenness to the world (Hegel, Moltmann and, with qualifications, Balthasar), the dualism determined the nature of thinking and the possibility for the conclusions of such thought. The dualism was inherited from early Protestantism, with its rejection or ignorance of the theological significance of Mary, the mother of Jesus, and its attenuated doctrine of creation. But, we need not construct a Christology upon the basis of such a dualism. In fact, to do so will always make Christ the Subject *par excellence*, the Monad defining all monads, the man-without-relation, the self-grounding one. Let me suggest a difference here between Subject and Person, subjectivity and personhood. Subjectivity, though not necessarily tied to a concept of the transcendental ego, is fundamentally concerned with discrete individuals. Personhood, on the other hand, is that sense of self that continually comes from being in relation, repeated, but non-identically with every action in and upon the world. Personhood involves always more than one; involves always transgressing notions of individualism by having to live ecstatically. Being made 'in the image of God' and, therefore, living *imitatio Christi*, Christian Persons are not replicas, but embodiments of Christ as Person. Persons, as such, are analogically related to each through Christ. Subjects, on the other hand, are atomised. They are monads. And theologies of Christ as Subject conceive other Christian Subjects as monadic replicas of the

114

same. This modern construction continually proceeds by way of two forgettings: first of Mary, his mother and, more generally, erasure of the feminine (Irigaray: 1997); and second, a forgetting of the trinitarian relations that deny such Christomonism. To construct a Christology differently is to shape an understanding of both Christ-in-relation to his mother, to other women, to his disciples, to his fellow Jews, and God-in-relation, God as an unfolding activity of giftedness, a trinitarian procession. Christology then becomes that which is performed between each of us in relation to Jesus Christ – not an attempt to define the nature of a supernatural Being, an *Übermensch* (as Nietzsche inverted the figure of Christ) – and between the Godhead and creation.

Furthermore, to figure Christology in terms of a founding dualism is to assume we know what either of the polar positions mean, that each position has a determinative identity that can be cashed in. Most particularly, it assumes that we know what being human is. But what we take to be 'human', what we define as those characteristics defining human being as such, are culturally and historically variable (Haraway: 1991). Likewise, since we configure God always and only within our own categories, in terms of our creaturely realities, and since these categories and realities are also culturally and historically variable – so what we take to be 'God' is never the same in any culture or historical frame.

The emphasis, in this chapter, on the transcorporeality of Christ, is a move towards a Christology-in-relation, a Christology that recognises the performative, historical nature of terms like 'Christ', 'man' and 'God'. Of course, this implies doctrines of Providence and election, which I have not sketched here at all, only assumed. But it takes as its starting point the historicity of Christ in Jesus of Nazareth, while also recognising that there is no unmediated, nor finalised, understanding of that historicity. History is written (Certeau: 1988; Ricoeur: 1984, 1985 and 1988). No appeal can be made to primary data, historical 'facts', concerning the Christ. Facts themselves have a history (Poovey: 1998, 7–16; Shapin: 1994). Again, to refer to the work of Judith Butler, what matters most about our very embodiment is always a matter also of the way we represent and produce our bodies. The same is true of Jesus' body: it is (and it always was) socially and historically constructed. The insight into what Foucault calls 'technologies of self' (Foucault: 1981, 127) and Teresa de Lauretis develops in terms of 'technologies of gender' (Lauretis: 1987, 1–30) – which involve processes of representation as well as specific practices or performances endorsed by specific institutions – affected Jesus' gendered embodiment, as it does our own. To examine how this body is represented and produced is not to deny the existence of the body as such. It is not docetic, until the body is forgotten. Bodies are written upon; these writings have to be read and reread, and this will change the nature of what is written, rewriting the body again. Tissue *is not* text, but there is tissue only because there *is* text. This means that Christology, in dealing with various textualities, is forever prone towards the forgetting of the body; but the pain, tiredness, orgasms, aches, delights, coughs, tearings, hiccups and itchings of our bodies, our embodiment, must constantly draw Christian theologians back to the matter that matters in the gendered Jew of Nazareth. That is why this Christological exploration issues from a reading of the Scriptural accounts of the life of God incarnate.

As such, I hope, we can move towards a Christology that is both cosmological and embodied; move towards that new construal of incarnation so longed for by some contemporary feminists (Irigaray: 1991; Jantzen: 1998), and glimpsed also by those involved in men's studies (Boyd *et al.*: 1996) and queer theory (Schehr: 1997; Carrette: 2000; Butler: 1990, 134–5). To do so, I have suggested, we need to think through the complex 'flesh' of Christ, and to view embodiment analogically. Those theologians framing questions such as 'Can a male saviour save women?' or engaged in investigating the sexuality of Jesus, fail, according to this argument, to discern the nature of the body of Christ; fail to understand the nature of bodies and sex in Christ. As Gregory of Nyssa points out, in his thirteenth sermon on *Song of Songs*, 'he who sees the Church looks directly at Christ. ... The establishment of the Church is re-creation of the world. ... A new earth is formed, and it drinks up the rains that pour down upon it ... [B]ut it is only in the union of all the particular members that the beauty of [Christ's] Body is complete' (Nyssa: 1979, 13, 1049B–1052A). After the Ascension the body of Christ undergoes a major transposition at Pentecost, when the Church is born within the space opened for redemption. The next step in understanding the body of Christ is to investigate the Church, that Spouse 'wounded by a spiritual and fiery dart of desire (*eros*). For love (*agape*) that is strained to intensity is called desire (*eros*)' (Nyssa: 1979,13, 1048A).[33] To continue would be to detail and discuss the body of the Church as the erotic community.

5

COMMUNITIES OF DESIRE

In societies where modern conditions of production prevail, all life presents itself as an immense accumulation of spectacles. Everything that was directly lived has moved away into a representation. ... [R]eciprocal alienation is the essence and the support of the existing society. ... The first phase of the domination of the economy over social life brought into the definition of all human realization the degradation of *being* into *having*. The present phase of total occupation of social life by the accumulated results of the economy leads to a generalized sliding of *having* into *appearing*.

(Debord: [1967] 1977, I: 1, 8, 17)

Introduction

One of the implications of the last two chapters is that the theological or analogical account of the body safeguards bodies as such – stops them disappearing. It does this by safeguarding the significance of materiality; viewing the material as suspended within a divine economy of love. Other accounts – biological, physical and philosophical – itemise and reduce the body and materiality. Not that the theological account is purely theological. This book is not an attempt to distil a purely theologically account of things from the pabulum of creation. The theological pertains to all things in an account of creation; it draws upon all discourses to substantiate its own *corpus* and to bespeak that which has been and is being revealed – as Aquinas informs us in the opening question of his *Summa theologiae*. In the last two chapters theology is also offering an anthropology and a metaphysics – albeit a Christian anthropology and a Christian metaphysics. As will become apparent in the chapters to follow, the theological is also implicated in a social and political account of being human. The claim I wish to pursue in these next chapters is that only a theological or analogical account of bodies safeguards the concreteness of community. To be bold: God founds society as those who are called to be in this time, with this particularity, for this purpose. Those called to be constitute the *ecclesia*. What we find, as increasingly secular parodies of *ecclesial* accounts of the

117

social emerge (Cavanaugh: 1998), is not only the disappearance of community, but the establishment, in that disappearance, of virtual or imaginary communities. The telecities and communities of cyberspace – explored more fully in Chapter 9 – are only a final outworking of a secular logic. The analogical account, on the other hand, specifies a certain being in communion (Zizoulas: 1985) – an ontology constituted in and by loving, erotic exchange. As the analogical account loses its credibility (and a geneaological account of this occurrence must form the basis of further study), as the construal of participation in a divine economy declines, so communities in which the desire for the good cultivates the virtues of theological citizenship, become libidinal communities – communities in which eros is read as a purely human drive. These communities foster 'the personal aesthetic and the relationship to the body … linked to the culture of individualism and narcissism' (Castells: 1996, 452) characterising contemporary Western, North American and Japanese society (Lasch: 1980).

This chapter explores the decline of the theological understanding of the social with respect to the rise of the modern subject of desire. It does so by, first, examining a cultural metaphor expressive of contemporary desire. Then it proceeds by sketching a genealogy of both the modern subject of desire and the modern communities of desire which gave rise to the cultural metaphor itself.

Let me take you on a trip into what I suggest is one of the most revealing and significant signs of our contemporary culture, inside a metaphor of contemporary desire. For if today what we acknowledge in our living is the glorification of consumer desire, seductive signs, illusory freedoms and hidden forms of power there are few places it is more in evidence than in that phenomenon known in the UK by a euphemism (significant in itself because its name conceals its nature), the Private Shop.

Privacy, political zoning (which restricts such shops to certain sections of the city) and interiority characterise these places. There are no windows. Or what windows there are are blacked out, even boarded up. To protect whom, one asks? The public? The shopper? The pornographer's business? The customer? Secrecy and enigma have been made a part of their allure, their design, their architecture – to risk entry is sexual in itself.

We enter. The light inside is artificial and intense. There are no shadows, no shades to harbour guilt, no pools of darkness for doubt or shame. There is a confidence, a brashness, but it as real and as thin as all other forms of staging. There are two security cameras and an office-cum-observatory, one suspects, behind a mirrored wall. Zygmunt Bauman writes:

> [today] the weapon of legitimacy has been replaced with two mutually complementary weapons: this of seduction and that of repression. … Repression employs surveillance. … Surveillance is indispensable to reach the areas seduction cannot and is not meant to reach: it remains

the paramount tool of subordination of the considerable margin of society which cannot be absorbed by the market dependency and hence,
in market terms, consists of non-consumers.

(Bauman: 1992, 97–8)

In the sex shop the distinction between seduction and repression is not so easy to
maintain. There is a sexual excitement about being watched. The voyeur is being
voyeured – the customer as consumer is also made to be a performer.

The room is a functional oblong; with nothing extraneous. The material is
displayed in serried ranks: desire is streamlined. The multiplicity of spectacle
offered is organised and catalogued according to three basic tastes. Anything to
do with animals and children, even in these places at the margins of civic life, is
understood to be outside. The Private Shop exists, then, in a certain penumbra
on the edges of the permissible and just within the bounds of legitimate daring.
But it borders also on the darker and more illicit. This too is part of their sexual
allure: one never knows just how far the material will go. Hence, as they keep
watch on their potential customers, others keep watch on them. There is always
the possibility of a raid, nevertheless in this way they are woven more securely
into the wider social fabric.

In the cataloguing of sexual taste, heterosexuality is dominant. It is a heterosexuality catering for and created by the male gaze. The male erotic gaze
structures the layout, and presides over the content, of these shops where women
are placed first – vulvas spread, inviting, sensual poses. Women in silks, in
feathers, in leather, in chains, shaven, large breasted, emaciated, plump. Women
with men, women with women, women with vibrators. This is a large section
accounting for probably more than half the material on offer. Then, once again,
one suspects, the male gaze structures the second section: the men – erect,
detumescent, circumcised, uncircumcised, anuses proffered, nipples tweaked.
Men in leather, in torn denims, in uniform, with other men in groups, indulging
themselves alone. Men with muscles toned, oiled and tanned, implicated in a
distillation of virility.[1] A medium sized section this, probably accounting for a
third of the material for sale. Finally, in the third section come the transvestites,
the bisexuals and the hermaphrodites with a panoply of wigs and costumes and
pantomime roles. There are bras stretched across hirsute chests, penises
protruding from lace pants and rising above suspender-belts. Make-up is much in
evidence, a theatricality, a self-conscious irony, a playing at gender games (see
Butler: 1993, 121–40, 223–42). This material presents the ludic and the outer
edges of what it is possible to obtain. We are bordering here on the chaotic, the
Dionysian, the realm of desire where anything goes. The ludic could at any
moment turn sadistic or masochistic – a violent, sexual energy simmers. This is
only a small section, next to the love-aids advertising the ultimate and most
prolonged experience, the most sustained and raunchy performance. Here are
the creams, the dildos, the inflatables, the thongs, the handcuffs, the straps and
the rings. Here is a complete technology of orgasm – the final orientation and

119

disciplining of one's identity towards the sexual, towards pleasuring the 'privates'.

In these magazines, videos and CD ROMs the world presented is exotic, glamorous, suggestive of luxuries untold and limitless credit. The bodies viewed from the perspectives of this material, with magnification and the freeze-framing of the orgasmic moment, are not available to human perception other than through technological means. The world presented is fabricated, engineered. Although there has always been pornography, this kind of pornographic world can only come into existence through advancements in reprographics, photography and telecommunications.[2]

'[I]n our time individuals are engaged ... first and foremost as consumers rather than producers ... [there is] the substitution of consumer freedom for work ... Reality ... is the pursuit of pleasure. Freedom is about the choice between greater and lesser satisfactions, and rationality is about choosing the first over the second' (Bauman: 1992, 49). As such the Sex Shop is a more explicit and less metaphorical example of the libido-driven nature of our culture. For the Sex Shop produces the *illusion* of immediate satisfaction. None of these people are really available to satisfy us. The material offered are simulations of relationality, simulations of sexuality, simulations of gratification. All is virtual. The material provokes desire, but it can neither maintain nor fulfil what it appears to promise. All is simulacra. Even if we model our experience around this material, allowing it to shape our desires and their satisfaction, sexual experience cannot be like the experiences suggested here. The Sex Shop produces nothing. It exists for the endless provocation of the desire to consume. Orgasm, in such terms, is customer satisfaction. The racing pulses and the rapid heartbeat of turning some of those pages, of watching that slow stripping away of clothing, is the equivalent of the shoppers' experience on the first days of the winter sales, the experience of the bargain hunter tracking down the almost-free gift. As such, the psychological design and mapping out of goods in hypermarkets, supermarkets and departmental stores are only variants on the culture of seduction most explicitly manifest in the Private Shop. As David Runciman puts it: 'Supermarkets are in the business of seduction and, as all seducers know, this begins with the right lighting. The average person blinks 32 times a minute; in a well-lit, well laid-out shop this can be reduced to 14 times a minute. Combined with gentle background noise and a uniform (cooked up) aroma, this has a mildly sedative effect. Zombie shoppers and splurge shoppers' (Runciman: 1996). In a similar way, some of the more recent advertising campaigns for the sale of perfumes, after-shaves, and even ice-cream, along with the renewed interest in the prurient biography, are further variants on the more obvious nakedness and invitation that constitutes the pornographic. What the Private Shop articulates – as customers are shut off from the larger market outside, sealed within mirrored walls, suspending within the fluorescent lighting – is a conviction that sexuality is the most profound and inner sanctum of human experience. What we are at base, these shops announce, is subjects of desire.

The subject of desire

I have argued in the previous chapters that Christian anthropology produces a person governed and disciplined by the twofold desire of/for God. What we need to explore here is how this modern subject of desire has come about and what its characteristics are such that they relate to, and yet also differ from, that Christian anthropology sketched earlier (and to be developed further). This is important because, in reading the signs of the times, I want to argue for the timeliness of pursuing the pneumatology of persons in Christ. The modern subject of desire has to be both challenged (by being shown the destructive nihilism and narcissism in which it is implicated) and enlarged (by being shown that the erotic economy need not be reduced to simply a libidinal economy). I propose to challenge and enlarge the modern subject of desire by producing two genealogies. The first is of the subject of desire itself, and the second is of the communities of desire in which this subject participates. The point of these genealogies is to allow us to recognise: (1) the metaphysical and socio-political corollaries of the modern subject of desire; (2) some of the cultural forces which governed its production; and (3) the alternative understandings of desire and its role in community-formation which can then be offered as other cultural forces with the potential to transform future persons-in-relation.

Sketching a genealogy of the modern subject of desire has been made easier by several contemporary critical theorists and the development of cultural studies. Many of the accounts available, whether from postcolonialists like Spivak, queer theorists like Butler or genealogists as different as Foucault, Certeau and Laqueur, provide detailed analyses of power, domination and legitimacy. And these analyses frequently focus on the nature and manifestations of desire and their encoding on the subject's body. Judith Butler explicitly founds her thinking upon a construal of subjectivity based within economies of desire. From *Subjects of Desire* (1987) to *The Psychic Life of Power* (1997) her work has undertaken an examination of the history, formation and subordination[3] of the subject. Her first book detailed the history of the subject of desire as it arose in Hegel and comes to dominate late-twentieth-century thinkers such as Lacan and Deleuze (Butler: 1987). The 'of' in the title is both objective and subjective – desire both structures subjects (externally) and pertains to the nature of subjectivity (internally); but where the line between the objective and the subjective lies is distinctly ambiguous. It is upon the basis of this historical account that Butler constructs her more famous work in gender theory and what she terms 'queer trouble' (Butler: 1990 and 1993, 226–30).

Other cultural historians, whose work concentrates upon the social construction of embodied persons – particularly those involved in feminist and masculine studies and historians of sexuality and medical science – have emphasised how the nineteenth century saw the rise of the homosexual and, subsequently, the heterosexual person; and how psychoanalytical attention to personality generated new discourses on sexual orientation and the morphology of sexual identity. It would appear that the medical interest in determining the nature of sexual difference (Laqueur: 1990) and the attention to perversions of the sexual 'norm', homosexuals, are central to the production of the modern (and normative) subject of desire. One notes the absence of any study of the feminine; this modern construal of subjectivity was shaped by patriarchal cultural forces. Foucault famously declared the 'homosexual' as a species first appeared in 1870 (Foucault: 1981), but the work of the historians Alan Bray (1982), David M. Halperin (1990), Bruce Smith (1991) and David Greenberg (1988) have made more subtle suggestions about the historical shift towards certain genital acts as characterising a whole lifestyle and identity. For Bray, the rise of the late-seventeenth-century/early-eighteenth-century 'moll' houses were the first indication that homosexuality was a distinct sexual practice involving a distinctive type of man (Bray: 1982). Certainly the work of Richard von Krafft-Ebing – *Manual of Forensic Psychology* (1879) and *Psychopathia Sexualis* (1886) – Patrick Geddes and J. Arthur Thompson – *The Evolution of Sex* (1889) – Havelock Ellis – *Sexual Inversion* (1897) and *Studies in the Psychology of Sex* (1899–1910) – Otto Weininger – *Sex and Character* (1903) – and Magnus Hirschfeld – *Berlins drittes Geschlecht* (1904) – all helped to establish a science of sexology to which Freud was much indebted. It was a science, on the whole, which was concerned with the 'pathological', the 'perverted' and the 'abnormal', and it was not until the publication, in 1910, of F.H.A Marshall's *The Physiology of Reproduction* that sexology took a decidedly medical and more universal approach (Porter and Hall: 1995, 155–201). Nevertheless, Freud's own famous *Three Essays on the Theory of Sexuality* appeared in 1905, and the opening footnote of the first essay – devoted to sexual aberrations – announces that 'the work is derived from' the analyses of sexuality made by his predecessors (Freud: 1961, 45). And after that first essay, his following essays – 'Infantile Sexuality' and 'The Transformations of Puberty' – sketch the outline for a general theory of sexuality 'adequate to the understanding alike of normal and pathological conditions' (Freud: 1961, 169).

Freud

It is undoubtedly with Freud that Hegel's dialectical and pneumatological subjectivity, which owes so much to patristic Christian anthropology (Chapelle: 1963–71; Shklar: 1976; Brito: 1979; Solomon: 1983; Dickey: 1988; O'Regan: 1994; Ward: 1999) is given its influential shape as a libidinal subject. Although the word 'sexual' as indicating a distinct human drive, goes back to early-nineteenth-century romanticism, it is with Freud that sexuality becomes foundational for human experience and personal development. With Freud's early analyses in those three essays on the libido, all subjectivity is related to sexual desire. But more than this, as Foucault observed, sex became associated with truth. Knowledge of our sexual desires became deemed the deepest knowledge we can have of ourselves; a knowledge of which we can be ignorant (and others enlightened). '[W]e demand that it tell us our truth, or rather, the deeply buried truth of that truth about ourselves which we think we possess in our immediate consciousness' (Foucault: 1981, 69). Further, for Freud, despite his analyses of narcissism, these desires were not simply self-contained. His subjects – divided within themselves between conscious and unconscious, id, ego and superego – were not autonomous individuals. They were intimately locked into an intersubjective theatre, fundamentally the histrionics of the family: the roles played or not played by the father, the mother, and siblings of the opposite sex in the Oedipal drama, for example.[4] Each divided ego was caught up in a complex weave of libidinal relations – an erotic community. Hence, as his thinking developed, Freud could move from the morphology of the individual to a collective and ultimately social psychology, publishing in 1913 *Totem and Taboo*, in 1921 *Group Psychology and the Analysis of the Ego* and in 1930 *Civilization and Its Discontents*. Desire remains constantly to the fore. In fact, the force and drama of sexual desire is Freud's final explanatory principle for the foundation and functioning of communities. Avoiding incestuous relations, in prehistoric communities (the descriptions of which rely on accounts of 'the most backward and miserable savages, the aborigines of Australia' (Freud: 1961, 2)), becomes the organising principle of their societies. *Totem and Taboo* proposed an aetiological narrative in which brothers within a single family, loving both their mother and sisters, form a mob, and commit the parricide (and consumption of the primal father) upon which the first community is founded (Freud: 1961, 119–61).[5]

In a move which rehearses Hegel's analysis of the family unit as the basic building block for the civic community (Hegel: 1977, 267–78),[6] Freud traces the beginnings of the 'social instinct' to the erotic dynamics of patriarchal family life. And, having defined the libido as 'the energy … of those instincts which have to do with all that may be comprised under the word "love"', and made explicit that the nucleus of what we mean by love is sexual, he makes the suggestion that 'love relationships … also constitute the essence of the group mind' (Freud: 1955, 90–1). Eros becomes a totalising power – at once, biological, psychological and sociological – which holds together the discrete elements of the community; eros as concomitant with what Monique Wittig termed 'the straight mind' (Wittig: 1992). In fact, having distinguished between natural and artificial groups, Freud analyses the Church (and the army) as communities in which the sexual impulsions of individuals are redirected. This redirection of libido from 'genital organisation' produces a series of identifications, introjections and substitutions, so that feelings of affection are linked to objects with which the individual can empathise and objects which stand in for an individual's ego-ideal. Interestingly, Freud locates the peculiarity of Christianity and 'its claim to have reached a higher ethical level' (Freud: [1921] (1955), 134–5) within a specific 'distribution of libido' in which there is identification not only with others in the group but with the object of the ego-ideal, such that one longs to identify with Christ and not just other Christians. Though Freud does not develop this, what his analysis of the libidinal organisation suggests is that, in Christian communities, love for one's neighbour as oneself is, simultaneously, becoming Christ-like. Here there is a certain healing of the psychic fragmentation that splits ego from object and ego-ideal. There is a certain *ekstasis* of self also. I will return to these ideas later, though I prepare the ground now for the development of this psychological redemption, theologically, in the chapters which follow. For the moment it is important to emphasise that, for Freud, what constitutes communities as erotic communities is that 'whenever we come across an affectionate feeling it is the successor to a completely "sensual" object-tie with the person in question or rather with that person's prototype (or *imago*)' (Freud: [1921] (1955), 138).

For Freud, then, subjects of desire dwell within an extensive web of relationalities – they determine and are determined by an ongoing libidinal reciprocity. '[C]ollections of men are to be libidinally bound to each other' (Freud: 1961, 122). And since the father has firmly set in place the taboo against incest, then these relationalities are not simply focused on the family, but move out exogamously, replaying the Oedipus complex, in a thousand different directions This ocean of erotic energies, at first chaotic because without aim or object, provides a conflictual dynamism in which commodities of desire are produced. Others become desirable; they become objects of affection and attraction. In the production and exchange of these objects one comes to recognise oneself as attractive, as the object of another's interest (loving or aggressive). The subject is itself commodified; it receives notice of its 'pulling' power. Such desire, which transcends because it is excessive to the individual and even the family within which the individual is situated, establishes communities, erotic communities – though where the boundaries of such communities lie and what constitutes such boundaries has yet to be defined. For Freud, who later came to extend his analysis of libido to the point where he argued that 'civilization obeys an internal erotic impulse which causes human beings to unite in closely-knit groups' (Freud: 1961, 133), all boundaries are artificial ones, created by the objects upon which ego-ideals can be projected. The oceanic and agonistic libido extends infinitely across the human plane.

There are three characteristics of this libidinal economy which structure a quite specific form of the erotic community. It is a form of erotic community which Christianity cannot endorse; and therefore challenges. First, it is patriarchal – founded upon and fostered by the figure of the father. As Juliette Mitchell has pointed out, in an illuminating exploration of Freud and Lévi-Strauss' work on kinship, the law against incest situates women within a structure of patriarchal exchange. Culture is founded upon the exchange of women subsequent to the law against incest (Mitchell: 1975). This patriarchalism is reinforced by the masculinity of desire itself: the Oedipus complex is a drama of male protagonists; the morphology of a woman's sexual identity is a negative form of the masculine plot line: it emerges out of lack and envy of the penis (Irigaray: 1985, 13–129). Secondly, this erotic community is heterosexual in its form, but homosocial in its content. By homosocial, I mean an ideology created by men about men with reference to the social activities of men; women are not figured in a homosocial account at all. Homosocial is not identical to homosexual. Though, with a pun, Irigaray will launch a critique against homosociality as a hom(m)osexuate culture. For Freud, homosexuality is deemed a species of primary narcissism – an immature fixation upon the mother. The direction of mature desire is male–female. Though, socially, the process of identification which binds father to son and is intrinsic to the morphological structure of 'becoming a man' results in a transgenerational male-bonding which reinforces the patriarchal production of culture. Thirdly, Freud's emphasis that, as Mitchell puts it, 'ontogeny repeated phylogeny' (Mitchell: 1975, 366), roots his psycho-analytical account in the biological sciences; a biological determinism generates the structures of all possible cultures. '[C]ivilization is a process in the service of Eros' (Freud: 1961, 122). Freud later qualifies this conclusion only by adding a congenital aggression, the death instinct, which struggled against the attempt to weave the world into one libidinal web. As we saw in the last two chapters, a Christian understanding of the body does not reduce it to Descartes' biological machine. And as we will see in Chapter 7, the family as the prime socio-biological unit is not a Christian teaching.

The contemporary culture of seduction, which constitutes various communities of desire, plays out these libidinal logics articulated by Freud. Even attempts to found alternative non-patriarchal, non-heterosexist communities (the gay family, the lesbian couple) are reinscribed into the dominant ideology as 'reactions' to it. For my argument it is important to recognise how this form of desire (libidinal) and the kind of communities it fosters has a genealogy and how the theological figures and is eventually erased within such a genealogy. As I said, Freud is indebted to Hegel, whose own subject of desire is Christological. But I would wish to argue that the communities of desire, dreamt and engineered by modernity, are parodies of the Christian *ecclesia*.

That these communities have been constructed out of Christian discourses on love, election, God's covenant with creation and the Spirit, has to be supplemented by *how* this has occurred. Christianity's own discourses on love, desire and the Spirit are, themselves, indebted to Platonic analyses of eros. But we need to understand how love, both divine and human, *eros* and its soteriological import, are transformed into a physiological and psychological science. So that, by the late nineteenth century, words like 'erotics', 'eroticism', 'erotically', 'erogenic' and 'erotica' are being coined and gaining currency. And this linguistic trend is developed in the twentieth century when we first get the words 'eroticize', 'erotology', 'erotomania' and 'erogenous' being used extensively. Similarly, the old use of 'sex' to describe womanhood or manhood in the sixteenth century, gives way to 'sex' as another word for sexual intercourse and 'sex' as a synonym for genitalia in the 1930s.

The outline of these modern libidinal and social economies is evident in earlier construals of the relationship between the social and the desiring individual in the sixteenth and seventeenth centuries (Macpherson: 1964; Macfarlane: 1978). It is significant that, in this period, we see the beginnings of the pornography industry (Hunt: 1993).[7] Before this period, the individual is not isolated from the social whole, isolated in a manner akin to the way an element in chemistry or a particle in physics is isolated in the development of the natural sciences. Individualism and atomism (where atomism includes both Newton's universe composed of particles of matter and society as composed of autarchic individuals) are inseparable (Freudenthal: 1986, 173–88). Before the early modern period the individual body was caught up in that network of analogical relations (relations which were cosmic, theological, economic and sociological) which we examined in Chapters 3 and 4. But, as Michel de Certeau observes, with respect to the break up of the analogically related cosmos: 'two complementary restoration projects have recourse to the same "ecclesial" heritage of a unifying whole, although they express it in henceforth specialised modes: for one, the reason of state, for the other, the "community of the saints" ' (Certeau: 1986, 87; see also Marin: 1989 and Kantorowicz: 1957). The dualism, implicit here, between state and ecclesia, comes later – though the ground is prepared with the emergence of another dualism, the public and the private spheres of action.

In the work of Thomas Hobbes and Benedict Spinoza it is still possible to see the erotic community as a civic yet also, by extension, religious community. Both offer accounts of commonwealths, albeit of contrasting kinds, in which the theological is still pronounced. The contrast between their societies, as we will see, issues from two different parsings of a similar secular logic. The road to the disappearance of God's covenant with creation as foundational for any commonwealth is paved by both of them. And the implications of their thinking will lead eventually to the state as a transvestite reading of its ' "ecclesial" heritage' and the emergence of imaginary (even virtual) commonwealths masking social atomism and acting as entertainments. We need to trace this history to understand: (1) where we have come from; (2) why the theological could so easily be erased as the secular state increased its own dominion; and (3) how the trajectory of this secular thinking on commonwealths which developed the libidinal subject leads us straight to the gates of the cities of endless desire.

The mechanistic and the organic commonwealths of desire

Both Thomas Hobbes and Benedict Spinoza begin from the premise that human beings are driven by desire. The positive construal of *libido dominandi* (Augustine's construal was negative) was Machiavelli's and Descartes' before it was their's (Descartes: 1984, 147). This is related to new understandings of the sexual subject emerging in the Renaissance and seventeenth century. For both, the individual's body extends to the civic body, and (with Hobbes) the national body and (with Spinoza) God's own body. Both present materialistic monisms. And, for both, what characterises desire is self-interest; a reactive response of assertion to the possibility of threat. This is the logic they share, though each present a different version of the commonwealth of desire which follows from it.

Hobbes

For Hobbes, arguing against the Cartesian first principle of the cogito and the dualism of mind/body which is concomitant with it, the I, and all its machinations, is an operation of matter. As such human beings are not blessed with the free will which becomes so important in the later writings of Descartes; human beings act because of the action of a contiguous body upon their own. 'Life itselfe is but Motion, and can never be without Desire, nor without Feare, no more than without Sense' (Hobbes: 1968, 130). All bodies exercise a motion natural to them; human bodies are driven by the natural law of self-protection. Hobbes' materialist monism conceives the natural condition as the play of forces which can be active or retroactive, causal or affective, attractive or repellent. These can work for peace (pleasure, delight, the good), but they can also work for war. There is no natural condition of either goodness or justice (or their opposites); life is contingent and the contingency unbounded and, therefore, arbitrary. Famously, Hobbes concludes, 'the condition of Man ... is a condition of Warre of every one against every one; in which case every one is governed by his own Reason; and there is nothing he can make use of, that may not be a help unto him, in preserving his life against his enemyes; It followeth, that in such a condition, every man has a Right to everything; even to one anothers body' (Hobbes: 1968, 189–90). What Hobbes calls 'mere nature' is, then, a state of 'anarchy' (343). In this state human reason seeks out the best means of satisfying its endless passions.

In his chapter on the passions in *Leviathan* (1.VI), Hobbes points out that desire is a general name (119). It includes within its ambit, appetite and love. But 'by Desire, we always signifie the Absence of the Object; by Love most commonly the Presence of the Same' (119). The economy of desire is privative. That which desire desires is felicity. The object of desire is therefore pleasurable, delightful and good. Many things can be the objects of desire and it is the object, for Hobbes, which determines the character of that desire. It is 'natural lust' when it is 'Love of Persons for Pleasing the sense onely', but desire to know why and how is an instinctive curiosity (123–4). Will, itself, is bound up with desire, so that all action can be said to be determined by either a desire for or an aversion against (aversion being a reactive form of desiring). Desire in and of itself is related to the more fundamental motion; it is a specific orientation of motion, and motion is simply what nature is. All that is is composed of corpuscles constantly moving. Hobbes, while not embracing Aristotle's cosmology, recognised his congruence with Aristotle on this matter (Hobbes: 'Dialogus Physicus', in Shapin and Schaffer: 1989). He remained unclear about where this motion came from and critics, like Robert Boyle, were quick to point out how, given Hobbes' materialism, dangerous theological consequences followed. For if nature was self-moving then it was taking on an attribute which was understood to be God's alone – nature was God. Or if God caused this movement then God too was material.[8] Desire, as a form of this motion, within animals and humans, had neither beginning nor end; it was complicit with the immanent forces of life

127

itself. It is in this sense that all are subjects of desire. Because, for Hobbes, the aggregate of all things constitutes one body such that the universe is composed of imbricated bodies, this desire is understood to operate in, through and across the atomism which is the natural state of things, binding all things into a endless relay of forces.

Within his own lifetime Hobbes was labelled an atheist; and some, like Bishop John Bramall, saw atheism as the logical consequence of Hobbes' position. But recently, A.P. Martinich has argued for a theological reading of Hobbes' plenism: 'Hobbes's determinism, which is often thought to indicate, or even entail, atheism, is not merely a part of his mechanistic materialism; it is logically tied to Calvin's doctrines of predestination and belief in the omnipotence of God' (Martinich: 1992, 3). Attention has been drawn to the theological ethics which Hobbes implies in his work. Having described the state of 'mere nature', Hobbes recognises that it is 'necessary to know what are the laws divine' (Hobbes: 1968, 343). The fear of the invisible drives people into forging covenants, so that Martinich can argue for a secondary nature in which God's laws operate through the obligations imposed by the state of nature (Martinich: 1992, 79). It is therefore possible to read Hobbes as viewing each person's desire for self-preservation as the basis for the common good. The human being as an autonomous monadic force is like God Himself, 'the first power of all powers' (Hobbes: 1888, 54). In this passion and human right, then, Hobbes presents a version of the *imago dei*. As such, a certain doctrine of analogy, based in God as the cause of all things, binds Hobbes' natural philosophy to a theological framework. It is an analogy of being as an analogy of power. Hobbes states that the best name for God is 'being' (Hobbes: 1976, 434). The power each body exerts participates in, because it is an expression of, the power God exerts. Human power is allied with passion, 'for passion, is power limited by somewhat else' (Hobbes: 1968, 352). God is without passion but we ascribe to Him a will 'as the power, by which he effecteth' (Hobbes: 1968, 352). The ordering of the world by chains of causes and effects, gives rise to a Hobbesian form of the design argument, whereby through the 'visible things of this world' we 'may conceive there is a cause of them which men call God' (Hobbes: 1968, 93, 95). Correspondingly, the Sovereign is God's representative on earth, to whom all people transfer their right to self-preservation that the Sovereign might govern.[9] The Sovereign, like God, stands outside the covenants by which the people transfer their right to self-interest. So the Sovereign, like God, acts mercifully and not out of any covenanted obligation himself. The Sovereign, like God as Trinity, represents, as one, a multitude (Hobbes: 1968, 486–9). Furthermore, in transferring their right to self-preservation, human beings are sources of grace (Hobbes: 1968, 121). It is divinely ordained, therefore, that human beings are self-preserving, just as it is divinely ordained that the people should dwell within confederacies governed by one Sovereign power who is an icon for God's absolute power. As Martinich puts it: 'the laws of nature are properly laws because they are derivable by reason as the laws of God' (Martinich: 1992, 127).

Furthermore, these natural laws operate within a universe governed by God as the absolute authority, so that Hobbes appends to his account of 'the natural kingdom of God, and his natural laws ... a short declaration of his natural punishments' (Hobbes: 1968, 356). The Sovereign's power is, then, underwritten by God's power, operating through creation, punishing those who break the covenant. Keeping the promise of the covenant is Hobbes' definition of faith; failing to keep the promise is the 'violation of faith' (Hobbes: 1968, 121). Punishment results from such a violation; for God's power can never be resisted. Here lies Hobbes' determinism as a variant of Calvin's doctrine of predestination.[10] God Himself remains the invisible, infinite and eternal power, never to be approached or understood, the perpetual fear of whom gives rise to the distinctively human capacity for religion (Hobbes: 1968, 94–5).

It is important to understand what Hobbes is doing here. The community or commonwealth which emerges is, as he himself states, an 'artificial man' (Hobbes: 1968, 81). Human beings have made Leviathan. Nevertheless, this is not what Benedict Anderson, discussing nations and nationalism, will call an 'imagined community': 'an imagined political community ... *imagined* because the members of even the smallest nation will never know most of their fellow-members, meet them, or even hear them, yet in the minds of each lives the image of their communion' (Anderson: 1983, 6). It is a contractual society, but it is also a covenantal society: God stands guarantor for the social order administered through the Sovereign. Subjects of desire are regulated by the community they are obliged to establish. As such desire itself is not productive, only the restraint of desire by enforced obedience. Desire does not function as that which weaves webs of relation between people. Rather it functions to maintain a strict divide between private pleasures and public conformity. Desire does not foster participation, sharing, co-operations, and so the resulting community is socially atomised. People are both isolated in their natural, embodied desires and obligated to an artificial external *corpus*. Despite, then, overcoming the Cartesian dualism of mind and body (for mind is body, for Hobbes), other dualisms, not unrelated to Descartes', between private and public, internal and external, natural and artificial are installed. And, like Descartes' dualism of mind and body, the installation prioritises one over the other. For the public, the external and the artificial is the superior value. Romanticism will go a long way to overturn this evaluation. But, for Hobbes, this set of dualisms is the basis for the psychology and politics governing his commonwealth. They are instituted and legitimated by an incomprehensible, eternal, and infinitely remote God whose power is irresistible. As Martinich rightly points out, once Leviathan has been created then 'God can be relegated to the background' (Martinich: 1992, 98).

The remoteness of God actually creates a space for the autonomous rule of the secular; this rule being characterised by endless and immanent agonistic forces. What prevents the autonomy of such a space, for Hobbes, is the analogical framework. Since the central concern of this book lies with the establishment of an analogical world-view, we need to understand the nature of this analogy and its theological implications. For Hobbes, the analogical issues from the way the divine law operates within the natural law; though not, like Aquinas, operating also within the civil or human law (which, for Hobbes, is artificial).[11] As such Hobbes introduces a univocity of being stretching out from the material bodies of the created order to the eternal and omnipotent, but nevertheless material, body of God. This is not strictly analogical, since a univocity of being reduces all things to the same immanent sphere (being), and so leaves no room for transcendence (and the differences vouchsafed and registered by transcendence). Nevertheless, this aside, opposing the logic of this immanent univocity of being is Hobbes' own insistence that the civil law is *constructed* with the aid of theological concepts: redefinitions of faith, grace and covenant, in particular. Directly contrary, then, to univocal participation of the divine law within the natural, is a specific nominalism. It is a nominalism which asserts an equivocity. This nominalism is evident where the theological language becomes detached from that which it names and is utilised in the construction of the artificial, in an act of persuasion which is self-consciously political. Ockhamist nominalism stressed, like Hobbes, the utter transcendence and, therefore, inscrutability of God. It deontologised language for the real, and the naming and knowledge of the real became distinct (Certeau: 1992, 123, 125–6). As Hobbes puts it: 'All names are imposed to signifie our conceptions' (Hobbes: 1968, 28). Words, like Sovereigns, are imposed and representative. The power of language to master 'not only objects but persons' (Silver: 1996, 332) is a significant theme in Hobbes, relating the exercise of power to knowledge (Skinner: 1996). But this means that illusion, deception and confusion among various struggling language-users is inevitable. Only the omnipotent God can guarantee truth; but He cannot be known other than by His effects; while His effects have to be judged *as* effects by means of our inconstant naming.

What we have here are two conflicting world-views: the natural (according to an 'analogy' of being) and the constructed (according to equivocity of nominalism). What is precisely absent is the analogical world-view that mediates between the immanentalism and the radical sense of the transcendent God. As John Montag has recently put it with respect to the Spanish Jesuit, and founder of modern metaphysics, Suarez: 'The divorce between words and things, coupled with the conflation of God and things, introduces a fundamental irrationality into what had been an ordered and intelligible realm of relations, an abyss between intelligibility and human intelligence' (Montag: 1998, 51). The work of Suarez was known to Hobbes and may well have considerably influenced him (Martinich: 1992, 134, 141, 379–80; Springborg: 1995, 503–31).[12] Montag demonstrates that Suarez held to the concept of direct propositional revelation from God confirming, *ad extra*, what is held by faith to be true. Hobbes, only too aware of the civil strife issuing from those with direct revelations of God, does not proceed down this route. Revelation is always mediated – through the Bible (subject to interpretation) and through the Sovereign who pronounces on these matters as head of the Church. The artificial man, created by men, speaks for both God and men. As such, salvation becomes a secular matter, effected through obedience to a material, but socially and linguistically constructed authority. The content of such salvation is public peace for private pleasures (among which are religious consolations). The commonwealth, as the Kingdom of God, is to be realised here. It is animated by desire and passion construed in terms of power relations rather than sexual relations. In fact, the sexual relations are not foregrounded though, as Moira Gatens points out, with Hobbes 'the modern body politic is based on an image of a *masculine* body which reflects fantasies about the value and capacities of that body' (Gatens: 1996, 25). It is not only the body politic, it is also the body ecclesial. The sexual relations are masked by a dominant and artificial homosociality which does not bind but atomises the subjects of desire.

The seventeenth and eighteenth centuries saw the rise of a number of artificial communities – societies, sometimes secret, always with restricted entry, which became parodies of the *ecclesia* or working models of the Kingdom of God. In Hobbes' time there was the Commonwealth Club (established in 1659) and Harrington's Rota Club. Above all, there was the founding of the Royal Society as an experimental community. 'The experimenters ... presented their own community as an *ideal society* where dispute could occur safely and where subversive errors were quickly corrected.'[13] The Rosicrucians and the Freemasons were to follow. Karl Barth traced the growth of *societas* to the Jesuit *Societas Jesu*, remarking that before this time 'there was in fact no such thing as a *societas*' (Barth: 1972, 62). He further noted the arbitrary nature of these communities: 'The meaning of *societas*, as distinct from an *ordo*, is *Gesellschaft*, that is to say it is an association of companions who meet by their own free choice, independently of the old institutions ... united by some common feeling, and for the achievement of some common aim' (Barth: 1972, 63). Communities are self-defining and self-serving. Hobbes' commonwealth still legitimates this through appeal to God, but Barth is aware that the Freemasons (and others) become 'the real and true Church, the veritable Church of Humanity' (Barth: 1972, 64). God is not absolutely necessary for the founding and maintenance of such communities.

Spinoza

It is known that Spinoza read Hobbes' 1642 volume, *De Cive*, though with respect to other texts it is more difficult to say.[14] The influence of Hobbes on Spinoza is a vexed question which I will not broach here. More important, for this study, are the similarities and differences concerning the role of an omnipotent God and the natural order in the construction of a commonwealth composed of subjects of desire. Two propositions from Spinoza's *Ethics* will guide my analysis of these similarities and differences. What will become evident is that with Spinoza we arrive at an alternative account of the relationship between God, the individual and the community, between the divine, the human and the civic bodies; an account which, in contrast to Hobbes' mechanism, can be termed organicist.

Proposition 3 of Book Two (Of the Mind) reads: 'In God there is necessarily an idea, both of his essence and of everything which necessarily follows from his essence' (Spinoza: 1996). An appended scholium remarks that often a comparison is made between 'God's power with the power of Kings', but that 'no one will be able to perceive rightly the things I maintained unless he takes great care not to confuse God's power with the human power or right of kings' (Spinoza: 1996). Proposition 57 of Book Three (Of the Affects) reads: '[D]esire (*cupiditas*) is the very nature, *or* essence of each [individual]. Therefore, desire (*cupiditas*) of each individual differs from the desire of another as much as the nature, *or* essence, of the one differs from the essence of the other' (Spinoza: 1996).

By 'individual' Spinoza does not mean the human subject. The world is composed of various individual bodies or singularities – from rocks and trees to animals, insects and humans. All these bodies are modes of God's body; their actions therefore are God's own actions. For God is Nature, and God as Nature is one undivided substance. Subjects of desire exist in/as the desiring divine. Since God can be understood according to two fundamental attributes – through (mind) and extension (body) – attributes which are not distinct and dualistically opposed, but inseparable, so too can other bodies. Desire, then, is not only a corporeal effect (appetite), for Spinoza, it is, at the same time, an intellectual effect (conscious of itself).

Accepting their differences with respect to the meaning of 'individual', Spinoza, like Hobbes, views the essence of each thing to be a particular form of desiring or striving. Each strives to preserve its own existence (Spinoza: 1996, Propositions 6,7 and 8 of Book Three). All things are tossed about on an open sea, driven by contrary winds (Spinoza: 1996, Scholium for Proposition 59 of Book Three). For both, then, social atomism is a natural law issuing from a cosmic atomism. The difference lies in the way, for Spinoza, the infinite variety of desiring individuals – each with their own strivings and understandings *vis-à-vis* the rest – is incorporated within the necessary self-expression of God. Desire has a telos, which is to arrive at the knowledge of the relation pertaining between God as substance and all other things as modes of God's attributes. For Spinoza, this is a second level of knowing. The first level of knowing is human opinion based upon the passions and the effects of desiring. There are always differences at such a level; but these differences are the product of a mistaken belief in the independence of the human will (Spinoza: 1996, Scholium for Proposition 3 of Book Three). Spinoza's third knowledge, his intellectual love of God, is an identification of the human with the divine, and absorption into the one.

The relation between the divine, the human and the civic is not then, as with Hobbes, caught between naturalism, on the one hand, and nominalist constructivism, on the other. Though Spinoza will concur with Hobbes that God too is material, this God does not exist at some infinite and inscrutable Calvinist distance from creation: God is immanent to creation itself. Furthermore, viewed *sub species aeternatis*, which is the only mode of true knowledge, all things are extensions of each other. So that human beings, who alone have power to reason, constitute a community of embodied rationalities.

An ontological agreement holds all human beings together. Their passions will separate them and cause conflict between them, but by the use of reason they will come to understand the way in which they coinhere in the one divine substance. They will come to understand also how each is caught up in a casual nexus far greater in complexity than the local strivings which issue from the mistaken belief in one's rights and freedom of will. Thus Spinoza can affirm, like Hobbes, that 'a man acts entirely from the laws of his own nature when he lives according to the guidance of reason' (Spinoza: 1996, first Corollary to Proposition 35 of Book Four) and yet, unlike Hobbes, can add that 'When each man seeks his own advantage for himself, then men are most useful to one another' (Spinoza: 1996, second Corollary to Proposition 35 of Book Four). What is most useful is what is good, for Spinoza, and what is good constitutes agreement and a recognition of interdependence. What is good is held in common. What is good is what is loved, desired and brings each one joy, and what is good is the possession and exercising of power (which, for Spinoza, is virtue) to preserve one's being (a power which is 'part of God or Nature's infinite power' (Spinoza: 1996, first Demonstration for Proposition 4 of Book Four)). Spinoza can then be said to be describing a commonwealth constituted by eros as logos and bios; a desire to love as the most reasonable and natural form of action.[15] This is where he differs radically from Hobbes, for whom reason could only serve to calculate how best to realise an individual's own desire. For Spinoza, reason participates in desire that individuals might create communities energised by the striving to understand their interdependence, from the imbricated forays of desire operative between each and all (Spinoza: 1996, Proposition 37 of Book Four). These communities are democratic because all things are equal with respect to their coherence within the one substance. Democracy is, therefore, the most natural and theological of political systems (Spinoza: 1958a, 137). For these communities, right down to the corporeal affects upon the individual human body, are ordered by a love for God. This love is the highest common good and dictate of reason (Spinoza: 1996, Proposition 20 of Book Five).[16] As such, the body, singular and social, is conceived to be 'contained in God and follow from the necessity of the divine nature' (Spinoza: 1996, Scholium to Proposition 29 of Book Five) and the love which it strives to perfect is 'part of the infinite love (*infiniti amoris*) by which God loves (*amat*) himself' (Spinoza: 1996, Proposition 36 of Book Five). Politically, these are democratic communities, but to proceed beyond politics (the realm, at best, of second knowledge) is to leave the body, singular and social, and all its passions behind. Ultimately, Spinoza's system has its telos in oblivion: that is, third knowledge, akin, as several scholars have observed, to Nietzsche's everlasting noon (Nietzsche: 1979; Yovel: 1989; Milbank: 1992, 30–44).

Certain Neo-Platonic elements are evident in Spinoza's marriage of rationalism and idealism, and in the significant return to the will as a determinative intellectual love. Again Spinoza differs from Hobbes here: for Hobbes, foreshadowing Nietzsche and in line with constructivism, the will is determinative of form.[17] In his earlier *Shorter Treatise*, the similarities between Spinoza's position on desire and the Good and Augustine's are even more pronounced.[18] These elements and similarities will become clearer in the next chapter and Chapter 9, when we examine the formation of persons in the city of God as Augustine portrays it. For the moment, it is important to determine the nature of this divine participation and its relation to the formalised commonwealth, the state and its government, in order to see *both* how it contrasts with Hobbes', and yet how they share the same natural philosophy: the immanentist logic – the univocity of being.

It is evident from: (1) Spinoza's own rejection of the term 'pantheism;[19] (2) the way we human beings (because of our own constitution) can only view the infinite attributes of God under the two attributes of mind and extension; and (3) Spinoza's insistence that God's existence is necessary, eternal and impassable, that God as substance is not the material out of which we and all other things in the world is composed. Nevertheless, according to his *Shorter Treatise*, reasoning operates by means of penetrating 'the property of proportionality' (Spinoza: 1985, 98). This form of 'analogy' by proportion presents a univocity of being such that, in the *Ethics*, the participation of intellectual love in God's own love for himself is deemed 'one and the same' (Spinoza: 1996, Corollary of Proposition 36 of Book Five). There is no true alterity. All otherness and difference is of imagination wrought; the knowledge of otherness is deemed inadequate knowledge. For Spinoza social atomism, therefore, is illusory for the conflict between bodies while being a conflict of desires, is not a conflict of rights, but a conflict between passions that need to be adequately understood. Foundationally, there is a natural harmony, even identity. The theological corollary of this is that God is knowable or, at least, approachable through reason. Since our minds and bodies exist within this God, a certain relationship between what is and how we represent what is pertains. Spinoza suggests Moses may have had to adapt his law code, Christ his moral code and the writers of Scripture their narratives in order both to accommodate 'the stupidity of the masses, and their failure to think' and win them to obedience and devotion (Spinoza: 1958a, 83, 103). But, the basic truth and reality being proclaimed is the same. The epistemological corollary of this is that, *although* we have no unmediated knowledge of the body in itself (and presumably other bodies in themselves) because our ideas arise from bodily affects (Spinoza: 1996, Proposition 19 of Book Two), *nevertheless*, by the employment of reason minds are capable of perceiving things clearly and distinctly. Therefore, foundationally, there is a correspondence between ideas and materiality because both are attributes of the one God. Furthermore, in knowledge of the third kind perspectivalism is overcome. There is not, then, Hobbes' infinite Calvinistic distinction between God and the world which promotes an epistemological and ontological vacuum to be filled by a sociology of knowledge.

Fundamentally, Spinoza's different metaphysical framework provides a different understanding of the nature of representation. This, subsequently, gives rise to different models of political representation such that Spinoza can deny any correspondence between God's power and the power of kings. His organic system rejects political absolutism in favour of 'a liberal pluralistic theory of the state' (Malcolm: 1987, 555). Nevertheless, there is an artificiality about Spinoza's commonwealth. For, like Hobbes, citizens are to give over their right to a sovereign power ruling on their behalf. And is it this artificiality that we need to understand. For Hobbes' inability to find a mediating principle such that equivocity and political absolutism (founded metaphysically upon nominalism) win out, cannot be pitched against Spinoza's univocity (founded in his naturalism)[20] – because, politically, Spinoza also requires contractual agreement. The state is created by human beings as the most rational way of organising other bodies in the world. It is the best way of facilitating self-preservation. Spinoza views the formation of associations as the outcome of understanding the interconnection of all things. Hence his insistence upon 'the principle of common life and common advantage' (Spinoza: 1996, Demonstration to Proposition 73 of Book Four). Nevertheless the common decision of the state institutionalises this interconnection, providing punitive judgements for those who cannot rationally understand the mutuality which exists at a higher level and who seek short term self-interest. The state's laws are, ideally, distillations of the natural and divine laws uniting that society. But the operation of the state is not universal, unlike the operation of God's laws; for states are spatially and temporally located.[21] States govern by consensus and laws are framed by convention; a convention that 'serves no other purpose than to preserve life' (Spinoza: 1958b, 71). Only within this constructed state can Spinoza demand the respect for difference (of belief, for example). Each is, ideally, provided with the security to pursue individual liberty within this domain; while, seen from the perspective of enlightened reason, there is neither liberty nor individualism at all.

As for the consummation of intellectual love in the third knowledge, this is, as we have already noted, a state beyond politics: a state of eternal blessedness wherein both mind and body dissolve into the one substance. As one recent commentator, assessing the character of subjectivity for Spinoza, explains: 'The inadequacy of self-knowledge could only be transcended at the cost of our ceasing to exist.'[22] In death, the mind like the body ceases to be and enters eternity with no possible awareness anymore of its one-time existence. It enters into what Certeau describes as 'white ecstasy' (Certeau: 1997, 157).[23] The erotic and rational community, participating in God's own infinite intellectual love, is, therefore, not identical with (in fact, exceeds in truth, reality and being) the civil community. The civil community is the pragmatic and localised way of handling the inadequacy of self-knowledge. This has repercussions for Spinoza's notion of subjectivity. In God, there is no subjectivity; for all individuals are modifications of the one substance. Ultimately, then, politics and ethics are simply local strategies working with illusions. Hegel saw this, and it constituted his own criticism of Spinoza (Hegel: 1974, vol. 3, 252–90). Put another way, political organisation, rather like the Palladian arches and porticoes of the same period, provides the elaborate, if not grand, scaffolding for an empty space, a space of indifference, a space for learning how to die well.

It is now possible to see the proximity of Hobbes and Spinoza, despite the different communities of desire they detail. For a certain equivocity creeps into Spinoza, not at the metaphysical or theological level, but politically. Metaphysical 'harmony' with respect to the one substance and 'harmony' in the united *polis* are not identical. One is natural and the other artificial. Furthermore, the first harmony requires the dissolution of the second (bodily participation in affective, passionate living in the city). Like Hobbes, then, Spinoza is politically a nominalist, for there is no participation of the sign in the thing it ultimately signifies. Nominalism and equivocity founds both Hobbesian absolutism and Spinoza's liberal contractualism. Furthermore, in its artificiality the liberal pluralistic state has no need for Spinoza's God. And so Spinoza's socio-political thinking can disassociate itself from his philosophy of religion – as contemporary advocates of Spinoza's corporate responsibility and sociology of knowledge, like Deleuze, Gatens and Lloyd,[24] have shown. But then to embrace Spinoza's God is to embrace death in order to enter into the All.

From this examination of the subject of desire in early modernity, and the socio-political communities it fosters, four significant characteristics arise. These characteristics will have to be re-examined when we begin to explore the kind of erotic community composed by the Church.

First, for both Hobbes and Spinoza desire is natural, negative and implicated in the will to preservation. It is negative insofar as, for Hobbes, it needs restraining, while, for Spinoza, it leads towards its own abolition (in the one). For both, though in different ways, desire provides the dynamic for relationality and the need for a politics of the body. But also, for both, desire has to be denied so that the body politic can emerge – either as Hobbesian absolutism or as Spinozist contractualism.

Secondly, for both Hobbes and Spinoza the embodied subject is under threat. Its extinction is all too possible. In Hobbes, the natural condition of subjectivity is agonistic. Subjects are atomised and in conflict. In Spinoza, subjects either disappear, when viewed with respect to God as their ultimate destiny, or are isolated in their own imaginary individualities and freedoms of will. The Hobbesian subject has singularity only in the face of unending opposition; the Spinozist subject has neither singularity nor opposition. For both (though Spinoza recognises a condition of natural interdependence), the community as the state is artificial. It is a virtual or imagined reality; a reactive defence against self-assertion.

Thirdly, their distinctive theologies (broadly, Calvinism and pantheism) legitimate the ontological nature of the commonwealths they conceive. But the role God plays is extrinsic to the state itself. The ontological bases (atomistic for Hobbes; monistic for Spinoza) are, then, fundamentally at odds with the institution of the state itself. For, in Hobbes, God is an at infinite distance from the commonwealth and, in Spinoza, God is so close to the commonwealth as to threaten to dissolve it altogether. For both, God has no positive and necessary role to play in the activities of the commonwealth. There is either too little God (in Hobbes) or too much God (in Spinoza). Hence, all authority exercised within the polis itself is pragmatic and arbitrary.

Fourthly, what is absent from both accounts is an analogical world-view, or a principle of mediation. In their different ways, both communities of desire are caught between univocity and equivocity. For both there is, then, either sameness or difference, either the natural condition or the artificially constructed one. In neither is there a coherent notion of participation (such that a real as opposed to an imaginary community can be constituted). In Hobbes, what all share is divisiveness itself, which has to be artificially subjugated; in Spinoza there are no subjects to participate, only a final identification of all as one.

These characteristics combine to create a certain kind of space: a space for the operation of the subjective will. It will become an increasingly godless space, occupied with the Promethean task of saving humanity by human means alone. It is within this space that the modern city of eternal aspiration is constructed. It is when this space collapses because it is seen for what it is – founded upon the virtual and the simulated – that postmodern cities of endless desire take over. One solitary voice stands out against this secular and nihilistic drift of desire. We must examine what he says since this voice is dominant in the trajectory of social and political thinking within which our contemporary community of desire is situated, as Judith Butler quite rightly recognised.

Hegel's community of the spirit

For it is Hegel who avowedly reinstalls a principle of mediation lacking in the equivocation and univocity noted in Hobbes and Spinoza. He does so in a way which gives emphasis again to the theological framework. Contrary to Hobbes, he views the civic society and the state (*Staat*, for Hegel meaning something closer to the Christian understanding of the Kingdom (Shanks: 1991, 120)) as the outworking, the actualisation of subjective desire as will and Spirit (*Geist*). Despite some of his right-wing interpreters, he would have viewed the imposition of sovereign absolutism as arbitrary and violent. For Hegel, it is the very incarnation of God, not God's infinite remoteness, that opens a theatre of operations for the Spirit (God's Spirit and the spirit of human beings working co-operatively). These operations are both rational and necessary such that through them the particularity of a subject receives what is most universally its own, its freedom. Hegel sacrifices none of Hobbes' emphasis upon materiality, but demonstrates how this materiality, this embodiment, is to be lived so that its universal truth can both be made manifest and understood as such. There is no room for atomistic individualism. Spinoza, of course, offers something similar: a depiction of the human working together with the divine; a certain concept of incarnation. But Hegel castigates Spinoza for asserting rather than demonstrating his axioms and collapsing all distinctions, claiming: 'What is requisite is to recognise God as the essence of essences, as universal substance, identity, and yet to preserve distinctions' (Hegel: 1974, 273). The human and the divine become conflated, so that every difference disappears into the universal. He sees the danger here lies in nihilism; the subsequent indifference that is, ultimately, destructive of community (Hegel: 1991, 39). With Hobbes we have the distinctions but nothing in common, and with Spinoza everything in common such that there are no distinctions. Hegel does not sacrifice Spinoza's ecstatic view of the subject – always having to live beyond itself, and live beyond itself in love. He does not sacrifice Spinoza's will as love, rather than (as in Descartes and Hobbes) will as the power to form. He does not reject the ethical *telos* of Spinoza's subject. But it is significant that the thinking of Hobbes and Spinoza was deemed, by their contemporaries, to lead to atheism.[25] And Hegel directly charges Spinoza with atheism. What is lacking, Hegel argues, is God as Spirit and, for Spinoza (whose Jewish identity Hegel foregrounds), 'the reason that God is not spirit is that He is not the Three in One' (Hegel: 1974, 288). Hegel, reinscribes the subject of desire, then, within a Trinitarian movement where difference is not dissolved but maintained by the Three in One. The dynamic of participation within both the world and communities of desire is, once again, pneumatological, and the principle of mediation becomes Christ. For the world is God's Other 'which, comprehended in its divine form is His Son' (Hegel: 1974a, 209).

'True Enlightenment has within it this *strain* of unsatisfied longing ... in passing beyond its individual nature to an unfulfilled beyond, the strain appears as an act and a process' (Hegel: 1977, 589). Within this act and process Hegel's subject of desire maintains itself in its own particularity, but cannot think that particularity as such. For, firstly, it cannot come to an understanding of anything at all without reflecting upon itself, objectively. The subject is mediated through its own self-reflexivity. Secondly, all reflection, as all thinking, operates in, through and as representation. The facility to represent belongs to the language-community in which one thinks. All identity is mediated, by reflection and representation. Thirdly, the subject can neither think nor represent without taking into account otherness – other persons, other things external to itself. Subjects are always then, and only identifiable to themselves when, in relation. Fundamentally it is a relation to all that is other, but given the temporal and geographical locatedness of each subject, then it is a relation to all that is other in the specificity of its own property, family, civil life and state. Subjects are, then, both individual and extended universally – first, with respect to themselves as thinking (about themselves); secondly, with respect to representation, which necessarily involves abstraction and generalisation (Hegel: 1991, 35); and, thirdly, with respect to the interrelatedness of their condition with all that is other. The subject is in continual process. It overcomes the dualism of subjectivity and objectivity, and makes meaningful for itself the subjective determinations of so many others, while remaining, at the same time, with itself as an objective particularity. It is dynamic, expressive of a certain grammar of being: the *in itself* which goes out of itself towards the other *for itself*, while yet remaining *with itself*; and the dynamic for this process is thought itself, thought as an embodied activity.

The mature Hegel calls this the 'will' – the will determines. In his *Philosophy of Religion* lectures he discusses at length the nature of this will. For it has two forms. The first corresponds closely to the natural inclinations of human beings found in Hobbes – a principle of selfishness, depravity and cruelty (Hegel: 1962, 48–9, 64). This is the natural, immediate will or desire; the evil will. For Hegel, those living at this level are not really human beings and are not subjects at all, for nothing is definitely desired at all (Hegel: 1962, 50). The will which determines the structure of human personhood is the rational will; the will for the good, the desire for freedom, which raises human beings beyond the natural and immediate. This will for the good is inherent – 'for he knows about the Good, and the Good is in him' (Hegel: 1962, 62) – and impels human beings towards the higher moral claims of their nature. Here the will is the drive of the spirit to love; thinking is the act of loving. It co-operates with the movement of the Spirit of God itself, coming to externalise its own freedom as the Spirit of God. The will here includes desire and drive (which Hegel views as the will's self-consciousness). It has both a sensuous element and a universality (Hegel: 1991, 52). To represent it as colonising, and therefore acting in its dominant self-relation as a power which denies the alterity of the other (the way the movement of the subject has been represented by many of Hegel's critics), fails to understand that all subjects are likewise engaged in such wilful determinations of their own, in accord with the universal.[26] Though, admittedly, some classes of subjects are understood to be more able to reflect upon (and universalise) their actions, and Hegel will turn these intellectual differentials into social and hierarchical differentials.[27] Nevertheless, the other is not colonised. It remains itself, in its own particularity and its welfare is inseparable from the good which is the essential character of the subject's will and which bears an unqualified obligation (Hegel: 1991, 161). What is appropriated is a certain translation of the meaning of the other for the subject. The other *as* other does not, cannot, appear – for there to be reflection, knowledge, or representation at all by subjects. Alterity is always and only mediated. But the mediation of otherness does not erase it; nor does the return, albeit differently, to the self-relation entail the dominance of the same. For this ecstatic subjectivity, this subject bound by a determinative identity that it cannot finally grasp, is, and always remains, in process and in relation.

Community is necessary; a community of love, of self-reflection, of Spirit in the way Hegel understands that word. Community is not a by-product of subjects of desire, but community is that which makes subjects of desire persons at all. Through the *geistlich* activity of the thinking subject there is participation in, and production of, the objective *Geist* – the concrete world of human relations. Operating in and through this objective *Geist* an absolute *Geist* is discernible which is the truth, the perfection of the self-relation. The absolute *Geist* is that which reveals the contingency of relations between the subjective and the objective *Geist* to be necessary. They are not only necessary, they are right in the way Hegel uses the word to cover civil rights, morality, ethics and 'world history' (which is closer to Augustine's construal of God as the Just, the True and the Good) (Hegel: 1991, 63). The specific inclusion of 'world history' is very important. The thinking self is not only implicated in a local politics and a global politics, she is implicated also in the movement towards the perfect externalisation of the absolute *Geist*. *Geist* as fully actualised (Hegel: 1991, 15). The particularity of the subject is taken up into the community, but the community is itself taken up into the perfection of self-relation; a perfection of self-relation which lives out eternally the three moments of *ekstasis* – the *in itself*, the *for itself* and the *with itself*. In this final sublation and community lies perfect freedom, true identity, universality and simplicity. The community, then, is located both chronologically (with respect to the operation of *Geist* in time as history) and cosmologically (with respect to co-operative interrelationships of subjective, objective and absolute *Geist*).

We could move swiftly here to the trinitarian community in which the Spirit draws the world into the loving relationship of the Father and the Son; the centrality of the incarnation of the historical Jesus as axiomatic for Hegel's understanding of history and mediation; and Christianity as the religion of freedom (Hegel: 1991, 51). But I want to stay with the human community and the economics of the confluence of wills, as here lie many of the difficulties and confusions of thinking with Hegel (Williams: 1998, 127–8). It is a spiritual community *as* a concrete community. It is an ethical community *as* each actualises desires whose end is universal. These performances of will (in Hegel's sense of will) are not blindly dutiful (as in Kant's ethical commonwealth), they are necessary because rational. The community finds its immediate form in the family, its mediated (and spiritual) form in civil society and its historical perfection in the state. These three spheres operate simultaneously and ideally to bring about the greatest externalisation of the freedom; where freedom is understood as conforming to that which is universal. The state is 'the divine idea as it exists in the world' (Hegel: 1956, 38). More expansively in *The Philosophy of Right*:

> The state is the actuality of concrete freedom. But concrete freedom requires that personal individuality (*Einzelheit*) and its particular interests should reach their full development and gain recognition of their right for itself (within the system of the family and of civil society), and also that they should, on the one hand, pass over of their own accord into the interest of the universal, and on the other, knowingly and willingly acknowledge this universal interest even as their own substantial spirit, and actively pursue it as their ultimate end. The effect of this is that the universal does not attain validity or fulfilment without the interest,

knowledge, and volition of the particular, and that individuals do not live as private persons merely for these particular interests without at the same time directing their will to a universal end (*in und für das Allgemeine wollen*) and acting in conscious awareness of this end.

(Hegel: 1991, 282)

Barring the reference to (or expanding the notion of) the family, this passage might have come from Augustine's *City of God*, as we will see more clearly in the final chapter. There is no subjugation of individuality to the state here, in fact exactly the opposite. There is no state without the externalisation of the subjective will and the reflective knowledge of the way that will accords with and produces what is universal. There is a certain diremption in the self-determination of each subject that Hegel will later speak of in terms of valour and sacrifice, but the state as the ultimate community of what all desire is neither totalitarian nor liberal. In fact, no one historical state (including the Prussian state undergoing its liberal reforms in the time of Friedrich Wilhelm III (see Wood: 1991, ix–xi)) incarnates the Idea. Hegel writes that: 'the state consists in the march of God in the world, and its basis is the power of reason actualising itself as will. In considering the Idea of the state, we must not have any particular states or particular institutions in mind; instead, we should consider the Idea, this actual God, in its own right (*für sich*)' (Hegel: 1991, 279). It is as though the state was a city of God, though not quite in the Augustinian sense of the singularity of that term. For in *Philosophy of Right* we move from this discourse of 'the state' to a discussion of states. There are then cities of God, plural. Hence Hegel examines international law and makes his infamous statement on the inevitability of war. But throughout there is a recognition that independent states 'have their truth and destiny (*Bestimmung*) in the concrete Idea as *absolute universality*' (Hegel: 1991: 376). The world spirit moves towards this ultimate exposition and actualisation of the universal spirit. (Even if, unfortunately, Hegel couches it in the last three sections in terms of the destiny of the Germanic realm.)

The ethical life, the discrete communities of spirit each express and maintain, is ultimately the one movement of the absolute and divine will unfolding itself through time. The mutual relations between these communities are 'the manifest (*erscheinende*) dialectic of the finitude of spirits. It is through this dialectic that the universal spirit, the spirit of the world, produces itself in its freedom from all limits, and it is this spirit which exercises its right – which is the highest right of all – over finite spirits in world history as the world's court of judgement (*Weltgericht*)' (Hegel: 1991, 371). The diremptive activity of the Spirit affects a global kenosis which brings about the sanctification of all. In his *Philosophy of Religion* lectures he explicitly states that 'The real Spiritual Community is what we in general call the Church' (Hegel: 1962, 123, 97). It is the ultimate unfolding of the Kingdom of God and its citizenship (Hegel: 1962, 84–90,102–3,109). In his *Philosophy of Right* Hegel is less explicit in his naming (an indication perhaps that

141

that is all we are handling, names, representations).[28] But in both accounts Hegel's story ends (as indeed Augustine's account of the city of God ends), by turning full circle, with the eschatological judgement in which all ethical communities will not only recognise their oneness but, in that recognition, come to the final knowledge of themselves as communities of love (Hegel: 1962: 88; 1974, 137). Olson notes: 'the *aufgehoben* of a strictly negative dialectic becomes, for Hegel after Frankfurt [after 1800], the *Aufhebung* of a positive dialectic in which first love and then Spirit emerge as the definitive reconciling agencies' (Olson: 1992, 59). It is a love which Hegel details as sublating all forms of human love – love of persons, the love of the sexes, the love of friends. Love is Spirit as such (Hegel: 1962, 106–7). It operates in and through all differences; acknowledging and requiring the particularities differences install (Hegel: 1962, 100).

There is much here that will be revisited with respect to my own account of the Church as the erotic community. Over the last thirty years considerable attempts have been made, by Hegel scholars, to examine and reinstate Hegel as the last great Christian metaphysician (Theunissen: 1970; Findlay: 1970; Lauer: 1982; Lakeland: 1984; Shanks: 1991; Burbidge: 1992; Olson: 1992; O'Regan: 1994; Crites: 1998), work from which I have gained much insight. Hegel's Pietist and Lutheran background have been extensively explored. And Hegel may well have been right, for his context; that is, he may well have provided a theological account of the world that was credible for that world. He is too comprehensive and complex simply to label wrong. There is much here that indeed reflects older, analogical world-views and Logos theologies (Olson: 1992, 16–24; Williams: 1998, 122). But it is at this very point that two questions emerge that may lead to differences between the community of the spirit delineated by Hegel and the erotic community of the Church that is central to the thesis of this book. These questions may also help us to understand why Hegel's community of the spirit was taken up in ways that advanced the secularisation of the social, rather than returned it to the provenance of the theological and cosmological. The two questions share a common difficulty.

The first question concerns Hegel's treatment of the state, particularly in *Philosophy of Right*. The second question concerns Hegel's consistent treatment of the Christian religion from *Phenomenology of Spirit* through the third part of the *Encyclopaedia* to the lectures which comprised his *Philosophy of Religion*. The concerns of both of these questions are related to the central teleological process in Hegel's thought – the movement from the immediate to representation to the concept to the Idea. The Idea is that which is immediate to itself and so there is, as is well known, a circularity about this process: a good infinite, in Hegel's terms. Within the circle an evaluative hierarchy is established. All stages are equally necessary. All stages are formally and logically equal. But qualitatively, and in terms of the actual offices and functions in the state that expresses them, they are not equal. Some people are able to think more clearly and rationally than others; some are more educated that others. Hence a certain intellectual meritocracy is established in the state that is not far removed from Plato's rule of the Philosopher-King or Aristotle's argument for the justification for slavery (and the position of women). The Idea is evidently superior overall, and the move from the immediate to the represented is the move into self-reflection, the move away from animality to humanity. That is an evaluative move, a qualitative move with respect to human life and the worlds human beings create. *A fortiori*, the move from representation to conceptualisation is a movement from self-reflected expression to knowledge. Knowledge is purer. The process of abstraction is a purifying process.

If we return now to the two concerns I raised: with respect to the state, I would argue, there is a certain slippage in Hegel between representations of the state and the state as the actuality of the ethical idea. Of course, any abstract notion of state Hegel would repudiate. The state is comprised of estates and standings, executive and legislative powers, constitutions and assemblies. The brave descent into the detailed mechanics of government in Part Three of *Philosophy of Right* is an attempt, by Hegel, to describe the lineaments of the ethical idea as it comes to be externalised and expressed. Knowledge wills. He is doing philosophy's job of raising this *Sittlichkeit* to a self-conscious understanding of itself: that it might understand the goals of absolute freedom to which it is attuned by the absolute *Geist*. For, according to his own logic, the state must implement 'what it knows in so far as it knows it' (Hegel: 1991, 275). Hegel is providing that reflection. In doing this he is expressing, to some extent, a form of state. As has already been noted, the shape and nature of government described by Hegel did not correspond to what was actually the case in Prussia at that time. It belonged to no one state. The description, then, is not neutral: it *advocates* and is, to some extent, *prescriptive*. Why is this significant? Because Hegel cannot be prescriptive. His method requires the encounter to have passed. The philosophical process of abstraction can only be retrospective. Yet what we find is that the need to avoid an empty abstraction of the ethical idea entails giving that idea content. But in giving that idea content representation *cannot be* sublated by the conceptual. That is, philosophical reflection cannot do what Hegel wishes it to do, provide knowledge, move from *Vorstellen* to *Denken*. Hegel would have to go beyond himself; beyond his own writing and, ascending Wittgenstein's ladder, enter into silence. Philosophical conceptualisation is not pure enough. It can only provide descriptions. And given what appears to be Hegel's emphasis – that philosophical reflections upon the cultural, the political and the social production of the ethical life are more universal because offering a conceptual grasp of underlying absolute structures – then description too easily can become prescriptive. In other words, in exalting the speculative as a moment in the economy of salvation (freedom) by and through the externalisation of the absolute idea, Hegel forgets that philosophy too trades in representations. Philosophy too is the product of a certain *Volkgeist* and, necessarily, implicated in disseminating certain ideologies manifest in that *Volkgeist*.

This leads us directly to examine that second concern. With respect to the Christian religion, Hegel consistently views it as the absolute (because revealed)

143

religion. Nevertheless it is a representation that needs philosophy to bring it to a full knowledge of itself (Lakeland: 1984, 93–6). Faith in this revealed religion mediates the Spirit (Olson: 1992, 34), the Incarnation renders explicit what has always been implicit about the relationship of God to human individuals (Shanks: 1991, 84). But the teaching of Christ belongs to the realm of figurative ideas (Hegel: 1962, 85). And while Hegel insists on the historical truth of Christ's death, resurrection and ascension (Hegel: 1962, 109), this history is a 'pictorial view', a 'representation' (Hegel: 1962, 95). This history passes and 'this sensuous mode must disappear and mount into the region of idea or mental representation. One of the constituent parts of the formation of the Church is that this sensuous form passes over into a spiritual element' (Hegel: 1962, 103). The sublation of the sensuous (and historical) is not its erasure, as Hegel insists, but akin to an inductive process in science – moving towards higher and purer levels of conceptualisation. 'This absolute truth, this truth in-and-for-itself that God is not an abstraction, but something concrete, is unfolded by philosophy, and it is only modern philosophy which has reached the profound thought thus contained in the Notion' (Hegel: 1962, 111). The philosopher's task is ultimately an apologetic one: unfolding the universal logic of the Christian faith as that logic manifests itself in the secular world.[29]

The danger in the sublation process is twofold: a certain forgetting and a certain philosophical hegemony. The material, that which singularises each body, is rendered complex in Hegel's process of idealisation; but its very substantiality could be lost, or forgotten. With respect to Jesus Christ, Hegel remarks that 'this individual man is changed by the Spiritual Community ... He is separated from substantiality' (Hegel: 1962, 115). Now this is right, in the sense that in the Church's thinking, speaking and writing about Christ that individual, historical figure is changed. He *is* separated from his substantiality. In this, the mediation of the body of Jesus Christ is no different from the mediation of all bodies. As we have seen, the givenness of the material is always already represented. But with Hegel's dialectical process, though the body is taken up (to use a positive description of the economy of *Aufhebung*), it is left unclear as to what remains of matter as such. The substantiality of Jesus as the Christ must not be simply discarded or allowed to be forgotten. For it is that historical substantiality which returns the Church again and again to check and guide its mediations on, and disseminations of, Jesus Christ. This is why the eucharist is also an act of remembrance, and why the liturgical cycle repeats, albeit differently, the founding events. We can link this tendency of Hegel's immanent and evolutionary process to forget the corporeal with the way gender figures within his rational system. For women, associated with the natural and the immediate (both in terms of the feminisation of Nature and the role women play with respect to the family – the natural and immediate locus for the human, male subject) are likewise mentioned only to be forgotten. They too are passed over. In the pursuit of the essential, sublation can effect a downgrading of the material that borders on rendering that material epiphenomenal. To counter this, more attention needs to be focused on the various social technologies of subjectivity; the various cultural disciplines which inform both the sexed body and the thinking of the subject.

Furthermore, a philosopheme becomes what Lyotard would term a grand narrative, such that all phenomena correlate: 'it belongs essentially to philosophy to get a grasp of what *is*, of what is actually real in itself' (Hegel: 1962, 112). A metaphysical ground is laid out by Hegel; and all things find their meaning and identity with respect to that ground. Personal development and social development are conflated with logical development. Philosophy provides a golden code, a genetic code. It perceives and evaluates that which governs all possible operations. With the Hegelian *corpus* a case can be made that this form of rationality is not tradition-free (Olson: 1992, 133). It is rooted in an understanding of trinitarian procession that renders consciousness itself a mystery. Revelation alone enables Hegel to think cosmologically. But all too easily can the immanentalism of Hegel's open-ended system be allowed to explain itself: and *Philosophy of Right* is moving in this direction. The process can be separated from its substantial and transcendent content (its origin in the specificity of Christ's death and resurrection as a trinitarian event) in further acts of intellectual refinement or correlation. The Idea can become History; and the new priests of this Idea are historians. Or the Idea can become a different transcendental operation, a transhistorical economy. And so History becomes the forefather to other more recent anonymous and transcendental dynamics: Nietzsche's impersonal will, Derrida's *différance* and Foucault's construal of power. '[O]nce one drops Hegel's nineteenth-century faith in progressive development of consciousness through history, and merely retains his contextualised conception of rationality, then historicism collapses into some form of relativistic scepticism, as there is now no standpoint at the end of history from which previous outlooks can be judged, and in which their culmination can be assured' (Stern: 1994, 146). With the dominance of the conceptual, we are on our way to what Derrida has termed (partly with reference to Hegel) 'the possibility of religion without religion' (Derrida: 1995, 49). By 'focussing on Hegelian "method" as something distinct from the "system" ' (Shanks: 1991, 140), Enlightenment thinking can continue to pursue its secularised eschatology. Which is why, perhaps Hegel's theological voice was, like his political theory, even when attacked, either misunderstood, secularised or both. Andrew Shanks, in his book *Hegel's Political Theology*, observes, with reference to Kierkegaard that he never 'appear[s] to have come to terms with the real theological challenge of what Hegel does say' (Shanks: 1991, 130). And of Adorno, Shanks states that '[h]is Hegel is, to all intents and purposes, a Hegel minus Christianity' (Shanks: 1991, 140). The French neo-Nietzscheans (Deleuze, Lacan, Foucault, Lyotard, Baudrillard), fed upon a Kojévian Marxist reading of Hegel, and Jean Hyppolite's questioning of the coherence of the Hegelian subject, all explicitly reject Hegelian 'method' without wrestling with the theological grammar upon which Hegel's thinking is founded.[30] Similarly, Judith Butler, with whom we began our discussion of modern communities of desire, reads Hegel not as the last Christian metaphysician but as the first phenomenologist of desire; Butler who considers Hegel at the forefront of our post-Enlightenment understandings of eros and subjectivity; Butler who is aware that without Hegel's metaphysical superstructure 'desire increasingly becomes a principle of the ontological displacement of the human subject, and in its latest stages, in the work of Lacan, Deleuze, and Foucault, desire comes to signify the impossibility of the coherent subject itself' (Butler: 1987, 6).

Hegel's community of the Spirit, stripped of the theological framework which attempted to relate subjects of desire to ecclesiology, left intellectual attention fixed upon dynamic principles (desire, will, time, power) that, like subatomic particles, move here and there creating arbitrary orderings for an increasingly insubstantial subject. Erotic communities, as ecclesial parodies, become imaginary and virtual; composed of contractual, imaginary and virtual relations. In the process desire becomes reduced to *libido*.

From imagined to virtual communities

In his influential study, Benedict Anderson provides us with both a map and a genealogy for the various forms of nationalistic desire and imagination which produce the contemporary world's 'nations'. He calls these political groups 'imagined communities', imagined insofar as they are culturally produced; they are artefacts existing in the minds of those who believe (who are also made to believe) they belong to them. '[T]he members of even the smallest nation will never know most of their fellow-members, meet them, or even hear them, yet in the minds of each lives the image of their community' (Anderson: 1983, 6).[31] For Anderson, what becomes fundamental in their production – and in their Western European origin – is the arbitrariness of the sign. From the moment when it could no longer be held that 'the ideograms of Chinese, Latin, or Arabic were emanations of reality, not randomly fabricated representations of it' (Anderson: 1983, 14), then the centre could no longer hold. Old sacral languages were gradually fragmented, pluralised and territorialised (Anderson: 1983, 19); signs could be produced and manipulated. The production and reproduction of the sign – in the novel and the newspaper, in the bank-note and the map, in the census and the museum – facilitated the birth of imaginary communities by representing and fostering the relationships that constituted such political units. Anderson observes, that since the onset of modernity 'Much the most important thing about language is its capacity for generating imagined communities, building in effect *particular solidarities*' (Anderson: 1983, 133). What he terms 'print-languages', standardised varieties of idiom and idiolect among vernaculars. Print-languages became the basis for print-capitalism. With print-capitalism the endless reproduction of arbitrary signs generates the power, value and meaning of those signs. But power, value and meaning is, then, a rhetorical effect. In this, 'language takes religion's place' (Anderson: 1983, 138) and we each become hostages to the Word (a Word which is Master and yet whose power is unfocused).

Anderson's thesis is painted in broad strokes, in a style which cherishes the epigrammatic and the aphoristic. Furthermore, he appears to embrace a poststructuralist tendency to hypostasise language as an anonymous, omnipotent power. The arbitrariness of the sign rules like blind fate or, to use a metaphor of Benjamin's that Anderson is fond of alluding to, an angel hurtling backwards into a future unseen and unknown while the past and the present collects as so much detritus at his feet. This emphasis has the effect of decorporealising his thesis – embodied agency is jeopardised. Nevertheless, Anderson's analysis is important for my own for three reasons. First, because what he compares to the arbitrary and imagined community is the older, sacral sodalities of premodernity. Second, because his thesis points to what has always been the weakness of contractual notions of the social (like Rousseau's based upon the individualism of *amour propre* and the collectivism of the *generale volonté*) – that is, the difficulties of ascertaining this general will and the extent to which any individual is ever concretely presented with a choice as to whether he or she opts in or out. Third, and most significantly, Anderson relates language to the production and promotion of these imagined communities. Language creates and endorses the fetishised object of the community; it generates the desire to belong and the allegiances which define community – making possible the sentiment of *dulce et decorum est pro patria mori*. The imaginary community is impossible outside of the desiring subject as the speaking subject, the libidinal subject as the wielder of rhetorical power.

To take Anderson's analysis further, we need to hear not simply the social but also the psychic associations of those words 'imaginary' and 'imagined'. To understand the complex relationships between language and belonging, we need to explore the way in which these imagined communities are composed of subjects of desire; bodies who compose, move and live through symbolic bodies of the nation or the polis while also inhabiting and performing other bodies, imaginary bodies which escape symbolisation. We have to relate Anderson's symbolic communities, generated and legitimated by the arbitrariness of the sign, to its imaginary. Making these connections between the symbolic community, its fantasies and its desire, on the basis of a Lacanian distinction between the Real, the Imaginary and the Symbolic, has been the specific work of the Slovenian philosopher, Slavoj Žižek (Ward: 2000, 162–9).

Entry into the citadels of the symbolic, for Lacan, is a necessary act following the sense of a lost unity or symbiosis. The symbolic offers forms of substitution, through signs, for this loss, for it promises the satisfaction of that desire for unity, the consummation of that desire, the achievement of what that desire projects, Lacan's *objet petit a*. The *objet petit a* is not what we desire, for we can never articulate what it is we desire, but it puts that desire into operation. Desire can only desire because the final *jouissance* is unobtainable; unobtainable because this consummation would involve our being consumed by the amorphous and traumatising arbitrariness of the Real itself (what Žižek terms 'the monstrous Life-Substance' (Žižek: 1997, 89)). In this way, desire produces meaning; a meaning which is not monadic, because it arises only in relation to other people, other objects in the world and a symbolic system which the I inhabits rather than possesses. For Lacan, as Žižek points out, 'fantasy is ultimately always the fantasy of a successful sexual relationship' (Žižek: 1994, 66). As such, desire produces symbolic communities; in fact our very notions of community. What interests Žižek is that which mediates between desire and the symbolic; the fantasy of *jouissance* in its various manifestations. What do our cultures of the symbolic betray about our fantasies; what ideologies are playing within and constructing the activities of our shared living?

Žižek reads films and other cultural products, social and erotic practices, historical events and their interpretation in order to map the fantasies of *jouissance* and explore the structures of their economies: the way in which the subject of desire produces and is produced by the various forms of imagined community (the army, the internet, the Stalinist and Nazi regimes etc.). What is important for Žižek is the thesis that fantasy sustains a subject's sense of what is real. In this way, the psychic is implicated in the civic, the sexual in the political. The community is still, as with Anderson, an imagined one – that is, a symbolically mediated and constructed one – but it is also an erotic one. For the ideal community, the fantasy that informs the utopic horizons for city, state and nationhood, is founded in ideally satisfied erotic relations. But erotic relations as such are always *manqué* and must remain so: the Imaginary sustains the Symbolic and screens the Real, but the collapse of the differences separating these three psychic fields would entail the demise of the subject. For example, Žižek points to the way Schumann, despite his profound love for Carla, kept the woman at a distance. The fulfilment of the erotic fantasy within the symbolic cannot be sustained. The actual erotic relation always compromises the fantasy so that when I make love to my partner there is never the complete surrender to the erotic moment, consciousness interrupts, makes me aware of that which counters my fantasy of the perfect *jouissance* – a smell of sweat, a prickling hair, an echo of another love scene played out elsewhere in a novel, a poem, a film etc. The erotic relation always and necessarily lacks its fulfilment. Hence, Žižek can point out:

> For animals, the most elementary form, the 'zero form', of sexuality is copulation; whereas for human, the 'zero form' is *masturbation with fantasising* (in this sense, for Lacan, phallic *jouissance* is masturbatory and idiotic); any contact with a 'real', flesh-and-blood other, any sexual pleasure that we find in touching *another* human being, is not something evident but inherently traumatic, and can be sustained only in so far as this other enters the subject's fantasy-frame.
>
> (Žižek: 1997, 65)

As such, the other is always and only a virtual other, not a real object of desire but a fantasised object created by the subject itself. As such, also, an asymmetrical power relation pertains to the erotic relation; each subject requires the other to submit to their 'fantasy-frames' in order for *jouissance* to be possible. Mapping this embodiment onto the wider social body, Žižek's work indicates that Anderson's imaginary community (the social-contractual bodies of Hobbes and Rousseau constituted, consolidated and maintained by communication networks) is underpinned by a virtual community. No longer a set of monadic subjects choosing, contracting or coerced, this community (and the identity of any position within it) is woven in and through the operations of desire. But since the *sine qua non* of this desire is its unfulfilment, the relation is a fantasy, a virtual reality. This has the effect of deepening the imagined reality (the symbolic realm) and creating a self-conscious awareness of the virtual nature of communities.

In an interesting essay on cyberspace and cybersex, Žižek discusses the contemporary fascination with, and New Age veneration of, virtual reality. He discerns two current perspectives on the phenomenon in its relation to notions of community: 'On the one hand, there is the dream of the new popularism, in which decentralized networks will allow individuals to band together and build a participatory grass-roots political system, a transparent world in which the mystery of the impenetrable bureaucratic state agencies is dispelled. On the other, the use of computers and VR as a tool to rebuild community results in the building of a community *inside* the machine, reducing individuals to isolated monads, each of them alone, facing a computer, ultimately unsure if the person she or he communicates with on the screen is a 'real' person, a false persona, an agent which combines a number of 'real' people, or a computer program … Again, the ambiguity is irreducible' (Žižek: 1997, 139). Either way, because of the irreducibility of the ambiguity, the communities created are virtual. We will return to this in the final chapter. For Žižek, relations in cyberspace – MUD or Multiple User Domains – become a metaphor for the relay of fantasised erotic relations without real objects – and therefore without real exchange or real participation – that sustains the symbolic realm of social and institutional contracts. Hence, he warns that the danger of cyberspace is the way it collapses the distinction between the Real, the Imaginary and the Symbolic. It does this first by bringing to a textual surface the underlying fantasy – 'that is, to fill in the gap which separates the symbolic surface texture from its underlying fantasy' (Žižek: 1997, 155). Thus the virtual is no longer virtual enough, for the distinction that enables there to be a 'virtual' no longer pertains. It does this, secondly, by presenting virtual spaces for exploration, experiment and discovery; a space for the endless operation of friction-free desire uninterrupted by the punctuating Real of the Other: 'when I am immersed in it, I, as it were, return to a symbiotic relationship with an Other in which the deluge of semblances seems to abolish the dimension of the Real' (Žižek: 1997, 156).[32] This is the realisation of the postmodern sublime: surrender to the flux. As Žižek observes, what is also surrendered is embodiment and the particularity of the participant's social position. '[T]he phantasmic kernel of our being is laid bare in a much more direct way, making us totally vulnerable and helpless' (Žižek: 1997, 164).

What is rendered comprehensible by this analysis is the highly charged eroticism of cyberspace – such that it is easy to understand why pornographic sites are the most widely used facility when surfing the internet. Cybersex and cyberspace become inseparable: virtual space offers a timeless, measureless domain for the vicissitudes of phallic, masturbatory desire. Furthermore, the expansion of cyberspace – concomitant with the expanding numbers of PC users and an increasing dependence upon digitalised information – only promotes the conscious virtual nature of erotic communities and the atomism of such communities. Zygmunt Bauman – taking his cue from Anderson – describes one of the conditions of postmodernity as neo-tribalism (Bauman: 1992, 198–9) and calls for a new sociological approach corresponding to the de-territorialisation of postmodern tribes in which the category of *society* is replaced with that of *sociality* (Bauman: 1992, 190). Žižek offers critique, but no constructive move beyond critique.

With Žižek's descriptive accounts of fist-fucking and fetishism, we return to the world of our Private Shop, our metaphor for the contemporary culture of seduction, our globalising community which operates, and defines its existence, in and through the erotic. Part of the pleasure of reading Žižek's own texts is the voyeurism of not knowing what will be encountered next, what new erotic pleasure, insight, will be unveiled over the page. But we return to the world of the Private Shop via Foucault. In doing so, we return to the creativity of hedonism, the aesthetics of orgasm – which is what is left in a virtual community where atomised bodies belong to no one, and are taught to enjoy their anonymity. In an interview, published by the American magazine *Advocate* on the 7 August 1984, Foucault said:

> The idea that S&M is related to deep violence, that S&M practice is a way of liberating this violence, this aggression, is stupid. We know very well that what all those people are doing is not aggressive; they are in-venting new possibilities of pleasure with strange parts of their body – through the eroticisation of the body. I think it's a kind of creation, a creative enterprise, which has as one of its main features what I call the desexualisation of pleasure.
>
> (quoted in Macey: 1994, 368)

But it is also Foucault who has emphasised how this subject of desire has been constituted by Christianity, such that today's secular construals of such subjectivity, and the cultures produced by such subjects, stand within an historical trajectory to which Christianity gave rise (Foucault: 1981; Gutting: 1994, 316). In this chapter I have sketched something of that trajectory and the eclipse of the theological ordering of the social. The virtual communities which sprawl and spread through our global cities and cyberspaces are aetiolated, idolatrous versions of the Church as the erotic community *par excellence*. If the Church is to speak in and to the present *Zeitgeist*, then it must recover its deliberations of desire and articulate again its theology of eros. It must do so in a way which learns from, but goes beyond, the contractualisms of Hobbes and Spinoza, and the hierarchical teleology of Hegel. It must do so in a way which maintains corporeality and emphasises the formation of substantial communities through shared practices.

6

THE CHURCH AS THE EROTIC COMMUNITY

> We are discontinuous beings, individuals who perish in isolation in the midst of an incomprehensible adventure, but we yearn for lost continuity.
>
> (Bataille: 1987, 15)

The fracture

There is a rich and complex liturgical interchange prior to the distribution of the eucharistic elements. It is called the fraction. The interchange has disappeared from the modern Catholic mass, through it is retained from the old Sarum Missal in the Anglican rite. The priest holds the wafer over the chalice of wine and breaks it into two saying: 'We break this bread to share in the Body of Christ.' The congregation respond with: 'Though we are many we are one body because we all share in one bread.' In this chapter I wish to unfold an examination of the Church as the erotic community through a reading of this interchange. For this small piece of liturgy focuses Christian thinking on the singularities of embodiment *and* participation. In doing that it announces something of the analogical order this book is attempting to construct.

Four aspects of this interchange concern us:

1.   Participation follows fragmentation; only on the basis of the broken body of Christ can the distribution of that body be effected. The fracturing here is positive, not negative. Developing what I suggested in Chapter 4, the fracture participates in and promotes the greater displacement of Christ's body such that there might be an expansion of the one body as subsequent other bodies come to share in it. Each fragment of the wafer is the whole body of Christ, being offered to and received by, each communicant. The interchange here between priest and congregation effects the eucharistic interchange between Christ and believer. 'Effects' does not imply a causal connection such that the first interchange causes the second interchange to be. For the first interchange is not outside and isolated from the second, even though the second has not taken place yet. The first interchange between priest and congregation already participates in the second interchange between Christ and believer. The participation is temporally

complex. It might be said to participate in it proleptically insofar as all things find their place in Christ eschatologically. It might be said that the participation issues from that which has been constituted (i.e. individual discipleship and corporate identity) through the practice of previous eucharistic interchanges. But the participation also takes place in and as the present performance. We will return to this temporal present, participation and presence later.

2.   The community of the faithful is established within Christ through the pronominal shifter 'we'. Here, and for the first time in the eucharistic exchange, both the priest and the congregation speak as 'we'. '*We* break this bread' and '*we* are many *we* are one'. The repetition of the 'we' by the priest and the 'we' by the congregation is not identical. The first 'we' is employed collectively by one on behalf of the many; it has the logic of synecdoche. It also bears the sense of instructing, demonstrating or teaching the faithful the meaning of the action. The words institute the fraction as a certain kind of action. Not that they need be announcing that 'we are involved here in a symbolic act' or that the words form a distinctive interpretation of the act. Rather word and act are both performative. But the 'we' because it is synecdochical is an ambivalent shifter. For who belongs to and makes up this 'we' when only one person announces it? The second 'we' is antiphonal and gives the historic and concrete content to the first 'we'. It is a 'we' of affirmation, of faith, the we of 'Amen'. We are the we. In the iteration 'we are many we are one' it is the 'we' which turns contradiction into a paradox that remains hidden in the mystery of 'sharing'. The 'we' bears us over the oxymoronic, the ancient problematic of the one and the many. It does so not as rhetoric – signs concealing an absence of content. It does so as performing an acceptance of the priest's 'we'. Furthermore, each speaker speaks the 'we'. There is no atomised individualism here. 'We' is the proper human subject, 'we' is an indication of personhood, not 'I' – 'we' as physical and psychological beings, as particularised male and female, sinner and saint, able and disabled, of this race and that, of this social class and that. Each speaking the 'we' voices an equivalence – all participate equally. This does not mean that distinctions are erased, for the we is many. But the distinctions are held within the tension of that mysterious paradox of the many being one. Distinctions are affirmed within the 'we', for the repetition of the rhythm 'we are' is not identical: 'we are many we are one'. Difference here is made possible by affirming similarity: relations emerge from the logic of analogy. It is an analogy which is enacted, practised. For the participation that enables each to speak as we, rather than a collection of 'I's', is performed in a number of different ways. It is performed by the verbal agreement with the priest's 'we' which is coupled with the action of the fracturing. Each affirms a part within that action. It is performed by the stepping forward and kneeling to receive: by participating in the liturgy, a participation that has been going on throughout the service. It is performed through the reception, the eating, the digestion of the elements: the physiological absorption of the one Body of Christ within the body of the believer, so that the two become one flesh. The interchanges announces a complex corporeality, a transcorporeality, in which

153

participation finds its ultimate figuration in erotic consummation. Becoming one flesh is the mark of participation itself. The recited 'we' affirms that the Church lives, moves and is nurtured as a particular type of erotic community.

3.   The community, while one, while many, affirms its location in Christ, but by that very sharing in Christ it participates in the displacement of the body of Christ announced in the breaking of the bread. This is a third aspect of the fracture, which is given more explicit expression in the final dismissal following the eucharistic feeding: 'Go in peace to love and serve the Lord.' To employ a distinction found in Michel de Certeau between place (*lieu*) and space (*espace*), the 'we' is not bound by the institutional place it finds itself in, nor the civic place that locates the institutionalised place. The 'we' walks and opens up spaces in and beyond the given and material locale. The we participates in a rhythm of gathering and dispersal that shapes its walking, its pilgrimage. The erotic community it forms transgresses all boundaries. It moves out in love and desire and produces a complex space which cannot be defined, cannot be grasped as such, labelled by sociologists, mapped by geographers. It is itself a fractured and fracturing community, internally deconstituting and reconstituting itself.

4.   Through the liturgical exchange the actions and pronominal assertions of identity employ, emphatically, a present continuous tense: 'we break', 'we are', 'we are' and 'we share'. Questions concerning time, representation, and the nature of participation (its relationship to mediation) all announce themselves in the use of this verbal mood. The use of the present tense parallels the verbal mood of the institutional narrative, rehearsed from its first utterance at the Last Supper, it is performed in the present and in every present enactment of the command to 'Do this in remembrance of me' enjoins: 'This is my body', 'This is my blood'. The deconstituted we is reconstituted by that making present again, albeit differently now, what was handed down to the community in the past and which it passes on into the future. For it is we who break the bread not just the priest, we who do not touch the wafer. The action is representative of our action in two ways: it *stands in for* something we cannot each individually do and it *describes* that very representative act. To the temporal, corporeal and spatial complexity I have outlined above, a mimetic complexity is added. These complexities are mutually implicated in and constitutive of each other.

It is on the basis of an exploration of the present tense of this liturgical interchange that the erotic nature of the ecclesial community can best be approached. As we saw in Chapter 2, our contemporary culture idolises the present, the seizure of the present, and that this seizure is a secular eschatology, a mimickery of eternity as the fullness of time. The eroticism of secular living is orientated around the experiencing of the present as such; implicated, that is, in a certain metaphysics of time and corporeality. By examining the nature of presence in the eucharist we can come to see what is different about the Church as an erotic community. The significance of the other three complexities of the fracture liturgy will emerge with respect to examining the theological relationship between the present and presence, time and participation.

What, then, is the relationship between this liturgical use of the present continuous and sacramental 'presence'? There are four possible answers to that question. First, that they are the same: the present tense presences because it performs what it utters or, as Marshall McLuhan taught: the medium is the message. Secondly, though 'present' (as in a verbal tense) and presence share an etymological root we are concerned with two different 'language games' or discursive categories, the one grammatical and the other ontological. That is, that just as there remains an unbridgeable gap between words and the world, between what is and the representation of what is, so the present tense names a presencing it cannot institute or be part of. We could see these first two options in terms of a see-saw we came across in the last chapter between univocity and equivocity. The third option, the postmodern option, is to describe the relationship between present and presence as undecideable, as part of an economy in which a trace of something arrives and is deferred simultaneously: the relationship is a differend, the economy one of *différance* – a Yes, a Promise which is also a Yes, Yes, a Promise of what is not yet. The final option is that there is some analogical relationship between the present tense and presence such that difference nevertheless participates in similitude.

Having already seen with Hobbes and Spinoza that neither univocity nor equivocity can form a theological basis for community, the last two options are the more important ones to examine. To some these options may appear to be identical (we can recall Derrida's ambiguous remarks concerning the construction by Levinas of an analogy *sui generis* (Derrida: 1991, 44–5)) and it is exactly here that a postmodern understanding of sacramental presence, and the communities it forms, must define itself. The first two options represent the two forms of linguistic philosophy which have been at the centre of the poststructuralist critique. On the one hand, there are the onto-theological resonances which Derrida baptised as logocentrism, which increasingly gained credence following Duns Scotus' *Expositio in metaphysicam* where all trandendentals, particularly existing and willing, can be predicated of God and creation univocally. On the other hand, there is the correspondence theory of signification which establishes the dualism between mind and world and the problem of how words hook up to what is out there which began to establish itself with nominalism. But before examining the *theological* implications of the postmodern criticism of these two options a more fundamental issue arises with respect to them. Heidegger pointed to it first, though not in this way: being has a history. What I mean by this is that 'the present' and 'presence' do not come to us as transparent, transhistorical concepts. They come to us bearing all the accretions of prior usage and transformation. This will be very important for what I wish to argue. For I will suggest that the current talk about the present and presence, whether in the Enlightenment longing for immediate knowledge which grounds the empiricisms and positivisms of the natural sciences (and engages the correspondence theory of language) or in the postmodern critiques of logocentrism and insistence upon the *graphe*, are both operating with very modern, and untheological, construals of these terms. In other words, the disappearance of the body and the creation of imaginary and virtual communities is predicated upon an understanding of a relationship between time and desire which must be theologically challenged if a new analogical world-view is to be constructed.

This can be put more succinctly with three examples. The first is Aquinas on what the Church will later term the real presence: 'in this sacrament he is present to be nourishment' (Aquinas: 1975, III a.q. 76.1). Later he emphasises: 'Christ is ... really present' (III a.q. 76.8). The second is Calvin, also writing about the flesh and blood of Christ in the eucharistic rite: 'we may confidently consider them as truly exhibited to us, as if Christ himself were presented to our eyes, and touched by our hands' (Calvin: 1936, 643). The third is Slavjo Žižek with respect to those worries he has about cyberspace: 'What brings about the "loss of reality" in cyberspace is not its emptiness (the fact that it is lacking with respect to the fullness of the real presence) but, on the contrary, its very excessive fullness (the potential abolition of the dimension of symbolic virtuality)' (Žižek: 1997, 155). What I am suggesting is that the use of the term present/presence in these three citations is implicated, for each, in distinctive historical, linguistic, social and metaphysical matrices. The words bears only a distant family resemblance to each other. If this is so then the postmodern deconstruction of present/presence, as Žižek performs it in his own Lacanian way, need bear little relation to the traditional understanding of presence or grace whereby the salvific life of Christ is shed abroad through the Church. The latter, in fact, may be used to critique the former: deconstructing the deconstructive economy itself – and redeeming the endless semiosis of sense by establishing an analogical order. That, *in nuce*, will be the argument of this chapter.

So taking these three examples, let me first sketch a genealogy of presence. Then we will see the implications of this genealogy with respect to the fracture liturgy and sacramental communion. Finally, we will see how the fourth aspect of that liturgy concerned with the present and presence has to be understood, can only be understood, with respect to the other three characteristics of the liturgical performance. Together these characteristics will enable me to define the operation of desire, the formation of persons-in-communion and the analogical nature in the Christian Church.

The birth of presence

Augustine / Aquinas

It has to be emphasised that other than the employment of the copula 'is' early accounts of the eucharist do not use the language of presence. The New

Testament accounts simply employ *estin*, and this is repeated in Ignatius of Antioch's statement in his *Letter to the Smyreans* that 'the Eucharist is the flesh of our Saviour, Jesus Christ' (7.1) and in Justyn Martyr's statement in his *Apologia* that that 'which nourishes our flesh and blood by assimilation is both the flesh and blood of that Jesus who was made flesh' (1.66). The question, then, arises whence did the language of presence emerge, and more particularly when did the adjective of 'real' preface the use of presence? For what is added to, what is being suggested by, the addition of that 'real'? What I will argue is that the employment of 'presence', and most particularly the term 'real presence', is not metaphysically innocent and places us on the road to Derrida's notion of logocentrism and Lacan's negative construal of that as the Real. The secular fixation upon the present has been partly produced from within the changing traditions of Christian theology.

Throughout medieval accounts of sacramental presence we are concerned with the nature of analogy. It is the collapse of analogy and the movement towards univocity, the transparency of 'clear and distinct' ideas, that can be traced in the difference between Aquinas' and Calvin's notions of 'presence'. As the analogical world collapses so the notion of 'participation' changes – as we will see. From out of the earliest discussions of what I have called the ontological scandal of that 'is' – the '*est*' in *hoc est corpus meus* – the language of appearance comes to be employed. The *Mystagogical Catechesis* gives us an instance of this: 'we consume these with perfect certainty that they are the body and blood of Christ, since under the appearance of bread the body is given, and the blood under the appearance of wine' (4:1–3). But the language of appearances is not to be identified with the language of presence, even more 'real presence'. Appearance is *species*, that is a mode of existing. Appearance is not divorced from the true; appearance is a participation in the true. Augustine emphasises this: 'This sacrament ... doesn't present you with the body of Christ in such a way as to divide it from you. This, as the apostle reminds us, was foretold in holy scripture: They shall be two in one flesh' (Augustine: 1993, 228b). We become what we eat. This is important, for the distinction between visible and invisible according to this logic does not constitute a dualism: the visible, when read theologically, manifests the watermark of its creator. The visible and corporeal is always suspended, and incomplete. Things cannot fully realise themselves in the present for Augustine. For having created, God maintains and sustains that creation throughout what we have seen Gregory of Nyssa term its *scopos*. The creaturely realm is always subject to time.

When we come to Aquinas, the key exponent of the eucharist, all this should be borne in mind. For despite the ubiquitous use of the words present/presence/real presence by translators, Aquinas does not employ that language in his account of sacramental realism. That he knows of the Latin *praesens* and *praesentia* is manifest. He uses the former in his discussion of time – the present (*praesens*) is a temporal location and God is omnipresent (Aquinas: 1964, I.q.8 a.3); he uses the latter with reference to Christ's bodily presence (*sua praesentia corporali*) in history. But he goes on to refute those who consider 'the presence of Christ's body (*praesentia corporis Christi*) as if it were present in a way that is natural for a body to be present (*prout est praesens per modum corporis*)' (Aquinas: 1975, III a.q. 75.2). The language of *praesens* and *praesentia* only have reference to temporal and historical corporeality and have to be understood analogically.[1] And there is a studied avoidance of using such language with respect to Christ's giving of Himself in the eucharist. So when we have statements like 'whenever this sacrament is celebrated he is present in an invisible way under sacramental appearances', the Latin is actually '*Invisibiliter tamen sub speciebus hujus sacramenti est ubicumque hoc sacramentum perficitur*' (Aquinas: 1975, III a.q. 75.2). There is no mention of 'presence' and the language of appearance is, again, the language of *species*. Aquinas will talk about how 'the very body of Christ exists (*verum corpus Christi ... existat*)' in the sacrament, and he will talk about how Christ is really there (*vere esse*). But throughout the whole of Quaestio 76 of the *Summa theologiae* – under a subtitle given by the editors of the translation 'Real Presence' – despite the repeated use of the term 'presence' by translators, the Latin *praesens* and/or *praesentia* is never used by Aquinas.

Two questions emerge at this point. Why does Aquinas avoid using the term and when did the term start getting used as a description of what Roman Catholics believe concerning the eucharist? I suggest the fundamental reason why Aquinas does not engage in a discourse concerning *praesens/praesentia* is because the celebrated theologian who had already done so, namely Augustine, had concluded that 'As for the present, it takes not up any space' (1991, XI.15). The Latin is even more resonant when we recall Augustine's concern with the nothing or *nihil* out of which God creates all things, and that all things are good insofar as they have being and evil insofar as they lack being: '*praesens autem nullum habet spatium*'. Augustine is thought to have been the first theologian to give theological consideration to the present as such, articulating a concept of the eternal as that which is complete all at once in the present without past or future (presence as divine onmipresence) (Teske: 1996, 22). This returns us to the discussion of 'appearances' and the relation of what is visible to the invisible: 'Nothing passes away in the eternal but is present as a whole. No time, however, is present as a whole (*sed totum esse praesens; nullum uero tempus esse prasens*)' (1991, XI, 11, 13).

Aquinas' understanding of time is indebted to Augustine's. For both, the temporal participates in and is made possible by the eternal. That is why Augustine goes on to elaborate, in that famous discussion of time, that in the soul (which participates in the eternity of God): 'The present time of past things is our memory; the present time of present things is our sight; the present time of future things is our expectation' (1991, XI.20). In creation, the present does not exist outside of the future and the past; time is a certain stretching (*distentio*) of the mind as it moves within the mind of the trinitarian God. To have a pure present, to have a discourse on presence, would be to reify something which has no existence in and of itself in the creaturely realm for Augustine.[2] Similarly, for

Aquinas, the sacrament while visibly present to the senses, celebrates the *anamnesis* of Christ's words in the upper room and looks forward to the beatific celebration to come. Its nature, then, as Aquinas states, is a *viaticum*. It is not the mechanism for some arbitrary deliverance of the now as grace. Neither is it a magical commodity, enchanting the material. It is not an object at all in the stasis of some objectively real, the stasis of 'the present time of present things'. The present *qua* present is the glorification of the visible as self-revealing, as in full possession of its own being, as self-validating. As we saw in Chapter 3, this is a fundamental axiom for empiricisms and positivisms. As we will see in Chapter 9 such a view of material existence is implicated in the metaphysics of light. For Augustine and Aquinas, created beings have no access to the purification of the present as such. To enter the daylight forever constitutes beatification. Only God as omnipresent views things in the eternal present. The language of *prae-sens/praesentia* is, therefore, I suggest, the language of idolatry (reifying that which cannot be plucked out of time and fully present to itself) for Aquinas. Hence, when it is employed – to describe Christ's visible and historically specific body and condemn those who cannot 'envisage a spiritual, non-visible' body – it is drawing attention to the way Christ is not present in the eucharist as *praesens* would suggest and, therefore, sacramental presence cannot employ the language of *praesentia*. We will examine this further with Calvin, for both Aquinas and Calvin have Augustine as their explicit source at this very point.[3] Access to things present in themselves is only available to God who knows all things and sees all things as they are eternally. Pretence to immediate access is illusory and evidence of a darkened understanding.

We touch here on a question which is central to understanding analogy and the way the word 'presence' or 'the present' function analogically. It is a question concerning the relationship between the Trinity and creation. We will examine this more fully towards the end of the chapter. For the moment let me suggest that we might understand Aquinas' reluctance to equate the presence of the historical body of Jesus Christ with the presence of Christ in the eucharist, in terms of God as Father not being present in the way God as Son is present and the presence of God as Son differing from the presence of God as Spirit. Karl Barth articulates something of these differences when he describes the triunity of the Godhead in terms of 'modes of being' (Barth: 1975, I, 359).

So when then did 'real presence' become current within Roman Catholic belief? The term does not appear in the Fourth Lateran Council's definition of transubstantiation in 1215. The reference does certainly appear in the decrees of the Council of Trent which, on 11 October 1551, opened its thirteenth session on *de eucharista* with the following discussion: 'On the Real Presence of our Lord Jesus Christ' and the English now does accurately translate the Latin, for the words are *'de reali praesentia'*. Furthermore, the contents of that first chapter pronounces that: 'our Lord Jesus Christ, true God and true man, is truly (*vere*), really (*realiter*) and substantially contained (*contineri*) in the August sacrament of the Holy Eucharist under the appearance (*sub species*) of those sensible things *(rerum sensibilium)*' (Schroeder: 1978, XIII.1). He is 'sacramentally present' *(sacramentaliter praesens)* to us. Now what is remarkable here is not only the employment of *praesens/praesentia* but also the adjective real *(reali/realiter)*. The word is often used to translate Aquinas' treatment of the eucharist, but is not found in Aquinas, who will use *vere*. It was a newly coined word in late medieval Latin. *Realiter* is found earlier, and used consistently by Aquinas as a synonym for *vere*, but *realitas* as thing *(res)*, or fundament *(fundus)* is only found in the discourse of jurisprudence in the early twelfth century. The earliest theological use of *realitas* and *realis* is in the work of Duns Scotus and William of Ockham. In Ockham's various treatises on the eucharist both *realis* and *praesens* are used, but not (as far as I have been able to ascertain) ever together. In a way that remarkably anticipates the language of the Council of Trent, in *De Corpore Christi* Ockham will writes about Christ being 'truly and really available *(vere et realiter continetur)* in the bread and the wine (quoted in Buescher: 1950, 9; see also Ockham: 1930, 166).[4] The dictionary of medieval Latin notes concerning the earliest use of *realis* that 'The precise sense is uncertain'. In other words, the language of the real was not available to either Augustine or Aquinas. In fact, its direct relation to 'thing' *(res, reipsa, reapse* and *revera)*, to the opacity and self-manifestation of an object, would only reaffirm their refusal to employ the language of *praesens/praesentia*. For the word idolises the visible, and such a reification, a commodification, is quite at odds with the understanding of the creation and the sacrament in Augustine and Aquinas. Significantly, it is Scotus and Ockham who also initiate, as part of their dicussions on the intuitive cognition of objects in the world, investigations into presence. *Praesens/praesentialiter* in Ockham, comes to refer to the definite location of things, to a certain rigorous spatialising[5] and to a specific and isolatable temporality, the now, the instant, the immediate.[6] Ockham registers a shift towards the modern obsession of seizing the present; a shift also towards space as location.

It is in following the Scotist and Ockhamist trajectories of scholastic thinking that we first discover the coming together of 'the real' and 'presence'. Commenting on the *Sentences* of Lombard in the early fifteenth century, the French Scotist bishop, Jean de Ripa, employs the terms *realis/realiter* with respect to distinctions in God. This is traditional, but Ripa develops a natural theology in which the distinction of personal properties in the divine essence '*sit recessus a summa ydemptitate reali*' (Ripa: 1957, 207). As Francis Ruello commentates upon this passage: '*la distinction formelle entre l'essence divine et les proprietes personalles peut-on inferer que leur identité réelle soit moindre que si l'on faisait abstraction de cette distinction*' (Ruello: 1992, 690). There are degrees of reality and God is the ultimately real, He is '*immensus causaliter*' (Ripa: 1957, 224) – a univocity of Being relates one to the other. When Ripa then turns to the discourse of presence although Ruello observes that there is a difference between '*la presence divine et la presence de la creature*' (Ruello: 1992, 734) it is a difference of degree. Among created things God '*est praesens huis quos per internam sanctificationem gratificat*' (Ripa: 1957, 223). It is in this sacramental and univocal universe that the words *realiter* and *praesens* come together for the first time. Ripa writes: '*Deus est realiter praesens infinito vacuo ymaginario extra celum*' (Ripa: 1957, 222).

One more link in the story can be made by examining the exposition of the Mass written by the fifteenth-century Ockhamist Gabriel Biel. Biel's role in the transmission of the heritage of medieval scholasticism to the early Reformers gathered around Luther is now well documented (Farthing: 1988). Significantly, the influence of Biel's theology on the Council of Trent had already been noted (Feckes: 1927, 55, 75). He might almost be quoting Ockham, when he writes: '*corpus Christi vere et realiter contineri in sacramento*' (Biel: 1965, 236). But whereas Ripa discusses God's 'real presence' in creation, Biel specifically speaks about a doctrine of the eucharist: '*corpus Christi realiter sit praesens per divinum beneplacitum*' (Biel: 1965, 232). Again, like Ockham, Biel will emphasise the way this presence punctuates the temporal with the eternal now. *Praesens* is concerned with time, the *nunc*, the *instans*, such that the eucharistic conversion is '*non successive sed instantance*' (Biel: 1965, 243, 247). The present is now a commodity to be abstracted, a property to be grasped.

The first English employment of the term 'real presence' is in the 1552 Book of Common Prayer where there is a direct refutation of the Council of Trent's doctrine of transubstantiation with regard to kneeling to receive the eucharist: 'It is not meant thereby, that any adoration is done … unto any real or essential Presence there being of Christ's natural flesh and blood.' Calvin does not employ the terms *realitas* or *realis* – only *vere*/*vrai*. The use of the word '*realis*' may well be at odds with the general sense of the Council of Trent's doctrine of the eucharist. For the language of appearance (*species*) remains, and *species* and *praesens* sit uneasily alongside each other unless the appearance is a veil behind which the presence hovers – which is the Calvinist understanding of the eucharist quite manifestly attacked in the seventh session of the Council of Trent, in canons 7 and 8 and repeated in canon 8 of session XIII. A change or transformation occurs in the elements such that a sacrifice takes place (cf. session XXII) for 'in it (the eucharist) the same God is present (*Deum praesentem in eo adesse*)' (XIII.5). Possibly the Council is adopting the theology of Ripa and the point is being made that only God can be present and/or real, for while all else appears only God is true Being (Ripa's *summa ydemptitate reali*). But since the metaphysics of the eucharist are downplayed – in favour of a pragmatics of liturgical execution – this is not explained and still runs contrary to Augustine and Aquinas' avoidance of the *praesens*/*praesentia* language. The nature of Christ's being with us in the eucharist has nothing to do with either reality or presence in the way these words came to be understood from the early fifteenth century onwards.

Calvin

The reification, and the literalisation, of presence affects understandings of corporeality and community, and orientates desire towards that which is available now. A sense of a haunting, an ectoplasmic aura behind or beyond the material will lead to an emphasis on 'spirituality' at the expense of the body – and eventually the emphasis upon solitary religious experience as the authentic mark of sanctity. The opacification of the natural prepares the metaphysical ground for the secular, demystified world-view (and later the scientific world-view and the capitalist cult of worldly goods). It prepares the ground also for the adoption of eucharistic language and liturgical *accoutrement* by state rulers for state ceremony (Marin: 1989). We are entering the society of the spectacle. Two key phenomena make manifest this new metaphysical trajectory such that the language of *praesens/praesentia* comes to be employed in order to describe the eucharist in early modernity. The first is the increasing attention to the visible display of power and charisma by the ecclesial institution, noted by both Henri de Lubac (1949: 281–88) and Michel de Certeau. Certeau observes: 'This Eucharistic "body" was the "sacrament" of the institution, the visible instituting of what the institution was meant to become' (Certeau: 1992, 83, 1949). He interprets this change as a crisis concerning the illegibility of creation which followed Ockhamist nominalism. Space is too short to follow his argument here. But the increasing emphasis upon the visible – which Augustine relates specifically with the presence of the present – led to the multiplication of fraternities of Corpus Christi, particularly in Italy in the early sixteenth century. Andre Duval notes '*l'affaissement progressif du sens du symbolisme sacramental au profit d'un goût excessif de l'efficacité – la disproportion entre une devotion envahissante à la Présence réelle et une mésestime pratique de la communion – l'obscurcissement, au sein*' (Duval: 1985, 57). Following du Lubac and Certeau, he finds in the late Middles Ages '*la ruin du mystére eucharistique*' (Duval: 1985, 57).

But the most determinative producer of the discourse of presence and the present is the fierce discussions among the various Protestantisms in which the eucharist becomes central for defining new ecclesial identities. Let us begin at the very heart of the matter for Calvin, Book IV of his *Institutes of the Christian Religion*, chapter XVII and section 9 where he details his view on the sacramental elements (bread and wine), sacramental presence and participation. Significantly, Calvin defines his own doctrine of the eucharist in contrast to all the other leading accounts and by rejecting all the interpretations of scripture which vouchsafed these accounts in favour of what his own inquiry 'into his (Christ's) genuine meaning (*de genuino sensu/le sens vrai et naturel*)' (Calvin: 1936, 668 (1,021/372))[7] – which presumably is that interpretation put forward (asserted) by Calvin himself. We will use the English translation, but I wish to examine the Latin text of 1559 (the last text Calvin revised) and the French translation of it which Calvin prepared. By consulting the Latin text it will be more evident how his Latin differs from Aquinas' (and therefore his understanding of the sacramental economy) and by consulting, when necessary, the French text we can gain some insight into how Calvin is using certain Latin terms, terms which he frequently shares with Aquinas. One passage is key:

the breaking of the bread is symbolical (*symbolum esse/le signe exterieur de la substance spirituelle*) and not the substance itself (*non rem ipsam*); yet, this being admitted, from the exhibition of the symbol we may justly infer the exhibition of the substance (*verum hoc poisto, a symboli tamen exhibitione rem ipsam exhiberi, rite colligemus/toutefois nous pourrons inferer de ce que le signe nous est baillé, que la substance nous est aussi livrée en sa vérité*); for unless any one would call God a deceiver, he can never presume to affirm that he sets before us an empty sign (*inane symbolum/un signe vain et vide*). Therefore, if, by the breaking of the bread, the Lord truly represents the participation of his body (*corporis sui participationem vere repraesentat/représente au vrai la participation*), it might not be doubted that he truly presents and communicates it (*quin vere praestet atque exhibeat/qu'il ne la baille en meme temps*). And it must always be the rule with believers, whenever they see the signs (*symbola*) instituted by the Lord, to assure and persuade themselves (*certo cogitant ac sibi persuadeant*). For to what end would the Lord deliver into our hands the symbol of his body except to assure us of a real participation of it (*verum eius participatione*). If it be true that the visible sign is given to us (*praeberi nobis signum visible*) to seal the donation of the invisible substance (*invisiblis rei donationem*) we ought to entertain a confident assurance that in receiving the symbol (*symbolo*) of his body, we at the same time receive the body itself.

(Calvin: 1936, 651 (1,009–10/357–8))

Calvin does not use the term 'real presence' to describe either his own teaching on the eucharist or the Roman doctrine. Neither does he use the word 'real (*realis*)', but consistently uses the term *vere/la verité/la vrai*. He also consistently uses, to define his own position, the verbs to represent (*raepresentere*) and to be present (*praesentere*), although in the passage above we have *praestare* and he will also use *exhibere*. What is evident in this central passage is a series of dislocations (and the word in deliberately chosen for the new spatial order Calvin evidences). The first dislocation is between sign (Calvin uses *symbolum* and *signum* interchangeably, as my polytext shows) and thing (translated substance but in Latin *rei*, not Aquinas' *substantia*).[8] The French maps this onto a second dislocation – between the exteriority of the sign and the spiritual, inner, materiality of the signified. The third dislocation is concomitant with both of these – that between representation (*repraesentat*) and presentation (*praestet* here which translates more accurately as 'to be ready at hand, to be available, to be waiting there', but on other occasions *praesens*). Finally, there is the fourth dislocation between the visible sign and the invisible thing.

Ironically Calvin will defend his teaching with respect to a distinction Augustine draws between the sign (*signum*) and the signified (*res*). But he fails to appreciate the Neo-Platonic logic that relates *signum* to *res* for Augustine, the dialectical relation between symbol and reality. Christ's body defines bread, Christ's blood defines wine, for Augustine. Aquinas, who also appeals to

163

Augustine on exactly this matter, understands the participation of the sign in the signified. Aquinas and Calvin appeal explicitly to an instance when Augustine does employ the language of presence. It is in his commentary on the Book of John, in his exegesis of Jesus' statement to his disciples that the poor you have always with you, but me you do not always have with you (Augustine: 1873, 50:13). Augustine explains that this statement does not contradict the final statement to his disciples in the Gospel that he will be with them always because, in the first saying he is speaking about his present body (*praesentia corporis sui*), the body available to sight for the forty days after his death. This body is no longer with us (*non est hic*), for Christ sits at the right hand of God. Nevertheless his presence remains (*hic est*) for his glorified presence is not withdrawn (*non enim recessit praesentia majestatis*). The way to interpret the Scriptural crux, then, is to draw a distinction between the present body (*praesentiam carnis*) and what is always with us, the presence of Christ's glory (*praesentiam majestatis*). The Church had the carnal body for a matter of days; it retains the presence of Christ by faith (*modo fide tenet, oculis non videt*).

It is significant that, for Calvin, this passage, which never once speaks of the sacraments, when he quotes in it section 22 of chapter XVII of *Institutes*, provides him with Augustine's understanding of the eucharist. Augustine authorises Calvin's discourse concerning presence, and the dualism between carnal and spiritual presence which Calvin's teaching about the eucharist centres upon. Aquinas, on the other hand, does not either read this passage back into an account of transubstantiation, nor make the distinction between the present body and the presence of Christ's glory. The difference between Aquinas and Calvin here relates to their doctrines of creation. Dualisms, for Calvin, deepen the opacification of the natural opening, a space between the subjective believer and the objective fact – bread, wine. He is obsessed with spatial determinants throughout his account of the eucharist. The body of Christ is in heaven, He descends to us, spanning the distance through his Spirit. We are below and every object, whether divine or creaturely, has its own proper location.[9] In the space between the subject and the object, observation, calculation, measurement and evaluation enter. In a move that predates the founding dualism of Descartes' *Meditations*, Calvin also anticipates the theological scepticism that waits in the metaphysical wings of such a dualism: 'for unless any one would call God a deceiver, he can never presume to affirm that he sets before us an empty sign (*inane symbolum/un signe vain et vide*).' Modern secular thinking is founded upon this ability to doubt.

The significance of accepting the possibility of 'an empty sign' – elsewhere described as 'a vain or ineffectual sign (*inani aut vacu signo*)' (Calvin: 1936, 651 (1,010)) – cannot be underestimated. It points to a nominalist metaphysics, but also to a curious tension in Calvin's description of the eucharistic communication. For elsewhere he insists on a form of analogy which suggests a univocity of being: 'We conclude, that our souls are fed by the flesh and blood of Christ, just as our corporeal life is preserved and sustained by bread and wine. For otherwise there would be no suitableness in the analogy of the sign (*Neque enim alitet quadraret analogia signi/Car autrement la similitude la signe ne conviendrait point*)' (Calvin: 1936, 650 (1,009/357)). The Latin verb *quadrare* and the French verb *conviendre* are frequently employed to define the nature of the analogy pertaining between Christ's body and the eucharistic elements: 'There would be no consistency in the signification, if the external sign were not a living image of the truth which is represented by it (*Nec vero significatio aliter quadraret, niri veritas quae illic figuratur, vivam effigiem haberet in externo signo*)' (Calvin: 1936, 656 (1013)). But these formulations structure a mode of analogical reasoning (by proportion) which, in the eighteenth century, became the basis for not only a natural theology, but inductive, *a posteriori* proofs for the existence of God. An onto-theology surfaces here. For the formulation seeks to demonstrate a mathematical relationship:

$$A = A1 \text{ or Christ} = \text{soul}$$
$$B = B1 \text{ or bread} = \text{body}$$

Christ is to the soul what bread is to the body, despite the dualism (indicated by the bar) separating Christ from external sign and the spiritual from the carnal. The Latin *quadrare* implies as much. So that, on the one hand, participation and communication are possible only the basis of a univocity $A = A1$ ('Christ truly becomes one with us') and $B = B1$ (he 'refreshes us by the eating of his flesh and the drinking of his blood').[10] While, on the other, an equivocal relationship holds between A and B ('the breaking of the bread is symbolical and not the substance (*rem*) itself (*le signe exterieur de la substance spirituelle*))' as between A1 and B1 ('the Holy Spirit transcends all our senses'). Calvin's position – which again demonstrates the collapse of analogical reasoning such as Thomas understood it – illustrates a tension Amos Funkenstein traces back to the Scholastics of the late Middle Ages, in which the 'movement towards a minimal construction of God's presence competed with a countermovement that sought a maximal construction in an ever more literal sense' (Funkenstein: 1986, 61).

This tension in Calvin also relates to the same tensions between equivocation and univocity, transcendence and immanence, that we noted in Hobbes and Spinoza. The collapse of analogy opens an aporetic space that the dualisms of modernity, establishing the instrumentality of reasoning, attempt to span. Dualistic thinking substitutes for mediation. It cannot itself mediate, but it establishes a logic that gives a definition to one thing (the objective, the natural, the public) only with respect to its diametrical opposite (the subjective, the cultural, the private). Calvin's analogical reasoning is not analogical at all (where analogy defines the mediation between similarity and difference, univocity and equivocity). This tension manifests itself in Calvin's formula of the participation *of* Christ rather than the participation *in* Christ and the description of the deliverance of Christ into our hands – presumably for either betraying (as in the first such deliverance) or embracing.

This instrumentality of reasoning issues, at times, in logical demonstrations (for all Calvin's insistence upon the sublime and infinite heights of the divine and the limitations of human thinking) against other interpretations of the eucharist. We must not dream, he warns, of such a presence of Christ (*praesentia Christi*) as the ingenuity of the Romanists has invented, because it is irrational 'that Christ annihiliates the substance (*rem*) of bread and conceals himself under its form' (Calvin: 1936, 654–5). And yet he admits that the descent of Christ 'to become nourishment to us' will not 'accord with human reason' (Calvin: 1936, 670). A certain form of reasoning counts here, while another form does not. A politics of the rational is evident, where appeal is being made to fixed and stable identities. In French, Christ's genuine meaning (*de genuino sensu*) is *le sens vrai et naturel*, 'true and natural'(Calvin: 1936, 668 (1,021/372)). What makes this reasoning possible is the presupposition of being able to define the nature of a thing (bread) by the human senses: 'What is the nature of a body? Has it not its proper and certain dimensions? Is it not contained in some particular place, and capable of being felt and seen?' (Calvin: 1936, 671) Things fully present themselves as themselves in definite locations and with definable dimensions. They are identical to themselves and in correspondence with (*propter affinitatem*) the names 'invented by men, which are rather emblems of things absent than tokens of things present (*imagines sunt reum absentium potius quam notae praesentium*)' (Calvin: 1936, 666 (1,020)). Therefore, to take this thing (bread/wine) as a symbol of, as a sign of, rather than simply its own self-authenticating presence, becomes a subjective act of consciousness, judgement-making. The 'seeing' has to be transformed by a 'persuading' and the entertainment of 'a confident assurance'. Christ offers himself, but our faith receives; the Spirit makes the offering effective, but our faith makes the reception of that effectivity possible.[11] Calvin does not proceed in detail here, but a psychology and phenomenology of reception lies waiting for future developments, future examinations of religious experience,[12] and the interiority of self-persuasion and self-assurance sails close to a voluntaristic emphasis in the reception and effectivity of the communication. In turn the subjectivity of judgement-making calls for external legitimation and authentication if the judgement is not to be simply an arbitrary but a true discernment.

But what are the implications of Calvin's discourse for the nature of presence? First, there is a commodification of presence and an investing of it with spiritual value. That which is present is that which is true; it is the authentic as opposed to the simulacrum, the real as opposed to the illusory, the immediate self-manifestation as opposed to the mediated representation. With Calvin there are two forms of this presence: the presence of Christ (which invests the eucharistic elements with a certain ectoplasmic aura, for those who have faith) and there is the concrete presence of things felt and seen. But since a common sense, a pragmatic reasoning, governs overall, then the way is prepared for the investigation of these things which are in and of themselves and for a new natural science. The discourse of presence is inseparable from reference to things (substance no longer bears the connotations of *substantia* but accords

166

rather to substance as in the phrase 'chemical substance'). Secondly, and concomitantly, this discourse of things present and subjects as separated observers, calculators and evaluators of this presence, promotes an atomism which is ontological (the world is composed of distinct entities which are themselves composed of smaller entities) and sociological (society is composed of distinct subjects whose judgement about things may or may not coincide).[13] Thirdly, this discourse of presence necessitates and produces a discourse of absence. Signs are 'invented by men, which are rather emblems of things absent than tokens of things present (*imagines sunt rerum absentium potius quam notae praesentium*)' (Calvin: 1936, 666 (1,020)). Signs can be empty. We have to persuade ourselves that we are not deceived. The discourse of presence and absence is indissociable from the new spatialising in which the distance opened between two points invokes the desire to span, invade, colonise (or, in Calvin's case, to be colonised (by Christ)). This spatialising produces an economy of desire based upon lack, as not-having, not-attaining, not-reaching. The consummation of that desire is the overcoming of that distance, that absence, that lacking, that difference between. Full presence is then the consummation, the teleology of desire. It is the annihilation of difference. Hence Calvin's early foreshadowing of the later concerns with the sublime in his discourse on the infinity of the divine; infinity being the absence of defining boundaries. Full presence borders here on the indifference of utter absence (which is articulated in Spinoza's third knowledge). As Derrida insightfully comments with respect to modernity's onto-theology, 'As soon as being and present are synonymous, to say nothingness and to say time are the same thing' (Derrida: 1982, 51).

Calvin creates a discursive body which both supplements the distance and absence of the longed for presence (of Christ) and yet maintains that distance and absence. It mimics his own doctrine of the eucharist. It keeps everything where it is while articulating, and by articulating embodying, the desire to be elsewhere. It evidences one more turn in the eucharist-as-spectacle that de Lubac and Certeau drew attention to. As Simon Oliver, discussing the nature and culture dualism in Calvin's doctrine of the eucharist emphasises: 'for Calvin, what might be termed the natural and the cultural elements of the Eucharistic liturgy … are mere theatre. … In truth, for Calvin, the Eucharistic liturgy is a virtual reality' (Oliver: 1999, 343). It leads to an understanding of the 'body' – physical, social and ecclesial – as a virtual community, as we saw in the last chapter. We will have more to say about this virtual reality in Chapter 9. For the moment it is important to recognise how the metaphysics of real presence has been produced, and the employment of the phrase *de reali praesentia* by the Council of Trent demonstrates an early *aggiornamento* mentality on behalf of the Catholic church (though one at odds with the traditional understanding of sacramental presence). Being and the present, presence and present are conflated. It is this real presence, dominating modernity, which postmodernism inveighs against.

Žižek

Žižek, is one of a number of poststructuralists who concern themselves with presence while not a believer in 'the fullness of real presence' or what Derrida terms variously phonocentrism or logocentrism. Jean-Luc Nancy, Jean-François Lyotard, Hélène Cixous and Jacques Derrida all have detailed analyses of presence, sometimes with and sometimes without the inverted commas. Žižek views the transparency of things being present to themselves (and the value attached to that transparency), which masks as naturalism, critically. As we saw in the last chapter, as an exegete of Lacan, what Žižek treats is the dialectic between the imaginary and the symbolic. He can only treat, then, the effects of truth. For the imaginary, which sustains desire, furnishes objects for what it lacks. The symbolic structures knowledge through chains of signifiers but a gap always remains between the explicit texture of such knowledge and the underlying levels of fantasy which support it. Furthermore, because for Lacan what desire desires is desire there is a paradoxical movement between wanting to attain the goal of one's desire and needing to forestall that final consummation. The imaginary and the symbolic must not collapse into each other – which would be the result of such a consummation. For then we would lose our very sense of reality (a reality which is always and only a symbolic virtuality). This is the inherent danger of cyberspace for Žižek. Nevertheless, as Žižek states, 'the status of what we have called the "real presence of the Other" is inherently spectral'. The Other, from whom the subject is detached and for whom the subject longs, haunts and organises the dialectic between the imaginary and the symbolic. He calls it 'the obscene ethereal *presence* of the Other' which is ultimately related to the third and most foundational of Lacan's psychic structures, the Real. The Real is the void which desire endless circulates. The Other is a little piece of the Real which bears witness to its 'presence beyond the symbolic order' (Žižek: 1997, 154). But all attempts to symbolize the Real, into which all meaning and virtuality dissolve, are 'so many attempts to avoid the true "end of history", the paradox of an infinity far more suffocating than any actual confinement' (Žižek: 1997, 154). The massive weight of the Real when it irrupts into the symbolic causes trauma, paralysis.

Now in sketching out Žižek's Lacanian concern for 'virtual reality' what I have tried to do is use his own descriptive terms and, in particular, point up the way he employs the language of presence and absence, real presence and the void or emptiness. For although, as I hope is evident, all truth is *méconnaisance* and we are constantly involved in saving the appearances of things, his analysis is made possible and structured by a dualism. Frequently he marks his employment of words like presence, real presence, sense and reality with inverted commas or by placing them in italics. But however much these words are 'under erasure' they are vital to the construction of his own – Lacanian – world-view. Significantly, the negative terms 'infinite', 'void', 'emptiness' are not so marked. For these are Žižek's truth, his negative ontology such that, as we have already observed, he can speak of the possible effect of cyberspace as: 'the phantasic kernel of our being is laid bare in a much more direct way, making us totally vulnerable and helpless' (Žižek: 1997, 164).

A metaphysics of presence, which is constructed on the principle of the univocity of being – Being as the *Grund* – and implicated in the onto-theological project where a divine *ens realissimum* completes (and causes) the great chain of being is, then, both necessary and reversed in Žižek. It is necessary as that against which he (and behind him stands Lacan, as behind Derrida stands Heidegger) posits his critique. But his critique is not an overcoming of such a metaphysics. In one sense it is the reaffirmation of the ineradicability of the metaphysical. For his critique reverses the metaphysics by offering a negative ontology, Nothing as a primary substance, an infinity of differences which renders difference indifferent and this fundamental Indifference as making all things virtual: the Void as the condition for possibility.

What is significant is that the similarity between the logical move made here in Žižek to the move made in onto-theology's account of full presence, renders Žižek (and those, like Žižek, who have poststructural critiques of full presence) vulnerable to the same criticisms launched against these metaphysics. Most particularly, Žižek is vulnerable to the criticism that the body, the material world is devalued. In the onto-theological project because what was given ontological priority and value was total presence, the transparency of the thing's self-existence, the self-grounded presentation of its complete meaning, then that which hindered or divided the subject from this 'presence' was devalued. Representation, signification were screens or even obstacles to be overcome. That which mediated the presence was epiphenomenal, not essential. A dualism was established between consciousness and the given which could only be encountered as an object of consciousness. Mediation – through the mind and then the signs which represented the contents of the mind – was always seen as lacking the full presence, even hindering access to the full presence. Signification operated according to an economy founded upon the endless striving for the presence that was longed for and deferred. Empiricism and positivism, in order to examine and exploit the presence of the given, either put aside questions of the mediation of their knowledge – their use of instruments to collect data, their interpretations of that data, the language used throughout the whole process of collection and evaluation – or treated each form of mediation as transparent channels for their knowledge.

In Žižek, what is prior is the negative version of full presence, the Void. That is the Real. What constitutes our knowledge is symbolic and virtual. And the same economy of lack, now a libidinal economy, governs the symbolic and the virtual – albeit with the added complexity that we cannot have what we desire because that would dissolve us and the virtual meaningfulness of our world entirely. The body disappears to give attention to the symptom and the phallus (which is not the penis) as the governor of desire.

I could repeat this analysis and suggest very similar results with respect to Derrida's thinking on *différance* (Derrida: 1982) or Jean-Luc Nancy's examination of *corpus* (Nancy: 1994) or Jean-François Lyotard's accounts of the sublime and the unpresentable (Lyotard: 1991, 1994). But what I wish to demonstrate by the genealogy of presence we have undertaken is that sacramental presence is not a mode of the metaphysics of presence (and absence). And hence it cannot be approached or understood in terms of this metaphysics or its crossing. We cannot proceed to understand the theological exchange within the eucharist via phenomenologies either Husserlian (Sokolowski: 1993) or Heideggerian (Marion: 1991a and Chauvet: 1995). Or, more accurately, if we do so proceed, we are framing theological accounts of what it is to be something, what it is to understand creation as governed by Christ and sustained by the Godhead, by metaphysical accounts which have reified and commodified presence and the present. In this reification they have perpetuated various atomisms (ontological, material, social) that open up nihilistic spaces, and function within various dualistic matrices which are ultimately gnostic. All of which we have seen embryonically there in the early modern (Calvin), and fully developed in the postmodern (Žižek), discourses on presence.

Eucharistic presence

Let us return to that question I posed at the beginning. What is the relationship between the present tense and presence? If eucharistic presence is not what is deemed presence in modernity how does it differ? Augustine's understanding of time is essential here: the present is not a distinct entity. There is no isolatable moment, no now that can be calculated and infinitesimally divided. We cannot experience the present as such. In modernity time is an endless series of distinctive nows, nows which because they are valued as such have to be grasped as such in order to get the most out of them. Participation is measured by and a mode of stimulation. To enjoy the instant is to experience the thrill, the buzz of being there. Orgasm, *jouissance*, becomes the measure of the moment which devalues eros. Since the now is commodified, and likewise access to the experience of the now, then getting the most out of what is becomes one of the metaphysical bases of consumer greed and one of the rationales for the erotification of consumer culture. And the endless deferment of the consummating now, articulated by so many poststructural thinkers, only fetishises that now even more. In fact the deferment itself can be invested with significance – the prolongation of desire endlessly produces it. Deferment of the now becomes itself part of a libidinal economy, part of the seduction. With poststructuralism, the now, the immediate becomes the unpresentable experience of the sublime, the final ecstasy of oblivion (the end of desiring) that awaits the other side of the endless chains of signifiers: the immediate beyond the frustrations and laws of mediation. Experiences of this now are revelatory 'events' – as Heidegger and more recently Lyotard detail them (Heidegger: 1972; Lyotard: 1991) – or ruptures – as Certeau describes them (Certeau: 1987, 37–45).

The present is not understood in this way in the tradition's accounts of the eucharist. The present is not a discrete and isolatable entity, as Augustine reminds us. If it is taken as such it becomes an idol, a pleasuring which is self-aggrandising and, therefore, self-absolving from the community of those who orientate their lives to each other and to God. Such possession of the present would be, for Augustine, a violation of time, a violence with respect to time, that would pitch the one who seizes the day outside the liturgical practice which engages the Church. For the eucharist participates in a temporal plenitude that gathers up and rehearses the past, while drawing upon the futural expectations and significations of the act in the present. In the same way as the Last Supper is both an enactment of the Passover Meal and rehearsal for the sacrifice on Calvary; so the eucharist is both an enactment of the Last Supper (and therefore a figuring of the Passover), a participation in the atoning sacrifice of Calvary, and a foretaste of the heavenly banquet at the eschatological wedding. In the fracture liturgy, for example, the congregational response is a reiteration of a Pauline formula from his first letter to the Corinthians and an affirmation of a oneness with the those who have gone, those who are and those who are to come. It is in this way that the activity participates in the eternal, for it belongs both to all times and to no one time. Hence the presence cannot be fixed into the present, a present which lies on the other side of representation. The eucharistic activity is implicated in various modes of figuration (of the past and of the future); its understanding of presence is always manifold and excessive to the present and sanctifies the various representations it is necessarily involved in because they are also, simultaneously, various embodiments. There is no space here for the reification, fetishisation, dualisms, atomisms and absences (the lacks, the deferments, the mournings and the arbitrary violences) which characterise modernity's (and postmodernity's) preoccupations with seizing the present as such.

We now have to relate the answer to this question back to those other three inseparable aspects of the fracture liturgy: a participation which disseminates; the constitution of the community of the 'we' as many and one; and the transgression by the 'we' of the institutional structures in which it foregathers. As we noted these aspects involve various complexities inextricable from the temporal complexity we have so far foregrounded: complexities of corporeality, space and representation.

Participation

The doctrine of participation, which is a doctrine of the Spirit, cannot be separated from a doctrine of time and a theology (which is also an anthropology) of desire. It is because the present participates in the eternal, in the way I pointed to above, that we who are time-bound, situated in specific temporalities or textualities of time, participate also in the eternal. But our participation is not simply formal. It is personal. For the eternal is not the endlessness of the infinite

– Hegel's bad infinite as the linear infinite (Hegel: 1991, 54). The infinite is the endless givenness of God in love. We are constituted as those who desire the freedom, goodness and beauty of being loved and loving. Our inclination to crave the other, what Augustine would term our fundamental *appetitus*, is an image of the divine appetite in which the Father craves the Son and the Son the Father, and both the Spirit who maintains the eternal craving open with respect to the world God created out of this excess of loving. We are, then, persons of desire. This is the image of God in whom we were created and we are constituted as persons through the operations of this desire (as Hegel saw). Our desire for God is constituted by God's desire for us such that redemption, which is our being transformed into the image of God, is an economy of desire. Our experience of time is inseparable from our desiring,[14] inseparable also from our longing to understand ourselves and our world.

Desire issues from difference; difference not satisfied in its own differential. There are three modes of difference such that desire is written into the nature of all that is. There is theological difference with respect to the persons of the Trinity. There is ontological difference with respect to the *diastema* which separates the uncreated God from creation. There is sexual difference with respect to the webs of attraction that draw us into one another such that one body is mapped onto several others. Difference can only be difference because it stands *in relation to* that which is other: which means that God is not wholly other (*pace* Barth) and Christian otherness cannot be transcendentalised as such (*pace* Levinas and Derrida). The kenosis of incarnation (and its possibility from the foundation of the world in what Balthasar terms God's *Urkenosis*) entails that otherness is always in relation. Difference extolled *as* difference, difference reified perpetuates atomism which can only produce indifference. Difference to be constituted and maintained *as* difference requires an analogical relation. It is that relation which we need to elucidate.

Two distinctions need to be made. First, we have seen already that modernity's subject of desire is implicated in an economy of lack. The lack arises because desire is object or goal orientated. I desire something or to be somewhere. In fact, the object is reified in the desirous look: the look which turns it into that which can feed and pleasure the one who looks. This would be what Augustine, with his understanding of the present for itself as feast for the immediate senses, terms *cupiditas*, and Jean-Luc Marion has examined recently in terms of idolatry (Marion: 1991a). It is a craving which lusts. It wants to possess, to put an end to the lack by subsuming that which is other (totally other in this economy). To employ Martin Buber's formula: this desire constitutes the I–It relation (Buber: 1958; see also Rosenzweig's comments). It is in this way that the libidinal economy is indissociable from consumerism, the exchange of 'goods' (the word is significant). Now the Christian economy of desire cannot do without locations for that which it finds desirable, that which it discerns as good, beautiful and true. The Christian as a subject of desire is attracted by that which is encountered. He or she responds in that attraction, which always has an embodied specificity. Christians desire this and that, him or her. That is why to desire or love God is not a divesting of the world of significance, to transcend the world in some pure *apatheia*. Rather to desire or love God is to invest the world with significance, a significance which deepens the mysterious presence of things. And so, in the Christian economy of desire, the object of desire can never be the terminus of desire. The object can never be made an end in itself without betraying the true nature of the thing (and the true nature of one's attraction to it). For the participation desire circulates within is far greater than any one location. The economy of desire is one of exceeding the object, exceeding the lack installed by the I–want which the object creates. As such, the object of desire takes on a certain density of significance, a rich materiality that cannot be exhausted, cannot be possessed. To employ again an Augustinian distinction, the object desired is to be enjoyed as gifted; rather than simply used, exploited, consumed. Of course, there is, in this enjoyment consumption and use. Enjoyment is not dualistically opposed to use, or lack dualistically opposed to excess. But neither lack nor use governs the operation of desire, such that desire finds its satisfaction in attaining. What is attained both satisfies and deepens the longing; what is used is both enjoyed and plunges joy into a more sublime wonder. Such that attainment and enjoyment require and produce a certain humility before that which is attractive, a certain surrender to the depth of its divine suggestiveness. There is always one more facet of the thing not revealed, always some mystery pertaining to any object that demonstrates how it exceeds in its significance that which it merely presents to the immediate senses. Objects do not exist in the seizable present; they exist in their contingency in a present that issues from an aorist and issues into an optative tense. Each object is located in a network of relation, invested both with past association and future potential. As Michel Serres puts it – and we will be exploring his work in a later chapter – objects are not inert (Serres: 1993). They are caught up in the motion and the communication of all things through the Spirit of Christ.

Secondly, we have also seen the atomistic communities that issue from economies of desire which define and produce lack: the contractual, the imaginary, and the virtual communities. And I have emphasised how Christian desire does not operate according to lack, exceeds the I–want lack installs. I desire not because I lack the other, but because the other is closer to me than I am to myself (and makes me aware that what I lack is, in part, myself). It is this logic which we need to elucidate; it is the logic of Paul's statement 'My life is hidden with Christ in God'. Another way of putting this – which relates back directly to Chapter 4 on the displaced body of Christ – is that our bodies occupy a space in Christ's body. Our desire is to understand and be conformed to that which we know we are, and yet also – because we have not the mind of Christ – know what we are not. We are not Christ-like; our redemption is the formation of that Christ-likeness which is ours truly insofar as we occupy this place *en Christoi*. The desire is orientated to that which exceeds what we think we know about ourselves and the world we live in. It is not orientated to what is absent, but to what is far too present; and because it is so present demands we take account of the yearnings it calls forth within us.

These two aspects of desire constitute our participation in the circle of divine trinitarian love; a love which cannot be limited by our words for it: *agape/eros* or *caritas/amor*. For where desire cannot be solely determined by object or goal, to what extent can we know whether the object or goal of our love (which defines whether it is *caritas* or *cupiditas*) is the object or goal itself or the sheer giftedness of that object in Christ? This is why the operation of love is always also *both and simultaneously* the operation of faith and the operation of hope. Most of the time Christians do not know, Christian believe and hope. Augustine is never consistent in his vocabulary of desire, which has frequently called forth criticism. There is a selfless giving love and there is a proper self-loving (*amor sui* as opposed to *superbia*). As such we can describe trinitarian loving as both self-transcending and self-referring to the extent that we can use the language of persons with respect to this mystery. In the same way, our loving as it participates within God's loving is always reaching beyond and forgetting itself, but, in that very activity, loving itself most truly. As with the Prodigal Son, the coming to oneself is also a movement towards the others one has separated oneself from in one's voluptuous greed for the world's 'goods'.

This twofold loving is the logic of the fracture: both celebrating the intimacy of oneness and taking that celebration out into the world: 'we *break* this bread to *share*'. In the breaking, the fracturing, the extension beyond a concern with one's own wholeness, is a sharing that will constitute our own true wholeness. To put this another way, the labour of love and the formation of self in love require the diremption of self in the formation of others. Hegel saw this. The one is also the many. This leads us directly to the constitution of that 'we'.

The pluralised body

At the opening of his own theological anthropology, Karl Barth wrote that the internal covenantal basis in creation issues from the truth that 'Man is no longer single but a couple' (Barth: 1958, III.1, 308). We will say more about this in the next chapter. The ego does not exist in and for itself – the goal of self-sufficiency taught by the Stoics, which has become both the fundamental axiom of modern epistemologies, liberal ethics, and Nietzsche's heroic *Übermensch*, is the utter denial and destruction of selfhood as it is theologically understood. As such social atomism is sinfulness. Hegel again: 'To be evil means in an abstract sense to isolate myself' (Hegel: 1962, 53). The privatisation of the self constitutes a turning back of creation to the chaos, the nothing from which God called it forth. It is the ultimate denial of creator and creation, and therefore the analogical world-view. The cult of celebrity, the production of personalities, the exaltation of the customised, the designer labelled – are not simply trading in illusions, trafficking in simulacra, they promote that which is evil. For they deprive this world's goods of their goodness; they negate and corrode the orders of creation. Utterly opposed to this atomism – which Augustine would see as founded upon fear, the fear of losing, of dispossession – is the I as We, the identity of the One as the Many. This is not the negation of selfhood or proper self-love. Levinas, critically developing Buber's I and Thou formula into I-as-hostage-to-Thou, as responsible for, responsive to, accusative in the face of the other (*autre* as well as *autrui*), puts the I always under erasure. As accusative – 'Here I am' – it is infinitely accused. The I is continually martyred, continually exiled from itself towards the totally other. But this is the other side of liberalism's optimism in moral autonomy; the critical reaction to the philosophy of humanism with its belief that all things can be resolved through dialogue. As such this reactive ethics works within and perpetuates the same logic (which is what we discovered with respect to the postmodern critique of presence). It does not announce an alternative logic of relations, for it demands a certain violence, even though it is the opposing violence of liberalism's autonomy. If humanism's self is ripped from social dependence, asserting its own rights and freedoms (and the exercise of its rights as the exercise of its freedoms), contracting out its own obligations to do that which authenticates itself as independent and sole author of its own destiny, then Levinas' denial of that simply asserts the priority of *ipseity* and *illeity*, the accusative and being accused for the other, which calls for a violence towards the self in its subjection to the absolutely other. The absolute authority of the I is exchanged for the absolute authority of the other: the same logic holds for both positions. And being infinitely responsible, abstractly responsible, as Hegel understood, is without content. I freeze before the endless possibilities for putting that responsibility into action, knowing that by being responsible here, for this, I am not able to be responsible there, with respect to that. Ethical action, as such, becomes arbitrary because its universalism overrides the particularity of where I am and the bodies I am *more* responsible for because of where I am.

The logic of the eucharistic relation in which the one is the many, the I as the We, refuses both the liberal ethical and the reactive ethical accounts of personhood. The love of the neighbour is correlative to the love of oneself. The desire for the neighbour's good is correlative to the desire for the personal good. And God is the true correlative of both desire and the good. The I is utterly singular. Called forth to be and to become in a specific time and in a specific social context, the narratives of that I are its own (though no one I can grasp anything but a minuscule number of them). The person is called forth to be and to become as a specific embodiment, a specific physiology, a specific genotype of a specific set of genotypes – given to the world in this locale. But the I is utterly dependent, what Schleiermacher rightly understood as absolutely dependent (for Augustine's account of this state see *De Genesi ad litteram* VIII.vi.12). The I does not belong to itself. Hence either the subjection of others to one's will or the assertion of independence are both violences again the divine order, both are expressions of the *libido dominandi*. Just as the present cannot exist in and of itself, but only in relation to memory and expectation, so the I is never the pronoun of an active continuous verb. In being utterly dependent it is always the pronoun of a deponent verb: moving between the self-assertive activity of modernity's ego[15] and the passivity more passive than the passive tense of Levinas' reaction to that egoity. The I is born *in relation to* and that is intrinsic to its being made *in the image of*, for God is also always and only in relation to. The I is given to the We for its own redemption (and perfection). Just as the I is given to the distended-present for time's redemption (and perfection); woven into the textualities and specificities of time as part of the We which celebrates its oneness in Christ as it also disperses, to expand the nature of the We-ness.

As one body mapped onto the sacramental and ecclesial body, located in and as the body of Christ, this 'expansion' is not concomitant with colonialism. Christian imperialism belongs to the perpetration of violence. We will look more at this in the final chapter. The expansion is only possible because, in creation, the space was opened *en Christoi* – and all other space is simulacra or, to use a distinction made by Certeau, space (*espace*) becomes rationalised as place (*lieu*). The eucharistic We is a pluralised and pluralising body that overspills defined places, opening up another space. It is at this point that, in our examination of the We, that we must discuss the way the fracturing and sending out of that We, transgresses institutional bodies that assist in defining, but can never confine, the body of Christ.

The body of Christ and the institutional churches

Institutions produce what, after Certeau, we can term 'rational utopias'. This is a place produced by the closed system, what Certeau will describe as 'a bubble of panoptic and classifying power, a module of imprisonment that makes possible production of an order' (Certeau: 1984, 111). It is the space of the voyeur, the observer, for whom only what is seen is what is valued, and what is seen is valued by locating it in a certain specified place, with its specified identity. We observed this construal of space operating in Calvin's understanding of both the eucharist and trinitarian operations. Descartes clarifies the notion of such space as the extension of what is – a body filled with other bodies which constitutes and produces its extension. Space is isomorphic with place in such a notion, insofar as space is made up of the sum of all places. Each place is composed, in turn, of discrete objects whose predicates (and therefore identities) can be detailed, calculated. What we observe in this new mathematical analysis of time, space and materiality is the overthrow of the analogical world in favour of the digital. Analyses of space now attend to atemporal structures and the calculation of this sum of all places and its properties.

There are certain presuppositions that such space requires for its rational examination. I will point to three which Certeau himself elucidates and a fourth as examined by Certeau's contemporary Henri Lefebvre. First, that all that is is visible; that there is nothing hidden, occult or mysterious. All things exist insofar as their properties are perceptible and an account can be made of them; as such, all things are inert. Again we revisit a non-mythical form of realised eschatology that returns us to our analysis of the present as fully present above. Secondly, and concomitant with this reification and immediacy of the thing, as Lefebvre tells us: 'The illusion of transparency goes hand in hand with a view of space as innocent, as free of traps or secret places' (Lefebvre: 1991, 28). Spatiality, like the materiality which composes it, is viewed in terms of light and intelligibility. We will see how this construal becomes fundamental for the virtual realities of cyberspace in the final chapter. Thirdly, and concomitant with the importance given to the eye in assumptions one and two, the one who sees is an autonomous unit, a conscious-ness, a *cogito*, who in thinking makes/passes judgement. Fourthly, that this space (now termed the world) is external to and independent of that judging *cogito* (or the mind), such that the mind acts within it not upon it and, primarily, is passively responsive to what is out there. Spatiality, here, is mapped in accordance with the dualism of object/subject – extendible to other dualisms such as body/soul, public/private, external/internal. As Lefebvre writes, 'the modernist trio, triad or trinity (is) readability–visibility–intelligibility' (Lefebvre: 1991, 96).

The churches as institutions produce such a spatiality and reproduce the metaphysics of such a spatiality; as all institutions do. This is not in itself a bad thing. It is a necessary thing. Only as institutions can they offer places for the organisation of a different kind of space, a liturgical space. In this liturgical space, activities are performed within a sacred world-view, and what is done is not an end in itself (a labour, the expenditure of a calculable energy for a definite purpose), but a creative act, expressing, being, a gift to what is other and divine. Liturgical activity opens up spatial possibilities, spatial complexities. Space, while not separating itself from and dualistically opposing place, is no longer co-extensive with it; it is excessive to location. In fact, as Certeau himself states: 'space (here) is a practised place' (Certeau: 1984, 117), and this place escapes all rationalist topologies.

Certeau examines the constitution of this second form of space in terms of textuality. Here spatial complexities are implicated in representational complex-ity. Practices are series of gestures involved in complex exchanges of signs. He calls this the 'space of operations', and to describe its economics he employs various terms like tactics, delinquency, wandering, and transgression. He examines this space of operations in two ways, each of which radically critiques those four suppositions for the rational, utopic space: the visibility and coherence of all that is; the unity of the subject; the objective facticity of the world. By looking at the practices of everyday, urban existence, he sketches an archaeology of spatial operations. By reading the writings of ethnographers and mystics, the paintings of Bosch, the accounts of demonic possession, he sketches a genealogy in which the space of an itinerary becomes the geographer's map – a genealogy, then, of spatial colonisation. A dialectic is established between rational and transgressional spacing, giving rise to a hybrid or hetero-spatiality.

Certeau wishes to invest this complex form of spatiality[16] evident in texts taken from the early dawn of modernity, with a contemporary significance and relevance. He wishes to advocate a relearning of this living in which 'Places are exceeded, passed, lost behind' (Certeau: 1992, 299), this walking within the contemporary city, which eludes the institutions of meaning. Like the monks Daniel and Piteroum, in the stories which open *The Mystic Fable*, this seems to be Certeau's theological task: 'to trace, in the symbolic institutions, an otherness already known to the crowd and that they are always "forgetting" ' (Certeau: 1992, 43). Having elucidated the nature of this hetero-spacing – which makes all of us mystics for Certeau, if, as he enjoins, to be a mystic is to be unable to stop walking – we can then access another spiritual spacing, a eucharistic spacing which operates as the possibility for space *as such*.

This is a line of analysis developing out of Certeau and, to some extent, against the grain of his thinking. For the world as fully present to itself – the realised eschatology of the rational utopia – is broken up by Certeau's profound analysis of loss, mourning and desire. With respect to our analysis of the churches – the proclaimed oneness of the body of Christ in which we share is fragmented into various institutional organisations. The 'One may no longer be found', as Certeau writes, in the opening pages of *The Mystic Fable*, but the kenotic desire which follows from this nevertheless 'is obviously a part of the long history of that *One*' (Certeau: 1992, 1–2). But the question then emerges, what makes possible this absence which provokes desire and peregrinage? What space, place, body (they are all related) is presupposed in order that there can be practices of everyday life at all? There is an 'elsewhere', there is another country which 'remains our own, but we are separated from it' (Certeau: 1992, 2). It is the manner in which Certeau alludes to that elsewhere – which circumscribes the nature of that other place – that is significant for our present analysis. We will discover there the final spiritual space and recognise it as none other than the eucharistic site.

All the stories of each I, that produce each sense of persons with respect to the We, organise spaces – self-consciously so in the internal geographies of St Teresa's *Interior Castle* or St John of the Cross' *Ascent of Mount Carmel*. What Certeau describes is the way in which the organisation of these spaces opens alternative spaces in historical systems of fact. They do so in two distinctive and deviant ways. Deviant, that is, in relation to the four suppositions of the 'rational utopia'. First, the We practises a manner of speaking from elsewhere – thus deconstructing the autonomy of the I and the priority of its judgements. Persons are produced, just as the soul is formed, disciplined or perfected, through welcoming and following the voice of the other. In various activities (liturgical acts of confession and acts of prayer which invest the everyday acts of writing oneself onto the social body with theological significance), these subjects reveal themselves as partly spoken from elsewhere. The 'I' becomes a shifter in a 'topography of pronouns', becomes a 'siteless site' (Certeau: 1986, 90). So judgements are not made easily, for the truth of what is seen has to be given to the subject, not simply read off from what is. Secondly, these activities make visible a spatiality – akin to the mansions, rooms and gates of Teresa's internalised Crusader castle[17] – which is invisible: thus subverting modernity's idolisation of presence as appearance. In this way the Word takes on a body; that which calls becomes enfleshed in the practices of living and the narratives of each one's itinerary. An alternative spacing is established in relation to a specific historical and cultural context. Certeau situates the work of Teresa and John of the Cross within a social context that had impoverished their aristocratic positions; within a church which was more concerned with the visibility of its powers than its spiritual truth; within a symbolic system 'which disintegrates at the end of the Middle Ages' (Certeau: 1992, 91).

But it is exactly at this point that we need to proceed more carefully with Certeau. What he terms his heterological spacing announces an aporetics, but what is this produced and productive alterity which forever stands in/as the penumbra? Ricoeur, at the conclusion of *Oneself as Another* maps out the problem (in a discussion of alterity in Levinas): is this other another person, or my ancestors for whom there is no representation and to whom I am so profoundly indebted, or God or an empty space (Ricoeur: 1992, 355). Certeau himself asks: 'Is this space divine or Nietzschean?' (Certeau: 1992, 175).

The first spacing, Certeau's 'rational utopia' perceived the world univocally: things were as they were named, and there was no reminder or mystery about what he elsewhere calls 'the positivities of history' (Certeau: 1992, 105). This is the world of institutional bodies like churches, bodies we pass in and out of. The eucharist, we recall, collects to disperse within such institutional bodies. The alternative spacing announces that the We as the interdependence and interrelationship of so many self-narratives, so many self-practices open up the rational place to produce a social space, an aporia within organised places. But Certeau goes on to suggest – though he does not develop his thinking here and therefore leaves himself open to the charge of nihilism – that the eucharist, the sacramental space offers a notion of body beyond the institutional and social which analogically relates the two. Conscious of Henri du Lubac's work *L'Euchariste*, he writes that before the thirteenth century there was that linear spatiality in which the Church as eucharist, God's Word in the world, produced 'the 'liturgical' combination of a visible community or people (*laos*) and a secret action (*ergon*) or mystery' (Certeau: 1992, 83). The hidden, the spiritual, the mystical was both other and yet part of the world. An analogical relationship pertained. The community participated in this alterity, and, as such, the practices of this community were all liturgical. Certeau writes: 'The fact is, the linear series extending from the apostolic origins (H) to the present Church (C) is sustained in its entirety by the sacrament (S), conceived as a unique and everywhere instituting operation (the "mystery"), linking the *kairos* to its progressive manifestation. Distinct time (H and C) are united by the same invisible "action". This is the paradigm of "the tradition" ' (Certeau: 1992, 83).

We can examine this another way. Complicit with the production of any spatiality is the production of a body. In the sacramental world-view, physical bodies, social bodies, ecclesial bodies, heavenly bodies, textual bodies, and the body of Christ all cohere palimpsestically. They do this because each of these bodies has permeable boundaries, fluid boundaries. This is the analogical world-view we have been sketching throughout Chapters 3, 4 and this one. As Certeau writes about the medieval copyist, distinguishing him from the Renaissance translator (who was also printer and typesetter): 'the copyist transformed his body into the spoken word of the other; he imitated and incarnated the text into a liturgy of reproduction. Simultaneously, he gave his body to the verb (*'verbum caro factum est'*) and made the verb into his own body (*'hoc est corpus meum'*) in a process of assimilation that eliminated differences, to make for the sacrament of the copy' (Certeau: 1992, 119).

Certeau concludes that the continuity of that tradition came to an end with the thirteenth century. But, first, Certeau's conclusion may be wrong. We may again, with the collapse of belief in rationally organised spaces that we traced in Chapter 2, be opening a space in which the tradition can once more be heard. That which brought about the changes from the thirteenth century onwards, are now being challenged; modernity is closing and new concepts of time, space and materiality are emerging. Secondly, this conclusion would not invalidate Certeau's observations with respect to the possibility of employing them to develop a theological account of the way the one body of the We, made up as it is of so many singular bodies, each, according to its desire, extended into and operating within various social and political bodies, produces a space which is excessive to those institutional ecclesial places. The Church is the body of Christ, but 'sustained in its entirety by the sacrament (S), conceived as a unique and everywhere instituting operation (the "mystery"), linking the *kairos* to its progressive manifestation' it cannot be fixed, God cannot be housed. That would be the greatest commodification of them all, the danger of which is evident in the *'reali praesentia'* of the Council of Trent. The institutional churches are necessary, but they are not ends in themselves; they are constantly transgressed by a community of desire, an erotic community, a spiritual activity. Within these places, organised by them, desire for God and God's desire for us opens a liturgical space which distends over all the other bodies which participate in and produce it. The body of Christ desiring its consummation opens itself to what is outside the institutional Church; offers itself to perform in fields of activity far from chancels and cloisters. In doing this certain risks are taken and certain fears can emerge within those who represent the institution. As Mary Douglas has noted with respect to the permeable boundaries of the body: 'Why should bodily margins be thought to be specifically invested with power and danger' (Douglas: 1966, 121)? But permeability being the nature of Christian embodiment (embodiment as such if Butler is to be believed (Butler: 1990, 79–141)) then the institutions of the body of Christ are serving a purpose much greater than their own survival. This is where the tensions arise. The structure institutions offer is simultaneously constraining and enabling. In this lies their potential for alienation, on the one hand, and reification, on the other (Giddens: 1984, 24–6). Alienating *and* reified, the institution of the Church becomes a mausoleum, drawing its power to attract more from the heritage industry and urban tourism.[18] The body of Christ lives on, beyond its precincts: each member of the eucharistic We writing God's name elsewhere in the world – redeeming it through desire. It is the erotics of that redemption that we must go on to sketch.

7

THE EROTICS OF REDEMPTION

Of course, the biological family is ubiquitous in human society. But what confers upon kinship its socio-cultural characters is not what it retains from nature, but, rather, the essential way in which it diverges from nature. A kinship system does not consist in the objective ties of descent or consanguinity between individuals. It exists only in human consciousness; it is an arbitrary system of representations, not the spontaneous development of a real situation. … [W]e are dealing strictly with symbolism. And although it may be legitimate or even inevitable to fall back upon a naturalistic interpretation in order to understand the emergence of symbolic thinking, once the latter is given, the nature of the explanation must change as radically as the newly appeared phenomenon differs from those which have preceded and prepared it.

(Lévi-Strauss: 1967, 50–1)

A critical reflection upon the last chapter might well have raised a significant question: why does the liturgical exchange in/of the fraction become the privileged site for making visible the Church as the erotic community, rather than the symbolics of the marriage service. I would suggest there are, for this project, two key answers to that question. First, that question can be answered through the attention in the eucharist to the breaking, exchange, absorption and dismissal of the body of Christ. It is the body of Christ, as I indicated both in Chapter 3 and 4, which governs a theological reading of bodies *per se*. The eucharist becomes then, as Aquinas recognised, the sacrament governing the nature of all the other sacraments – including the sacrament of marriage. Further the fraction is the liturgical hinge between the consecration and the distribution which both articulates and constitutes the nature of the community. It is, I argue, erotic in its movement from breaking to union to dispersal. Second, that question is answered through what I wish to present in this chapter in elaborating the erotics of redemption. That is (1) a critique of the marriage liturgy, and the place, politics and ideology of such heterosexism within Christian dogmatic thinking and ecclesial practice; and (2) the refiguring of a much broader Christian erotic relationality. In brief, the character of marriage at the moment, I

182

will argue, privileges one form of relationship over another, constructs gender along the lines of biological, reproductive difference, and reinforces a social policy that needs to be challenged and transformed. The politics of the heterosexual family are predicated upon an unreflective biosociality which renders unnatural (if not even criminal) homosexuality and, what is possibly worse, reifies two models of sexual orientation within which all human being is situated. I will argue that kinship is a symbolic, not a natural, arrangement, and that there are many genders as there are performances of being sexed. Marriage, as the Church conceives and practices it today, sacramentalises an exclusive relationship between two positions, one biologically male and the other female. I argue for the need for a redemption from such an erotics and outline the economy such a redemption might take.

Sacred sex

The association of the sacred and the sexual has a history that dissolves into the mythic and primeval. The association issues from a close relationship between sexual and religious ecstasy such that the divine and the human can become conflated. A univocal libidinal economy is announced. Bataille examines and endorses such a perspective in his classic *Eroticism*: 'communication is always possible between sensuality and mysticism, obedient as they are to the same motive force' (Bataille: 1987, 284). But the erotic economy as it operates in Christianity does not sketch a natural theology in which human eros and divine pneuma are identified. It does not endorse such univocalism. On the other hand, the development of agape and eros as two conceptually distinct categories by Anders Nygren and, later, Karl Barth, creates a dualism, an equivocal order. And a Christianity which takes incarnation seriously cannot accept equivocation either. When Nygren sets out to examine the 'problem' of agape and eros and the way in which, in the course of history, they have become 'thoroughly bound up and interwoven with one another', his purpose is to demonstrate how they are 'two fundamentally opposed motifs' (Nygren: 1953, 30). Eros is described in the scholastic terms of *amor concupiscentiae* and *amor amicitiae*, acquisitive love or the love of friends but, in contrast 'Measured by the standard of Divine love ... human love is not love at all in a deeper sense, but only a form of natural self-love, which extends its scope to embrace also benefactors of the self' (Nygren: 1953, 96–7). As such, despite recognising that love of neighbour cannot be isolated from love of God without a certain perversion (Nygren: 1953, 97), he nevertheless abjures all construals of the significance of self-love (Nygren: 1953, 100–1). In this way he ontologises eros and agape as two 'entirely separate spiritual worlds' (Nygren: 1953, 31). These are the worlds of Plato and St Paul, the worlds of the natural and the theological. The first of which, in both cases, is a domain of deception. Mediation, co-operation, becomes impossible and so Christology becomes a profound paradox. Barth only modifies this dualistic ontology – finding space for sexual love or 'sanctified eros' in marriage (Barth:

1961, III.4, 222). Here Barth endorses a 'true *eros*' and a 'genuine *eros*' in which there is self-giving and legitimate desire (Barth: 1961, III.4, 219). Nevertheless, in a love which is distinct from mere desire, sympathy and affection, Christian lovers are 'united not merely in *eros* but also and primarily in *agape*, in the Lord and in the community of His brethren' (Barth: 1961, III.4, 223). *Eros* is policed and disciplined by marriage and the community of His brethren, and the implication is that the Church itself is not an erotic, but quite emphatically an agapaic, community.

Now certainly, Nygren and Barth are right to observe that eros is never mentioned in the New Testament. And agape as a noun is more frequently found in the epistles of St Paul than anywhere else. Furthermore, this studied avoidance of the language of eros probably has something to do with Eastern mystery cults in which sexuality and religion danced seductively about each other. But there is some research to suggest that the particular form in which the sensual and the spiritual are associated with death in Western culture (as is most certainly the case with Bataille) arises only in early modernity: 'Notoriously, though, the Renaissance was also when eros and thanatos began to be associated in new and disturbing ways' (Dollimore: 1998, 62). Eros begins a certain semantic journey towards its current degraded form – the form most evident in the Private Shops examined in Chapter 5. Nygren and Barth seem to view the operation of these words eros and agape as atemporal, as outside cultural variation and transmission. They name two transhistorical economies of love. But this is not so. The medicalisation and the psychologising of sex in early modernity onwards takes us on a journey through Bernini's statue of Saint Teresa to Lacan' s employment of it as trope for female *jouissance* (Lacan: 1982, 147). Love, sex and agape (along with friendship, intimacy and desire) are culturally and historically specific and not necessarily dimorphic.

This being so, my own argument in this chapter is opposed to *both* the univocalism that renders orgasm and revelation the same thing (or two forms of a similar self-transcendence) *and* the dualistic separation of the eros and agape that leaves the human passions unredeemed, at worst, or okay-but, at best. Put briefly, there is nothing natural about God – not in the way we have come to construe and capitalise Nature since at least the time of Francis Bacon. What Gregory of Nyssa called a *diastema*, an interval or distance, remains between the uncreated God and creation: an ontological and theological difference pertains. Divine desire and human desire are not the same, though human eros, rightly understood and directed, can participate in the greater movement of God's desire for the salvation of the world. Building upon what was expressed at the end of the last chapter – difference to be maintained as difference has always to be difference-in-relation – the concern of this chapter is the way this ontologi-cal difference, founded in trinitarian difference, relates to sexual differences (plural), such that desire can incarnate redemption and build the kingdom of heaven.

By not accepting the conflation of divine and human spirit – the univocity of desire which has repercussions for much that goes under the name of 'spirituality' today – the logic of certain libidinal construals of God is avoided. I need not argue against the view that God is the necessary product of an illusory father-figure, an alter-ego, produced on the basis of a libidinal economy – to keep that fermenting libido in some kind of check. The worship of God is not simply a desire to return to the mother from whom we are now eternally separated, while being threatened with castration by the father. Neither do I need to explain the economy of desire in terms of a spiritual longing, a search by Osiris for a lost penis – that final signified which will condense all the floating signifiers and constitute a complete image of who I am. This second account is Lacan's (Lacan: 1977, 281–91) and through Lacan Julia Kristeva's (Kristeva: 1988). All these accounts in which religion is a projection of an anthropological *a priori* with a specific erotic groundbase, all these accounts which conflate eros, bios and logos, are Nietzschian in inspiration, and forms of *Lebensphilosophie*. Orgasm, made philosophically respectable by being called *jouissance* or bliss, remains what Nietzsche first described as the Dionysian moment 'in which we become one with the immense lust for life and are made aware of the eternity and indestructibility of that lust' (Nietzsche: 1956, 103). The problem with Nietzsche's position, and modern accounts of the erotic economy as a redemptive economy, is that the structures of such thinking appeals to and rests upon an indifferent flux, a malleable flow of molten energies out which everything is constructed. As Nietzsche realised, in this ontological nihilism all differences are dissolved, all identities, all individualities. A 'philosophy of wild and naked nature' (Nietzsche: 1956, 67) announces 'the shattering of the individual and his fusion with the original Oneness' (Nietzsche: 1956, 56). Nietzsche's position is only a development of the erotics of romanticism, typified in Schleiermacher's view of the heterosexual couple fusing, through sex, the horizons of their difference to inform a synthesis, an androgynous unity. Desire and embodiment are transcended in this economy as they are also transcended in the production of a Christian dualism between eros and agape.

The difficulty with the Nietzschian position is both logical and existential – there can be no desire where there is no difference. Difference constitutes desire. Indifference, nihilism as the undetermined flux of Being itself, cannot account for desire let alone act as the ground of desire. Read theologically – against the currents of liberalism where anthropology and pneumatology are extensions each of the other, and against the currents of conservativism with its apartheid of desire – there can only be desire for God and a desire from God on the basis of difference. Liberal theologies which collapse the difference between the divine and the human only play into the hands of Feuerbach and Freud – as Karl Barth realised. Conservatives who divinise difference leave us equally indifferent to the historical and material which differentiates. As Roland Barthes has pointed out: desire is always a dialectic.[1] The communicated bliss is only available because of the pleasure, sympathies, abrasion, ruptures, shocks and disturbances which constitute the brio of encounter. Barthes also demands an unassimilable alterity.[2] Difference provides that which is necessary for movement, for economy, for time, for history and, therefore, difference is intimately related to soteriology.

While deconstructing the bipolarity of agape and eros we must not, then, dissolve the difference between *Geist* human and *Geist* divine. Neither must we dissolve that which is fundamental to embodiment: the sexual differences between male and female, male and male, female and female. I emphasise the plurality of these differences because much has been written recently by both feminists and those involved with pro-feminist men about sexual difference (singular) (see Jardine and Smith: 1987); as if this was the great discovery at the end of the twentieth century. French feminist, psychoanalyst and philosopher, Luce Irigaray, opens one of her seminal works with the statement: 'Sexual difference is one of the major philosophical issues, if not the issue, of our age. According to Heidegger, each age has one issue to think through, and only one. Sexual difference is probably the issue in our time which could be our "salvation" if we thought it through' (Irigaray: 1993, 5). And I too, in my time, have championed the recognition and welcoming of the other which attention to sexual difference invited us to think. But, as Thomas Laqueur reminds us: 'no one was much interested in looking for evidence of two distinct sexes, at the anatomical and concrete physiological differences between men and women, until such difference became politically important' (Laqueur: 1990, 10). Sexual difference is produced. It was produced by certain cultural situations through a specific set of epistemological concerns. Modernity's medical practices and investigations into sexual difference constructed this difference as biologically foundational. Sexual difference, then, is part of the ideology and biopolitics of heterosexuality (Laqueur: 1990,193–243). Because of this entrenched dimorphism, attention even to the symbolics of sexual difference – which Luce Irigaray has been foremost in alerting our need to think through – continually gets entwined with a biological essentialism it is wishing to transcend. Irigaray is constantly questioned by her critics as to whether her descriptions of the utopic horizon maintained and made visible by the recognition of difference (which does not move towards fusion or synthesis) is not, ultimately, theorising (and reifying) heterosexuality. Representations of sexual difference can too easily become embroiled in, and reduced to, chromosological differences – even when this is not intended.

Furthermore, and as a consequence of focusing upon the uniformity of sexual difference, what Teresa de Lauretis has called (after Foucault) the 'technology of gender' can be masked (Lauretis: 1987, 1–30). What she points out is the way gender is constructed through discursive practices. Some of the practices she examines are the representations of women in films orientated towards the male gaze. But discourses on sexual difference are also practices, rhetorical practices. As such they are practised by embodied, gendered speakers/performers, with respect to being received and interpreted by other speakers/performers. Gendered subjectivity is constructed through such

186

practices. Attention, then, to sexual difference must also ask who is seeking this attention – from what culturally, racially, socially and sexually embedded position? For these positions will affect the technology of gender with respect to sexual differences.

To summarise the theological and sociological complexity here: diastema, distance, interval, the other cannot be synthesised into a monistic whole. Ironically, therefore, there is no doctrine of reconciliation without difference. But there can be reconciliation, there can be mediation, only because the differences do not stand incommensurably over against each other. They are differences (trinitarian, ontological, sexual), differences plural, but they are always differences-in-relation.

A theology of desire

According to the work of Emmanuel Levinas in *Time and the Other*, there is neither time nor salvation without the desire engendered, literally, by sexual difference (Levinas: 1987, 84–97; see also Ward: 1996, 153–72). In terms of the Christian economy of redemption, eschatology becomes indissociable from pneumatology and soteriology and hence, mapping these economies onto sexual difference we arrive at the erotics of redemption, or sexual healing, as Marvin Gaye once sang it. True desire is eschatological. Later, having expounded the theology of this more closely, I wish to develop the consequences for perspectives on the specific ethical situations of homosexuality and the celebration of same-sex unions with respect to the Church as the erotic community. That is, from my analysis of the theology of sexual difference I will argue that there is no such thing as homosexuality, only narcissism. And that, because this is so, the time is ripe for the Church to celebrate same-sex unions.

A theology of desire begins with God's desire for me (a prerequisite for any doctrine of election and hence redemption) and my desire for God. This theology of desire has to be constructed with relation to (1) sexual differences and hence erotics, (2) the ontological difference between the divine and the human and, finally, (3) trinitarian difference. What I will concentrate upon is the relationship between libidinal economies of desire (and I say economies because I want to avoid the idea there is only one – Freud and Lacan's masculine desire) and a theological economy of desire, normally understood in terms of pneumatology, eschatology and a doctrine of salvation. Theologically, this account of sexual and theological difference, of libidinal and pneumatic economies, must issue in a doctrine of marriage or the becoming of 'one flesh' which, in its widest application, constitutes the basis for ecclesiology open to an eschatological horizon. But within this eschatological and matrimonial horizon other forms of relations – friendships and a variety of different partnerships – evidence lines of communication and communion within the Church as an erotic community. Thus through the operation of desire the Kingdom of God on earth comes to be 'as it is' (*hos hen* Matthew 6.10) in heaven.[3] Difference

187

remains fundamental, and cannot be transcended. Sexual difference, in its endorsement of both separation and relation, constitutes human creatures as *imago dei*. In attraction-in-difference is reflected the difference-in-relation in the trinitarian God. In the character of that reflection lies a whole doctrine of analogy. There can be no analogical world-view without difference. It is a world-view constituted from above – we reflect, we are not the prototype. It is the expression of the difference-in-relation of the Incarnate Christ, the revelation of God, the Man-God, as Calvin frequently refers to Him. But I am now proceeding too quickly.

The examination undertaken in this chapter will proceed intertextually. That is, it will proceed on the basis of a commentary and critique of another text: this text weaving its way in, through and beyond that other. This is a way of announcing that none of us write on a *tabula rasa*. We each stand within a tradition of some sort, with a legacy of some sort, and we are rereading it. Any Christian theology of sexual difference works in and upon that which it has received. Primarily contemporary theology has received a legacy from the romantic theologies of Schleiermacher and Hegel and the conversative theologies of Barth and Balthasar. We will be examining, in the main, the latter two, for they, more than any other twentieth-century theologians, recognised the importance of sexual difference for theology. Schleiermacher and Hegel both treat sexual difference in terms of the fall of man into self-consciousness. Eve, in both cases, represents the natural order which must be overcome, what Schleiermacher terms 'the independent activity and revolt of the sensuous element that develops so readily upon any external incentive by way of opposition to a divine command' (Schleiermacher: 1989, 303). Hegel specifically develops sexual difference in terms of his theology and politics of the family, the natural, immediate ethical state that the male has to transcend in order to become truly moral and participate in the *Sittlichkeit* of civil life. 'The difference of the sexes and their ethical content remains, however, in the unity of the substance, and its movement is just the constant becoming of that substance. The husband is sent out by the Spirit of the Family into the community in which he finds his conscious-being' (Hegel: 1977, 276). The implication here, as with Schleiermacher, is that woman, in herself, does not or does not need to find her own self-conscious being. She is redeemed through her oneness with the man.

Both Barth and Balthasar carry within their work echos of Schleiermacher's and Hegel's positions, but they complicate the symbiosis of natural, metaphysical and theological. Neither of them overcome that early romantic symbiosis, as we will see. It is not without significance that both of them suffered and enjoyed close relationships with women which scandalised their churches. Barth with Charlotte von Kirschbaum, his secretary, and Balthasar with Adrienne von Speyre. Since much attention has already been paid to sexual difference in Balthasar's work (see Beattie: 1998, 95–103; Loughlin: 1998, 143–62; Ward: 1999; Moss and Gardner: 1998, 377–401 and 1999; Muers: 1999, 265–79) we will work through a critical assessment of the theology of sexual difference as

Karl Barth describes it, and draw attention to parallels with Balthasar thought where they occur.

Barth's theology of sexual difference

Barth develops his teaching on the theology of sexual difference with reference to ecclesiology, anthropology and ethics in volume 3 of the *Church Dogmatics*. In III.1, discussing the nature of the image of God, the Garden of Eden, and Adam and Eve he articulates his understanding of 'The Covenant as the Internal Basis of Creation'. In III.2, in developing his teaching on being human as being-in-encounter and therefore human beings as constituted to be covenant partners, he discusses the analogy of relation that holds between man and woman and between human beings and God. In III.4. in the context of examining human freedom in its relation to God's command, and therefore ethics, he discusses the nature of human fellowship between man and woman, culminating in his teaching on marriage. Now let me sketch the main joists of his theology of sexual difference. Three points in a developing narrative emerge.

1. Creation itself is a separation from God, that which is different from Him. (I use Him only because of Barthian precedence. It is a metaphor.) Barth says of the creature that it was not created other than to be the recipient of God's love: 'it does not exist otherwise than as the recipient of this gift' (Barth: 1958, III.1, 230). In the beginning, then, there is *diastasis* – a divinely ordained distance or separation between creation and the uncreated God. And for Barth this difference is overcome only because of a freedom in God to give, to give His love. The medium for this giving and the means whereby human beings can receive this giving, is God as Spirit. The Holy Spirit, not being identical with the human spirit, maintains both communion and separation. On this basis there is an eternal covenant whereby, as Barth puts it 'God fulfils the will of His free love' (Barth: 1958, III.1, 231). Human beings are, therefore, dependent upon God for their existence, although the nature of this existence cannot be read off from our existential condition. The life breathed into Adam can only be understood in terms of the life which raised Jesus Christ from the dead. We live such a life, an eschatological life, by the will of God and our freedom is the freedom to obey. That is the nature of our dependence – and how Barth's understanding of dependence differs from Schleiermacher's. Anthropology has a pneumatological basis. Not that human *Geist* and divine *Geist* are identical, but the Spirit becomes the condition for human corporeality. As Barth writes: 'Yet it [human reality] is soul and body as Spirit comes to it, as it receives and has Spirit, as Spirit has it and will not leave it, but grounds, determines, limits it' (Barth: 1960, III.2, 356). What this means – and in this Barth points up his own critique of modernity – is that material bodies, materiality itself, can only be understood theologically, spiritually. The world of nature created by science, since Duns Scotus onwards (see Balthasar: 1991, 16–21 and Alliez: 1996, 196–238), in which the world is composed of discrete, self-grounding, self-defining objects 'out there', is a world-

view Barth rejects as false and idolatrous. In the footsteps of Hegel, corporeality is viewed as spiritual by nature, and to be understood as such it must be understood theologically, not on its own immanent and secular terms.

2. What Barth calls man, as man made in the image of God, is neither male nor female, but both (*Mensch*). God created man, Barth tells us, 'in the unequal duality of male and female' (Barth: 1958, III.1, 288). I will return to this inequality later. The male is only completed in his humanity by God bringing to him the woman; the woman would not be complete in her humanity without being given to the man. Hence, as we observed in the last chapter, Barth, to complete the internal covenantal basis in creation, will state that 'Man is no longer single but a couple' (Barth: 1958, III.1, 308). There is no abstract masculinity nor woman-hood, he emphasises, the couple reflect the hierarchical difference between God and creation. In their difference, what brings them together and demands their mutuality is twofold – their vocation as male and female is to be for the other, a vocation that is divine and therefore communicated through the Spirit; and their desire for each other. The sexual difference reproduces an ontological difference.

There are two quite separate economies of desire here. They indicate the kinds of relatedlessness and yet distinctiveness between creation and creator which are important for assessing Barth's analogical perspective. They are important and cause Barth endless intellectual dilemmas. The first economy is of God's love – the economy of the gift – which is not based on any lack in God but rather the very excess of love that pours itself out towards the other. It is love as generosity, as lavish expenditure beyond anything that might be demanded. It requires, establishes, perpetuates and affirms difference. Following Hegel again, the economy of desire here is kenotic and corresponds to the intradivine love of the Trinity. Barth calls this 'free love' or agape. The second economy is a desire structured into the very nature of being human. Human beings are, on their own, incomplete. They desire completion and completion is only possible through the creation and maintenance of the I–Thou relationship. Barth describes man alone as not knowing what he lacked specifically, although knowing he was unsatisfied. Woman, he states, 'With her special existence … fulfils something' (Barth: 1958, III.1, 296) which he cannot; 'woman as the one who is near and indispensable to man, as part of himself which is lost' (Barth: 1958, III.1, 301). What man does for woman is not described in anything like the same detail. The economy of desire, linked to eros, is an economy based upon (male) lack and need. It is an economy of privation. This is the libidinal economy of masculine desire found in both Freud and Lacan; all of whom are indebted to that metaphysical economy of desire in Hegel outlined in Chapter 5. This desire has a quite specific aim (unlike the economy of giving which can have no aim beyond the action of giving itself). The aim is to have one's demand satisfied. Its aim is possession and incorporation of the other, the eclipse and erasure of difference. Hence Barth comments, and it is here that the problems begin, that 'As the desire of love, true eros, desire is legitimate … when it is preceded by self-giving' (Barth: 1961, III.4, 219).

A third, internally unstable, economy of desire suggests itself here in which the self-giving, free love of agape makes possible the incorporation and oneness of true eros. Barth goes on to develop this ecclesiologically, as we noted: the lovers as believers are 'united not merely in eros but also primarily in agape, in the Lord and in the community of His brethren' (Barth: 1961, III.4, 223). The Church, then, occupies a space in which the dualism of agape and eros, kenotic and possessive desire, is deconstructed. The agapaic enables the proper realisation of the erotic, and yet the proper realisation of the erotic (the completion of the couple, their incorporation) stands in tension to the more general self-giving of one to another in the community. In fact, it would appear that the non-erotic relation of fellowship among the 'brethren' (Barth's masculine terminology) is more akin to the nature of God's own love. We will return to these tensions later. For the moment, it is important to recognise that they arise because of the separation and hierarchising of the two antithetical economies of desire, named agape and eros. The tensions could only be resolved by first, a more adequate account of desire in the intratrinitarian community of love; second, a developed notion of participation between this intratrinarian community and the ecclesial communities; and, third, by a recognition that the creation and antithetical employment of the terms, agape and eros, are human and historically located. Barth's understanding of eros (like Nygren's) is culturally determined. At the moment, trinitarian difference and sexual difference operate at odds with each other.

The question of analogy (mediation and participation) comes to the fore when we examine the way in which two economies of desire relate to two ontological orders, two forms of *analogia entis*, two ways of conceiving relationship-in-difference. The first is the intradivine form of God's three modes of being – as Father, Son and Spirit – which constitutes a twofold difference (of Father and Son and then of Spirit to Father–Son) related through a shared ontology. The second form is between the male and female who also share in a common ground of existing. Therefore, in their relationship too there is both a recognition of similarity and difference. Barth writes that man 'finds the basis of this recognition and welcome in the fact that [he] can and does find in [the woman] something of himself, and yet not only something of himself, but a new and independent being planned and moulded by God' (Barth: 1958, III.1, 299). In this sense, though the nature of the being is not univocal between the divine and the human, yet there is no room in the economies of desire for a third set of similarities-in-differences between the divine and the human communities. Each shares the same word, being, though distinctively. Each do not share the same desire because one functions in an antithetical direction towards the other – eros to agape. Both forms of *analogia entis* are related through Barth's development of the *analogia fidei* or *analogia Christi*. This is a form of correspondence initiated by God on the basis of the incarnation of the second person of the Godhead. God creates the correspondence Himself through the Spirit of Christ communicating with human beings by taking up and informing systems of signification. The

Church operates in the space opened and made comprehensible by the *analogia Christi*. In this space the Church participates and co-operates within the divine order of being, in resurrection life. Therefore, genuine human being is Christic being. But we must note here how, just as trinitarian difference operates at odds with sexual difference, so ontological difference is also at odds with sexual difference. For true eros is not participation and co-operation in divine love. And that leaves unresolved the question of embodied and gendered agency with respect to the work of the Spirit of Christ in the redemption of the world.[4]

3.   The discipline of Christian marriage and its ethics, for Barth, issues from and gives expression to these two antithetical economies of desire, and these two, but not antithetical in their own spheres of operation, orders of being. Marriage creates the temporal space and the moral field for creative interaction, one with the other – so that alterity is respected and difference maintained within the erotic relation. The external covenant (of God with human beings) and the internal covenant (of human beings with each other) co-exist. Where the radical difference between these two economies of desire, and two forms of *analogia entis* come together is in the text and tissue of history and ecclesiology. Marriage as life-long partnership, expresses this coming together while also promoting both history and ecclesiology. Marriage is a narrative, a textuality of Christian time. The economy of salvation worked out through history and ecclesiology is governed by the call and election to universal reconciliation that marriage announces. The married couple, then, act out their relationship and their sexual difference within the cosmological drama of redemption. As such, sexual difference is placed at the crux of a horizontal relation with time and a vertical relation with eternity.

It is significant that throughout Barth's examination of sexual, trinitarian and ontological difference he has drawn upon biblical narratives which demonstrate the co-existence of the antithetical relations, the correspondence-in-difference. This is wholly as a consequence of his theological method – expounding Scripture which bears witness to God's revelation through the work of the Spirit. His theology, then, will always take the form of expanded commentary. Or, to employ a more contemporary term, his theological discourse and method is intertextual. He develops his understanding of the operation of God's love within us and our love for each other through analyses of the Creation story, and he explores the eschatological implications of the movements of these two currents – the kenotic and the erotic – through a reading of the *Song of Songs*. 'It is in this book alone ... that Gen. 2 is developed' (Barth: 1958, III.1, 312).

What maintains the 'eros for which there is no such thing as shame' (Barth: 1958, III.1, 313) together with the faithful love of God for His people, in the *Song of Songs*, is the language and the tradition of its interpretation. Earlier, in his analysis of Genesis 2, and later in III.2 discussing the basic form of humanity, Barth frequently translates and metaphorises sexual difference by rephrasing the relationship between the male and the female in terms of 'partnership', 'fellowship', 'covenantal relationship', 'helpmeet' or the one appropriate to him or her, 'encountering the stranger', the recognition of the 'other', the 'Thou' which is 'immanent to I' (Barth: 1960, III.2, 245). The erasure of the specific biological difference issues, I would argue, from reading the relationship of the male and female from a theological (rather than a medical or sociological or anthropological) point of view. Where the true understanding of creation's ontological order comes from a participation in the operation of God's being, the biological – nature as it has been conceived since the seventeenth century as an independent realm of self-grounding, self-defining entities – has no value. Corporeality is such because it is materiality informed by the Spirit. To handle the corporeal as if it were not also spiritual and theological is a form of idolatry; a consequence of sin, ignorance and human arrogance. Barth preaches this. Left to ourselves, human beings simply traffic in the inventions of the all too human heart. 'God is the prius of all cognition and everything known' (Barth: 1958, II.1, 197) in the world. From the perspective of the revelation of the Godhead, then, it is not only orders of existence and the nature of bodies that are redefined. Sexual relations and identities are redefined also. From the point of view of revelation the difference is read in terms of a covenant constituted through reciprocal desire. It is this covenant through desire for the other that constitutes the image in us of the nature of the Godhead itself and the economy of relations created by reciprocal desire within the Godhead. It is not biology *per se*. Put another way, God does not see male and female, God sees human being in partnership, in covenantal relationships of I and Thou, One and the Other reflecting His own Triune nature. He views the couple as human being, not male and female. In the couple, male and female, Barth writes 'He makes a *copy* of Himself. Even in His inner divine being there is relationship. To be sure God is One in Himself. But He is not alone. There is in Him a co-existence, co-inherence, reciprocity' (Barth: 1960, III.2, 218). Thus Barth will add, '[o]nly what takes place between such as these [the couple, the fellows, the helpmates] is humanity' (Barth: 1960, III.2, 271).

In his examination of the language of the *Song of Songs* and the tradition of its interpretation, Barth points up this transfiguration of biological difference. For at the heart of the text the male and the female are also Yahweh and His people as 'one flesh'. Yahweh is Israel's husband and Israel is Yahweh's wife, so erotic love and marriage are transposed into kenotic giving and covenant. The former is established as an analogy of the later by the power of God alone. Only post revelation can there be a recognition of the divine relationship in the human one. Of course, Barth then transposes the Yahweh/Israel relationship into the relationship between Christ and his Church. So now we have three levels of typology, which Barth maps clearly out for us. 'the divine likeness of man (*Mensch* – humanity) as male and female which in the plan and election of God is primarily the relationship between Jesus Christ and His Church, secondarily the relationship between Yahweh and Israel, and only finally – although very directly in view of its origin – the relationship between the sexes. It is because Jesus Christ and His Church are the internal basis of creation, and because Jesus

Christ is again the basis of the election and call of Israel, that the relation between Yahweh and Israel can and must be described as an erotic relationship' (Barth: 1958, III.1, 322). We must read sexual difference, then, not simply biologically, but theologically. That is, we must read it as the product and promoter of corporeality and history (in terms, then, of the doctrines of vocation and providence). We must read it eschatologically (in terms of universal reconciliation in the coming of the Kingdom); soteriologically (in terms of our redemption in Christ); and ecclesiologically (in terms of I–Thou, Self–Other relations which build up the community of Christ here on earth). In fact, we only read sexual difference aright when we read it from the theological perspective, rather than the biological, sociological and anthropological perspectives. In the narrative of God's story, male and female are tropes. That does not stop them being corporeal, but then tropes too have a materiality. Neither does it condemn erotic love as wrong, for erotic desire constitutes the anthropological basis for the internal convent. But corporeality and eros have to be read in the wider perspective of God's revelation and purpose in creation. When we are talking about redemption we are talking about bodies and redemption through bodies. And bodies have no stable or autonomous identity. Bodies are not self-grounded and self-defining. A person's physical body, the 'one flesh' of the nuptual body, the Church's ecclesial body, the eucharistic body and Christ's eschatological body map one upon another.

Corollaries and critique

All this we can take from Barth, and yet ... there is that highly ambivalent clause 'only finally – although very directly in view of its origin'. What does 'very directly' refer to? Does it refer to the relation of sexual difference to the ontological difference between God and humanity? The German is even more emphatic: '*her nun doch auch ganz direkt das Verhältnis des meschenlichen Geschelcter ist*'. But Barth's *analogia fidei* would refuse a 'direct' correspondence between these two orders. That would pave the way for natural theology. The relation cannot be direct, only mediated. So what is going on here? I want to suggest that Barth did not follow through his theological interpretation of the semiotics of sexual difference (based upon his doctrines of *analogia fidei* and *analogia relationis*) when it came to writing III.4 of *Church Dogmatics*. And that here, in this ambivalent clause which speaks of a 'very direct' relation between sexual difference and ontological difference, we have an early indication of such a slippage in his thinking.

Let me frame the case I will make with some more general remarks about theology and the current gender debate. For whether the debate surfaces in feminist, masculinist or queer theory, it has continued to revolve around the polarity of biological essentialism versus social constructivism. Though both what is understood by essentialism and constructivism have been made ever more complex (see Vance: 1995, 37–48). Having distinguished between a person's sex (a physiological distinction), sexuality (the orientation of their libidinal economy) and gender (the social meanings attached to, produced and cultivated by the interplay between sex and sexuality) – the burning question is which has the upper and determinative hand: biological or socio-historical factors? When we emphasise the social construction of sexual identity then we can all too easily lose sight of subjects, motivation and agency. When we emphasise the biological we can all too easily assume access to an essential, natural state, a body which simply receives cultural inscriptions of various kinds. The more sophisticated thinkers, developing notions of gender as performance, attempt to find a way of moving beyond this polarity and the distinctions between sex, sexuality and gender. Both Judith Butler and Teresa de Lauretis develop complex accounts of how gendered embodiment takes place and proceeds. We have examined something of Butler's account with respect to the body of Jesus Christ, in Chapter 4. For Butler materiality itself is constructed. It is 'the effect of power, [as] power's most productive effect' (Butler: 1993, 2). In fact, Judith Butler, following the work of Foucault, Lacan and Irigaray on the relationship between power and language and the morphology of identity, raises the profile of representation and politics as they shape both the biological and the cultural. She wishes to discuss the formation of sexed personhood as a production that takes place within a symbolic field. Gender is performed. 'The more a practice is mastered, the more fully subjection is achieved. ... [T]here is no subject prior to their performing; performing skills laboriously works the subject into its status as a social being' (Butler: 1997, 116, 119). This continual process of self-expression (which has echoes of Hegel (see Butler: 1997, 31–62)) is culturally and historically embedded, but this does not render the subject passive before determining social forces. Subjectivity is twofold – both subjection and self-expression. Such performances and productions of sexed embodiment, she insists, always exceeds anatomical determination, establishing agency and direction in the cultural formation and signification of sexual relationships. 'Language and materiality are fully embedded in each other, chiasmic in their interdependency, but never fully collapsed into one another,' she writes in her seminal essay 'The Lesbian Phallus' (Butler: 1993, 69). She concludes: 'The anatomical is only "given" through its signification, and yet it appears to exceed that signification' (Butler: 1993, 91).

Her thesis is extremely complex and very challenging, but the point I wish to make here, in relation to Barth, is that 'male' and female', for Butler, in their gender performances, are inscribed within a temporality, a social context and an historical movement which causes the 'meaning' attached to those nouns to exceed their biological definitions. 'Male' and 'female', because they are identified in and through language, are caught up in wider fields of signification than simply the anatomical. Hence, in moving towards analyses of the symbolics of gender performance, gender narratives, she moves beyond the polarity of essentialism and constructivism towards a site at which both sides of the antinomy reciprocally define and continually redefine each other. Neither biologically nor socially and linguistically constructed bodies remain stable.

In her later work, which pays increasing attention to the reproduction of rules embodied in social 'rituals of actions', she relates performance to the production of belief. 'The notion of ritual suggests that it is performed, and that in the repetition of performance a belief is spawned, which is then incorporated into the performance in its subsequent operations. But inherent to any performance is a compulsion to "acquit oneself" ' (Butler: 1997, 119). Belief is left abstract here, and part of Butler's argument is that the coherence of gay and lesbian identities both repudiates and requires the social rules of heterosexuality. But she offers two insights important for the nature of embodied formation as it is performed and produced in the Church as the erotic community. First, she articulates the logic of that performance/production that deepens what we have seen suggested in Barth's theology of sexual difference. For Barth's work emphasises the way biblical discourse on the male and female views the anatomical as participating in a much larger symbolic fields. Sexual difference not only also, but primarily, signifies the cosmic and theological differentiation between I and Thou, Self and Other, Yahweh and Israel, Christ and His Church. The discourse on sexual difference continually exceeds its anatomical reference by being related to other, more fundamental (because hierarchically arranged) contexts. There is the historical context of the history of Israel and the Church; there is the eschatological context of the final marriage of the Bride of Christ; there is the ecclesiological context of vocations being worked out in Christian communities in terms of fellowship and mutual responsibility; there is the physiological context of sexual desire. In each context, 'body', the material and contingent, the extended and spiritual, is being redefined and its meaning continually opened up towards an eschatological horizon. This is pushing Butler's analysis in a theological direction, a direction she herself makes possible by likening performance to ritual. Male and female become two differentiated positions within a divinely ordered sociality that signify partnership, covenant, fellowship and helpmates. They are symbolic positions within a divine narrative. Their life together constitutes the very fabric of Christian time. As such their performances are corporeal. Symbols are corporeal. Secondly, Butler points up the processes of identification – how, in and through these performances not only is the body engaged in larger symbolic operations, but it comes to identify itself *as* this person, this unique performance, this *believer*. In terms of the liturgies and social rituals of church-going, the Christian only comes to an understanding of himself or herself as this particular embodied Christian by engaging, by practising and acquiring an understanding of what it is to be a member. As such one comes to be a person in Christ; and to grasp something of what that person in Christ is. This identity is continually in process because the erotic economy of redemption is always a movement – there are always other people to engage with, other situations to negotiate and 'dress up for' (in the way Butler regards drag as the self-conscious staging of and resistance to culturally encoded sexual identities).

Thus far can Barth, read in tandem with queer theory, get us. It is a pity, then, that in III.4, having rejected in III.2 stereotyped roles for 'male' and 'female' (Barth: 1960, III.2, 287) and having insisted that the divine command 'frees man and woman from the self-imposed compulsion of ... systematisation' (Barth: 1961, III.4, 153), Barth defines their ethical and social vocation in terms of their biology alone. It is as if he returns to a natural theology his whole theological system is set up to refute. Hence, same sex relations are perversions not of the theological but of the natural order. '[A]s a man he can only be genuinely human with woman, or as a woman with a man. In proportion as he accepts this insight, homosexuality can have no place in his life' (Barth: 1961, III.4, 166). And, furthermore, in this new biologically based metaphysics of heterosexuality 'the business of woman, her task and function, is to actualise the fellowship in which man can only precede her, stimulating, leading and inspiring' (Barth: 1961, III.4, 171). Let's rub some salt here into an opening wound. Woman, he adds, 'is in her whole existence an appeal to the kindness of man' (Barth: 1961, III.4, 180–1). And, central to his doctrine of marriage, is the thesis that 'marriage can be for the husband the foundation of his professional life, for the wife the normative ratio of the home to be administered and inspired by her' (Barth: 1961, III.4, 189). This is an echo again of Hegel. Barth returns to an affirmation of a natural and social order (orders highly convenient to him, serviced as he was by two women)[5] that runs contrary to his theological thesis that there is no independent natural or social order to which appeal can be made. Our knowledge of what is natural and social has to be a knowledge revealed to us by God. We read nature and society not in terms of what we see around us, but what is revealed to us following the resurrection of Christ.

So what has happened? What has led Barth to reaffirm the socio-sexual status quo? A critique of the type Luce Irigaray employs with reference to Freud and Plato may assist our enquiry. As we noted in Chapter 5, Irigaray argues that there is a culturally pervasive 'hom(m)osexuality'. That is, a sexuality inscribed from the perspective of men (*les hommes*); in other words, a phallocentrism. It is evident in Plato, it is axiomatic in Aristotle and it dominates the structures of the Freudian psyche (Irigaray: 1985). The consequences of this hom(m)osexuality is that no genuine sexual difference can be established, because the other sex is always interpreted from the perspective of the one, monolithic sex, the male. The female is only a variant of the male; his other half, that which fulfils and supports him. To quote Hélène Cixous, 'Either woman is passive or she does not exist' (Cixous: 1975, 118). Now, I suggest, this is exactly what is going on in Barth and what brings about a certain incoherence in his theological reasoning. He wants difference. He wants sexual difference to be paradigmatic of the radically, unassimilable difference between I and Thou, Self and Other, Yahweh and Israel, Christ and His Church. But he reads this sexual difference from the male perspective. Though he voices a respect for the feminine, she is defined only in relation to what the male lacks – she is the helpmeet for him. His other is not really another at all. It is the other of the same. In Hegelian terms, the woman provides the consciousness with a reflection of itself that it might have a sense of its own identity. And even if Barth should claim (albeit much more weakly) that this operates for the woman *vis-à-vis* the man, still the homosexual logic of the other-of-the-same, is evident.[6] Man precedes, woman follows after, Barth writes (III.4, 167–172), while maintaining that this 'does not mean any inner inequality between those who stand in this succession' (III.4, 170). The problem is the 'equality' is always being gauged from a male, homosexual (Irigaray's 'hom(m)osexual') perspective. The relation he wants between the I and Thou, the Self and Other, Israel and Yahweh, the Church and Christ, is where the latter ruptures the autonomy of the former, questioning the authority and privilege of the former. But the hierarchy of the male/female relation means that the female (though in some sense other) is in no position to question. She can only, as with Balthasar, answer (Balthasar: 1992, 260–330; Gardner and Moss: 1999, 87–9). She does not stand *with* man, or *before* man as other, she stands *for* man. In other words, I suggest, Barth is not able to establish the sexual difference his theology requires. His male and female are not a couple. They are not a partnership. The desire in operation, in Irigaray's terms, is hom(m)osexual, narcissistic. The woman has a function only within the economy of the male desire wherein she functions as complement, not difference. This maps onto a biological determinism whereby the male is a strong, active, performer on the public stage and woman is weak, passive and creates a space (both in terms of the home and her womb) to support and promote male productivity.[7]

I suggest Barth is brought to an endorsement of the biological and social orders, contrary to the direction of his theological thesis, because of the way he has set up the economies of desire – agapaic and erotic. We need to return to the complex and conflicting relationship between trinitarian, ontological and sexual difference, outlined earlier; to the stubborn dualism of agape and eros that lies outside the participation and co-operation of the created order in the divine made possible by the *analogia Christi*. The consequences of this are profound – for what cannot be taken up into Christ cannot be redeemed by Him. By the dualism Barth isolates the erotic economy which, as he examines it in its sociological and ecclesiological forms, develops into a hom(m)osexual economy. It becomes saturated with the male perspective which cannot establish the true difference he requires. The erotic becomes an economy to restore mutual lack. Where does the Holy Spirit of agapaic desire enter this self-fulfilling erotic economy? Where does the economy of God's desire enter this homosexual economy to disrupt it and keep it open, in hope, for fulfilment in Christ? That homosexual logic of erotic desire – which Hélène Cixous relates to consumerism, the desire to possess, capitalism, systems of exchange and relations of power (Cixous: 1990; Ward: 1996a) – is not taken up into, governed and transformed by, a divine eros; a trinitarian erotics in which true difference between the first and the second Person is maintained by the second difference of the Spirit. The Spirit keeps open, while maintaining the unity of, the trinitarian relations of love.[8] It is the isolation of the erotic from the agapic, the lack of participation and co-operation of the two desires, grounded in the intradivine love, which leaves Barth simply peddling the male perspective, with its biological and sociological repercussions, when he comes to examine the relation of man to woman in III.4.

Towards a theology of sexual difference

Now, let me propose a thesis, which develops Barth's theological position without reducing male and female to either biological categories or social roles, and which also moves us beyond the dichotomy of those two economies of desire, the agapaic and the erotic. We need, then, to take those three theological positions with which Barth began. First, the divine call to difference mediated by the Spirit – the trinitarian difference and the ontological *diastema* between creator and creation; secondly, humanity created as the *imago dei*, in and through sexual difference, a difference mediated by desire; thirdly, Christian life-partnerships as the narrative of the performance and operation of the divine kenotic and the human erotic giving, a narrative which possesses soteriological and eschatological value in terms of the reconciliation of the world and the coming of the Kingdom. It is, I suggest, the third of these aspects which allows us to glimpse the truth of the first and second. In particular, it is the category of narrative or performance which we need to examine. For love, desire, personhood, gender, and sexuality are all practices. They are all textualities of time, subject to and modifying a particular set of contextual forces. They are only identifiable as performances within specific socio-historical conditions. And performances, to be evaluated and examined as performances (evaluated or examined philosophically or theologically, for example), have to be recorded; they have become texts. To recall Butler, they are 'given' to us through their signification. To recall de Lauretis, they are practices through which a gendered embodiment is produced for us and by us; practices by which that embodiment is represented for and by us. Our gendered and embodied performances and practices are texts themselves, of course, in the widest understanding of gesture and action as expression, as social semiotics. As such, any performance or practice has to take the form of a narrative, a semiotic chain starting (however pragmatically) here and ending (however pragmatically) there, in which is marked the passage of time and the development of an action. Hence both Butler and de Lauretis examine film, novels and short stories. Within such narratives male and female figures are condensation points or metaphors for a density of signification above and beyond their anatomical specifications. The dynamism behind the economies of such narratives can neither strictly be identified as kenotic (the lavish outpouring of a self-giving love) nor erotic (the desire to acquire in order to satisfy a particular demand). The feminist theologian Mary McClintock Fulkerson, in her book *Changing the Subject*, has examined the significance for feminism of examining discursive contexts within which women are found and by which they attest their own identity (Fulkerson: 1994). Without a concern for the theological implications of his work, R.W. Connell has examined in a similar way the discursive contexts in which men are found and by which they attest their identity (Connell: 1995). What they both emphasise is how the particularity of any such discourse moves beyond universalist answers to the questions 'What is a woman?' 'What is a man?' and 'What is a woman's experience?', 'What is male experience?' – questions around which much theology of gender has been galvanised. I suggest, by examining the discourses concerned with sexual difference, love stories if you like, as they are handled theologically, we will reinforce what Hélène Cixous' work repeatedly draws attention to – 'a question of the mystery of "woman" and "man" ' (Cixous: 1991, 78–103).

It is that mystery which same-sex relationships open up. Same-sex relationships displace (in the way I have used that term of the body of Christ in Chapter 4) heterosexist symbolics, revealing a love which exceeds biological reproduction. Of course love between men and women can do that also; their love does not need to be restricted to reproduction. But there is nothing surprising about the attraction of opposites that manifest their opposition in appearances. In *Symposium*, Plato could already draw upon stories of human beings born with both sexes only to be sundered apart and predestined to roam the earth in pursuit of their lost other half. But as feminists have pointed out, and Barth's thinking illustrates, the attraction of opposite sexes maps too easily onto the logic of those who have and want more and those who lack and are dependent. The mystery of attraction, the deconstruction of 'male' and female' as self-grounding, biological positions, the opening of 'male' and 'female' to recognise a certain mystery and malleability of the body – this becomes more evident in same-sex relations, that disrupt the *Magic Flute* rationality which deems that every man wants a woman and every woman wants a man. Attraction arises still in difference, in opposition, through alterity. As we have recognised, there is no desire without difference. But exactly what is other in a relationship between two 'women' or two 'men' becomes less easy to define, to catalogue. Their embodied relationship is maintained in an elusive grace (Williams: 1996, 58–68); their materiality is, perhaps, more recognisably suspended, awaiting a judgement that can only be eschatological. That there is alterity is not to be gainsaid, for desire in both gay and lesbian relationships is both autoerotic and directed towards the other. If this is doubted read Joseph Olshan's *Night Swimmer*, where swimming long stretches of the ocean at night becomes a metaphor for the erotic search. Many men offer themselves and are found to be available, but the central character, Will, loves what is impossible and the finding of that love is something of a miracle. The last phrase is simply the description 'I was praying' (Olshan: 1995, 212). In fact, it has been a point made by several gay and lesbian apologists that same-sex relationships are entered into with more difficulty, more self-questioning, more consideration because it is constantly framed by the world-view of the 'straight mind' (Wittig: 1992). They can offer, then, theologically, a sense of grace, of vocation, of miracle that might too easily be forgotten in the sheer 'naturalism' which surrounds heterosexual courting and engagements. Same-sex relationships have suffered from the nineteenth-century label of 'homosexual', a product of those romantic erotics which announced the metaphysics of heterosexuality, predicated on medical investigations into the biology of sexual difference (Greenberg: 1988, 397–434; Laqueur: 1990, 52–3; Halperin: 1990; Trumbach in Duberman: 1991). 'Homosexuality' was linked to narcissism, introversion and self-indulgence. When Barth describes the 'malady of homosexuality' as 'the physical, psychological and social sickness, the phenomenon of perversion, decadence and decay' (Barth: 1961, III.4, 166), he is following in the wake of psychologists like Havelock Ellis and Paul Nacke who examined homosexuality in terms of narcissism, love of the same (see Freud: 1957, 73–102). But on the account I am sketching here there can be selfdesignated 'heterosexual relationships' whose structure of desire is homosexual, and so-called homosexual relationships whose structure of desire is heterosexual. True desire, that is, God-ordained desire can only be heterosexual. Hence the first of my two assertions at the beginning of this chapter: there can be no sexual economy respecting difference and alterity, respecting the interval which separates, which is homosexual.

Irigaray writes: 'Desire occupies or designates the place of the interval ... Desire demands a sense of attraction: a change in the interval, the displacement of the subject or of the object in their relations of nearness or distance' (Irigaray: 1993, 8). In a further essay she develops this idea: 'If desire is to subsist, a double place is necessary, a double envelop. Or else God as subtending the interval, pushing the interval toward and into infinite ... the irreducible. Opening up the universe and all beyond it. In this sense, the interval would produce place' (Irigaray: 1993a, 48). The 'place' Irigaray speaks of I have termed space (after Certeau) in the last chapter. It is a space opened up by the distending body of Christ (Chapter 4). The desire Irigaray speaks of I wish to read theologically, as I believe Barth also wished to do. My account, then, would run something like this: What is loved in love is difference. Such love of difference, in difference, from difference, to difference operates according the economies of both kenotic and erotic desire. In fact, agape and eros can be seen as two perspectives within the same dynamic, moments of giving and receiving where giving is also receiving, and vice versa. They are both creaturely names given to processes that enfold creaturely existence, and therefore, exceed our ability to grasp their essence and operations such that distinctions can be clearly drawn with respect to divine operations. While there can be so many different degrees of attraction (and repulsion); while the mystery of why we form a friendship here, a connection here, but cannot form a friendship there or a connection there remains; while in each day a thousand micro-relations, flirtations, and exchanges of eye-contact are made – so that there are, in the Church, a panoply of different relations: nevertheless, there can be no kenotic love which is not erotic also. There is a desire to give and a diremption in receiving. The endless giving without reception announces a demonic and nihilistic logic, under the ideology of which many women and gay men have suffered in silence. Endless giving becomes indifferent to itself. The labour of trinitarian love – of difference, in difference, from difference, to difference – prescribes the relation of the Godhead to creation and the relation that is possible between two women, two men or a man and a woman. Such a labour of love far exceeds, in its significance and influence, the biological. Marriage is not the rite of synthesis – the dissolution of the difference worshipped by and through love. Marriage is the narrative of the creative interval between two bodies, maintained by the labour of loving as it moves in hope towards the eschatological coming of the Kingdom, which is redemption – personal only in as far as it is also ecclesial. It is time, then, for the Church to recognise that for far too long it has remained enthralled to, and fostered, a biological essentialism and hom(m)osexual economy (in Irigaray's understanding of the term). The Church must sanctify difference, must examine and discern difference in all the relationships it sanctifies. For it is from difference that the Church receives the power to be and participates in the power to become. The Church must sanctify, then, genuine sexual difference through its liturgies – whether that sexual difference is evident between two women, two men or a man and a woman.

The sanctification of such unions, along with the celebration of relationality *per se* – of friendships and neighbourliness, of kinship (by both blood and by law), of colleagues and co-workers – becomes the means for the kenosis and enrichment of the Church as the erotic community. Founded and refounded continually upon its eucharistic site – upon the dynamics of fracture, union and dispersal – sexual difference participates analogically in trinitarian difference, while maintaining the ontological difference which enables the suspension of all that is and becomes in this world within the perfection of God's own transcendent being.

Part III

THEOLOGY AND THE PRACTICES OF CONTEMPORARY LIVING

8

CITIES OF ANGELS

> They would rather proudly be able to do what an angel can than devotedly be what an angel is.
>
> (Augustine 1963, VIII.5)

Over the last five chapters I have been outlining the central columns of a Christian systematic theology which attempts to configure and be configured by an analogical world-view. The basis of the analogical structure is embodiment and the manner in which the physical body, situated in the space opened by the continual displacement of Christ's own body, maps on to other bodies and so constitutes the ecclesial and sacramental body of Christ. In the last chapter I was concerned with showing the theological dynamics of those co-implicated bodies with respect to redemption and the work of the Spirit. That is, how the physiological differences of sex and sociological gender differences, never distinct and separable, participate in the dissemination of eucharistic grace which, ultimately, is grounded in intratrinitarian love. Throughout these five chapters, we have been examining the body in terms of the grammar of the Christian faith, taking seriously what it would mean to begin with a theological understanding of embodiment. These chapters, then, constitute an internal reflection upon the practices and productions of Christian believing and gendered Christian personhood. But we started from, and must return to, the contemporary city. For it is not just an internal account of Christian coherence that I wish to construct; that would be opening one more chapter in a conversation among theologians for theologians. As I said in Chapter 1, the city has a theological role to play in the economy of redemption. It is towards the establishment of a city of God that Christian redemption moves. The city is not accidental to Christianity; it is a means of grace and an analogue (however fallen or remote) of eschatological possibilities. From the internal reflection, then, on a theology of embodiment and desire we need to move to a consideration of the way those physical, ecclesial and sacramental bodies and desires relate to the social and political bodies of civic life. We need to consider how this Christian materiality, spatiality, temporality and mimesis (examinations of which have been key to the theology I

205

have been outlining) relate to what Certeau called the practices of everyday life. In particular, how do they relate to the materialities, spatialities, temporalities and forms of mimesis evident in that postmodern city examined in Chapter 2?

Today's angelic hosts

I suggest there are three significant configurations of the human embodiment evident in contemporary culture; all of them are representations of *Übermenschen* expressive of Nietzsche's will to power. They each occur frequently in the media, in advertising, in books and interactive computer games and each have their own theological heritage. Each are parodies of Christian configurations. These are: the vampire, the cyborg/clone and the angel. The vampire, as so many telling moments in Francis Ford Coppola's *Bram Stoker's Dracula* revealed, is an inverted Christ figure: taking rather than giving His blood. Vampire stories are eucharistic stories played out negatively, as the attempt to create and maintain a family, in Neil Jordan's *Interview with a Vampire*, suggests. The cyborg/clone is the new superman or superwoman figure. They are eternally young, Kung-Fu fit, lithe, beautiful, day-glo intelligent and infinitely capable. They are transhuman or perfected human beings, like Lara Croft of cyber-games fame or Signorney Weaver in *Alien Resurrection*. They are frequently messianic figures like Neo in *The Matrix*. They are the people who governments want to produce out of all of us – that we might be more efficient, demand less state-sponsored health care, cause less accidents, be more clear-sighted about our goals, and more transparent (from their point of view). The angel is more complex, even more approachable, because the angel is not the source of the power itself but an emissary, a mediator. It is with the host of contemporary angels that our move beyond the doors of the Christian Church and back into the city will begin. For what each of these ex-theological configurations demonstrate is the commodification of the theological as one aspect of contemporary culture. I suggest we need to investigate and understand the nature of this commodification. It is a sign of our times. We need to interpret its significance. That is what I attempt in this chapter, and suggest that today, amid this new angelic host and a certain (albeit commodified) re-enchantment of the world, Christian theology has an opportunity to have a public voice in a way it has lacked for centuries.

Our cultural horizons are crowding with hosts of angels. Concentrated no longer around the season of Christmas and its commercialisation, they have multiplied; Christmasing our cultural scene with glitter and glamour and consumer promise. It is a cultural scene that is fast observing the erasure of seasons. Angels are box-officed by Hollywood; compact-disced by vocal artists; and promoted in literature.[1] Angels are the subject of a new philosophical hype in the thinking of Luce Irigaray, Hélène Cixous and Michel Serres. Gilded cherubim, putti and seraphim hang from the ceilings not only of religious bookshops and stores for church furnishings, but of department stores up and down the country. They are part of the current pomading of consumer space with scented candles and incense. They are part, more generally, of a re-enchantment of culture which, rejecting the scientism of the machine age and mystified by the IT age, produces dreams of transcendence. The magical realism of the 1970s has deepened and now pervades our perceptions of the very ordinary – employed to promote vodka and even yoghurt.

Meanwhile, the brocaded, fabulous couture of Gautier, Versace, McQueen and Galliano is producing angels of all of us. Our bodies are becoming prisons for angelic souls: concepts and construals of the perfect corporeality are disciplining us in what we eat and binding us with fears of infection. The cult of sport, with its glamourisation of sweat, flesh-not-fat and sculptured muscularity; the marketing of cosmetic surgery, facial injections to erase the effects of ageing, breast implants – all demonstrate that we are perfecting the techniques for turning each of us into angels. We are manufacturing and manufactured by a contemporary angelology.

The American sociologist, Robert Wuthnow, recently observed:

> The mysterious has become a growth industry.
>
> One manifestation of this growth is the enormous interest in angels. In only three years, Sophy Burnham's *A Book of Angels* sold 450,000 copies. So many readers wrote letters to the author reporting their encounters with angels that her edited anthology of these letters (*Angel Letters*) sold another 175,000 copies. Joan Wester Anderson's book, *Where Angels Walk*, proved even more successful, selling more than a million copies ...
>
> As if to capitalise on the popular interest, in 1993 First Lady Hilary Rodham Clinton decorated the White House Christmas tree entirely in angels, declaring 'this is the year of the angels'. ... Overall, the number of books on angels (according to the Library of Congress) rose from 20 published between 1971 and 1975, to 31 between 1976 and 1980, 34 between 1981 and 1985, 57 between 1986 and 1990, and 110 between 1991 and 1995. During the last of these periods, total sales of angel books were estimated to exceed five million copies.
>
> (Wuthnow: 1998, 120–1)

What we need to ask here is a question we asked about the credibility of Christian theological response in Chapter 2; a question about the politics of believing. A space has been produced in which talk about angels, television interviews with those who have been visited by angels, websites on angelic experiences and, more generally, acceptance of the possibility of angels is rendered credible. What, to the Enlightenment mind and the modern scientific mind, would have been consigned to folklore – like the stories of fairies in Victorian England – is suddenly, again, gaining credence (and, therefore, reality).

In attempting to analyse the contemporary commodification of theological motifs (which is not limited to Christian motifs for there is a commercialisation of the Jewish tradition and there has, since the 1960s, been commercialisation of the Eastern traditions) I wish to examine and 'explain' this phenomenon. The inverted commas around 'explain' are there to emphasise that I claim no epistemological validity, no objectivity for the rationality of my argument. The argument, the very discourse, is caught up with the production and expansion of that space open for the credibility of angels. But the focus of my 'explanation' is why it is that angels, which seemingly disappeared from the systems of belief which created the space termed modernity, are making a dramatic comeback in the new cultural spaces, temporalities and materialities (complex and heterogeneous) of postmodernity. Once we did not, could not, believe in angels any longer because angels produced no space; they did not give themselves as objects organising a certain perspective within which they could be viewed or figure forth something meaningful. Put another way, they were no longer visible because of what determines, for us, those three foundational categories that Henri Lefebvre alludes to in *The Production of Space* – 'social existence', being 'real' and spatiality (Lefebvre: 1991, 53). But Lefebvre's analysis opens up alternative possibilities, because if we accept the production of social existence, what is considered 'real' and space, then there may be (may have been and may will yet be) forms of social existence, reality and spatiality in which angels can again appear (and be believed in). And maybe we are heralding again a time of advent. So we need to enquire why this might be so and to understand what angels are figuring for us today.

The release of hybrids

Angels are not the only 'creatures' experiencing a revival of interest, as I have said. They are part of a cultural context which, in witnessing the implosion of modernity, is welcoming again the hybrid and making the claim that 'We have never been modern (not really)'. We can take a cue here from the historian of science, Bruno Latour who, in his book entitled *We Have Never Been Modern* distinguished one of the fundamental trajectories of modernity to be the aspiration for purity. The production of this purity is complex, for Latour. It requires socially acceptable places of production – laboratories and law courts for example – and, because of the dualistic distillations that it brings about (nature/culture, domestic/foreign, object/subject, transcendent/immanent, private/public etc.) it requires processes of translation. That is, sites where the separation is maintained and yet mediated. These two activities guarantee the modern constitution. Latour makes it quite plain that these activities of purification and translation are implicated and replicated in theological concerns, notably an emphasis upon the utter transcendence of God (who cannot, therefore, interfere with the processes of nature as it is under construction) and an equal emphasis upon the spiritual presence of God in the hearts of individual believers. 'By playing three times in a row on the same alternation of transcendence and immanence, the modern can mobilise nature, objectify the social, and feel the spiritual presence of God, even while firmly maintaining that nature escapes us, that society is our own work, and that God no longer intervenes. Who could resist such a constitution?' (Latour: 1993, 34). As Latour points out, modernity, then, both 'allows the expanded proliferation of the hybrids whose existence, whose very possibility, it denies' (Latour: 1993, 43). The effect of this was the production and yet the suppression, or erasure, or fear of *the hybrid*. That which did not conform to the rules of conduct or the laws of science (which the ethics of natural law conflated) was criminal, pathological, or perverted. These types were produced only to be publicly, clinically, and scientifically exposed and shown to be in need of reformation, healing, or disciplining. The natural was the understandable, the rational, that which conformed.

What took place sociologically was the production of an underworld: a world of the prostitutes, the transvestites, the sodomites, the paedophiles, the criminal, the insane, the vagabonds, the gypsies that haunt Victorian novels. What took place, imaginatively, was the development of the dark side of the romantic: the gothic, creatures of the supernatural, the demonic, the pornographic, the suicidal and the sublime. Here Wagner's *Niebelungen* and Rhine Maidens, stalked the same lands as Shelley's Frankenstein, Byron's Cain, Stoker's Dracula, Le Fanu's Uncle Silas, the Golem myths of Judaism and Goya's witches. Angels too had a place here: in the esoteric writings of Lavater and Swedenborg, in the paintings of the Pre-Raphaelite brotherhood and, following the revival of medievalism, the fashion for gilded cherubim in the homes and the cold marble angels at the head of graves. Unlike the romantic 'monsters' their faces were more publicly acceptable. For rather than exemplifying the hybrid – which they might well have done since Old Testament scholars in the nineteenth century recognised that angels were imported into ancient Judaism via Babylon, where *kerub* (from which we derive *cherubim*) were bulls with wings and the faces of the human beings – angels became figures for modernity's obsession with the pure.

Writing in Germany in 1827, Carl Hase in a book entitled mysteriously enough *Gnosis* wrote: 'Those who have a heart for the beautiful and the ideal will gladly think of angels. It was the desire for a living creature better than ourselves yet benevolently participating in our human joys and sorrows which first heard the angel-song in the quiet night' (quoted in Barth: 1960, III.3, 377). The title of the book is significant, for gnosticism is associated with the exaltation of the spiritual above the material, in fact, with cosmic mythologies in which the binary principle of good and evil is mapped onto the binary division between spirit and flesh. The angels of romanticism were figures for the ethereal and sublime. Furthermore, they were gendered feminine. Since Winklemann and the development, in Germany, of the gymnasium, the male body had been undergoing a Hellenisation of its own in which slender, hairless, feminised bodies were sought after (Mosse: 1996). Romantic angels of the male gender were either children or feminised. A paradox is articulated by these gendered figures, therefore, as representations of the beautiful and the ideal body they are escapes from actuality of embodiment, rejections of corporeality. As Grace Jantzen and other feminist thinkers have emphasised this production of the eternal feminine (by and in dialectical opposition to the masculine), this divinising of woman as the perfect other with whom synthesis is sublime (witness the end of *The Flying Dutchman*) is a manifestation of the male fear of death (Jantzen: 1998, 128–55; Cavarero: 1995). The body beautiful, particularly the idealisation of feminine beauty, was implicated in a complex paradox of necrophobia and necrophilia. The necrophilia is evident here in the association of: angels and the afterlife, angels and the other shore; just as, the necrophilia is figured in the ultimate consumption and realisation of the total present (see Chapters 4 and 5 and Pickstock: 1998, 101–18). This paradox of the necrophobia/nercophilia, like these figurations of the pure (that required disciplining of the body to replicate them), are profoundly gnostic.

What has changed in today's interest in the hybrid and in the angelic is twofold. First, the hybrid is no longer the monstrous other out there, the other that must be kept out there, kept at bay (like Stevenson's Mr Hyde). The hybrid is part of the social; we are all recognised to be hybrids now for the natural order has buckled and warped. With our implants, pacemakers, false teeth, cosmetic surgeries, contact lenses; with our diet over years of genetically engineered food; with our notions of hygiene; with the pharmaceuticalisation of our bodies and the electronic extension of those bodies (mentally with computers, physically with cars and planes and space shuttles) – we are already becoming cyborgs (see Haraway: 1991). The question of what now is human is a real question. The collapse of liberal humanism in the wake of twentieth-century atrocities, galloping social atomism fuelled by advanced market economics and the explorations of the dark, violent side of the psyche has launched that question into the black holes of deep space (quite 'literally' in terms of the Hollywood film industry).

The alien lives among us – the *X-Files* finds that frighteningly true, the film *Men in Black* exalts in the playful possibilities this opens up (though violence and threat bubble up through the laughter). *Men in Black* in fact plays also with the relationship between the extraterrestrial alien and the terrestrial one: the Mexican immigrant, the black detective. The profound racial intermixing, particularly in those places whose histories are deeply associated with colonialism and immigration, puts ethnic cleansing high on the list of contemporary priorities. The alien is us. Witness our voyeuristic fascination with the mind games of Hannibal Lecter, in *Silence of the Lambs*, which reveals that the vicious predatory nature (invoking 'cannibal', Hannibal the rapacious Hun and *lector*, the reader, the thinker, the cultured one) cannot be expunged from society and isolated behind bars. Our voyeuristic fascination with the sheer rationalised evil of Lecter is itself an indication that he dwells within us, as us. Michel Serres has one of his characters state: '[O]ur televisions don't transmit good news any more. With

210

every meal, we're forced to eat dead bodies and drink spilt blood ... We've become cannibals again. Man devouring man, in untold numbers. Human beings on the butcher's slab' (Serres: 1993, 156). We are the other who is no longer distinct and ostracised from us.

This is the change ushered in under such labels as postmodernity, late modernity, and post capitalism. In Ridley Scott's *Blade Runner*, the human beings are trying to annihilate ('retire') a small group of genetically cloned human beings ('replicants') who have now turned against their creators. They are wishing to maintain the separation between culture and nature. The four replicants are killed, but at the end of the film the hero (Harrison Ford) flies off into a Hollywood sunset with a more advanced model of a replicant, disappearing into the naturalism of heterosexual sociality.[2]

The first change, then, is that the hybrid is not the exception. We are all hybrids. Secondly, the angel, while figuring still within utopic horizons does not evoke a spirituality in opposition to a corporeality. The angel is weighed down again with the gold brocade vestments of medieval Annunciations (for Gabriel) or Botticini's sheaths of amour (for Michael). The angels have been earthed. They no longer figure a transcendent, cosmological purposiveness; other worldliness as modernity conceived it. In fact, they confuse and deconstruct modernity's forced separations – nature/culture, matter/spirit, empiricism/idealism, the sciences/the arts. They have joined the other hybrids which escape categorisation and are valourised for being on the boundary, in the margins, at the threshold. They are figures of the in-between, the indeterminable. They are figures of unstable identity.

The Protestant theologian, Karl Barth, writing about angels in his *Church Dogmatics* in the late 1940s strikes a contemporary note. While attacking as a biblicist, on the one hand, the speculative nonsense of those great angelologists of the Christian tradition – Pseudo-Dionysus in his *De hierarchia coelesti* and Thomas Aquinas (nicknamed the 'angelic doctor') in both his *Summa theologiae* and his *Summa Contra Gentiles* – Barth attacks, on the other, those liberal theologians seduced by positivisms and keen to demythologise the Bible's record of angelic hosts. He writes that 'when the Bible speaks of angels (and their demonic counterparts) it always introduces us to a sphere where historically verifiable history, i.e., the history which is comprehensible by the known analogies of world history, passes over into non verifiable saga or legend. That is to say, when it is a matter of angels in the Bible, we are in the sphere of the particular form of history which by content and nature does not proceed according to ordinary analogies' (Barth: 1960, III.3, 374). With angels the material orders scrutinised and tabulated by modernity – nature verifiable by number and all ready to be digitalised – are questioned; and with that also is questioned what it is we 'know', the nature of analogical knowledge (knowledge built upon seeing thing *as* other things, and *in relation* to other things) and, therefore, the production of the 'comprehensible' itself. We no longer speak of knowledge, we speak of the production of knowledge, and we speak of the

211

politics of belief, the spaces for credence. As Wittgenstein puts it in his ironically entitled book, *On Certainty*: 'The difficulty is to realise the groundlessness of our believing'; 'What I know, I believe'; 'Knowledge is in the end based on acknowledgements'; 'At the end of reason comes persuasion' (Wittgenstein: 1974, propositions 166, 177, 378 and 612).

With the waning of modernity a certain order of being and knowing passes also. New multiple, rhizomatic orders announce themselves in the chaos theories of science and the collapsed geometries of architects like Frank Gehry. Serres writes: '[O]ur world, which is fluid, fluent, fluctuating, is increasingly volatile. ... *Volitatis* is the Latin word for things that have wings' (Serres: 1995, 44). Furthermore, the hybrids, angels among them, are giving birth to new complex discourses. Discourses which cannot be bound (or seized upon) by one academic discipline, owned by one academic department. These are discourses of migration reflecting our own heterogeneous cuisines where a Thai chicken main course is complemented by a melon and Parma ham starter, a crème brûlé dessert, a Chilean chardonnay and a New Zealand Pinot Noir. Such are the discourses we will be examining as contemporary forms of angelology: the philosophy/politics/fiction/imaging of Michel Serres' and Luce Irigaray's work and Wim Wenders' cinematography. Angels have returned, then, as the virtual realities of modernity and are being seen for what they are: productions. This opens up the world to new and self-confessed virtualities or kitsch realities (Ward: 2000b) and the order of simulacra. We will examine three such annunciations in order to probe more deeply into what this return to the angelic host signifies – for contemporary society and for Christian theology.

Michel Serres and the tongues of angels

Serres' *La Légende des Anges* was published in 1993 and translated into English in 1995 as *Angels: A Modern Myth*. The translation 'myth' does not capture the connotations of the French *Légende*. For Serres' book is concerned with languages, speaking, messages, communication, translation (in its various meanings), transmission and transmutation. These are all aspects of his angelology, his talk about angels. The Latin *legere* (to bind or collect together as well as to appoint, or send out on a commission, as well as to read aloud or cite) can be heard in the French *Légende*. *Legens* the Latin participle can be used as a substantive meaning 'reader'. The French *Légende* is also linked to citation, as well as meaning 'key' or 'caption' beneath a painting or map. Serres plays with the associations of the word with 'key' and 'caption' and, in a volume richly illustrated, draws attention to the phrasing beneath paintings or encompassed by a photograph. *Légende* is much richer in meaning than 'myth' allows. In a dialogue between two characters, female and male, named Pia and her brother Jacques, Serres writes: 'Jacques says derisively: "But angels are fictitious beings." Pia counters, learnedly: "Take them in a figurative sense. And remember that both your 'fictitious' and my 'figurative' come from the same Latin root" '

(Serres: 1993, 121). Just as Michel de Certeau uses 'fable' with the associations not of fiction as opposed to fact, but *facere*, to make, to do, Serres emphasises the construction and the production of what we know. Knowledge is *poiesis*. For Serres we compose our world in and through our employment of figures. Not only compose, but we also discover we are immersed within a world that speaks in, to and through us. We dwell within the endless relays and interchanges of language in transit – language understood widely to include the exchange of signs, the making of gestures, the production of rhythms and complex patterns of chains of activity (geological as well as technological). Hence the series of dialogues which constitute the text is staged in an airport, a place of transition with the coming and going of several people speaking several languages.

Angels, for Serres, are like the convexed mirrors at the back of certain seventeenth century Dutch paintings which reflect back upon the painter painting. They are figures of a self-reflexivity in which communication is conscious of itself. They are not mythic. Like the word Barth uses for the genre of the discourses in which the actions of angels are described, 'saga', which bears within it the German *Sagen*, '*Légende*' is not simply being used generically by Serres. The word is being used to suggest the whole history of the transmission and commission, the speaking about or citation of these figures. Serres' book stands within that transmission, mediating and passing it on into another future.

The book, then, is not only about angels it is angelic. Taking up a traditional notion of angelic intelligence and mechanics, in which they move as fast as they can think, the movement of the thought in the book tracks the passage of angels. The direction of the thought is governed by the 'good news' that angels are commissioned to tell out. The twilight of the angels comes then when the good news arrives, when the Word becomes flesh. This insistence upon incarnationalism structures the book which shifts liturgically through the day and through refigured scenes of the Scriptural narrative of the birth of Christ. The dawn opening sketches an annunciation scene between Pia (a doctor at the airport's medical centre) and her lover Pantope (who flies constantly all over the world as a travel inspector for Air France). With the birth of Christ refigured as a midnight mass and the birth of a child to an Israel woman in the airport, in the final section entitled 'Noel', the work of the angels is accomplished and they take their leave:

> Angels will still be able to continue expressing their language, writing and singing, transporting and coding messages ... but henceforth their role will be subaltern, their age will have come to an end, and both their role and their end will have been fulfilled, because the message is here ... Throughout the whole world, all the networks are crying out about hunger, are screaming a thirst for incarnation, in a situation where the body is horribly lacking. But at last, the Good News: the Messiah, the message, is flesh, immanent.
>
> (Serres: 1993, 285)

It is the movement towards this incarnationalism which bears the ethical and political significance of Serres' appeal to angels. The *'Légende'* bears us, on messianic wings, towards a utopic horizon in which there is a new respect for the corporeal. At the moment 'the body is horribly lacking', Serres comments. That is, a limited number of bodies are being pampered and cared for in what he calls Newtown (the city founded upon informational technology by those who know how to access, use and profit by it) by exploiting and then disregarding the violated, abused and disfigured bodies of those still in Oldtown. The death of a destitute man called Gabriel, at the beginning of the book, announces these tidings. He announces by his very presence and act (for there is no distinction between the messenger and the message if the angel is good) the systematic destruction of humanity. Newtown is ruled over and organised by the fallen angels (where, in the distinction between messenger and message, the messenger wants to be glorified above or in place of the message). These fallen angels constitute powers, thrones and dominions; the realm of the false gods who work to create simulacra of paradise and angelic existence for its best citizens. Not that Serres embraces a gnosticism here, the volatility of angels means there is always the temptation for rising or falling and a difficulty in assessing the good from the fallen. What is required then is mercy and love. The operation of the former (countering the effects of social Darwinism) is then associated with the angel of consolation (the archangel Michael with the Small Foot); the operation of the latter, which brings about rebirth, is associated with entering 'the triangle of the seraphim' (Serres: 1993, 274).

Not only new bodies will be formed (and therefore a new ethics and politics governed by a recognition of the interdependence of all bodies), but new knowledges and states of being will be formed also. Serres' angelology announces these new knowledges; for they figure forth a new enchantment of the real. This re-enchantment has to arise from the sublation of what Serres has viewed as socially dangerous and violent from his early writings: the cultural dominance of the hard sciences. Max Weber first described the advance of technology as withdrawing mystery from the world and dis-enchanting it. Serres' angelology is one more strategy for calling forth new knowledges by bringing together the so-called natural sciences and the social sciences or humanities. Hence throughout the book a series of analogies are created establishing new connections: information theory is related to Hermes as a forerunner of the angels; spectrograms of the human voice are paralleled with Jacob's ladder and the continual ascent and descent of the angels upon it; the greenhouse effect with the myth of Prometheus; Los Angeles is related to the heavenly Jerusalem. In another work, *Le parasite* (Serres: 1980), he draws together literature, parasitology and sociological analysis. A hybrid and intermixing of discourses which seeks to constitute new relationalities in our thinking, establish a new holism, is fundamental to Serres' work. Only this creative activity of making connection, of communicating one thing to another, one discursive world to another, will, for Serres, stall the accelerated dis-enchantment of the world which exploits in its death-drive to control. Newtown is established here: it is these uncontrolled technologies that produce 'the aggressive hell of commercial advertising' and a new form of global city 'which allows us to place our hopes only in itself and in its achievements. Furthermore, people can only enter it if they know how to access it everywhere' (Serres: 1993, 72). Such blatant forms of power-to-exclude and segregate manifests, for Serres, the problem of evil.

The new knowledges of angels bring a recognition of 'a state of intercon-nectedness' (Serres: 1993, 55). It is a recognition that must produce humility; because it understands that the pursuit (and achievement) of personal glory, power and excellence is at the expense of others. But Serres goes further than this, as indeed he must. For he needs to expound the basis upon which the holism he propounds (and the analogies he constructs) is possible. What the re-enchantment of the world through angels suggests is that ultimately what holds all things in place, for Serres, is a theological world-view. The book, which draws together (*legere*), encyclopaedically, so many different fields of reference, that moves between popular science, literature, philosophy and sociology, is finally framed by Christian theology. All the connections can only be made, all the relations only hold, if a third and transcendent party is honoured above and beyond the analogical communications themselves. The angels announce a pantheistic world of immanent fluxes, a world in which the Word is to be made flesh. But beyond the angelic hosts is the Most High or the All High God to whom all glory is due: 'if our will becomes sufficiently good for us to make an agreement between us to accord the glory only to a transcendent absent being, then we will be able to live in peace' (Serres: 1993, 288). The book concludes: 'This unique solution to the problem of evil thus leads not to a demonstration of the existence of God, but to the fact that it is necessary for him to exist, and to the refutation of polytheism, which is what dominates us today. Without a God who is one and unique, and without his exclusive glory – these being the sole foundations for peace – the war of all against everyone will continue to rage' (Serres: 1993, 290).

I pass no comment on the Hobbesian element here – the social contract guaranteed by a covenant with the Almighty God. The utopianism is unabashed, but then Serres' work is to implement transformation by being angelic, performing the creative bridge-building that will incarnate our words by making us all messengers who live out absolutely our messages. The angelology arises as the repressed voice of Enlightenment rationality, with its social Darwinism and its scientific reductionism. The angels in Serres' work call for and create a new spatiality within which there can be optimism and *renaissance*. In an interview with his pupil and colleague, Bruno Latour, he said: 'Hiroshima remains the sole object of my philosophy' (Serres: 1995, 19). Doxology is recognised as the only way of redeeming Hiroshima.

Wim Wenders and the knowledge of angels

In one of Wim Wenders' most recent films, *The End of Violence* (1997), a detective (Doc) who is tracking down a film director (Mike Max) who has gone missing and is thought to be a murderer, tells the director's wife (Page): 'I think everything's connected. Did you know that in nuclear physics if you look at a so-called particle you change it? Imagine, just by looking at something you can actually change what it is. ... We're connected and we've never even met.' The film explores that interconnectedness which is graphically portrayed in shots of a major road intersection outside Los Angeles and dramatised in the prominence in the narrative of video surveillancing of the city. The interconnectedness is both reassuring – the detective finds the woman he loves and the main character is cleared of a murder because the event is caught on camera – and disturbing – the voyeuristic intrusion of surveillance evokes the sinister threat of a power controlling the narrative. Connectedness is also narrativised in terms of computer links, video conferencing, the use of e-mail and mobile phones. Wenders' world is Serres' global city. In fact, Serres himself uses Los Angeles as a metaphor for his infotech Newtown; his city of the fallen angels. In Wenders' world the intricate networks of communication and the continuous relays of information, artificially relate human beings. For most of the characters are isolated atoms, immigrants, refugees, men (always) on the run. They make small gestures of belonging – on the run Mike Max finds refuge among the Mexican family who services his Beverly Hills mansion; Ray, who supervises the observatory (which controls the city's surveillance cameras) begins an affair with a South American refugee who acts as a cleaner. But the belonging never lasts: the cleaner betrays her supervisor, who is shot; the film director's wife leaves him and then threatens him with a gun when he returns. The absence of connection is dramatised in terms of the four plots running concurrently, linked through what is caught on camera (and those who are controlling what is caught on camera, in the observatory). What connections are made can appear either planned (and therefore possibly sinister) or arbitrary. For the connections themselves are tangential (at no point do any of those involved in the four plots understand their complicity one with the others).

At the end of the film, though, Mike has escaped (by leaving his wealth and position as a film director behind) the networks of global connection (which constantly threaten violence and intrusion). He stands facing the Pacific Ocean while another level of the plot unravels: the South American cleaner is about to be assassinated by those who control the surveillance cameras because she knows too much, while her daughter stands by and begins a conversation with Mike. Their conversation concerns Spanish words, how many he knows and how to pronounce them.

MIKE: Los Angeles
GIRL: [*correcting his pronunciation*] Los Angeles
MIKE: Sky?

GIRL: Cielo.
MIKE: I thought cielo means heaven.
GIRL: Cielo means both heaven and sky. [*Pause*] They're watching us.

The camera zooms out and sweeps the promenade. We see (without commentary) that the mother is allowed to return to her child and the threat of assassination reprieved. In what is almost a trademark of Wenders' film a voice-over (Mike's) accompanies the camera's movement as the shot pulls smoothly to a distant point in the sky and panoramically surveys the sunlit Californian coastline, serene and blue. 'Funny, just when you think you've got it all figured in a heartbeat it changes again. (*Pause*) Thing is, all those years while I was waiting for that sudden attack, *I* became the enemy. And when the enemy I expected finally came, they set me free. Strange. (*Pause*) Now when I look over the ocean I don't expect nuclear submarines, alien attacks anymore. I see China now. And I hope they can see us' (*Fade out*).

The violence, threats and paranoia dissolve into an appeal for omniscience. Bathed in sunlight, desire finds its *jouissance*, its sabbath rest. Movement – at least Mike's movements in this film – serves to escalate violence. Angels, like the satellites which comb the world and record what they see, like cameras passively watching, offer hope for a utopian future. They act as guarantors that someone knows what is going on. Their knowledge protects all of us. The close intimacy of the voice-over reassures us, but the panning long shot of the ocean comes from no where. Freed from the secular forms of tracking and surveillance, exiled from the social, Mike seems to place himself in the hands of transcendent all-seeing powers which are benevolent. He seems to place himself in the hands of angels, and an omniscience which is innocent (affirmed by the words and perspective of a child).[3] If Serres' concern with communication is with the word as flesh, the message, then his focus is upon the tongues of angels whereas, for Wenders, for whom communication is fundamentally visual, attention is given to the knowledge of angels.

What the knowledge of angels, or the camera, seems to give Wenders is a transcendental authority to direct films. For Mike Max, the filming-within-the-film, and the intrusive, voyeuristic cameras controlled from the observation tower, all suggest power and its potential for abuse; its potential for generating violence rather than ending it. The director is guilty, not of the crime for which he is being hunted down, but for allowing himself to become the focus for power. His seeing changes the world we see in the same way perception changes the nature of particles in sub-atomic physics. A guilt appends to Wenders seeing and making us see. He is not confident that his seeing facilitates a redemption of the real – to quote the subtitle of Siegfried Kracauer's important book from the early Frankfurt School on film-making. In accepting the exile from globalisation and the film industry's implication in it, in handing his studios and production over to his estranged wife, Page, in surrendering his vision for the seeing of the angels, the director enacts a kenosis and receives the grace of absolution.

217

The End of Violence suggests a new development in Wenders' exploration of the knowledge of angels which explicitly began ten years earlier with *Wings of Desire* (1987) and continued in its sequel *Far Away, So Close* (1993). These two films form a diptych. In the first the angel Damiel falls in love with a woman and, leaving his friend Cassiel, falls to earth to create a relationship with her. The film is shot in West Berlin, and the Berlin Wall and Germany's Nazi past are constantly alluded to and revisited in documentary clips. In the second film, Cassiel, who comes to earth to join Damiel in his family bliss, finds the human, technicolor world (the angel scenes are shot in black and white) painful and violent. He eventually returns to the angelic realm. The film is shot in the former East Berlin, the Wall has now been torn down, Germany is still affected by the fruits of past events though Cassiel's interventions redeem the possible present violence of those fruits. He manages to smuggle away a hoard of Nazi guns, for example, from a group of arms dealers. A little girl held at gun point by the arms dealers is saved by Cassiel, who is killed in saving her but then returns home to Raphaela, his angelic friend.

In both films, Wenders plays with the political rather than engages and critiques it. The darkness, despair and guilt of post-war divided Berlin in the first film is portrayed, self-consciously so when Peter Falk, as himself, is flown into Berlin to star in a film being made about the Nazi concentration camps. But the darkness is constantly juxtaposed to the main focus of the film, the romance between the circus woman and the angel. In his notes for the film, published as *The Logic of Images*, Wenders wrote:

> One day, in the middle of Berlin, I suddenly became aware of that gleaming figure, 'the Angel of Peace', metamorphosed from being a warlike victory angel into a pacifist. ... [T]here have always been child-hood images of angels as invisible, omnipresent observers; there was, so to speak, the old hunger for transcendence.
>
> (Wenders: 1991, 77)

The political is inseparable from the aestheticised, and a utopic horizon relates them both: the end of violence is the annunciation of an age of peace. Berlin's Angel of Peace rules over all.

Far Away, So Close opens with one of Wenders' circling, flying shots of Cassiel on the top of the Angel of Peace. And, once more, in this film, after the kenosis of Cassiel to the hell of earthly living and his crucifixion on behalf of a child (whom he had already saved from a fatal fall over the balcony of her apartment earlier in the film – a salvation which brought him to earth), the film ends with shots of the barge carrying the Nazi armaments towards their final resting place in the sea. It is dawn, the river is misty, the colours are blue and violet touched by an orange sunrise and the view is panoramic. A voice-over, a duet composed of Cassiel and Raphaela speaking together, repeats, in an extended form, the opening lines of the film: 'You. You whom we love. You do not see us. You do not hear us. You imagine us in the far distance, yet we are so near. We are the messengers who bring closeness to those in distance. We are not the message. We are only the messengers. The message is love. We are nothing. You are everything to us. Let us dwell in your eyes. See your world through us. Recapture through us that loving look once again. Then we'll be close to you and you to Him.' This is very close to the utopic ending of Serres' work.

In his film notes, Wenders self-consciously constructs a myth for these angels: 'When God, endless disappointed, finally prepared to turn his back on the world for ever, it happened that some of his angels disagreed with him and took the side of man, saying he deserved another chance. Angry at being crossed, God banished them to what is then the most terrible place on earth: Berlin. And then he turned away. All this happened at the time that today we call 'the end of the Second World War' (Wenders: 1991, 78). It is a cosmic myth which does not map onto the films themselves. Particularly in *Far Away, So Close* Cassiel falls to earth because of his love, not his will (as Damiel) and, as the final voice-over suggests, the intention is to return the world in love 'to Him'. Earlier in the film, in a dialogue between Raphaela and Cassiel we are informed that humankind has hardened its heart and is now unable to see and hear the angelic presence. It is the world, not the angels, who have fallen. The redemption of that world lies in recalling these angelic figures, giving their knowledge (their way of seeing) cultural space. Luce Irigaray would concur.

Luce Irigaray and the flesh of angels

As a philosopher of sexual difference, Irigaray has been concerned throughout most of her work with, on the one hand, a critical project (deconstructing a male-centred cultural symbolic) and, on the other, a constructive project (transfiguring the cultural symbolic in a way that takes account of women). In the last chapter we examined something of her critical project. It is with reference to the second of these projects that she develops her angelology. Her understanding of the constitution of culture as a field of symbols issues from her critical engagement with Freudian and Lacanian psychology. For Lacan, the development of subjectivity requires the entry into language and the exchange of signs. These signs give representation to the subject's imaginary (that realm in which a subject's experience of the world is internalised in terms of various images, rhythms and intuitions). But the order of the symbolic, according to Lacan, is governed by the phallus and phallic-driven desire: 'The phallus is the privileged signifier of that mark in which the role of the logos is joined with the advent of desire' (Lacan: 1977, 187). The phallus is a metonymy for stabilised identity, full self-present meaning, the Word of God. This consummation of identity is never possible; the journeying towards it and the mourning for its absence goes on till death.

Irigaray's writing on angels, like Serres', arises from a concern for a new kind of incarnationalism: the Word made flesh in a way that owns the sexuate nature of all flesh and the sexual difference necessary for all fleshing at all. '[Angels] are not unrelated to sex. There is of course Gabriel, the angel of the Annunciation. But other angels announce the consummation of marriage, notably all the angels in the Apocalypse and many in the Old Testament. As if the angel were a representation of a sexuality that has never been incarnated. ... The fate of all flesh which is, moreover, attributable to God. ... They proclaim that such a journey can be made by the body of man, and above all the body of woman. They represent and tell of another incarnation, another parousia of the body' (Irigaray: 1993, 15–6). Where the lapsed Catholic Wim Wenders pays homage to St Thomas Aquinas, in both emphasising the significance of the knowledge of angels and presenting them as not having material bodies and therefore unable to sense and limited in the impact they might have upon the world, the lapsed Catholic, Luce Irigaray, employs them as figures for the Christian construal of the resurrected body.

There are two distinct stages of the 'journey [that] can be made by the body'. The first of these relates to Irigaray's feminist project: the becoming divine or the incarnation of the woman. In her seminal essays 'Belief Itself' and 'Divine Women', in order to disrupt and transform the male symbolics of the body, she figures woman, she speaks of woman (*parler-femme*) as associated with the elements – earth, water, fire and air – and as hybrids. Divine women are 'half-creatures of the sea, half creatures of the air' (Irigaray: 1993, 60). By means of this figuration, women's fecundity is rendered cosmic. But something more is needed: a God is necessary to facilitate the infinite, to operate as the ideal, the Form to which divine woman aspires. Men have such a God, as Feuerbach had pointed out. In fact, men have a whole hom(m)osexual community of Gods in the Trinity. 'We have no female trinity. But, as long as woman lacks a divine made in her image she cannot establish her subjectivity or achieve a goal of her own' (Irigaray: 1993, 63). The embodied subjectivity of woman, the transfigura-tion of woman's flesh from fish to bird, requires this transcendental ideal. This female god has not yet come, but it is being imagined (through Irigaray's deconstruction of the male-focused god) and it is being symbolised in terms of alternative models of subjectivity. And so, pointing to the lacuna in Freud's account of the development of sexual identity, Irigaray posits the morphology of an identity around the two, vaginal lips of woman as different from the phallic morphology of men. And, having critically examined the Christian tradition, asks: 'Does respect for God made flesh not imply that we should incarnate God within us and within our sex: daughter–woman–mother' (Irigaray: 1993, 71). Here are alternative genealogies, new possibilities, a good news for women.

But who is to deliver this good news to the Church? For 'Theology and the ritual practices [of the mass] it demands would seem to correspond to one formulation of all that is hidden in the constitution of the monocratic patriar-chal truth, the faith in its order, its word, its logic' (Irigaray, 1993, 27). Who is, then, to ensure both its proclamation and reception? It is answering this question, in writing what elsewhere Irigaray will term 'the epistle to the last Christians' (Irigaray: 1991, 164–90), that the hybrid bodies of those half-fish and half-bird become associated with the transfigured flesh of angels. Three angelic sites are visited in Irigaray's exposition of this transfigured flesh: the Old Testament account in Exodus of the Ark of the Covenant between God and the tribe of Israel in which two sculptured angels are described as facing each other; the Annunciation scene with the Virgin Mary; and the Apocalyptic bridal banquet. The Annunciation, in particular, is concerned with the transmission of messages, but in all three scenes 'a mediating angel or angels come to give us news about the place where the divine presence may be found, speaking of the word made flesh, returning, awaited' (Irigaray: 1993, 36). Evil angels, like Serres' demonic hoard, are those who block the mediating process by drawing attention to themselves. As figures for mediation, the angels, then, incarnate the condition of representation and presentation – that which makes the message possible, the speaking and writing as woman. The enfleshment of angels is found in the very practice of speaking and writing, representing and presenting. For the angels mediate 'by keeping a space open and marking the trail from the oldest days to the farthest future of the world' (Irigaray: 1993, 40).[4]

The Virgin Mary represents the woman who receives the angelic message and brings it to birth within her own body. In this way, Mary represents becoming divine, she incarnates what Irigaray will term the 'sensible transcendental' without whom there is no Christ and only with whom can there be redemption (Irigaray: 1998: 198–213). In modernity's refusal and rejection of angels, the message they enflesh goes unheard or is distorted. That is why Irigaray calls for the rethinking and rebuilding of 'the whole scene of representation' (Irigaray: 1993, 42), beginning with speaking as woman (*parler-femme*). Only then can the second stage of the 'journey [that] can be made by the body' be entered upon. This second stage is the realisation of sexual difference and the divinity it presences. Men too are now brought into this transfiguration and the utopic age of the Spirit or the Bride dawns.[5] This is what the Apocalyptic angels figure, for Irigaray. This is what the two angels that stand at the two ends of the mercy seat which covers the Ark of the Covenant figure, for Irigaray. A new forgiveness, a reconciliation, is announced by the way in which their wings reach over but never touch each other; and it is in this way that they 'guard the presence of God'. The guarding has two directions: towards human beings and towards God. For the 'doubling of the angel ... would keep Yahweh from being closed up in the text of the law. ... They guard and await the mystery of a divine presence that has yet to be made flesh. Alike and different, they face each other, near enough and far enough for the future still to be on hold' (Irigaray: 1993, 44–5).

Angels, and here Irigaray returns to a more orthodox angelology, represent the movement of thought itself; thought which is always embodied, impassioned and sexuate. They figure the speaking and writing of Irigaray herself who, in receiving them, who in standing with the Virgin Mary in her Annunciation, proclaims 'the production of a new age of thought, art, poetry, and language: the creation of a new *poetics*' (Irigaray: 1993a, 5) when the horizons of the world are constituted in terms of sexual difference.

Cultural metaphors

We cannot conflate these three contemporary angelologies. They are far from being identical as my headings – 'The speech of angels', 'The knowledge of angels' and 'The flesh of angels' – suggest. Serres (whose father was a converted Catholic, though he associates himself with the Cathars) and Irigaray think angels within a broadly Christian schema – downplaying the historical particularity of Christ while insisting upon the incarnation of the more nebulous Word made flesh. Confusingly, Irigaray also seems to espouse the immanent logic of Feuerbachian projectionism. Wenders has his film *Far Away, So Close* open with the passage from Matthew's Gospel about true seeing: 'If therefore thine eye be single, thy whole body shall be full of light' (Matt. 7.22). Nevertheless, he detaches himself from any biblical framework. Theologically, though, there are close correspondences between his depiction of angels and the descriptions of them deduced by Aquinas. For Aquinas will insist also that the bodies of angels are non-corporeal, that their substance is spiritual, and that they can only, then assume human bodies to communicate, not become them. Serres and Irigaray pass from human bodies to angelic ones easily, with Irigaray quite emphatically stating that the angelic body is the perfection of human corporeality. Angels announce, for both of them, the incarnation of the spiritual that we must give birth to. Although, what Irigaray would observe, despite Serres' account of relationality, participation and reciprocity – which she would embrace – he still hierarchises the angelic realm. What Serres would observe in return is Irigaray's lack of concern with technology (she is more forthcoming on all the four natural elements (Irigaray: 1992)). For Serres, our ability to become angelic is linked to our increasing capacity to evolve technically, particularly with telecommunications. Wenders, like Aquinas on angelic materiality, is more dualistic – as his employment of technicolour for the human world and black and white for the angelic world, makes visible. Neither Irigaray, Serres nor Wender espouse an institutional commitment to religion, for all the emphasis upon communication (or, in Wenders' the lack of communication) there is only the eschatological hope of communion (although Wenders again presents loving communities at the end of both *Wings of Desire* and *Far Away, So Close*).

But the question remains how we account for this resurfacing of the Christian imaginary in postmodern culture? Nostalgia for the Middle Ages and the hegemony of the Church? Both Serres and Irigaray will recognise the appeal of the medieval: 'Is it not true that in this age of sophisticated technical apparatus we still frequently turn to the Middle Ages in search of our images and secrets?' (Irigaray: 1993, 58). Serres informs Bruno Latour that 'we are living today (and even more so in the United States than in Europe) closer to the Middle Ages than to the salons of the Age of Enlightenment' (Serres: 1995, 25). If this is not nostalgia for the liturgical cosmos of the medieval Catholic Church, then it certainly does claim to speak for a culture which has come to the end of the Age of Enlightenment, a culture disillusioned with the wielding of technical power for its own sake, a culture that is post-industrial and post-liberal. How then do we read this cultural metaphor of the angels? As New Age spirituality, as a response to the rootlessness, the heady irreality, the crisis of legitimation, authority and validation which characterises postmodernity, a culture caught between the virtualities of cyberspace and the TV soap? Does the hyperventilating experience of postmodern living lead to *fin-de-siècle* fantasies; fantasies which are comforting, drugging, utopian, and dripping with the red and golds of millenarianism?

No doubt sociological, psychological, ideological and historical explanations can be produced. But the production, not simply the fact, of these contemporary angelologies exceeds explanation. For they are not retreats into illusion or fantasies and away from a hard and rational reality, a normalcy. There is no hard reality for any of our three thinkers – no benchmark of the brutally given to appeal to. Each announce a world of constantly exchanging signs, the real as the production of a shifting commerce of messages written, delivered, stalled, distorted, misunderstood. The ontology is soft (Vattimo: 1998; see Introduction). – matter, time and space have liquefied – making belief possible, maybe even necessary. Belief itself is produced, as Irigaray, like Certeau, points out (see Chapter 2). But what are we producing belief in? What we are witnessing here is the manufacture of new urban mythologies, a longing for transcendence, the fabrication of new cosmologies, a desire to become divine while being constantly reminded by Hiroshima (Serres), the German death camps (Wenders), continuing exploitation (Irigaray): the results of our attempts to play God. In the culture of the death of God, we replaced him. Nietzsche tells us it is we who killed him. Now new negotiations with the divine are opening. Or are they? Something stirs the contemporary passions, and who can say whether this is an hysterical hope for security or the Spirit of God blowing on the cold embers of souls who are remembering something whispered from their past, and who had forgotten how to sing of anything but loss? Serres, conscious of the difficulty of distinguishing the good from the bad angels, desires the purity of mediation, and writes a series of dialogues as if he is not there. He plays, silently, with omniscience, dreaming his new electronic cosmos. But he *is* there – he receives the royalty cheques. And so an impurity in the new angelic mediation is evident. Wenders employs film stars like Natasha Kinski and William Defoe to play his angels, his films always reflecting back upon their own production and the guilt he feels about that production. Irony stipples his vision. Irigaray's *parler-femme* is self-consciously utopic and mimics the very stereotypes of the feminine (element-bound, ineffable, dreaming of other worlds, the mystic as hysteric) she is attempting to subvert. Paradox installs itself in the heralding of her new age of the Bride. But ultimately all three of our contemporary angelologists enjoin us to celebrate the ambivalence itself. They are upbeat and doxological in their acts of persuasion. To return to Lefebvre, the ambivalent, it seems, offers new spacing. It offers space for the sacral. Today the undefined is again taking on the gravitas of grace – as 69 per cent of Americans believe in angels, according to a poll conducted for *Time* magazine in 1994 (Wuthnow: 1998, 120).

Theological conclusions

Space, time and materiality, then, are being transformed in the cultures of the postmodern city. The transformation is shot through with theological colouring, resonant with theological memories and recitations. A great semiosis is generated in which aporia, instability, the unpresentable, the undecideable and the ambivalent are turned into transcendental principles that re-enchant the world. Or, at least, those parts of the world which import and export these cultural productions. God-talk is everywhere, again, *à la mode*. But what kind of God is being produced here? No longer the God of the gaps, but God as the gap – as a naming of the aporetic as such. And the difficulty with transcendentalising (even divinising) the aporetic as such is that for all the talk of passage and flight, for all the images of the roads and airports in Wenders' films and the economics of the sign, of desire, of the market, all movement is virtual. For in the infinity of the undecideable there is no direction, no place by which to register movement or change or transformation or, indeed, history. The economies become virtual like the journeys into outer space on the SS *Enterprise* which are not journeys at all towards or away from anything, only changes in dramatic encounter. Travis (pronounced 'Travers'), the main character in Wenders' evocative film *Paris, Texas* (1984), issues from and returns back to the desert, alone (albeit he walks *from* the desert but drives *back* into it).[6] We enter the eternal reoccurrence of the same. And so, in this infinite semiosis, sense, meaning, identity, in being endlessly deferred, is endlessly dissolved, which must dissolve also embodiment, singularity, particularity, difference (and, therefore, relation). The interconnectedness, love, participation, incarnation, and shared liturgical practices theorised, photographed, appealed to and traced in these discourses is also, then, virtual – caught up, that is, in the massive drift of signification. We have seen this as a problem throughout – how to keep the body, the material, from disappearing while suspending judgement as to the final, eschatological understanding of embodiment, materiality, spatiality and temporality. Theology has become a public discourse again. The theological imaginary is being revisited as a marketable product. But it is a virtual theology. It is a use of the terminology but an evisceration of the contents. It installs a 'religion without religion' (Derrida: 1995). The theological rhetoric is evacuated of the analogical vision that provides, most profoundly, mysteriously and concretely, a theological account of creation and human being as part of that creation. The time is ripe then for a *theological* intervention that speaks of the content that is being lost. It is time for an intervention that embraces semiosis, the aporetic and the undecideable, but orientates them towards a new analogical world-view that allows differences to be differences, and singularities to retain their singularity. Only the analogical world view will prevent the disappearances of the material, the spatial and the temporal in their contemporary overdetermination and complexity. By preventing the disappearances, while embracing some of the radicalness of contemporary insights, theology can offer a redemptive economy for the healing of the nations. A real economy, not a virtual one.

224

9

CITIES OF THE GOOD

The redemption of cyberspace

Furthermore, it is from the likeness of things up there that all the different kinds of things in this lower creation were made, even though the likeness is a very remote one.

(Augustine: 1963, XII.2)

Following the ancient parallel between the human body and the city (Sennett: 1994, 31–123), we began in Chapter 3 to develop a theology of corporeality as such so that the physical body might be understood as mapped onto the body of Christ. In Chapter 4 I explored this further with respect to the displacement of Christ's body such that all human bodies participate in this one body and this participation and belonging constitutes the ecclesial body, the Church. To forward the examination of the nature of this ecclesial body as an erotic community founded within and sustained by the desire of God, Chapter 5 mapped out various models for the erotic community which have come to dominate our current understanding of ourselves as socio-sexual beings. Chapter 6 then began to conceive of a theological account of the sacramental body, emphasising its relationship to the distention of time and also its continual fracturing and coming together within that distention. The distention of time was the temporal axis of the spatialised corporeality of displacement in Christ. Chapter 7 developed this account of the sacramental body with specific reference to sexual embodiment and the performance of gender. Then Chapter 8 began to sketch the relationship between this sacramental body and the contemporary city of angels, pointing out how the figure of angels operates as an index of certain contemporary desires for a frictionless and perfected communication. Thus with this chapter we began to move back to the focus of this book, the contemporary city and a theology partly produced by, but also hopefully productive within, the city that we sketched in Chapter 2, the city of endless desire, the postmodern city, the city that followed the city of eternal aspiration, the modern city. And now we come to the final drawing together of the global city and the city of God (made up as it is of the multiple implicated bodies we have examined throughout) and the depiction of the relationship that binds and bonds them. What has been important throughout is that time is God's grace, and that it comes to us as a gift not of the present alone, but as the pull of both past and future within the present. The city of God is not then imposed upon us in some arbitrary now, some future rupturing event. It is continually being given us to live in and build. It is only possible to separate it from the kingdom of this world, the secular city, by divine judgement. We may speak then of two kingdoms or two cities, as Augustine and later Luther did, but none of us can know the extent to which one is independent of the other. None of us have that true knowledge of where we are at any given moment, or where anyone else is. None of us can know the extent to which any activity we are engaged in is a work in God, and therefore good and true and beautiful, or a work of self-reference, and therefore nothing but the swollen bruising of an injury to the body. There is faith, hope and charity which operates by seeing through a glass darkly.

The Book of Revelation speaks of the final city as one which 'descends out of heaven from God, having the glory of God' (Revelation 21.2). It is described not in the similitude of a Bride and the wife of the Lamb (the similitude is 'prepared like a bride'), for one of the seven angels instructs John to 'Come, and I will show you the Bride, the Lamb's wife' (Revelation 21.9). No similitude is involved. We have moved beyond similitudes, and this is suggested by the way the symbolism – of marriage and liturgical stones, sacred geometry, Jewish Passover, Christian pastoralism, Eden's garden, Jerusalem past and future and Ezekiel's river – buckle under each other with the weight of what they bring from the past and carry into the present. The Bride returns us to the erotics of redemption and the symbolics of Adam and Eve, Israel and Yahweh, and the eschatological wedding. The city is a multi-gendered body and a garden and a liturgical space. No sooner has John seen it than he is in it, walking its street, observing its entrances, recognising the globalism of its space. Here all nations are gathered and healed.

It is important to distinguish between this city and utopia. Utopia is 'no where', without a place (*topos*). This city is to be historically realised. Unlike Plato's ideal state, which depends upon establishing an education system to train and discipline human beings to understand the common and supreme Good, and therefore is forever dependent upon the vicissitudes of human frailty, the Christian city descends as a gift from God. With this city we are not concerned then with sketching institutional structures, political, social, economic and cultural arrangements that will be the conditions for the possibility of the city. The institutional structures etc. in the Christian city must emerge from the responses to God's grace, the good practices which such responses call into existence. On the other hand, the Christian city, like Plato's Republic, is immanent to the forms of all cities, the ideal form that does not float divorced from the cities of the everyday – like Aristophanes' ideal city of birds.[1] This city makes possible the cities of the everyday; and makes possible their redemption. This is the informing idea in Augustine's theology of the city; an idea lost in Luther's theology of the city. As we move towards summing up a Christian theology of the contemporary city it is through Augustine that we must proceed.[2]

Augustine's city of God

As we saw in Chapter 7, Calvin read the distinction Augustine drew between the *signum* and the *res* dualistically, in the nominalist line of word as distinct from thing. It may be that Luther does the same with respect to the distinction Augustine makes between Jerusalem and Babylon, the heavenly city and the earthly city in *De civitate Dei*. As I quoted in the Introduction, 'Of these, the earthly one has made to herself … false gods whom she might serve by sacrifice; but she which is heavenly and is a pilgrim on the earth does not make false gods, but is herself made by the true God of whom she herself must be the true sacrifice (*cuius verum sacrificium ipsa fit*)' (1972, XVIII.54). Furthermore, these two cities are founded upon two antithetical economies of desire, both of them erotic:

> the two cities were created by two kinds of love (*civitates duas amores duo*): the earthly city was created by self-love (*amor sui*) reaching the point of contempt for God, the Heavenly city by the love of God (*amor dei*) carried as far as contempt of self … . In the former, the lust for domination (*dominandi libido*) lords it over its princes as over the nations it subjugates; in the other both those put in authority and those subject to them serve one another in love (*serviunt inuicem in caritate*), the rulers by their counsel, the subjects by their obedience. The one city loves its own strength (*diligit virtutem suam*) shown in its powerful leaders; the other says to its God, 'I will love you (*diligam te*), my Lord, my strength.'
>
> (1972, XIV.28)

We must note Augustine's evocative Latin prose here. For while distinctions are drawing the two cities apart, certain key words (*amor*, *diligo*), the very Latin grammar, alliteration and assonance of the phrasing (where the balanced clauses of either and or are governed frequently by the same verb) and the syntactical repetition bring them back into association. In the language only one distinction remains: *amor dei* becomes *diligam te* through all subjects serving one another *in caritate*; while *amor sui* becomes *diligit virtutem suam* through acts of subjugation issuing from *dominandi libido*. The difference between the kenotic disposition of *caritate* and the despotic disposition of *libido* emphatically remains. In fact, its remaining is rendered more emphatic because of the parallelism governing the passage. One is the perverse imitation of the other.[3] But otherwise the erotic economy, the love (*amor*, *diligo*), in either city is what Augustine will call, with regard to the relationship between these two cities and the temporal goods they both enjoy, *permixtum*, inextricably bound each to the other. And if this is so, if it is difficult to distinguish *amor sui* from *amor dei*, then it must also, by implication, be difficult to judge whether the relationship between those in authority and those who serve them is *in caritate* or the exercise in *dominandi libido*.

Augustine's theology of the interwoven, *permixtum* and his doctrine of distorted representation, *perverse imitatur*, have implications for his account of civic life and a Christian understanding concerning it. In the passage from Augustine's *De Genesi ad litteram*, also quoted in the Introduction, the two forms of love, one holy and the other impious, are described as sociable, on the one hand, and self-centred, on the other. The word for self-centred is *privatus* – that very characteristic so safeguarded by Western liberalism: the concern for the individual's freedom as such. *Amor sui* is the source of social atomism; a perverse individualism that corrodes the possibility for social order. Augustine opposes community to social atomism, concern for 'the common good for the sake of the heavenly society' to the subordination of the common good to self-interest, the sociable *amor* which is characterised by its giveness in friendship to the perverse *amor* 'which isolates the mind swollen with pride from the blessed society of others' (1972, XI, 15). Only the operation of the former can bring about justice and the just society. The proud desire privacy in order the better to please themselves. The coiling in upon oneself that marks the disposition to *privatus* is evoked so clearly in Augustine's *Lalia sua superbia sibi placuerat* (see Markus: 1994, 245–59). There can be no justice where such privacy reigns. Furthermore, it is this same *amor sui* which gives rise to distorted representations of the divine, parodic simulacra of theological truths.

Like Aristotle and Cicero before him, Augustine accepts the classical understanding that human beings are sociable by nature. But his Christian acknowledgement that human nature is fallen leads him to be more sceptical than they of the capacity of human beings to control the power of the *amor sui* that rages to protect and nourish itself: 'all men desire to be at peace with their own people, while wishing to impose their will upon those people's lives' (1972, XIX.12). This is the paradox of being human. And though these philosophers rightly espouse a virtue ethics in which a human being's happiness subordinates all desires to a final Good, while the Good itself is desired for its own sake, Augustine is alert to the fact that the pursuit of the virtues does not 'ensure that the people in whom they exist will not suffer any miseries' (1972, XIX. 4). The philosophers cannot guarantee the happiness that underwrites a human being's pursuit of the Good. Furthermore, what is the Good? 'For we do not yet see our good, and hence we have to seek it by believing; and it is not in our power to live rightly' (ibid.).

It is the play of scepticism and knowledge in Augustine's theology of the city which is significant (see Burleigh: 1949, 184). On the one hand, he sets out to demonstrate that Cicero's definition of *res publica* – a society 'bound together by a mutual recognition of rights (*coetum juris consensus*) and a mutual recognition for the common good (*utilitatis communione sociatum esse determinat*)' – was never fulfilled, because only in Christ can true justice be established and a common weal such that all goods are being used in the same way (i.e. to glorify God). On the other, he emphasises the suspension of judgement in this world on eschatological grounds:

'Therefore do not pronounce judgement before the time, before the Lord comes, who will bring to light the things now hidden in darkness and will disclose the purposes of the heart' (1979: 130.2.4). Distinctions are drawn, judgements rendered, by Augustine, only to submit them subsequently to the hidden and inscrutable operations of divine providence. A theology of commingling has to accept a certain provisionality about its statements; preaches a necessary agnosticism. A doctrine of representation has to accept that it too will not escape producing simulacra of divine truths.[4] So that, in an age when certain Latin theologians, inspired by Theodotus' closure of pagan sites and championing of the Christian faith, were outlining a theology of history in which the Roman conquest of the known world lay the foundation for an *imperium Christianum* now imminent, thus conflating the political with the ecclesial,[5] Augustine both resisted the translation of God's kingdom into sociological, historical and political practices, and the temptation to identify the Church with the Heavenly city.[6] The Church is also a human and earthly institution. Insofar as it is ordered towards the worship and love of God, and participates in the triune operation of that God (both in the natural world and in and through the willed actions of human beings), then it is the heavenly city. But Augustine is also aware that those who make up the ecclesial community are subject to the same desires and temptations of those espoused to the *civitas terrena*. As such a distinction has to be drawn between Christ's true body (*vero corpus*) and Christ's commingled body in this world (*corpus permixtum*), for 'that which will not be with the Lord in eternity should not really be called his body' (1995, III, 32, 45). There is no room, therefore, for either a theocracy or a theopolis.

Augustine, then, both discerns and details the differences between the pagan and the Christian, the impious and the pious, the earthly and the heavenly, the profane and the sacred, the unrighteous and the righteous – while simultaneously confessing the impossibility of translating these distinctions into concrete historical and sociological realities. Hence *amor* is not the only word used in a 'commingled' sense. *Ius* – as both depicting the basis of Roman social order on rights established and defended by law in the *civitas terrena* becomes *ius* as righteousness established by the grace of God in Christ. Virtue, people, community, the good, peace are similarly employed in a double sense, employed both as social, political or moral terms in one city and as theological terms in another. It is this double use which produces the necessary ambiguity, the verbal correlate of the 'unavoidable ignorance' which pertains to knowledge in this world. This is central to Augustine's doctrine of representation: the two cities use the same language in different ways until 'they are separated by the final judgement, and each receives her own end' (1972, XVIII.54). Both cities therefore come under divine providence, God working in and through them towards God's own purposes. It is because the two cities share not only the same temporal good and temporal adversities, but also play a part in God's unfolding providence, that analogical thinking is required. The analogical world-view is axiomatic.

The logic of analogy is here caught up with the logic of parody and the doctrine of the fall. For when love, justice, society and peace are predicates of the *civitas terrena* then they are parodies of predicates of the *civitas dei*; they find their true significance in relation to Christian eschatology. It is a significance which subverts (or restores) their meaning in the *civitas terrena*. But as Oliver O'Donovan has pointed out with reference to the relationship of the political and the spiritual, for Augustine 'disorder is predatory on some order' (O'Donovan: 1995, 143). In other words, the use of these terms parodically in the *civitas terrena* is made possible by the reality of what these terms mean eschatologically: the perverse imitation is the result of the fall when living onto God (*amor dei*) became living for oneself (*amor sui*). Justice, love, peace, sociability and, presumably, the exercise of authority (since there is a 'serving one another *in caritate*') were part of the order of creation, the order disrupted and thrown back towards the *nihil* by the fall. But as the 'natural'[7] order, they constitute the condition for the possibility of the parodies which follow. The heavenly city itself must make possible the earthly city, such that in the *saeculum* 'city' is used figurally, virtually. Augustine suggests as much when he informs us that the two societies of human beings that are the concern of his book 'I also call these two classes the two cities, speaking allegorically (*mystice appellamus civitates duas*)' (1972, XV.1). The Latin again is important. For what Augustine is alluding to here is a way of interpreting the Scriptures, inherited from Origen via Ambrose, by moving beyond the literal or historical towards the spiritual or mystical meaning of the text.[8] He goes on in the same chapter of Book XV to comment that Cain, the murderer, founded the first city, whereas Abel, the pilgrim did not because the 'the City of the saints is up above, although it also produces citizens here below, and in their persons the City is on pilgrimage until the time of the kingdom comes' (1972, XV).

Michel de Certeau offers something of a contemporary inflection of this figural reading of the city, in developing a distinction we have already used concerning the institutional body and the cultural body, a distinction between place (*lieu*) and space (*espace*). Probably, influenced by Roland Barthes' essay on the Eiffel Tower, where the city of Paris is laid out as a text before the elevated observer, certainly influenced by Merleau-Ponty's examination of space in *The Phenomenology of Perception* (Merleau-Ponty: 1962) and the development of a Marxist geography by Henri Lefebvre, in one celebrated essay, Certeau looks down upon New York from the 107th floor of the World Trade Centre. He views the city as a vast text. It is a text that not only writes upon the human body, as an organised place, but a text produced by the human body as it pursues its own individuating desires within the network of streets and the city's totalising planning. 'I shall try to locate the processes that are foreign to the "geometrical" or the "geographical" space of visual, panoptic, or theoretical constructions. These practices of space refer to a specific form of *operations* (ways of operating), to "another spatiality" (and "anthropological", poetic and mythical experience of space), and to an opaque and blind mobility characteristic of the bustling city. A migrational, or metaphorical, city thus slips into the clear text of the planned and readable city' (Certeau, 1984: 93). Certeau's exploration of alterity – the other voice (heterology) and the other space (heterotopia) – issues from this awareness of how each of us subverts the logic of the logical and linear through the distinctive practices of our living, through the individual inflections and declensions of the situating grammar. For Certeau – as probably for Barthes (who wrote his essay on the Eiffel Tower in 1970) and Foucault (who published his influential essay on Bentham's panopticon in 1975) – the questions concerning subversion and a totalising spatiality emerged following what Certeau called the symbolic revolution in Paris in May 1968. The rationalisation of the city, of the space organised and surveillanced by the government, was broken open and recognised as arbitrary. 'The city becomes the dominant theme in political legends, but it is no longer a field of programmed and regulated operations. Beneath the discourses that ideologise the city, the ruses and combinations of powers that have no readable identity proliferate. … The Concept-city is decaying' (Certeau: 1984, 95). Thus any given place or site (*lieu*) is unstable, for it is constantly being displaced by the mobility of any individual's walking or action. To walk is to lack a site, to interpellate the rented spaces 'haunted by a nowhere or by dreamed-of places' (Certeau: 1984, 103). He draws two conclusions: 'Haunted places are the only ones people can live in – and this inverts the schema of the *Panopticon*. … To practice space is thus to repeat the joyful and silent experience of childhood: it is, in a place, *to be other* and *to move toward the other*' (Certeau: 1984, 108–10).

Let me draw two consequences from Certeau's conclusions with respect to our own examination. First, the city, for Certeau, can only ever be a virtual reality. Its structures and organisations are mobilised both by time and subjective desire. To begin with, the city as place is always invested with a certain utopianism – reflecting the goal of human desire as it is fashioned by, and fantasises, in modernity: the ideal of transparency and control, manifesting its own rational system. Bentham's panopticon is reformulated in the dreams of Le Corbusier for a Radiant City, the obsessions of Frank Lloyd Wright for Broadacres, the functionalism of Bauhaus and the glass monoliths of Mies Van der Rohr. Here, as we saw in Chapter 1, salvation is envisaged as issuing from the engineered alignment of a subject's body and mind with the spatial harmonics they walk through and live within, a harmonics regulated and intensified by the maximal use of light and the suggestion of infinite openness. But this utopianism is forever crossed, for Certeau, by the wandering, the tactics, the walking that installs subjects-in-process, subjects subjected to a narrativised identity forever updated and modified. These practices (Butler would call them performances) of individual walking link various sites within the city, articulating the style of the city whilst also making the city for each walker. Certeau explicitly characterises this walking as a form of utterance. A personal and civic voice issues from the way any one figure both confirms the established spatial order – dictated by its call to gather in squares, its cultural zoning and the prohibitions of its walls and *cul-de-sacs* – and, simultaneously, displaces or invents other spaces. '(S)ince the crossing, drifting away, or improvisation of walking privilege, transform, or abandon spatial elements' (Certeau: 1984, 98). A style of usage becomes a way of being, a manner of being, itself as mobile as the spatiality it produces and is produced by. If the city is recognised as a language – and Certeau likens the geometric space of city-planners and architects to the 'literal meaning' constructed by grammarians and linguists – then each of us speaks that language differently and comes to represent what is differently. All these differences would be related, as Wittgenstein observed (also employing the city as an analogy) by a network of 'family resemblances'. Cities as 'haunted sites' are metaphoric. That is, they are places of constant transferral and transit. They are both site and non-site simultaneously. Their actuality is crossed by both the utopianism of city-planners and architects and the heterologia of their inhabitants.

With this in mind we can return to Augustine's own account of the city as a haunted site. In doing so we see an important difference between the way in which meaning is set adrift in Certeau and Wittgenstein and the way that drift maintains a certain order in Augustine. This will be significant for what follows, because in accepting the semiosis of postmodernity (and therefore speaking with its voice), Christian theology must also point to the divine order which maintains this semantic drift of the sign. The move from one meaning to the other, from the earthly city, peace, love, justice, community to the heavenly forms which are the condition for their possibility is not available by inductive reasoning or inference. In the *saeculum* as such all meanings are equivalent – there is this use of love and that, this use of peace and that etc. – because all comparisons and contrasts are immanent.[9] There is no absolute difference, only relative differences. So that, any hierarchy of values established between a series of family resemblances – this form of love, peace, justice, society is better than that one – is based upon a judgement that is also always established immanently. It is only on the basis of the theological difference that transcends the immanent order, that the equivalence becomes evident and the hierarchies can be critiqued as simply subjugation.

We can see this logic unfolding in Augustine's debate with Cicero's notion of a *res publica*. For Cicero, political association was founded upon *ius* as right established by law and the utility of goods held in common. Augustine critiques the hierarchy, calling into question both Cicero's concept of justice and shared goods, revealing that the hierarchy is not based in natural dominion, but on the purely human power to dominate. As such communities come to be defined as 'the association of a multitude of rational beings united by a common agreement on the objects of their love' (1972, XIX.24). Each grouping would have its own languages, local customs historical memory and shared values, but since only one object of love, for Augustine, is the true and right object, namely God, the language of good and bad, worse and better, worst and best can only have reference internal to the organisation and life of the community in question. Pluralism, equivalence and relativism necessarily follow.[10] But,

232

significantly, it is the theological difference which makes possible this judgement, makes possible the distinction Augustine draws between the facts of the case and what really is. The theological difference makes possible the figural reading of the city. It establishes an analogical relationship because it establishes true difference with respect to various similarities. It is an analogy based upon faith: 'the association, of people, of righteous men lives on the same basis of faith, active in love, the love with which a man loves God, as God ought to be loved, and loves his neighbour as himself' (1972, XIX.23).[11] Hence it is that the final relationship that physical, social, ecclesial and eucharistic bodies have with the body of Christ is an analogical relationship. There is no progression or extension of these created bodies into the uncreated body of Christ, just as, for Augustine, there is no progression in history towards a Christian world order, nor any progression either, *pace Plato*, from the sexual erotic to the theological erotic. Neither, though, are there two distinct orders of being. For Augustine such a suggestion of ontological dualism would be Manichean; it was against such a notion of dualism that he argued against Donatist separatism. There are not two kingdoms[12] – the *civitas terrena*, like Augustine's famous understanding of evil itself, is a *privatio bone* – it has no real substance; it is virtual. In fact, Book XIX ends by translating the two loves and the two cities into 'the final states of good and evil (*ad hos autem fines bonorum et malorum*)' (1972, XIX. 28). Having no true substance does not mean that we deny what is received by and through our senses (Augustine warns against such activity) no more than we deny the existence of things which are evil. But we do not fully understand what we see. For only in the eschaton will we be able to judge rightly and understand rightly, and thus have knowledge of anything but in the most provisional of senses.

It is at this very eschatological point that we must pause and raise a question which divides scholarship on Augustine and relates back to other cruxes in his thinking. As *De civitate Dei* enters upon its final three books, the eschatological judgement becomes more pronounced, the separation is developed in detail, and it becomes evident that analogy is replaced by equivocity. That is, while the analogical relations can pertain while both cities share in time, space and materiality, come the eternal we have to recognise that the theological under-standing of love, peace, justice, community is absolutely distinct from any social, historical or political understandings of these terms. The language may be the same but the meaning now is equivocal, not ambivalent, not subject to unavoidable human ignorance nor the inscrutability of God's ways. And this may well seem as if the influence of Mani remained with Augustine: the pilgrim community now perfected as the heavenly city in another life. Is this not a Christian version of the Socratic learning to die well? Labouring in this world while we wait for the deliverance from such labours in life on the other side of death? Is creation simply to be eclipsed? Does the Christian life only begin when this life comes to an end and the Christian is translated elsewhere? We can relate this to a paradox (or contradiction) we came across in Chapter 6 concerning Augustine's conception of time. Because of the absolute distinction drawn between the temporal and the eternal and the characterisation of the temporal as a painful distension, then what is God's relationship to the created order? Why create a painful distension (since time was created with the world, not with the fall)? Hence O'Donovon remarks, 'This (the second feature of Augustine's political thought – that it lacks a theory of progress) seems to me to fall considerably short of what is meant if we speak of the "transformation" of cultural institutions ... What appears to be civilisational progress is, in fact, on the moral and spiritual level, self-defeating' (O'Donovan: 1995, 146–7). It is all too easy to see how in developing a doctrine of the two kingdoms Luther would understand himself as being true to Augustine, and why comparisons can be made by some modern scholars between Augustine and Karl Barth.[13] Barth's *analogia fidei* is also founded upon a radical distinction between the God who is wholly other and the fallen creaturely existence.

The question is whether Augustine's understanding of analogical relationships is similar to Barth's. For while Augustine was composing *De civitate Dei* he was completing *De trinitate*, a book which celebrates and elaborates a doctrine of divine participation in creaturely existence, through a developed analysis of God in time: Christ as the incarnated Logos, the mediating missions of the Son and the Holy Spirit, and an account of human beings as *imago dei*. He is concerned in this book with many of the themes found in *De civitate Dei* – justice, community, fallen human creatures, *amor sui* and *amor dei* – but the model for the operation of analogy in this book is more Platonic. As with human beings in the earthly city, the divine remains invisible and the person will only be able to think and perceive masses and space, little or great (1963, Book VII.3). But Augustine's advice to such people – which parallels his own testimony in the much earlier *Confessions* – is to believe that there might come about an understanding of himself or herself as ' "to the image" because of the disparity of his likeness to God, and "to our image" to show that man is in the image of the trinity' (ibid., VIII.4). Human beings as made 'to the image' of the Trinity is significant for civic relations, for the Trinity is a community of co-equals. Being made 'to the image' of the Trinity returns us to Augustine's affirmation that we are human beings insofar as we are social; the good ordering of the social therefore stands in relation to the image and the glory of God.

With regards to that relation let us examine one of the ambivalent and central concepts of *De civitate Dei* as it is considered in *De trinitate* – that is, the concept of justice. For Augustine asks explicitly how do we know what is just if we are not ourselves just. To become just requires a desire towards that which is just, but whence comes our knowledge of that which we should desire (and will desire because the just is a good, 'a sort of beauty of the mind' we are attracted to)? Augustine deduced that it comes from within ourselves. It is not something in our minds because we have learnt about it by experience, or even imagined it. It is there as a 'form which they behold, in order to be come formed by it and become just minds' (ibid., VIII.4). Justice is living justly and conducting oneself justly as a consequence of beholding this 'form' – for in loving this form human beings love one another because they give to each his or her own. In loving one another they love themselves justly. The Platonic language or 'form' or idea is apparent, and likewise the operation of the psychic within the civic. But Augustine then tells us that 'it is in God that we observe that unchanging form of justice which we judge that a man should live up to (*incommutabilem formam iustitiae secundum quam hominem vivere oportere iudicamus*)' (ibid.). Moving, without categorical distinction, between the nouns *dilectio*, *caritas* and *amor* and the verb *diligo*, Augustine makes the same claim with respect to 'love' (for love is the dynamic for justice). He begins his discussion making a point that seems to parallel the equivocation of *amor* in *De civitate Dei* – that love is only properly called love when it is true love. But then he goes on to demonstrate how love of neighbour is indistinguishable from love of God, so that 'if a man loves his neighbour, it follows from that above all he loves love itself (*consequens est ut ipsam praecipue dilectionem diligat*) ... above all he loves God' (ibid.). The apostrophised observation 'Oh but you do see a trinity' (*vides trinitatem*) if you see charity (*caritatem vides*)' (Book VIII.5) may seem as if we can move from the earthly to the heavenly form directly (as Plato seems to believe in his analogies of the line and the cave).[14] But the discovery of a triad is not necessarily the discovery of the *imago dei* (ibid., XII.1). We learn that we come to understand and discern charity, that charity is possible at all, because the Trinity is the very structure of loving (that is, structured as the endless circulation of lover, what is loved and loving) which *informs* all loving. This renders significant the movement towards understanding evident in *Confessions*: the young Augustine's faithful love towards his concubine and intense love towards the unnamed friend who dies are not repudiated *as such* in his confession to God. They are experiences intrinsic to the movement of God's Providence and the earthly means whereby Augustine is led to understanding divine love as manifest in both love of self and love of neighbour (1991, Books III and IV). *Amor dei* does not deny the value of these other loves, it puts them into perspective because they are 'harmoniously adjusted to this form (*formae coaptatam et congruentem*)' (Book VIII.5) and, in this way, facilitates a correct judgement concerning them. This harmonious adjustment, this understanding of an object, or an action, or a desire with respect to God, is redemptive. Surely this has to be the significance Augustine draws from his confessions – that the life with his concubine is part of the economy of his (and maybe her) redemption. As Augustine writes in *De trinitate* : 'we make the reasonable use of temporal things with any eye to the acquisition of eternal things (*aeternorum adipiscendorum contemplatione faciamus*), passing by the former on the way, setting our hearts on the latter to the end' (1972, XII.3).

To return to the city: several scholars have argued – though not necessarily with appeal to *De trinitate* – that, for Augustine, civil society *must possess* inherent moral validity, and conclude, then, that Augustine does not reject previous classical traditions (from Plato primarily), but baptises these traditions. For our purposes we do not need to resolve paradoxes in the interpretation of Augustine. Augustine may help us by offering the most sophisticated theology of the city, a theology some aspects of which I wish to revisit and reinvest with contemporary significance. But we are not asking Augustine's questions in Augustine's context and, furthermore, following a line a inquiry opened by the hermeneutics of suspicion, we have to question whether the 'Augustine' we have examined, quoted and critiqued is not a production of my own. Mine is not the Augustine who advocated orthodoxy by coercion or who wishes to extol sexual continence as a higher erotic way, for example. And although, even on my reading, the sectarian nature of Donatism, the dualistic cosmologies of Manichean gnosticism and the focus upon the individual will in Pelagius might all be deemed theologically inadequate, mine is not the Augustine of Christian polemics. Nevertheless the Augustinianism argued for (and constructed) here, I suggest, rather than any of the other theorists of the erotic community we have looked at – Hobbes, Spinoza, Hegel, Freud/Lacan – points the way towards a contemporary theology of the city, by celebrating a trinitarian participation. What I take from this Augustine is the observation that only theology can/has envisaged the other side of secularism. Only theology can, therefore, give to secularism a legitimacy that saves it from nihilistic self-consumption, from the atomism of *amor sui*, from the drift into the disorders of the *nihil*. Protestantism at the Reformation lost sight of this, and we now need to retrieve it although in a different way.

The question we now have to ask concerns the relationship between the Church as the erotic community and our contemporary city. This is the question towards which we have been moving throughout the book. Four points need to be clarified on the basis of the ground we have so far covered.

The first one is that, given an analogical world-view, I have no need to argue *for* a relationship between the ecclesial body and the civic. The relationship is already there; a participation already exists on the basis of the intratrinitarian community which causes other analogies of itself, however fallen and however remote, to be. A doctrine of analogy is also a doctrine of participation and causality. We could develop this causal element in analogy much further, with reference to Aquinas. But it is not the elaboration of the logic of analogy with which we are concerned, more the cosmological operation of the analogical with respect to materiality, temporality, spatiality and mimesis.

The second point of clarification is that given the levels of interdependence and interrelationship (they are not the same thing in secularity's immanental thinking, as we will see with communities in cyberspace, as they are in trinitarian thinking); given also the practices of our daily living and the way these impact on and shape the practices of other people's daily living (even if only reactively) – Christians living out their faith (as anyone else living out their implicit or explicit beliefs) *will* contribute to the social energies and the symbolic fields outside the specificities of their ecclesial institutions. Christians *will* contribute: they will reproduce, produce and disseminate a certain social semiotics that are believed to have analogical significance.

The third point of clarification follows directly from this. I have spoken about the Church and I have drawn attention to Augustine's fundamental trinitarian insight that makes possible analogical relations between the earthly cities and the heavenly city. The earthly is situated cosmologically. But we are speaking here of *one* eternal city. How is it possible to avoid the charge of imperialism with respect to those other beliefs systems within which the Christian communities disseminate their gospel? More pointedly, how does a Christian relate to the practices of faith from other theological communities? We are not, as Augustine was (though he was ambivalent about its advantages) at the threshold of a new Christendom. We are at the end of the Christendom which Ambrose, in Augustine's time, and later Gregory the Great promoted. But, we are also beyond pluralism. Pluralism, that is, that recognised different faiths as species of the one generic religion or even different symbolic world-views that were all ultimately grounded in and expressive of the one simply, existential reality. We have moved beyond pluralism because there is no view from no where, no objective knowledge; the view from no where is itself a cultural ideology – often Western, white, and male.

The final point of clarification is a development of this. As we have seen, with Augustine we are not treating of utopia when we examine the city of God and its relation to the cities of the world. For that very reason, while the Book of Revelation ends upon the visionary glories of the New Jerusalem, we return to the present, existing as it does between commemoration and anticipation. The glories of the final city – which John, the writer, does not appear to withdraw from to represent, for he is caught up and remains, as narrator, traversing its heavenly spaces – are not yet. The body is not yet one, not yet whole, not yet healed. I cannot, then, conclude on the knowledge of angels; staring in astonishment, like Dante, at the three eternal rainbows, the constellations of trinitarian love. Christians anticipate this end with every theological analysis undertaken, with every practice (academic or otherwise) in which we are involved. Just as we recall and rehearse the words and actions of the hosts who have gone before us; living out the lives they once lived, in another way. We are, as such, in communion, eucharistic communion, with those before and those who will follow. The final city (a city without an altar, a city in which the eucharist no longer requires a fracture) is the consummation of communion; a space which governs and sustains the Christian sense of community. But it is with today's city, that still requires our theology of the fracture, that we must conclude. For it is here that theology, the theology informing this book, must be practised.

With these four clarifications the question of the relationship between the ecclesial body and the contemporary cultural body remains. I suggest we can move towards a 'thicker description' of the relationship by (1) returning to the specificities of urban living today; (2) offering a theological and critical reading of the root or key metaphor of its culture; and (3) responding to the openings and spaces given, in that culture, for specific theological response.

Millennial Manchester

Let me begin with a personal experience of one morning in May when I was on my way to deliver a 9 o'clock lecture. Oxford Road, a main arterial route in the city and along which the university is situated, is quiet at around 8.15. It was on Oxford Road that Friedrich Engels lived, over a hundred and fifty years ago, observing the slavery and suffering of industrial Manchester that formed the core of his *The Condition of the Working Class in England*. At this time in the morning the traffic has not yet built up, clogging the side streets. The shops have not yet opened. And most of the student population housed between UMIST, Manchester Metropolitan, the Royal Northern College of Music and the University of Manchester are still in bed. As part of the major 'renewal and rebuilding of Manchester City for the new millennium'[15] Oxford Road is caught, at the moment, between the ferocious urban decay that Manchester experienced when manufacturing industry came to an end and the new urban developments as money pours in to constitute it as not only a 'European regional centre'[16] but as 'a leading international city of the future'.[17] I was passing through a cruddy bit just before approaching the new olympic-size pool being built in preparation for hosting the Commonwealth Games in 2002. It was an ugly wet morning, when I came across a body stretched out in the doorway of a functional branch of the UK's leading international bank. Nothing unusual in that – someone sleeping rough. One day walking from one end of Oxford Road to the other I counted seventeen people asking for money, all below thirty years old, some not even in their teens. Among them were four sellers of *Big Issue*. Some sit sprawled across the pavement, some walk from one person to another, some stagger with drink, some lie silent with a notice nearby saying 'Homeless', some are attached to a dog, some beg for money politely, some aggressively, some with a smile and a look which suggests payment in kind is available. But what held my attention with this person – who was so completely dug down into a filthy sleeping-bag that there was no telling whether it is was a man or a woman, alive or dead – what held my attention here were two objects at the side of the figure. One was a half-finished bottle of Chianti and the other was an old copy of Hegel's *Philosophy of Right*.

Now I have seen *Rear Window* (both versions). I know it is only too possible to construct fabulous scenarios around details taken out of context. But it would not alter the significance of my immediate response if it did turn out that the objects had been placed there deliberately to win the attention of people like myself approaching the University of Manchester. What held my attention was not that this figure might have been me, or any number of academics I know who enjoy a glass of red wine and an intense read about the ethical life, social justice and the state. No, what held my attention was the fact that this scene summed up an enormous cultural fragmentation – bits of life that came from various places seemed tossed together randomly. Everything could be catalogued, itemised, but nothing made sense. An undefined body in a dirty, sleeping-bag, a bottle of okay Italian wine, a philosophical classic all out there on the pavement framed by dereliction on the one hand, and international finance on the other, all reduced to the same level not just of banality, but disrespect, degradation.

Manchester has increasingly become what the geographer Saskia Sassen, with respect to London, Tokyo and New York in the 1980s, has termed a global city. The global city is a new type of city manifesting new forms of sociality in a cosmopolitan culture. '(T)oday's global cities are (1) command points in the organisation of the world economy; (2) key locations and marketplaces for the leading industries of the current period, which are finance and specialised services for firms; and (3) major sites of production for these industries' (Sassen: 1994, 4). Following Sassen's analysis of how such cities function, Manchester is now a commanding locus in the organisation of the world economy, a locus in which manufacturing industry has been replaced by specialised service firms and financial corporations. Manchester has more venture capital providers than any other city in Europe according to a report from the Manchester Business School.[18] The city is home to more than sixty banks – clearers, merchants and overseas – augmented by specialist corporate finance boutiques, large account-ancy operations like Ernst and Young and Price Waterhouse, internationally acknowledged corporate law firms, numerous independent finance houses and large insurance corporations.[19] It is a site of both production in these new industries (services and financial goods) and a market for the consumption of these products (Sassen: 1991, 3–6). It is a city woven into an international network through telecommunications and digital services[20] (the National Computer Centre has its home here), housing twenty-five consulates, and locating the regional headquarters or significant operations of multinational corporations (ICL, Siemens, British Vita, T&N, Ciba, Sharp, GEC). It is a city where, in the massive decentralisation of production around the world, co-ordination takes place which has strengthened the city's position as a regional node in a global economy.

There is a hierarchy of such cities both globally and nationally. Globally, Manchester is in the second order rather than the first; nationally, it is one of the top two (Birmingham is often cited as its closest rival) outside London. In the wake of the collapse of manufacturing industry, the economic crises of 1970s and 1980s and decline in population, Manchester has been reinventing itself as an international city, a telecity, and attracting large foreign investment. As the regional capital to the North West of England, it now boasts 2.56 million people and a GDP of £18 billion. So successful has been this reinvention that it was able to submit to the Olympic Games Committee its bid to hold the games in the millennial year 2000. The bid, though not successful, nevertheless helped their successful bid to stage the Commonwealth Games in 2002.

The government has been pleased at the partnerships between the public and private sectors which have facilitated this flourishing. With Birmingham and London, Manchester was asked to take part in the City Pride Initiative and draw up a visionary blueprint of Manchester for the next ten years. The model can be viewed in the local government offices in St Peter's Square. Investment has poured into the city as a consequence, and a new international wealth is evident in its streets. Sprawled across the pavements of several main thoroughfares, like Deansgate, St Peter's Square, Albert Square and Piccadilly, are now a flotilla of street-cafés and theme-pubs offering a dash of Irish or Italian or French or Spanish or Greek to civic living. Between St Peter's Square and Piccadilly lies a China Town as large as London's own, decorated with the largest arch outside China. From the University of Manchester southwards towards Rusholme stretches the Indian curry centre of Britain. Elsewhere, there has been the development of hotels and leisure amenities. And, as the city with the largest student population in Europe, the number of overseas, temporary residents adds to a city already culturally diverse through several waves of immigration.

Sassen's thesis returns us to several of the aspects of post-Fordist or late-capitalist urban regimes noted in Chapter 3. In Manchester we recognise the concrete results of such a shift in the social fabric of the city and its urban culture. As Sassen opines:

> Conceivably, this core of leading industries in the premier cities of the world economy could have the overall effect of raising the quality of life and the quality of jobs for large segments of both the work force and the rest of the population in these cities. And conceivably, the profits and tax revenues these sectors have generated ... could have made it possible for the governments of these cities to help support those in the population who could not share in this new economic order.
>
> (Sassen: 1991, 195)

But, having investigated the social order of the global city, we come back to Oxford Street, Manchester on that morning in May. For the internationalisation of the city has led to a growing inequality of earnings and an inflation in real estate prices. High-income jobs are created but there is 'a much larger share of low-wage jobs than is the case with a strong manufacturing-based economy' (Sassen: 1991, 244). Despite an expansion of the highly-educated and trained work force, income is polarising and employment is increasingly becoming temporary, part-time and contracted. The post-Second World War boom in manufacturing provided housing, roads, shopping centres, schools; the economic revival saw an increase in public goods and utilities. It produced an expansion of the middle-class which deterred and reduced tendencies towards inequality by 'constituting an economic regime centred on mass production and mass consumption' (Sassen: 1994, 101). But the new global generation of monies and the expansion and deregulation of the consumer market comes with greater job insecurity and the dismantling or underfunding of public goods and utilities. New professionals, managers, brokers, mediators and executors set unprecedented levels of high earning power which demands customised goods and informalised labour patterns 'which represents a direct profit-maximising strategy, one that can operate through subcontracting' (Sassen: 1994, 107). Such informalisation, on the one hand, and demands for luxury items on the other, is, as Sassen points out, a phenomenon of third-world cities (Sassen: 1994, 106) now part of most major cities in highly developed countries. As Sassen sharply observes:

> The uncomfortable question is whether the sudden growth in homelessness ... the growth of poverty generally, the growth of low-wage employment without any fringe benefits, and the growth of sweatshops and industrial homework are all linked to the growth of an industrial complex orientated to the world market and significantly less dependent on local factors.
>
> (Sassen: 1991, 334)

Socially, this exponentially developing polarisation maps onto class, gender, ethnic and racial divisions (Sassen: 1991, 244, 248, 318–19; 1994, 99–117). Geographically, this has led to the development of new sites of centralisation and marginality in which there are spatial concentrations of poverty and decay and greater residential segregations accelerating what Sassen describes as the 'white flight to the suburbs' (Sassen: 1991, 253). Furthermore, in this new urban geography the sharp increase of foreign and domestic capital in luxury commercial and residential housing, high-priced refurbishments and redevelopments 'has also contributed to a sharp increase in homelessness' (Sassen: 1991, 254). Every week new billboards in Manchester advertise the conversion of erstwhile warehouses, the refurbishment of office space to designer specification, and apartments with luxury fittings. Segmentation, segregation, polarisation, ghettoisation are the flip side of a new gentrification with its demands for designer styles and fashionable accessories, its 'ideology of consumption' (Sassen: 1991, 317). This consumption is quite different from anything in the past and 'represents a massive appropriation of public resources and urban space' (Sassen: 1991, 317).

The poor, the destitute, the socially and economically and culturally damaged – there are many. And, given the analogical world-view, the Christian cosmology, I have been outlining throughout this book, I am neither innocent nor myself undamaged. The smell of poverty in certain parts of Manchester makes me retch. The hardened features of the desperate, the indifferent and the ones who cannot bear to look is both brutal and brutalising. My briefcase swinging at my side, I head for the halogen lights, fluorescent colours, plastics, tinsels and giant video screens of the Arndale Shopping Centre. I head for the perfumed warmth of the department stores, the smells of rich continental coffees, the racks of fine wines and fine foods on offer in Tesco and Marks and Spencer.

A paradox with enormous social consequences emerges in the global city, and in globalisation more generally. It has at least three faces. First, the more decentralised and globally interdependent economies become, the greater the need for centralising nodes of operation, control centres. Second, the more we acquire the capacity to work as a unit – a global economy 'is an economy with the capacity to work as a unit in real time on a planetary scale' (Castells: 1996, 92) – the greater the production of inequalities (racial, gender, ethnic, geographical, social) and the greater the competition between different atomised sections. Third, the more advanced communication systems become – the faster the relays of information and the flows of capital – the more atomised, segregated and imaginary are the communities they no longer serve but produce.

The city, having undergone major plastic surgery in the late eighties and continuing until today, is disseminating itself. It is living beyond itself in cyberspatial virtualities and global markets. It no longer belongs to or is constituted by its citizens. '(P)lace no longer matters and ... the only type of worker that matters is the highly educated professional' (Sassen: 1994, 6–7). Traditionally rooted in its region and traditionally analysed in terms of its contribution to the nation, cities involved in transnational economies are disconnecting from regional or national urban systems. Floating internationally, global cities are dissolving the age-old analogy between family–polis–state – the scale of interdependencies which remains the paradigm for much political, economic, social thinking and planning (Castells: 1989; Daniels: 1991; Sassen: 1991; Castells: 1996; Sassen: 1994, 29–52). They have to live beyond themselves because what happens on the stockmarket in Tokyo could effect their whole livelihood. '(C)ivil societies shrink and disarticulate because there is no longer continuity between the logic of power-making in the global network and the logic of association and representation in specific societies and cultures' (Castells: 1997, 11). What remains is fragmentation, the dislocation of interests, and a concentration upon the present (again, that commodification of time as the grasping of the present as present) that facilitates an appalling forgetfulness (Virilio: 1991,139–40). Severing connections with the grassroots of the people, catering for the needs of an increasingly mobile and short-stay populace, the polis becomes a panopticon surveying the international scene, speculating here and there on its future aggrandisement. It increasingly can become unmindful of those below, of those who are left behind, of those it cannot retrain, of those it cannot force into new labour disciplines, of those who lack the energies required to turn and turn about in the market, of those who cannot participate in the nervous hyperactivity of its contingent celebrations. In an imaginary community, there are some (maybe many) who are left out because they cannot imagine themselves, and are not imagined by others to be, a part of it. Where the city's most important forms of continuing existence lie in the circulations of electronic data – from the digital images of its wonderful new stadiums and hotels cabled by satellite throughout the world, to the informational and monetary relays on the net that keeps its companies ahead of the race – it is becoming cyberspatial.

The Matrix

The 1999 film by the Wachowski brothers, *The Matrix*, commodifies both the fears and hopes of living in a cyber city; and does so with specific reference to

Judaeo-Christian teachings. First, the city (New York, though it was shot in Sydney) and all its bustling activity is literally understood as a simulacrum. Thomas, alias Neo, the computer hacker, who pirates programs, hiding them in a hollowed-out volume of Baudrillard's *Simulations and Simulacra* – is contacted by a group of figures (led by Morpheus (from the Greek, the male-maker or creator of form), abetted principally by Trinity (introduced as a god among hackers)). He is given to understand by this group that what he believes to be life in 1998 New York is in fact a simulation generated by forms of artificial intelligence existing in 2098 (or thereabouts, since chronological time is now suspended). The program generating the simulation – down to the taste of meat and the neural reactions during orgasm – is called the matrix. Discussed in messianic terms, Neo is the one Morpheus has been looking for to save the city which is tantamount to saving the real as utterly distinct from the virtual. The real is encoded in another framework called Zion. Neo incarnates this programme, which is superior finally to the Matrix. But we only come to understand this, as Neo comes to understand his own misson, by returning to the cyber city, now intellectually trained (through various computer-generated simulations) in a battery of Japanese martial art skills. In a visit to the Oracle (who can determine whether Neo is the One) Morpheus is captured. In a logic of sacrifice-as-gift (a Judaeo-Christian logic), Morpheus surrenders his life to the agents of the Matrix within the cyber city. Neo rescues him and reveals that he is programmed from a different framework than the Matrix, a more powerful and, seemingly, more humane and transcendent framework, draped in Judaeo-Christian imagery, shot through with a Buddhist spirituality and a Hellenic paganism (the Oracle has over her kitchen door, as a Delphi, albeit in Latin *Nosce Tiepsum*). In the last scene, which follows the resurrection of Neo from the dead by the love of Trinity, a decidedly heterosexual love, Neo sends a message to the Matrix which signals, on screen, as the screen, the failure of its system: 'I know you are out there, can feel you now. I know that you're afraid. You're afraid of us. You're afraid of change. I don't know the future. I didn't come here to tell you how this was going to end. I came here to tell you how it's going to begin. I'm going to hang up this phone and then I'm going to show these people what you don't want them to see. I'm going to show them a world without you. A world without rules and controls, without borders or boundaries. A world where anything is possible. Where we go from there is a choice I leave to you.' Then, leaving a telephone-box in downtown Sydney he ascends through the air in dark glass and a full-length black leather coat like Superman-as-Dracula.

This is a complex, postmodern (that is, overcoded) film. The real, the truth as opposed to the virtual, and as represented in Morpheus and his family (he is portrayed as the Creator-Father), remains dependent upon cyber-simulation and telematics. It is difficult, then, to understand what Neo means by 'a world without'. The cyber city remains, Neo returns to it to show 'these people' what its possibilities are. The film does not break free of the power games it depicts. The salvation promised, as suggested by the closing lines, is a negotiated one.

The change and fear-of-change theme expresses a certain neo-Darwinism with which the film is complicit. For the film itself is dependent upon the computer-generated simulations that give it its pace, special effects and drama. It is a visual, multimedia extravaganza, immersing many of one's sensations (touch, taste and smell are continually appealed to through various images) in a new Hollywood style. It produces and reproduces the cyber city, bending, playing with and commodifying its virtuality. It is itself, and it displays, 'A world where anything is possible', an enchanted world. And yet a world fraught with paranoia, violence and the electric tensions of twisted lines of power. It is difficult, then, to understand what Neo means by 'a world without you'. A world without rules and controls, without borders or boundaries. It would be too easy to say this was a film about film. Rather I would return to a connection I made at the beginning of this book with *Metropolis*: film is a medium made possible by, and continually reflecting upon, the city. It is, fundamentally, an urban art. As such *The Matrix* capitalises on, as it expresses (and what better form of advanced, adaptive, versatile capitalism than one which commodifies even its own ideologies and critiques) the new fears, speeds, spaces, materialities and self-conscious virtualities of contemporary urban living. So that ultimately, a theological response to the contemporary city has to be a response to cyberspatiality itself, to virtuality itself. For the cyber city is not a new invention, but the coming to consciousness of what modernity always knew – without God community is always and only virtual. Self-grounding secularity, that is, a secularity grounded upon its own self-reflected knowledges (fundamentally, its mathematical, scientific knowledges of itself) is founded upon a digitality which cyberspace reinforces and renders fully visible.

Communities in cyberspace: a metaphor

'(T)he rapid growth and disproportionate concentration of producer services in central cities … are thoroughly embedded in the most advanced information technologies' (Sassen: 1994, 65). Manchester was the first UK city to announce its telematics strategy, back in 1989. It has a Manchester Telematics and Telework Partnership with an aim to make Manchester a digital city. This will be the image that is projected across every continent with the Commonwealth Games of 2002. Contemporary globalism is inseparable from the continuing expansion of cyberspace. Few have analysed this association better than the French urban sociologist Manuel Castells in his magisterial and exhaustive triptych *The Information Age: Economy, Society and Culture*.

Castells characterises our new social and economic realities as configured by networks of processes, productions and operations. These networks are global and totally dependent upon access to technological know-how. 'Networks are open structures, able to expand without limits, integrating new nodes as long as they are able to share the same communication codes' (Castells: 1996, 470). These information and telecommunication based networks not only dramatically reorganise power relationships, they reconstitute our notions of time and space. Castells analyses space in terms of flows, in which places and local cultures are superseded. He emphasises that it is not placeless, but the logic and meaningfulness of place, rootedness, and an urbanism generating cities of collective memory (see Boyer: 1994) is absorbed into the 'flows of capital, flows of information, flows of technology, flows of organisational interaction, flows of images, sounds, and symbols' (Castells: 1996, 412). For the dominating cultural ideal is to be cosmopolitan. The space of flows is organised by managerial elites. Space, then, becomes ethereal, and time follows suit.

Castells examines the development of what he calls 'timeless time' (Castells: 1996, 429–68), a cultural phenomena which is close to what I have drawn attention to throughout this book – that is, the secular desire to experience the eternal by experiencing the presence of the present. The production, through information technologies, of simultaneity or the compression of time, is the production of timelessness. He points to a paradox in this production: for 'in a universe of undifferentiated temporality of cultural expressions' the culture is 'at the same time of the eternal and of the ephemeral' (Castells: 1996, 462).

What is created overall, and what the network most fully instantiates and maintains is a culture of virtual reality. For the network generates 'a digitalized audiovisual hypertext' (Castells: 1996, 476) that works upon the imagination, consciousness and social behaviour as real experience works on dreams. Again a paradox emerges for advanced communication systems and media diversification both globalises – to the extent that programmes and websites produced anywhere in the world can be relayed to anywhere else in the world at any time – and yet localises – to the extent that there is more targeting, more customisation, increasing segmentation and mass decentralisation (see Sabbah: 1985). The internet constellation, employing the universality of digital language and the pure logic of the network creates the conditions for horizontal, global communication (Castells: 1996, 352), but, simultaneously, ruthlessly atomises, itemising each customer sitting before their VDU constructing their 'home-page'.

> In the mid-1990s it [the internet] connected 44,000 computer networks and about 3.2 million host computers worldwide with an estimated 25 million users, and it was expanding rapidly. According to a survey of the United States conducted in August 1995 by Nielson Media Research, 24 million people were internet users, and 36 million had access to it ... there is a convergence of opinion that it has the potential to explode into hundreds of millions of users by the early twenty-first century.
>
> (Castells: 1996, 351, 354)

Christians stand at a point in time, then, when reading the signs of the times brings with it the recognition that we are all immersed in symbolic processing. Many of us in advanced countries are living in symbolic environments. I

245

CITIES OF THE GOOD

emphasise 'advanced countries', for Castells has significant maps of the world which demonstrate how several huge landmasses just do not exist on the map of global communications, and an examination of what he calls the 'Fourth World' (Castells: 1998: 70–165). These parts of the global body are disappearing, while, in the advanced countries, we are caught up in a massive drift of overdetermined, digitalised meaninglessness. Castells, while, like Certeau, recognising potential for local resistance and political interpellation (Castells: 1997, 68–242), is frank about the nihilism: 'The issue at stake is not the medium is the message: messages are messages. And because they keep their distinctiveness as messages, while being mixed in the symbolic communication process, they blur their codes in this process, creating a multifaceted semantic context made of a random mixture of various meanings. ... They make virtuality our reality' (Castells: 1996: 371–2; 1997; 354–62). The significance of this is that globalism is a self-conscious myth. It is a production – that we are involved in. There is nothing real about it. It exists only to the extent that our symbolic production-line exists. It is co-terminus with it. With globalisation economics becomes metaphorics. The sites of power are now within people's minds.

For the Christian theologian the implications of this cultural shift are enormous. Some of the key concepts organising Christian social ethics and liberation theologies are no longer available. The concept of scarcity has been fundamental to the development in the past of theological economics (Preston: 1991). It is axiomatic in construals of distributional justice. But scarcity is about the finite resources of objects and the optimal use of these resources. It is associated with a concrete world of finite things. For its operations to be defined and its opportunity costs calculated, it is assumed that both the exchange of these finite things and the world in which they can be exchanged can be represented transparently, objectively. That world no longer is there; that mode of representational innocence is no longer there – if, even with modernity, it was ever there. For, as we saw in Chapter 5, virtual and imaginary communities go back to the early years of modern thinking. When scarcity is named we now have to ask where and what is being named, who is doing the naming, how the calculations of resources and their optimal use are being made, what is being left out of these equations (since something always is) and for what reason. 'Scarcities' are produced, they are disseminated, they are ideological freighted. They are not seen and identified from nowhere. They are shifting and shifted throughout global transactions: not fixed. The old concept of scarcity belongs to an identity politics, to a world of locatable agents and calculable goods that cannot operate in a virtual world. In fact, the virtual world – manned (quite literally) in the majority by cosmopolitan elites – knows no such concept as scarcity. Its operational logic is excess and abundance: everything is available, at any time (Cooper: 1997). And therefore, as a corollary, what does distributional justice mean in a network society where distribution belongs to flows of space, flows of information, flows of signs. flows of persuasion? What does social mean as distinct from cultural?[21] What does public policy mean when the public is no longer an identifiable and discrete group of people, and when the power for policy-making, when power as such, is radically decentralised.[22] As Zygmunt Bauman has been continually saying: we need a postmodern sociology; we can no longer simply compose sociologies of postmodernity – the categories do not fit (Bauman: 1992).

If identity-thinking is not available in our advancing cyberspatiality then the kind of Christian communitarian ethics which responded in the late 1980s and the 1990s to the advancing pluralism will also have to change (Brown: 1999). The narrative-bound Christian identities announced by Ronald Thiemann (1985), George Lindbeck (1984) and, albeit covertly, by Alasdair MacIntyre (1981 and 1990, 127–48), which attempt to draw up the bridges and demarcate the boundaries of confessional communities, have to embrace fully the *poeisis* that narrative installs.[22] Narratives truck and trade in signs. Traditions are not static. Therefore the narrative-bound identities of Christians are enmeshed in the larger symbolic processes that characterise Castells' network society. The boundaries cannot be patrolled, the sites of Christian community cannot be mapped and labelled (as Augustine recognised). Christians have no control over the language used and the traditions rehearsed. I repeat the claim I made earlier in this chapter with respect to Augustine's understanding of the city of God: we must necessarily make judgements with regards to all sorts of things and we must, with equal necessity, confess our ignorance. What Sassen and Castells point up is that today, when we consider the analogical relationships binding the physical body to the ecclesial and eucharistic body, when we consider inhabiting, and producing by that inhabiting, the body of Christ with respect to the social and political body, then we have to consider the relationship between these theological bodies and cyberspace. Local theologies have to relate to global, virtual communities in order to understand and redeem the nature of their singularity, their embodiedness. For as Castells notes, with the culture of real virtuality 'The final step of secularization of society follows' (Castells: 1996, 375).

The redemption of cyberspace

The internet 'represents not only fifty years of computer design, but the scientific solution to the death of God' (Interrogate the Internet Group: 1996, 125). Another point of view asserts : 'VR suggests we "see visions" when we close our eyes to the outside world. These visions, I argue, are Ideal ones confirming the "correctness" of the Neo-Platonic associations between light, "vision", and an originary source of truth. This truth source, once widely associated with a "god on high", is now understood as part of technology's praxis: as a result, emerging optical technology itself becomes truth, and, for some, even a god' (Hillis: 1999, 25). Both these statements offer entry points for the Christian theologian to investigate cyberspace. For the Christian theologian these observations require two distinct examinations: the first concerns how we arrived here and the second concerns the resources in the Christian tradition (which, as I have argued, is many but also, formally, one) that might address the nihilistic post-symbolics of death, atheism and idolatry with which cyberspace seems to be invested. The age of what Michel de Certeau termed the scriptural economy, the age of writing that became the age of printing, is giving way now to the age digital enlightenment. Each successive development – from oral to written, from written to print, from print to broadcasting, from broadcasting to virtual reality – refigures the spatial, temporal and material organisation of social life. It refigures the orders of our existence and the way we perceive and read it. It therefore also refigures how we perceive and contemplate God. With Castells' observation that we have taken the final step in the process of secularisation, let me suggest three things: (1) that post/modernity itself, because it is so implicated in the production and expansion of cyberspatial realities, has no resources for rethinking cyberspace critically; (2) that the ethos and therefore the ethics or *Sittlichkeit* of cyberspace perpetuates the pernicious atomism with profound implications for political involvement and social justice; and (3) that theology's contribution comes in the form of reinstating the analogical and participatory world-view that counters, by contextualising, the reduction of the real to the digital. With this last point, a distinction has to be made between theological ideality and idealisation.

In order both to demonstrate the bankruptcy of modernity's resources to think cyberspace differently and enable the inscription of cyberspace within a theological discourse, it is important to recognise that cyberspace has a history that we began tracing in Chapter 5. Conceptually, it goes back much further than the invention and creation of the internet by getting first two and then more computers to communicate electronically with each other. It goes back further than the 1985 science fiction novel, *Neuromancer* by William Gibson, in which the term is first coined and used. It is important to trace the lineaments of this history for the virtual worlds which cyberspace commodifies have been with us a long time: in terms of television and, more generally, broadcasting; in terms of theme parks and shopping malls; in terms of the immersing aesthetic experiences of film, opera and science fiction; in terms of the illusions of *trompe l'oeil* painting and the operation of a transcendental reasoning that constructs the cosmos through the categories of the understanding; in terms of utopian thinking from Plato to Bacon and Montaigne; in terms of kingdoms conceived which are not of this world. Cyberspace is produced out of a certain destiny of thinking, dreaming, hoping, and awaiting. It goes back to ancient and modern metaphysical speculations. It is implicated in these metaphysics and produces a specific cultural ethos with respect to them. It is the history, metaphysics and ethics of cyberspace that we most need to consider. By the redemption I specifically want to suggest that there is a need here for reading this cultural phenomenon (which threatens to absorb and endlessly reproduce cultural phenomena *tout court*)[23] in terms of Christian construals of salvation and so redirect its role in terms of Christian praxis.

For cyberspace is a praxis. It is not a state, a realm, a space at all – these are only the metaphors we use to describe it whose metaphoricity seems to disappear in the electric bombardment (Nunes: 1997, 163–78). It is a practice in telecommunications; a participation in a medium. As we engage in e-mailing, surfing the web, chatlines, downloading or word-processing so we create this 'other' place and make it relate to the times and spaces of our lived existence. It is a continuing exposition of the logic of the Enlightenment's three dominant ideals; fulfilling these ideals in ways which require theological interrogation – because VR is not innocent, not neutral, not just a tool like other tools honed for us by advancing technology.

First, it is another promise of being able to grasp and capitalise on the moment – fulfilling the ideal of total presence. Its metaphysics is indissociable from the modern conception of time as a chain of discrete instants, each immediate and self-contained, whose potential is there is to be realised – a conception of time we examined in Chapter 6. The gratification of human desire comes in the experience of the presence of the present. There is no remembrance in cyberspace, only a memory bank for the retrieval of arbitrary pieces of information. The compression of time in cyberspace, the erosion of the time-lag difference between thought and its representation, imagination and the real, the symbolic and the concrete, that is a characteristic of working in cyberspace, is concomitant with modernity's ideal.

Ethically, the result is atomism: the gratification of monadic desires in discrete locations divided one from another. One VDU, and hence communicant, is electronically networked one into another such that space too becomes compressed: I can interface (in 'real' or 'asynchronic' time) with anyone, anywhere else in the matrix; I can order books shipped from a hundred different international publishing houses. Everyone is my near-neighbour, the divisions lie only with the finitude and limitations of my own choosing. The divisions and distances are subjective, in fact, locking each monadic unit in the very subjectivity of its own limitations. Because the divisions are not spatial, they do not announce a geography that can be mapped; and that makes the divisions more problematic because they are rendered invisible. The divisions can never therefore be overcome because radical decentralisation is axiomatic for the operation and production of cyberspace. They are continually reaffirmed. As such there is no other in cyberspace; only different terminals logged into the same matrix which produces the same material in any number of distinct places; only projections and fantasies of the other in a relay of mind-games. The thinker who has done more to prepare the West for the electronic age, Paul Virilio, observes, critically: 'The specific negative aspect of these information superhighways is precisely this loss of orientation regarding alterity (the other), this disturbance in the relationship with the other and with the world. It is obvious that this loss of orientation, this non-situation, is going to usher in a deep crisis which will affect society and hence, democracy' (Virilio: 1995).

Hence the notions of self-transcendence in virtual-reality involve a category mistake. The consciousness can be displaced or diverted into a cyber reality, as its focus can be softened with various drugs, or lack of sleep or the low flickering of fluorescent light in supermarkets, but one cannot author one's own transcendence. Nor can the body be left entirely behind as the mind races down the superhighways of technicolour information: gloves are worn, mice are clicked, joysticks are handled, suits are donned. The seeming erasure of the interior and the exterior does not constitute self-transcendence: only a psychedelic consciousness which remains, albeit stubbornly, one's own.

Furthermore, this monadic dispersal which connects me *de facto* to everyone, everywhere, who owns a computer and has access to the internet, constructs relationships established on the basis of the production/consumption of information. The virtual community it establishes exists in and as the endless exchange of signs divorced from embodiment. The larger the pseudo-space gets the deeper the social and political aphasia it fosters.

The second of modernity's ideals to which cyberspace approximates is the ideal of total knowledge – the knowledge not only of the angels, but the access to the omniscience that pervades the Enlightenment pursuit of the ultimate encyclopaedia, Hegel's dialectical drive towards the absolute, Wagner's *Gesamtkunstwerk*. As such cyberspace offers the illusion of unlimited control, control beyond the limitations of the physical body. Cyberspace promises the sublime experience such that one can lose oneself as one appears to move through a vertiginous infinite at a speed which makes the heat beat quicker in a friction-free accumulation of knowledge. Part of that transcendental allure is the experience of DVD clarities which improve upon the real world by filtering and abstracting from the perceived and experienced in order to produce the digital ideal.[24] Immersed in a million choices of scintillating direction and not wishing to leave any single avenue unexplored, any treasures unconcealed, the adrenaline rushes towards a state of hyperventilation. Jaron Lanier – who coined the term 'virtual reality' – speaks of it as 'technology as ... an experience of infinity' (Lanier and Biocca: 1992, 156). Michael Heim discusses the 'esoteric essence' of VR as the experience of 'the sublime or awesome' (Heim: 1993, 123, 137). The promised total enlightenment has its analogue in Spinoza's third knowledge examined in Chapter 5, where God is one substance and the mind strives to enter the eternity and infinity of God's own intellectual love. Hence its links with death or the annihilation of the self. Transcendence is becoming one with the whole, experiencing the diffusion of self into the sublime. Cyberspace holism promises the same ultimate freedom. The holism is predicated on a radical immanentalism: cyberspace produces and reproduces itself. It is a self-sustaining universe. In this lies its true identity: the apotheosis of the secular. Hence, again, the need for a point from which to interrogate its lack of alterity. Hence also the need to examine its power with respect to new forms of fascism – fascism without a charismatic *Führer*. For as Philipp Lacoue-Labarthe, in his exploration of the aestheticisation of the political observes: 'the *Gesamtkunstwerk* is a political project ... that finds its truth in a "fusion of the community" (in festival or war) or in the ecstatic identification with a Leader who in no way represents any form of transcendence, but incarnates, in immanent fashion, the immanentism of the community' (Lacoue-Labarthe: 1989, 70). Fascism is the final expression of the secular desire for total knowledge.

Thirdly, cyberspace approximates to modernity's Promethianism – the vision of human potential that finds early expression in that oration by Pico della Mirandola in 1486 where human beings 'can become whatever we will', even children of God. This is the ideal of total power. The lure of cyberspace lies in the endless opportunities it promises for new spaces, new sites, new sensations and new adventures. Advocates like Mark Poster, emphasise virtual reality as a 'realm of plenitude and self-presence' (Cooper: 1997, 103; Poster: 1994 and 1997). The desire is evoked to experience one's own power, one's own being. Being as power, the actualisation of one's own being as and in the act of being powerful, is axiomatic for the allure of cyberspace to operate; it redirects the *libido dominandi* behind imperalisms, fascisms, colonialisms, and enterprise initiatives towards the cultivation of an inner space. As 'the scientific solution to the death of God' VR is the dawning of a messianism without the Messiah. In fact, we each are our own messiahs. Physical bodies will be resurrected as 'a unique and immutable body will give way to a far more liberated notion of "body" as something quite disposable' (Randall Walser quoted in Rheingold: 1991, 191). And so, the eschaton arrives for we save ourselves by 'becoming what we will.' We save the world at the same time because the monad participates in the illusory production of a technosociality, a technodemocracy in which all bodies (now virtual) belong to and make up the one global body, the virtual community, the internet. If some of the apocalyptic voices warning us about cyberspace are true then it not only produces and maintains the frontier-spirit, but by that production and maintenance it is self-colonising, emptying (by consuming) the world of reference and the real, replacing (by producing) it with digital simulacra. As such, cyberspace trades upon absence: substituting the authentic for the replica to the point where the authentic loses its value or is even forgotten. The modern subject of desire – Hegel's subject, Nietzsche's, Freud's, Lacan's – receives its final form as divine, omnipotent and omniscient in virtual reality. For that reason cybersex has such a significant presence in virtual reality. The desire to conquer and possess is erotically driven; and so, as we saw in Chapter 5, cybersex provides the fantasy space for such consumption. Michael Heim speaks of the erotic ontology of cyberspace (Heim: 1993, 107). Pornography and sex-oriented chat-lines focus this ontology most precisely, revealing the dialectic of desire and need that perpetuates communication, even stimulation, founded upon absence. The production of a virtual reality itself is the ultimate substitutive act of the libidinous subject. Such Prometheanism demands the death of God in order to appropriate what Regis on the transhuman condition describes as 'the power to remake humanity, earth, the universe at large' (Regis: 1990, 7).

The logic of the move from cities to cyberspace becomes clear. For cyberspace is announcing that it can provide what those modern cities of aspiration and those postmodern cities of endless desire both promised. Cyberspace is the outworking of modernity's dominant modes of thinking with respect to space. It is the final development in secularity – that is, the belief in the self-validation and self-containment of this world, a world without transcendent values, a world to which God is dead. But it is more than that. In the volume of essays entitled *Radical Orthodoxy* (1998), John Milbank, Catherine Pickstock and myself, as the editors of the volume, spoke of the implosion of secularism which characterises contemporary West European and North American society. Cyberspace is a profound expression of this implosion in which the values of secularity – humanism, contractualism, freedom, democracy, liberalism, progress, dialogue, consensus – have collapsed upon themselves and, now inverted, are celebrated in and through simulacra. In other words, the reality that secularity sought to establish, the reality without God, proclaims itself in cyberspace for what it always was: virtual. But now we face the most acute problem, for cyberspace also subverts the old dualisms upon which traditional metaphysics and the ideals of modernity, are founded – subject/object, symbol/signified, idealism/realism, name/thing, mind/world, soul/body, infinite/finite, immanence/transcendence, active/passive, public/private. It does not erase them: digital coding is binary based. The dualisms are internalised and rendered invisible to the participant. In fact cyberspace is a gnostic world-view where minds operate at a vast remove from bodies. But this internalisation and invisibility of the dualisms upon which modernity was founded is significant with respect to the need to think it differently. Cyberspace trades in post-symbolic worlds, but the non-realism of modernity metaphysics was always balanced by an appeal to real 'out there', things in themselves. Reference has always been problematic, more so since the divorce between words and things gained cultural purchase in the late medieval period, when the word *virtualis* was philosophically debated by Scotus and Ockham in connection with logical possibilities (Cunningham: 2000). But the hyperrealities of cyberspace no longer engage with the nominalist divide between sign and thing. The sign is the thing; the thing is composed of digital signs processed at electronic speed. There is a social constitution of the digital – a history, a metaphysics, a technological practice – but now there is a digital constitution which transforms desires, perceptions and imagined possibilities in the social. Such that, while the social still frames the VDU, the digitally simulated and the concrete particular mutually effect each other. Two thousand computerised satellites in outer space currently monitor and control our lives on earth. The categories structuring modernity's metaphysical questions concerning epistemology are transformed as knowledge becomes the absorbing or, at least, collection, organisation and storing of bytes of information. There is no operation of transcendental reasoning here, no dialectic between perception and conception, thinking and experiencing, naming and quiddity, noumenal and phenomenal, reference and sense. Cyberspace renders modernity's concern to make knowledge conform to its object so that truth is determined by the adequacy of knowledge to the one reality 'out there', redundant. The knowledge is already pre-packaged and comes complete with a date of manufacture (or updating) and a breakdown of its components (each of which, if clicked on, provides another informational site). Knowledge as such is atomised, so that the world of cyberspace is a world completely catalogued and known. And since, for some time now, as we have seen, the factuality of the concrete has been founded upon the atomisation of distinctive properties and the digital simulation is likewise founded upon the principle of atomisation, there will be enough common ground for one to slide towards and into the other. As talk of the real has to be placed in scare quotes because it is recognised as always socially constructed and endlessly aporetic, talk about the virtually real as distinct from the real becomes precarious. The virtual is not the other of the real; the virtual is not a parallel world to the real one: they are mutually constitutive. Drawn one to another their difference dissolves. As we have seen, for some time now modernity has been producing a weak or hermeneutic ontology where all experience of reality is fictional and indissociable from metaphoricity, cyberspace is the ultimate encoding of soft ontology. Modernity then no longer has the resources to critique virtual reality. The radical critiques modernity fostered to reflect upon its own creations – the critiques of those masters of suspicion – have now lost their critical force because cyberspace has imploded and internalised modernity's programme. The postmodern critiques avail little either. Baudrillard can only conceive that we need to think simulation, seduction and simulacra through to their very end. Derrida and Lyotard, in their different ways, can only transcendentalise aporia. Mark Poster writes, significantly:

> The Internet resists the basic conditions for asking the question of the effects of technology. It installs a new regime of relations between humans and matter, and between matter and non-matter, reconfiguring the relation of technology to culture and thereby undermining the standpoint from within which, in the past, a discourse developed – one which appeared to be natural – about the effects of technology. The only way to define the technological effects of the Internet is to build the Internet.
>
> (Poster: 1997, 215–16)

Technology is no longer an aid, a tool, a prosthesis extending human capacity. It is an environment, a culture that is re-enchanting construals of the real and the world.[25] The slide of the analogical world-view into univocity, equivocity and dualism opened a space in which the digital world-view was waiting to happen. There are no mysteries, except for the technologically mystified – for all is pre-programmed by the 'Gods', formatted, with access to the superhighways of information controlled, and toll charges all along the route. Communication, cyber-relationality, is time-charged. This is important when considering again the ethos of cyberspace: it produces (and reproduces) a certain technocracy which correlates with income-generation and develops new forms of class division, new kinds of poverties civically, nationally and globally distributed. Once more, there is an *ethical interjection* that can obviously be made, but to *redeem* the situation means rethinking this analogical world-view with respect to its digital reduction and simulation; rethinking creation in terms of its creator: a creator who maintains and validates its reality and its standing. Only theology can do this; for only theology reflects upon the relationship between the uncreated creator and creation *on the basis* of what the Godhead has revealed about both itself and its desires and designs with respect to creation. The theological makes differences different, makes particularities singular and concrete. It is the theological which opens up difference as such (as Hegel understood). The analogical world-view recognises the traffic of signs and its own involvement with it. It recognises also the semiosis that is inevitable in such production and exchange. But the analogical retains a sense of the created order, a transcendent order; a logic beyond its own logics which shepherds meaning and establishes judgements about what is true, good, beautiful and just. The most successful secular critiques of cyberspace are made on the basis of identity politics – the critiques of gender, ethnic and class blindness (Wise: 1997; Burkhalter: 1999; Donath: 1999; O'Brien: 1999; Wakeford: 1999). The theological critique would still require these, but it can go further. These critiques, as I have argued above, are criticised themselves for employing categories of substantial identity that are considerably weakened in a culture of real virtuality, a culture of metaphor, narrative and allegory; they still rely upon the existence of the liberal if not Cartesian subject. Furthermore, they are local and call for modifications to, or extensions in the availability of, the system. The theological critique is more global and works with a transcendental, rather than immanent, construal of the other. It can offer critique and re-envisaging; it can offer a notion of the common good on the basis of a theological rather than cultural or political anthropology. It can resituate the virtual with respect not to the nihilistic post-symbolics of death and atheism, but with respect to the living God and the communities of the faithful.

This theological interpellation to redeem cyberspace would situate the digital, the virtual, the secular – which are profoundly interconnected, as we have seen – with respect to the analogical. There are entry-points where such an interpella-tion is possible. If the modern, as distinct from the classical, concept of democracy is heavily indebted to Christian construals of the Kingdom and the eschatological community (for in classical antiquity social, economic and sexual hierarchies visibly maintained the democratic space) – then the Pauline description of the inclusive body of Christ as a place where there are no racial differences (between Jew and Gentile), class distinctions (between slave and freeborn) or gender inequalities (between male and female) fulfils the promise that promotes and extends the frontiers of cyberspace (and the globalism it makes possible) redemptively. Advocates of the internet, like US Vice-President Alan Gore, have preached the new democracies of on-line interaction where gender, race, class, age or aesthetic (ugly/beautiful, fit/unfit) differences are erased. I can speak (or write) with a global freedom. Unfettered from my socio-economic placing I can participate in e-mail and discussion lists, various bulletin board systems (BBSs) employed by newsgroups to which I can belong, Internet Relay Chats (IRCs) and Multi-User Domains or Dungeons (MUDs). And in this way I can mix with experts and professionals, students, civic library users, anyone who has access to a terminal and is linked into the internet either through an institutional or a commercial server. I can enter 'rooms' in 'real time' and exchange advice, offer opinions, contribute to a discussion and none of the other users will know whether I am black, female, in this income bracket or that, Irish, Muslim, disabled, brain-surgeon or farmer.

In his book *The Virtual Community: Homesteading on the Electronic Frontier*, Howard Rheingold compares the relays in the on-line community to a gift-exchange system where useful information or advice is offered, information or advice which one would have to pay to receive in the 'real world' (Rheingold: 1993). This exchange differs from Maussian gift economies, where the gift establishes an obligation to reciprocal giving between two particular people drawn into a personal bonding, so that the on-line 'system of sharing is both more generous and riskier than traditional gift exchange' (Kollock: 1999, 222; see also Bell: 1991 and Carrier: 1991).[26] The obsessions of self-interest, characteristic of contractual models of society such as we saw in Chapter 5 and the solipsism of terminal interfacing with terminal, have to be viewed alongside the narratives of co-operation among members of communities in cyberspace (Mele: 1999, 290–310). Furthermore, on the net, everyone has equal access to the information, so the sharing has a much wider distribution potential (though a greater potential also for those who wish to free-ride on the backs of others without contributing themselves to the production of a more public good). Phil Patton, suggests: 'computer-mediated communication ... will ... connect us rather than atomize us' (Patton: 1986, 20). This is important, for I have been concerned throughout this book with demonstrating the acceleration of social atomism and its nihilistic consequences for both the city and constructing a theology of the city. I would put Patton's observation in the conditional – without the analogical world-view the basis for resisting that atomism is itself insubstantial. We would be relying on 'communes of resistance identity' (Castells: 1998: 351) which are neotribal units easily vanquished in the divide and rule logics of the market. Globalisation and the network society in its various forms offer, potentially, a certain interconnectedness – though not interdependence (because it lacks a transcendental economy of participation). It is not analogical, and the digital alone makes both bodies and persons disappear (Der Derian: 1998, 2); but contextualised by the analogical world-view it makes manifest and substantial the difference-in-relation binding the material, the anthropological, the cultural, the sacramental, the ecclesial and the theological, argued for throughout this book.

We need not, then, cynically dismiss the potential of the internet by suggesting that at the very point when our own world seems prey to ecological disintegration, social and political anarchy, and cultural banality, another world is founded to which we can all digitally migrate and start again. We need not picture the future as becoming one with the machines we have created, cyborgs, entering the domain of ultimate plasticity and friction-free fantasy where heaven (no longer figured as lying by green pastures, surrounded by loved ones, basking in the sunshine of triumph over death) is the endless adventure of second generation Star-Trekkers participating in the perfect democracy of the *Enterprise*, intrepidly surfing the pleasures, surprises and beauties of an electronic universe. Such depictions of cyberspace can only come about when the digital world replaces actual communities, and telecommunication networks erase the significance of social networks. We are heading in this direction if the Haraways and Posters, the Sassens and Castellses, the Featherstones and Harveys, the Baudrillards and Lyotards, the Vattimos and Baumans, the Nancys and Žižeks, the Urilios and Giddenses are to be believed. But we need not. Power today, the power to change human behaviour, the power to change minds, lies in the dissemination of information, the use and abuse of modes of representation by various forms of media. Theology is not either without access to this power or free of its problems. Theology can speak. It can argue for the establishment of an analogical world-view in which the materiality of bodies is maintained and sustained by a theological construal of creation. It can amplify and transform what other, non-theological discourses are announcing as the direction in which we are heading. Analogically contextualised, the internet and the virtual communities it establishes, could then supplement our social relatedness and we would employ the computer prosthetically. This vision would constitute the theological response, and interjection, to the culture of virtual reality which is the non-foundational foundation of the contemporary city.

Epilogue

Castells observes that:

> people still live in places. But because function and power in our societies are organised in the space of flows, the structural domination of its logic essentially alters the meaning and dynamic of places. Experience, by being related to places, becomes abstracted from power, and meaning is increasingly separated from knowledge. It follows a structural schizo-phrenia between two spatial logics that threatens to break down commu-nication channels in society. The dominant tendency is toward a horizon of networked, ahistorical space of flows, aiming at imposing its logic over scattered, segmented places, increasingly unrelated to each other, less and less able to share cultural codes. Unless cultural and *physical* bridges are deliberately built between these two forms of space, we may be heading toward life in parallel universes whose times cannot meet be-cause they are warped into different dimensions of a social hyperspace.
>
> (Castells: 1996, 428)

The argument of this book has been that only the construction of an analogical world-view is able to build those bridges, and stop that liquidation of space and time and the disappearance of the material. It is the analogical world-view that I have being reconstructing. Theologically, it is an explicitly Christian analogical world-view in which, beginning with the physical body of Jesus the Christ, all other forms of body – sacramental, ecclesial, the gendered human body, the social – find their place in the continually expansive Christological *corpus*. Other accounts of the relationship between the divine, the human and the created order – Jewish, Islamic, Hindu, Buddhist – will construct their own analogical world-views. They have different resources for that construction which means that they will construct them differently. But in analogy, difference is only different because it is in relation to. As we have seen, difference cannot be hypostasised (and commodified) without falling into indifference. Because of the nature of analogical world-views, there can be no tight and policed boundaries around any of them. Christianity, the practice of the faith that I can speak for or from, comes in a diversity of forms and is continually defining itself, on the one hand, *against* other positions and, on the other, *with respect to* other positions. As both ideologies and praxes, theologies are culturally produced and productive. The interdependence and interrelationality of all things, which is what I have argued for throughout this book, cannot defend the walls of some medieval notion of Christendom. Christendom is over; and with it Christian hegemony. To return to Augustine, the body of Christ exists virtually in and through other bodies – social and political. These physical bodies that everyday or every week or every month or every year partake of the eucharistic body, belong to various ecclesial bodies, view and read their lives with respect to dwelling in the body of Christ, and also participate in social practices, also dwell in social spaces occupied by those who dwell in other theological worlds, with, at the very least, equal faith and equal integrity. The city is a collocation of shifting networks of relations in which I live with my Jewish neighbour, I eat with my Muslim friend, I listen with the Quaker who sits and listens with me, and I slowly learn about the religions of South Asia, a world I approach cautiously through a critical self-awareness facilitated by postcolonial theorists. I can and do remain a Christian, but my body is continually mapped onto other bodies; bodies which have no theological affiliations (political groups, cinema clubs, community welfare programmes) and bodies that are involved in practices of faithful living in theologies not my own.

From Augustine I take the insight that we need to suspend judgement. I take it in a way that differs from him. As Christians we have to suspend judgement concerning other faiths. In this middle place (as Christians interpret time between the Ascension of Christ and the eschaton), we must necessarily make judgements with regards to all sorts of things and we must, with equal necessity, confess our ignorance. We must suspend our judgement about those who pursue love, mercy, justice, and righteousness in other practices, in other communities, with other liturgies and symbolic exchanges. We must sink ourselves deeper into our own traditions, meditating upon the grammar of the faith we live, the Scriptures that embody that grammar, and we must not be afraid that others do things differently, not only elsewhere but here, in the urban spaces we share and produce. We share even before we come to appreciate the differences. We share so much. We participate in so many different levels of social interaction, so that my assertion of exclusivity debilitates us both: both of us are injured, both of us are violated. To deny relation is to act against the theological condition of things. The real questions about the relation of different faith communities and traditions only emerge as we learn to live together without fear. We cannot presuppose the outcome, as liberal Christian pluralisms did in their neo-Kantian espousal of different symbolic takes on the one ultimate reality. We cannot solve the complexity of the relation before the real questions have emerged. And the real questions only emerge in the practices of our everyday living alongside each other. Then, having dwelt together, maybe we can sit around a table and, looking each in the eye, describe how we have been put through this trial, we have been blessed because of that, we have been pained by this persecution, lived through that darkness, experienced this hope and yet, in the simplicity that hallmarks truth lived out, each can announce that throughout God has been faithful. Our God – whatever we understand by that.

In the meantime, as Christians, we belong to a community that is open-ended and, therefore, continually has to risk. This is the communitarianism I am advocating – confessionalism which accepts, embraces, *poeisis*; that believes in teleology without being able to predict the future. I join my voice to others, like Homi K. Bhabha, who writes: 'What is theoretically innovative, and politically crucial, is the need to think beyond narratives of originary and initial subjectivities and to focus on those moments or processes that are produced in the articulation of cultural differences. These 'in-between' spaces provide the terrain with for elaborating strategies of selfhood – singular or communal – that initiate new signs of identity, and innovative site of collaboration, and contestation, in the act of defining the idea of society itself' (Bhabha: 1994, 1–2). Bhabha speaks primarily of ethnic and cultural differences and movements beyond our narratives. I speak of a movement beyond the narrative which binds Christian practice and formation through a deepening sense of the rich interpretative openness of that narrative. The Christian community always waits to receive its understanding, waits to discerns its form. It is a community that produces and occupies a space transcending place, walls and boundaries, a liturgical, doxological space opening in the world onto the world. It is a community whose admission of not-knowing, whose admission of different modes of knowing, substantiates its wisdom. Not that the pursuit of knowledge is wrong. We must continually strive to understand, for it is not just we, but the faith we live that seeks understanding, seeks clarification in the movement towards true judgement. But we must recognise that our knowing, thinking, and representing is time-bound, situated and, therefore, incomplete, open to what is more and limited by that which cannot yet arrive – the questions of tomorrow. The suspension of time, space, and materiality demands the suspension of judgement. We do not know how the story ends and we do not know how far we have come in the plot. We do not know how many other characters have yet to appear, have appeared, appear already. We do not know whether we are a leading player or in a supporting role. We do not know what we say when we say 'Abba', 'Lord', 'Christ', 'salvation', 'God'. We see so few of the connections which make up our lives, and so few of our connections with other lives. We see so few of the consequences of our smallest actions. We cannot even begin to calculate the chains of circumstance which have delivered us to this point. Our certainties are persuasions; our facts are selections from the data available; our dogmatisms speak more about our fears than our aspirations. There is no room for Christian imperialism; crusades in the name of the triune love misconceive the kenosis of that love. That love is poured out eternally *on behalf of* not *against*. It works alongside, transfiguring the ordinary, transforming the mundane. It persuades; it does not coerce. It bears witness, and ultimately that is what we all do – Christian, Jew, Muslim, Hindu, Buddhist, atheist, agnostic – we each bear witness to that which we believe. The judgement of the witness lies elsewhere.

Christians constitute something of the city in this place; the collocation of interdependent bodies located here rather than there, and yet always extended beyond ourselves – even to the furthest shores of the most distant sands. Cyberspace mimics this analogical connectedness; the engineering of the real (the possibility of which designers of the modern city dreamed) encrypts, in mathematics, space and matter reduced to inert stabilities. In cyberspace the cities of aspiration and the cities of endless desire are revealed for what they lack – truth, authenticity, justice, goodness and beauty. They are and always were simulacra. They were always virtual; that is, abstracted to the point of commodification. And this concealed the mystery of connectedness and the profoundity of co-operation and the sacral ethics of responsibility that is, ultimately, not to one another, but in and through one another to God. And, yes, we do not know what we mean by God. And yes that assertion 'I am a Christian' is not an identity statement. For my intellectual grasp upon what it is to be a Christian is weak, hermeneutical. I follow. I do not know what it is I say when I say 'Christ'. I give myself over to that which I have come to recognise is more than I and dearer.

We constitute and continue to prepare what the psalmist in Psalm 107 calls a 'city of habitation'. The city of habitation gathers out of every land, receives those spirits who have sunk, rescues the troubled from their distress, satisfies the thirsty and fills the hungry with good things. We make visible a theological statement about embodied redemption. That body on the street of Manchester accuses me, calls out, not like the blood of Abel, for vengeance, but like the blood of Christ for justice, for righteousness, for a new relationality. Alone I have no answer to give my accuser. I cannot begin to conceive how I alone can change the economic, the political and the cultural promotion of social atomism. And I am as seduced as the next person by the bright new goods in the tastefully lit windows – the calls to how I should look, should dress, should accumulate, should spend, should protect my own best interests. The theologian's task cannot be one which provides the solutions. The matrices of power – economic, political, cultural and historical – that brought about and continue to produce alienation, solipsism, incommensurate and unequal differences, are complex. The theologian's task is to keep alive the vision of better things – of justice, salvation and the common good – and work to clarify the world-view conducive to the promotion of those things. As such, the theologian prophesies, amplifying the voice of the accuser. But the theologian is also mother, brother, lover, son, child, church-member, neighbour, friends, cousin, taxpayer, resident, employer, colleague. Alone I have no answer to give to my accuser, and because of his or her own silence, his or her own degradation, then I can pass by and, muttering an apology, pat my pockets of loose change. But something in me dies with such a denial. And so I must find a way not to be alone before that accusation. I must find a way of not being paralysed by the accusation, and frozen into the condition of being permanently accused. I must speak. I must respond. I must not be afraid of the differences. And I must find a way of joining with those who are also ashamed. *There* is the beginning: the reappropriation of analogical relations, the delineation of a theological cosmology, the constitution of cities of God, the recognition that I only belong to myself insofar as I belong to everyone else – insofar as I have been given to this situation, in this context, with these questions, and this task *saeculum saeculorum*. Given, thank God, by God, in God, suspended …

St Thomas Aquinas Day (28 January) 2000

NOTES

INTRODUCTION: THE SIGNS OF THE TIMES

1 I am more than aware these are not representative cities, if, indeed, any single city can be generically representative. I cannot speak for cities in Latin America, for example, on most of the African continent. I speak of Western European and North American cities specifically and that must severely qualify large statements about civic life in the opening of the third millennium.

2 Others have attempted to answer that question for different times. We will be exploring some of their work. Most recently Harvey Cox, in the States, and Jacques Ellul, in France, asked, in their different ways, what is the meaning of the contemporary city.

3 'Church Going' in Larkin: 1955.

4 Though the 'I' in *The Confessions* is what the linguists call a 'pronomial shifter'. Augustine does not proleptically conceive of the 'I' as a Cartesian ego. Though the history of this 'I' is always Augustine's, by our speaking this 'I' in reading we see through the eyes of this I and participate in the formation of Christian personhood. I enter into Augustine's I and come to understanding in him our place in Christ as persons. See also O'Donovan: 1980 and Ruokanen: 1993.

5 The writing begins with the inscription of boundaries that found the city, the first ploughed furrow and the rituals (frequently sacrificial) accompanying the demarcation. See Rykwert: 1988, 27–71 and Ward: 2001.

6 Michel de Certeau will call the city a text that demands to be read. See 'Walking in the City' in Certeau: 1984, 91–110. Italo Calvino draws attention to Balzac's intuition of the city as a language in his 'The City as Protagonist in Balzac', Calvino: 1989, 182–89. See also Peter Preston and Paul Simpson-Housley: 1994.

7 Intersubjective meanings are 'ways of experiencing action in society which are expressed in the language and descriptions constitutive of institutions and practices'. To interpret them we 'have to understand the language, the underlying meanings, which constitute them' (Taylor: 1985, 38). Common meanings are not the same as intersubjective meanings, though there is considerable overlap. Common meanings are what any community of intersubjective meanings find significant – the expectation of the coming Messiah, for example, among Christian congregations..

8 Indebted to both Augustine and Denys, Hugh describes the process of reading God's Book of Creation through God's biblical Word: 'we come through the word to the concept, through the concept to a thing, through a thing to an idea, and through its idea arrive at Truth' (Hugh of St Victor: 1991, 122). For the medieval construal of the Book and concerns with signs and signification and *grammatica* (the first of the seven disciplines composing the liberal arts education), see Jesse M. Gellrich: 1985.

9 For Aquinas' understanding of the sign in which the Eucharist makes it possible to trust in signs by being the condition for the possibility of signification, see Catherine Pickstock: 1997, 261–2.

10 David Macey has argued that 'it is anthropology which provides the ground for stating that the unconscious is structured like a language' (Macey: 1988, 155). For Lacan – like Lévi-Strauss – is claiming the discovery of the symbolic structure for the foundation of the social order, and using the term 'unconscious' to refer to that which is *a priori*. The word is coloured with a philosophical, in fact, Kantian, hue. Of course, Freud's work could itself be read as a form of neo-Kantianism (just as Kant's demonstration of the regulative ideas which govern human understanding can be read as a development of Descartes' innate ideas in the ego and viewed as neo-Cartesian). Furthermore, Freud's psychoanalytical investigations into the operations of the unconscious was never divorced from his anthropological and cultural investigations as both *Totem and Taboo* and, later, *Civilisation and Its Discontents* bear witness.

11 For Saussure the bipolar axes were synchronic and diachronic in relation to which language could be examined as either *la parole* (an actual speech act) or *la langue* (the resources of a language, and its continual development, as a whole).

12 Elizabeth Roudinesco and David Macey disagree on this, but certainly Lacan only began an in-depth reading of Saussure in June 1954. Whereas Lévi-Strauss had introduced Jakobson to Lacan in 1950, and from that time Jakobson was a frequent guest in Lacan's house. See Roudinesco: 1990, 271–7; Macey: 1988, 129.

13 Macey is right to draw attention to the precise ways in which Lacan misreads Saussure (Macey: 1988, 131–9). Saussure only divides the sign into the signifier and the signified in principle, *de facto* they are a unity. The signifier cannot then, for Saussure, take precedence over the signified. Here Lacan is carried away by the Freudian distinction between the manifest and the latent meaning of the dream. Of course, Lacan saw such misreading as inevitable. In fact, *méconnaissance* is axiomatic in his project.

14 '[T]he formal laws of the poetics associated with Jakobson are ignored or flouted' (Macey: 1988, 160).

15 See Quinn, 1991, 56–93. Quinn argues that the metaphors we use to think through and organise our experience of the world are based upon certain cultural models of shared understanding. The structure of these models themselves Quinn leaves embarrassingly open (93), but suggests they may be schemas of images or metaphors themselves.

16 I do not see a contradiction here between the plurality of traditions and the singleness of orthodoxy. The orthodoxy is the measure of Christ's own truth; the various traditions (which historically cannot be denied) are all formally related to each other by the constitutive orthodoxy in Christ.

17 See Mary Douglas: 1966 for an examination of the way in which the physical structure of the body furnished analogies for the social body such that there was a continual exchange of meaning between the physical, the social and the cosmic body.

18 By employing the adjective 'holographic' I wish to emphasis that the Augustine I am conjuring, and whose thinking has shaped my own, bears some relation to the late-fourth- and early-fifth-century Bishop of Hippo. But that relation, while historically true, is tenuous. I have learnt too much from Gadamer to pretend that my Augustine or interpretation of Augustine is Augustine or the true interpretation of Augustine. I have produced a certain figure from the texts I have read and meditated upon, and this figure bears the traces of the historical bishop on that North African coast.

NOTES

1 CITIES OF ETERNAL ASPIRATION

1 At best it offered what Elaine Graham has rightly called a 'theological functionalism' in which 'the status quo is believed to be ordained by God; particular cultural phenomena are regarded as permanent institutions of creation rather than contingent and particular products of specific human relations' (Graham: 1996, 184).

2 The truth of this remark has been challenged by Patrick McGilligan: 1997, 108–9.

3 London, New York, Paris, Berlin, Manchester and Birmingham are among them.

4 Martin Golding draws attention to the way city-life is also related to photography (Golding: 2000: 55). The aesthetic values of photography, he argues, concern the tension in the photograph between the captured unique presence of the object or event and the endless possibilities for the reproduction of that presence. This installs a certain mourning for what has passed; the photograph becoming a memorial to presence. Cinematography is different. Its aesthetics are concerned with the immersion of the visual and auditory senses in a simulated drama. Cinematography installs participation in the virtual, in part as a voyeur, in part as a receiver of affects. As a medium it offers less in the way of critical distance than the photograph and plays with elements of transcendence: the transcendence of time and space as commonly experienced. It plays back and reinforces the immersion in urban life, while offering the illusion of control.

5 I owe this observation on the way Freder, without appeal to any outside authority, proclaims himself to be the fulfilment of Maria's prophecies, to my colleague, Professor Elaine Graham. In fact, the way the male positions usurp control over the plot of this film, stealing it from Maria, is a striking demonstration of gender-based power, and what Luce Irigaray terms the hom(m)osexuality of Western culture. See Chapter 7.

6 See Chapter 2 for a similarity here with the Disney cities. These too are built on vast platforms beneath which a labyrinth of passageways is used only by those worker-actors who are part of the Disney production.

7 The film also plays with the fantasy of the human as a machine. Descartes had begun to view the body as a machine in his *Meditations* and Engels observed that one of the consequences of the Industrial Revolution was the turning of human beings into machine parts ([1845]1987, 52). But it was in the twentieth century that the fantasy of combining the organic with the mechanic began to have cultural significance, and drive scientific research. *Metropolis* rejects the fantasy at the level of the narrative, but nevertheless the robotic Maria is at the very centre of what makes the film of perennial interest. She constitutes the fierce erotic and creative dynamic that Lang puritanically polices.

8 See here Tönnies' book, *Gemeinschaft und Gesellschaft. Community and Association* (Tönnies: 1955). Between 1920 and 1926 Tönnies' book ran through five editions; its popularity, as an analysis of social conditions, concomitant with the search for a new liberal regime for the Weimar Republic. Tönnies' distinction between community and society is an expansion of Hegel's contrast between the domestic and the civic, the private and the public. Marriage is the prototype for community, and religious associations (imaged, frequently, in terms of Roman Catholicism). For Hegel and the metaphysics of the heterosexual family see Chapters 5 and 7.

9 '[I]ntellect in natural will attains its fruition in the creative, formative, and artistic ability ... whereas, on the other hand, rational will is most frequently characterised by consciousness. To the latter belongs manufacturing as contrasted with creation' (Tönnies: 1955, 17).

10 One might even suggest that Freder brings together the masculine power of his father with the feminine principle of loving and caring embodied in Maria. There is a certain androgeny about Freder which, of course, does nothing for the feminine as

such. His androgeny only more deeply masks the presence and role of the woman in civic society.

11 For a more detailed account of the figure of the city in the Old and New Testaments, see Ellul: 1970, 1–182. This will be discussed later. Also Wilson: 1986; Meeks: 1986; and Smith: 1986; Seitz: 1997, 11–27.

12 On this distinction and its erosion, see Tönnies: 1955, 77–80.

13 Where faith went public, it frequently did so by being championed by evangelical men employing a military vocabulary.

14 For an exposition of this paradox so foundational to modernity – the demands for separation, on the one hand, and synthesis, on the other, see Bruno Latour on hybrids in Chapter 8.

15 We must also include here hospitals and schools and, in doing so, interrupt any merely negative appraisal of modernity and secularism. This is important because Christianity does not speak unambivalently in public. The Christianity I give voice to is very much a product of my own Western Europeanism. There are places still – Greece, for example – where the liberations and desacralisations of modernity are still desired and viewed as emancipatory. Modernity was not some blip in the divine providence to be outreached or outnarrated. Certain things of divine and salvific importance came about in and through the projects of modernity. Such things cannot be passed over lightly or effaced by a contemporary call to orthodoxy.

16 For Le Corbusier's view of religion see his strange book *Poème de l'angle droit* (Le Corbusier: 1989).

17 The late eighties and nineties saw a reaction against this approach to Thomas. Several scholars argued for a separation between theology and philosophy in Thomas' writing and denied he could be employed as the basis for a natural theology in the way we have come to view the 'natural' since the seventeenth century. See Di-Noia: 1990, 499–518.

18 Soleri: 1970, no page references can be given because the text is not paginated. See Soleri: 1969.

19 For an overview of these cities with reference to the history of utopian city-planning see Helen Rosenau: 1972.

20 What Barth's approach shares with American fundamentalism is that for both the 'idea of apologetics is not to translate the gospel into the mental categories of modernity, but to change the modern mental categories so the gospel can be grasped. They are culture critics and political theologians despite themselves' (Cox: 1985, 61; Castells: 1997, 21–7).

21 *Theology in the City* attempted to develop the notion of 'local theologies', which Harvey saw as an implicit but embryonic theological approach in *Faith in the City*. How the local can maintain its singularity and concreteness in the context of globalisation and cyberspace will be examined in Chapter 9.

2 CITIES OF ENDLESS DESIRE

1 What scope there is for resistance – namely a deconstructed socialism of local resistence – he sketches in the closing section of his article 'Flexible Accumulation through Urbanization: Reflections on "Post-modernism" in the American City' (Harvey: 1987, 260–86).

2 Charles Jencks dates postmodernism from the first of these events (Jencks: 1984, 8).

3 Harvey characterises Fordism as a commitment to rationalism, functionalism and efficiency.

4 For detailed analyses of the impossibility of distinguishing between the libidinal and the political economy see Deleuze and Guattari: 1984 and Lyotard: 1992.

5 We can see this in the gendering of urban relations in *The Full Monty*, for the film focuses on male sexual anxieties of castration (or impotence). Female desire is governed entirely by the phallus (the male strippers). In one significant scene a group of women invade the men's toilets and one of them pees standing up against the urinal. She is completing the castration of the male (she is being watched by one of the men), but in carrying that castration to completion her own sexuality is denied and erased even more.

6 There are wide variations in the nature of these relations. For example, with respect to gender, masculinity means something different among the working class and unemployed youth of Salford to what it means among the young high-wage-earning employees of international corporations in the city of London. There are what Doreen Massey, who has done much to examine these differences, calls 'local gender cultures' and they cannot be divorced from the economics and geographies of the new cities. For work on gender and urban space see Fainstein: 1996, 456–60; and Doreen Massey: 1994, 183–272. In her essay 'Flexible Sexism' (212–48) Massey gives a critical, feminist reading of two of the guru analysts of the new capitalist city – Edward W. Soja and David Harvey.

7 This crisis in urban planning was also partly because of the amorphous nature of planning theory and its distribution over several professions (architects, business developers, town planners). In practice planning was becoming increasingly disregarded. Even in the mid-1990s the only justification for trying to found planning theory on scientific (that is, culturally legitimating) principles was that it 'allows one to see the conditions of this "pragmatism" ' (Campbell and Fainstein: 1996, 2).

8 For the difference between the organisation and operation of Enterprise Zones in Britain and the States see Butler: 1991, 27–40.

9 '[T]he decentralisation of population have largely removed the previous social basis for working-class organisation and the advancement of working-class interests in policy formation. The new, much more fragmented working-class, divided by ethnicity, gender, and its location in smaller and/or nonunionized workplaces, has not been able to replace the organization which previously existed' (Harloe and Fainstein: 1992, 249).

10 As I write I read that a casino in Las Vegas has unveiled its own reproduction of the Eiffel Tower.

11 Featherstone is drawing upon the work of the French cultural critic M. Maffesoli. See Maffesoli: 1988.

12 One might read the ending of Ridley Scott's *Thelma and Louise* – where the two women catapult their car over the edge of the Grand Canyon, raising joined hands in a symbol of sororal triumph – as an expression of this euphoric acceptance of death as the dispersal of all significance, the experience of zero degree.

13 For Foucault, and geographers like Edward W. Soja who have developed Foucault's notion of 'heterotopias', it is an anxiety about the complexity of space that fascinates our present culture and defines postmodern geopolitics. (See Foucault and Soja in Watson and Gibson: 1995; see also Harvey: 1990, 201–323 for an account of how time also changes.)

14 These are cities of spectacle and spectacle as we have seen is one of the characteristics of the contemporary city. It is also one of the fundamental features of cinematography. It is no coincidence that the film industry of Los Angeles feeds upon the city's own investments in the spectacular.

15 See Taylor: 1999, 168–201. He describes the development of a project called Holy Land, a Scripture theme-park just outside Las Vegas, reminding us forcefully that 'Vegas is, among other things – many other things – *about* religion' (170).

16 Bryant Fraser. For this and many other reviews of the film see The Internet Movie Database <http://us.imdb.com/Reviews>.

NOTES

17 These fantasy buildings can take more subtle forms: the current nostalgia, for example, for the mock Georgian houses, at Richmond, or the imitation Dutch seventeenth-century houses in the Docklands.

18 Mike Davis, *City of Quartz* (London: Verso, 1990).

19 It is evident from the increasing interest in New Age cults and sects, like Scientology, that various forms of believing without belonging are being developed and supported in the postmodern city, but it is not the religious response that is the concern of this book, but a Christian theological one.

20 We find Tawney emphasising the need for individualism. His argument throughout *The Acquisitive Society* is founded upon the complex communities which emerge from the fact that 'happiness is individual, and to make happiness the object of society is to resolve society itself into the ambitions of numberless individuals, each directed towards the attainment of some personal purpose' (Tawney: 1921, 32). In his concluding chapter, *Porro unum necessarium*, inspired by Dante's medievalism, he enjoins the need to be united by overmastering devotion to a common end (240) that the Church should preach. Asserting a central liberal tenet, he writes: 'membership involves duties as well as privileges' (237). While Tawney has to be admired for the manner in which he passed theological judgement on the acquisitiveness of industrial society, he was undoubtedly a better economic historian than a Christian theologian. And the extent to which either the Church had the power to enforce a sense of corporate responsibility, or that a 'common end' was readily available for consensus after the First World War is doubtful. A deeper appreciation of the *Realpolitik* was necessary. This is why, in its time, the critical and analytical mind of Ronald Preston was important, theologically (Preston: 1981; 1983). What is impressive about Preston's latter work was the acknowledgement that the world was changing and his own thinking in need of modification also. What is striking is the way *Faith in the City* repeats so many of the ideas and moves in Tawney's work.

21 This dynamic and unified sense of tradition can also be found in Talal Asad: 1993. He writes: 'if tradition is thought of as a rejection of any idea of reasoned change, then such an understanding would be mistaken. ... I have tried to show that Islamic tradition is the ground on which that reasoning takes place.' Furthermore, 'There are, it is true, several Islamic traditions. ... But the several Islamic traditions are related to one another formally, through common founding texts, and temporally, through diverging authoritative interpreters' (220, 236).

22 Appeal can be, and has been made in the Christian (particularly Protestant) tradition, to the self-authenticating nature of revelation: that is, revelation comes carrying its own conviction of truth. But such a view of revelation makes the operation of grace arbitrary; it is concomitant with the metaphysics of secularism – the grasping of a fully realised present.

23 *Faith in the City*, inspired by a commitment to grassroots communities, called for the development of local theologies. As Michael Northcott has recently pointed out 'the report was curiously silent on the actual shape and content of urban theology' (Northcott: 1998, 3). The contributions by Andrew Kirk and Anthony Harvey in *Theology in the City* attempted to develop the shape and content with appeal to the work of Robert J. Schreiter, *Constructing Local Theologies* (Schreiter: 1985). What I am attempting in the following chapters is to present a theological account of how the local is also the global and the universal. I do not reject the development of local theologies, but I want to supplement and, hopefully, enrich it. For vigilance is necessary: talk of 'local', like 'community', is a postmodern rhetorical panacea, which is at home with fragmentation and exclusion. Even *Faith in the City*'s own segregation for special attention of the UPA area from the rest of the urban fabric is a move within the cultural politics of post-Fordism.

266

3 TRANSCORPOREALITY: THE ONTOLOGICAL
SCANDAL

1 For another discussion of this scandal, as it was discussed by the Port-Royal grammarians of the seventeenth century, see Louis Marin's essay 'The Body of the Divinity Captured by Signs' (Marin: 1989, 3–25).

2 This return to a Dionysian ecstasy which seizes the present while tearing it apart is a recurrent theme in contemporary writing. See Thomas Pynchon: 1963; Patrick Süskind: 1987; and Donna Tartt: 1992. In all these novels *speragmos* plays an important, ritualistic role where immanence turns upon itself. In pure immanence all bodies are dissolved.

3 I place this word in inverted commas because of the way 'becoming' is axiomatic in immanent economies whether Spinozas', Hegel's, Marx's or process theologians'. I do not intend 'becoming' in such a way. I intend the activation, the *dunamis*, of being; a being that is gifted by a God who is the pure actantial giving. My 'becoming' should be read theologically. That is, as process associated with trinitarian procession. See Chapters 7 and 8.

4 *Energia* is often translated as 'operation' or 'working', from the Greek verb *energeo* 'to be operative' or 'to be at work'. *Dunamis* is often translated 'power', power, that is, which resides in a thing by virtue of its nature. Both these terms are used technically and philosophically first by Aristotle. For the relationship between Aristotle's ideas and Gregory's see Ward: 1999.

5 The Greek word used by Gregory is often translated as the 'mark' or the 'goal' one has in view. The English word 'scope' derives from it.

6 Translates as 'those things which compose or make up any object' from the Greek verb *poieo*, to make.

7 *Upo* is a Greek suffix meaning 'under' and *keimai* is the Greek verb 'to lie'. The noun *upokeimenon* has a philosophical use approximating to what might be translated 'the ultimate reality'.

8 This is a very important word for Gregory – as it was also for Basil, another of the Cappadocian fathers. It translates often as 'conception' but refers to the faculty in the mind which operates upon what the senses immediately perceive. For a further, and more detailed, examination of this word see Schaff and Wace: 1979, 249.

9 This Greek word is often translated 'age' or 'from of old'. From Plato's *Timaeus* onwards it took on the associations of a realm independent of time, the eternal realm, and this is how Gregory uses the term.

10 This is the Greek word for 'Being' because it derives from the participle form of the verb *eimi* – to be. But the word is freighted with philosophical usage and is sometimes translated 'substance'.

11 The Christian doctrine of kenosis issues from a baptismal hymn incorporated into Paul's letter to the Church at Philippi (Philippians 2.5–11). Here is described the descent of Christ from heaven to earth and, following his death, his return to the Father who gives him 'a name which is above every name'. For a further examination of the association of kenosis with naming and discourse see Ward: 1999.

12 This, of course, raises an highly important question: why does Nancy continually make appeal to Christian rhetoric in order to describe his concept of the body or the community? Why does *The Inoperative Community* move, inexorably, towards a final chapter, entitled 'Of Divine Places' where he insists that 'we shall not call this presence "god", we shall not even say it is divine' (Nancy: 1991, 150)? Why does this demythologising discourse which attempts the stripping away of mystery operate through and upon Christian discourses concerning the mysteries of incarnation and transubstantiation? Is this the repressed other of French intellectualism, a Catholic

imaginary informing the symbolic at every level? As theologians we have hardly yet begun to ask these questions. See Ward: 2000.

13 'Metalepsis' is the Greek word for 'a taking' or 'participation'. With Quintilian it became a term in rhetoric, rather like metonymy – it means an act of substitution (of one word for another).

14 See Ward: 1999 for a discussion of Hegel in the context of modernity's fascination with taxidermy.

15 See the catalogue for *Sensation: Young British Artists from the Saatchi Collection* (Saatchi: 1998).

16 To a certain extent, this will also be a critique of postmodernism in its philosophical guise. It can point up the way philosophical postmodernism pushes beyond the secular and employs theological language to do so, but it will also have to announce the impossibility of philosophy to move beyond itself. Postmodern philosophy eventually flounders upon an implicit metaphysics which it is continually trying to avoid and evade.

17 I find illuminating here a comment made by Conor Cunningham on an earlier draft of this chapter: 'Postmodernity dissolves the body and modernity ossifies it.'

18 These are all words employed theologically by the Greek Fathers in the basis of New Testament texts. *Meta* is the Greek suffix for 'with', *metousia* is the sharing in one substance, *metexein* is the verb 'to participate', *metalambanein* is the verb 'to be made a partaker of' and *metanoia* often translates as repentance, but more accurately means a transformation of one's mind.

4 THE DISPLACED BODY OF JESUS CHRIST

1 I am quoting a question that forms the subtitle of a chapter in Rosemary Radford Ruether: 1983, 116–38. I do not intend this essay to be an attack on Ruether herself. Rather I am attacking the biological essentialism which lies behind many of the recent moves by feminists to a post-Christian perspective and attempting to show how a masculinist symbolics can be refigured in a way which opens salvation through Christ to both (if there are only two, which I doubt (Herdt: 1993)) sexes.

2 The question was opened, and the investigations began, because sexuality and Christianity had become so divorced from one another. The topic had become taboo as Tom Driver suggested at the outset of his article 'Sexuality and Jesus' (Driver: 1965). Stephen Sapp, in a chapter of his book *Sexuality, the Bible, and Science* (Sapp: 1976) entitled 'The Sexuality of Jesus' developed the discussion. Driver and Sapp, in their attention to this sexuality – and by calling into question dogmas such as the virgin conception and birth – employ medical materialism to offset a potential docetism. Both of them needed to go back to Tertullian and a cultural epoch when eros could still be theologically valued beyond its implications for sexuality. Ruether joined in with her own note 'The Sexuality of Jesus' (Ruether: 1978).

3 I employ this word because of its associations with patristic theologies of Christ's flesh. These patristic theologies understood bodies more fluidly than we who have inherited notions of body following the Nominalist (and Atomistic) debates of the late Middle Ages, the Cartesian definition of bodies as extended things (*res extensae*), the seventeenth-century move towards unequivocation, and Leibniz's understanding of the individuation of matter. See Amos Funkenstein: 1986, 23–116. Although even Leibniz developed 'a doctrine of semi-substances in order to lend precise meaning to Christ's real presence in the Host' (109). See also Daniel Boyarin: 1993 for an examination of the body and sexuality in the Hellenistic and Talmudic Jewish periods. Elliot Wolfson takes us on from there in his detailed study of the symbolism of sexual differences in the Jewish Cabbalistic tradition (Wolfson: 1995).

NOTES

4 The deferral of this corporeal identity can be related to the variety of names and titles given to Jesus, most particularly in John's Gospel. Attention has frequently focused on the title 'Son of Man' – its relation to Daniel 7 (Schnackenburg), the gnostic saviour (Lindars), the humanity of Christ (Pamment), the Primal Man (Borsch). But the appellation 'Son of Man' stands, especially in John's Gospel, alongside a series of other titles: Logos, Light, the Only-Begotten, Jesus Christ, King, Lamb, Lord, Rabbi, Teacher, Jesus of Nazareth, Son of Joseph, Son of God, Messiah, *ego eimi*. Furthermore, as scholars of John's Gospel have pointed out, Jesus performs actions which are explicitly associated with his Jewish forefathers: he is compared to Jacob, Moses, the heavenly Adam, the Suffering Servant. The deferral of corporeal identity is paralleled, therefore, by a plethora of names and designations for this man, such that his identity is always excessive to any single appellation. For an examination of these titles in relation to the early formation of doctrine see James D.G. Dunn: 1989. I also find it significant that John's Gospel has received attention recently from at least one feminist scholar interested in his feminine descriptions of Christ as Sophia (Jasper: 1998).

5 *De Carne*, xvii. Tertullian, polemically engaging with various gnostic heresies – the Ebionites, Valentinians and Marcionites – suggests that copulation changes corporeality. He speaks of sinful flesh, angelic flesh and virginal flesh, besides spiritual flesh (or 'flesh from the stars'). Gregory of Nyssa will make a distinction between true human nature and the postlapsarian human nature which is forced to wear a *garment of skin*, that is a corporeality subject to mortality and corruptibility. See *de Anime et Resurrectione*. Christ's body wears a *tunic of incorruptibility*.

6 Tertullian notes that Mary is both virgin and not a virgin, a virgin and yet mother, a virgin and yet a wife, married and yet not married (*De Carne*, xxxiii).

7 For Athanasius (who Frances M. Young understands as 'Apollinarian in tendency' (Young: 1983, 80) see *de Incarnatione Verbi Dei*, 17: 'The Word was not hedged in by His body, nor did His presence in the body prevent His being present elsewhere as well. When He moved His body He did not cease also to direct the universe by His Mind and might.'

8 'the Father from whom [out of whom *ex ou*] every fatherhood in the heavens and upon the earth is named'.

9 Butler: 1993. While Butler understands how the material is informed by the way in which we represent it, and how gendered embodiment is performed with respect to that complex materiality, she does not take this further to ask what then is the nature of materiality itself. Butler does not relate it to a wider genealogy to show the way in which representations of the corporeal, the philosophical notion of substance itself, is historically situated and theologically indebted. Her concern is with bodies now. But these bodies now have been given to us through a history of embodiment. See Martin: 1995; Roussell: 1993; Laqueur: 1990; and Mosse: 1996.

10 The doctrine of the ubiquity or omnipresence of God starts here. For the way in which these theological notions change and become secularised (becoming the feared omnipotent God of the Nominalists; see Funkenstein: 1986 and Michael Allen Gillespie: 1996, 1–32).

11 *De Carne*, iii.

12 The Renaissance architect, Vitruvius, is a forerunner. The geometric perfection of the cosmos is mapped onto the body of a well-built, male adult as his famous diagram of the outstretched, naked man embraced by a circle, demonstrates. See 'Utopic Rabelesian Bodies', Marin: 1989, 84–113.

13 For a phenomenology of the invisible within the visible, the iconic beyond the idolised, see Jean-Luc Marion: 1991a, 11–46.

14 This form of the sublime differs from the sublime as it features in romantic aesthetics and, more recently, the work of Jean-François Lyotard. The sublime here is not

registering the frisson of the unpresentable, the abyssal, the ineffable. The sublime here is more like Longinus' sublime: it elevates, it ennobles the soul, it leads to reflection and examination, it 'exerts an irresistible force and mastery' (Longinus: 1965, 99–113).

15 Gregory of Nyssa makes a similar claim while simultaneously distinguishing Christ's body as immortal from the mortality of our own: 'that body to which immortality has been given to it by God, when it is in ours, translates and transmutes the whole into itself' (*The Great Catechism* 37.x).

16 Cinematographic accounts of this scene enable us to appreciate the erotic charge of the action, because they place us (as none of the disciples were placed) as voyeurs, observing the playful abuse perpetrated. See Franco Zeffirelli's *Jesus of Nazareth*.

17 In bringing back this Christian witness, we too, as readers, are no longer voyeurs, for we identify with this witness and claim it as our own. We claim it not unproblematically. The memory of having been caught up in the kinetic energies and a communal slaughter remains. We are not innocent. Our hands are not clean.

18 My thinking here has been profoundly influenced by the work of Hans Urs von Balthasar: 1990.

19 Turner recognises here how 'novel configurations of ideas and relations may arise' (97) from such liminality – the liminal space opens up the potential for new births.

20 See the work of Carolyn Walker Bynum.

21 The terms real, imaginary and symbolic are Jacques Lacan's. I am not using them in his technical sense, particularly his understanding of *réel* which we will return to later with respect to Žižek's comments upon cyberspace. Here, I am employing the terms in the looser manner of Moira Gatens: 1996. The real bodies are the empirical and historical, medical and material ones to which we have no access other than through the 'images, symbols, metaphors and representations ... the (often unconscious) imaginaries of a specific culture: those ready-made images and symbols through which we make sense of social bodies and which determine, in part, their value, their status and what will be deemed their appropriate treatment' (viii).

22 Of course this transgendering or making women virile – which goes back to the gnostic *Gospel of St Thomas* – is part of a masculine ideology. I do not wish to suggest in the late antiquity or medieval periods there was a cultural openness such that men being figured as women and women as men were equally valued.

23 See Kant: 1983 in which he gives a philosophical interpretation of the fall. Kant reads the Genesis story again, albeit differently, in *Religion within the Limits of Reason Alone* (Kant: 1960).

24 Lacan writes about *objet petit a* which symbolises lack. This is where the subject, in order to constitute itself, posits an object outside itself. The *objet petit a* substitutes for the lack of the phallus. With this substitution, the entry in the symbolic, Lacan (more than Freud) views the death instinct as encoded within libidinal desire. In *Écrits* (Lacan: 1977), he writes: 'what is primordial to the birth of symbols, we find ... in death. ... It is in effect as a desire for death that he [the subject] affirms himself for others' (105). For an excellent discussion of the nihilistic metaphysics governing Lacan's project see Henry Staten: 1995, 166–85.

25 '[T]here is nothing of which we are more certain than the feeling of our self, of our own ego. This ego appears to us as something autonomous and unitary, marked off distinctly from everything else' (Freud: 1961: 65–6).

26 Luce Irigaray refers to the holiness of this spacing, which she likens to the sacred hiatus which is constituted by sexual difference, in her essay 'Belief Itself' (Irigaray: 1993, 5–53). 'Those angels ... guard and await the mystery of the divine presence that has yet to be made flesh' (45). See Chapter 8.

27 This returns to Gregory of Nyssa's notion of *scopus*. Nyssa distinguishes this growth or movement from the cyclical one, which is inferior and immanent to the orders of

creation. This second movement is a movement of expansion or *epectasis* – the perpetual growth in goodness as the human nature is redeemed. For a more detailed examination of *epectasis* see Jean Danièlou's Introduction to Herbert Musurillo: 1979, 56–71.

28 An inference of this is not that Christ can be identified with Derrida's *différance*, as John D. Caputo has demonstrated. The only inference is that the logic of *différance* parallels the logic of Christ and talk about Christ. But insofar as, for Derrida, deferral is infinite there is a difference between Derrida's suspension of all things in and through semiosis and Christianity's suspension of all things in Christ as the true, the good and the beautiful to be fully manifest in the eschaton. Derrida has no appraisal of the eschaton as the telos of all things. *Différance* has no teleology. Furthermore, Christianity has no concept of the infinite as endlessness, as *en abyme*. The eternal is not the same as modernity's conception of the infinite (see J.V. Field: 1997 for the historical development of our concept of infinity from medieval mathematics and optics to Descartes' work on geometry). The eternal is an aeon; a temporality and an order. It is not spatialised.

29 See the narrative theologians for a more detailed exposition of this: the work of George Lindbeck: 1984; Ronald F. Thiemann: 1985 and Gerard Loughlin: 1998. See also Paul Ricoeur: 1992, 203–39.

30 Certeau was one of the founder members of Lacan's *École freudienne*. His work reflects some of Lacan's categories. This gives his understanding of Christianity a certain undecideable negativity. See Ward: 1999a for an account of this and a more detailed bibliography.

31 Calvin: [1559] (1864), IV: 17, 'The Sacred Supper of Christ and What it Brings to us'. See Chapter 6 for a more detailed discussion of Calvin's conception of the eucharist.

32 This ubiquity is not compromised by what appears to be the mutability of assuming other bodies. God is immutable. But the displacements of the body involved in transcorporeality must be understood as variations on a single theme, as moments within the *scopos* of the divine unfolded love. Creation – and human nature as part of the created order – is placed within the operation of the Trinity, such that the Trinity informs embodiment.

33 Herbert Musurillo comments, significantly, 'In this passage *eros* would seem to be merely [!] a more intense, less satisfied form of *agape*,' (Nyssa: 1979, 297).

5 COMMUNITIES OF DESIRE

1 See Tim Edwards: 1990, 110–23. Edwards argues that, following the Stonewall riots, gay men wanted to show that they were 'real men' too, not effeminates. This led to what he terms a 'machoisation' in gay culture, an emphasis upon hyper-masculine images and cloning.

2 Advances in telecommunications, the creation of the internet and cyberspace will actually cause the Private Shop to disappear from public, civic space. Its privacy will become even more internalised as no objects will be owned or purchased – not as videos or magazines. All the objects will be available only on-line, accessed through the home computer and financed through the credit card. The Private Shop will be global not local, constructing and promoting economies of desire throughout the world.

3 Subordination is not viewed negatively, but as 'central to the becoming of the subject' (Butler: 1997, 7). See Ward: 2000 for a more detailed examination of Butler's work and its implications for theological studies.

4 *Group Psychology and the Analysis of the Ego*: 'In the individual's mental life someone else is invariably involved, as a model, as an object, as a helper, as an opponent; and so

from the very first, individual psychology, in this extended but entirely justifiable sense of the words, is at the same time social psychology' (Freud: 1955, 69).

5 See Girard: 1977 for a recapitulation of this Freudian idea. We might have taken Girard's work as another example of the exploration of the erotic community, for he too construes people as subjects of desire.

6 In Hegel's account there is an emphasis upon the negative or sacrificial moment when the man leaves the tight embrace of the family to enter into a self-conscious ethical life. Similarly Freud's account both of the morphology of the sexual self and the move from the individual to the collective mind stresses certain *volte face* events.

7 Hunt's 'Introduction' and Margaret C. Jacob's analysis of the relationship between philosophical materialism and pornography, 'The Materialist World of Pornography', are excellent.

8 For an account of Boyle's theological accusations against Hobbes see Shapin and Schaffer: 1985, 202–7.

9 On the history of this analogy see the magisterial volume by Ernst H. Kantorowicz: 1957. For the nature of this analogy and its representation in the seventeenth century with respect to Louis XIV, see Louis Marin: 1989.

10 For a brief account of Hobbes' Calvinist roots see Martinich: 1999, 137–9.

11 *Summa theologiae*, I–II, 91,4.

12 For an account of Suarez's own political absolutism, based upon the transfer of the power by the people to the Sovereign and the analogical relationship pertaining between the human body and the commonwealth, see Howell A. Lloyd: 1991, 292–7.

13 Shapin and Schaffer: 1985, 298. Shapin and Schaffer examine, in this book, the way in which this all-male society organised itself as a regulated group composed of socially worthy witnesses involved in the production of scientific facts and knowledge by consensus. Shapin went on to detail further the relationship of science to the rise of gentlemenly society in his *A Social History of Truth: Civility and Science in Seventeenth Century England* (Shapin: 1994). His findings concur with Genevieve Lloyd: 1993, about the rise and domination of the *man* of reason.

14 See William Sacksteder: 1987, 125–49. For the influence of Hobbes' work in the Dutch Republic see Catherine Scretan: 1987 and, '*La reception de Hobbes aux Pays-Bas au XVIIe siècle*' in the same volume, and Noel Malcolm: 1987, 545–50.

15 With this argument Spinoza counters those critics who held that each one seeking their own is a recipe for immorality and atheism. It needs to be noted that Spinoza might object to 'eros' here. 'Love' *is* Curley's translation of *amor* (which is the Latinate form of eros), and 'desire' is Curley's translation of *cupiditas*. There is then an erotics here, despite the fact that, like Anselm and Aquinas, the bond of love Spinoza advocates strongly is called 'friendship' *between men*. See the Demonstrations for Propositions 70 and 71 of Book Four of *Ethics*. Aquinas would call this *caritas*.

16 This ordering of the good life by a love for God is often forgotten by those wishing to secularise Spinoza and employ his conception of community to advocate new forms of liberal society. This would be my criticism of Moira Gatens' book (Gatens: 1996).

17 See Gillespie: 1996. Gillespie argues for the origins of this human will and its absolute I in Descartes and examines the romantics, where nihilism 'is the result of the assertion that man is an autonomous, self-creating I, free from both God and nature' (64).

18 See Part II, Chapters XIV and XVI, 'Of Longing' and 'Of the Will' in Spinoza: 1985, 118, 121.

19 For a brief account of Spinoza's letters to critics see Richard Mason: 1997, 31.

20 In this Spinoza is opposing the equivocation of Descartes' understanding of substance: where substance is defined as that which exists without dependence upon anything else. So, for Descartes, there is 'only one substance ... namely God'. Thus 'the term "substance" does not apply *univocally*, as they say in the Schools, to God and

to other things; that is, there is no distinctly intelligible meaning of the term common to God and his creatures'. Nevertheless, there is 'common concept' of 'corporeal substance and mind' (Descartes: 1985, 210).

21 It is on this basis that Spinoza explains the uniqueness of the Jewish people: their political organisation (Spinoza: 1958b, Chapter III).

22 Genevieve Lloyd: 1994, 25. Lloyd, though, does wish to advocate, countering Hegel, that Spinoza does offer a significant account of embodied individuality. She ends her thesis by pursuing Spinoza's thinking with respect to sexual difference and socialised subjectivities. But in doing this she has to put to one side the God who not only sublates all differences and individualities, but is, strictly speaking, the only agent.

23 See Certeau's essay 'White Ecstasy'. He describes the sublime and nihilistic experience of pilgrims searching until 'they bear this dazzling death, speechless from having seen without knowing it .... the whiteness that is beyond all division, the ecstacy that kills consciousness and extinguishes all spectacles, an illuminated death' (Ward: 1998, 155–8). On the nihilism of modern and postmodern understandings of the sublime see John Milbank: 1998, 258–84.

24 All three present Spinoza as a counter-tradition to the Cartesian autonomous will, viewing Spinoza's thought as offering new spaces for embodied and socialised human beings working together, in their differences. Gatens makes no references to the God who holds the Spinozistic system together (Gatens: 1996, 108–24); Deleuze rejects the God of Spinoza, recognises that without this God, there is endless flux with only localised, relative meaning in 'sociabilities and communities' and rejoices in the Dionysian (Deleuze and Guattari: 1988); and Lloyd asserts that we cannot return 'to the Spinozistic certainty of our status as parts of a rationally ordered whole' (Lloyd: 1994, 174), but does not recognise the metaphysical consequences of the non-foundationalism this position entails.

25 With regard to Spinoza and the charges of atheism, see Nadler: 1999, 295–8. For an account of Spinoza and Hegel see Shanks: 1991, 54–8 and Yovel: 1989, vol. 2, 27–50.

26 See Hegel: 1991, 119–22 for a discussion of how the free will in and for itself *cannot* be coerced.

27 But then what else could he do? More than all the transcendentalists Hegel knew he wrote for his times about the signs of those times, in and through the signs available in those times. Of course, he reflects a certain cultural *status quo*, though he is not uncritical of it. In fact the hermeneutical dialectic which Hegel's thinking engages in enables there to be a reflection beyond it (see Wood: 1991, viii–xi). Culture too is in process; it can be raised beyond itself and transformed.

28 Hegel, like Augustine, does not view the institutional churches as the final externalisation of the Idea. For the complex relationship between religion and the state in Hegel see Lakeland: 1984, 87–93.

29 See Olson: 1992, 157–8 for a detailed account of Hegel's doctrine of representation and Ricoeur: 1982.

30 Of course, the exception here was Heidegger who saw Hegel's thinking as the apotheosis of onto-theology.

31 Anderson does not mention it, but the term 'imaginary', as associated with communities was first put forward by Ferdinand Tönnies. *Gemeinschaft* possesses an organic life but *Gesellschaft* was conceived of 'as imaginary and mechanical' (Tönnies: 1955, 37). This is essential to Tönnies' distinction between community and society. Where there is a difference is Tönnies' understanding of 'state' does not parallel Anderson's 'nation' – for Tönnies (writing on a growing tide of German nationalism), 'state' is the greatest of corporate bodies and comes under the category of *Gemeinschaft*.

32 Of course, this is an idealisation of cyberspace as any user will know. We do not have instant access – downloading takes time; VDUs still occupy a small proportion of space within any room such that the context still impinges; and programmes frequently crash or are interrupted. So Žižek's fear that the subject will lose itself entirely, disengaging from contact with external bodies, surrendered to the pure flux of desire is itself a fantasy. Furthermore, we are not simply constructs of desire – even within the Freudian and Lacanian worlds of Žižek. Our psychic life is also composed of somatic needs which desires and drives may suspend, but not erase. Žižek enjoys playing with while criticising the postmodern void and selling the frisson that comes from gazing towards the apocalyptic. There is a kind of pornography going on here.

6 THE CHURCH AS THE EROTIC COMMUNITY

1 'Medieval theology in most of its varieties viewed with intense suspicion any doctrine that took God's presence in the world too literally' (Funkenstein: 1986, 25).
2 This may partly explain why Anselm's ontological proof was ignored in the medieval period but picked up avidly from the seventeenth century onwards.
3 Augustine's teaching on Christ in the eucharist is fragmentary, hence both Aquinas and Calvin can cite him as an authority in markedly different ways.
4 For Ockham's conception of the eucharistic, which drew upon him much criticism, see Buescher: 1950 and Stump: 1982.
5 *'quod est praesens alicui primo et postea manens non est praesens illi loco, necessario transfertur de loco ad locum'* (Ockham: 1930, 294).
6 *'Et hoc facto, corpus Christi essst praesens in illo loco immediate. Igitur eodem modo nunc est praesens immediate, non mediante illa specie'* (quoted in Buescher: 1950, 7).
7 The second and third sets of numbers relate to the pages in the Latin and French texts respectively.
8 As the commentator to the modern French edition of the *Institutes* points out: '*Calvin emploie a plusieurs reprises le mot substance – dans ce chapitre, mais il ne lui donne pas le sens philosophique ou théologique. La substance est pour lui synonyme de presence – vivifiante*' (Calvin: 1958, 349). Missing also in Calvin, and related to the avoidance of *substantia* is an account of appearance *species*. In its place is a language of 'corporal signs/*corporealis signis*' (Calvin: 1936, 652 (1010)), 'earthly signs', 'carnal presence/*carnalem … praesentiam*' (Calvin: 1936, 656 (1012)) figuration and exhibition (*exhibitione/bailler*).
9 Compare Augustine's understanding of space and materiality as he views the body of Christ as extendible: 'He didn't depart from heaven, when he came down to us from there; nor did he depart from us, when he ascended to heaven again. I mean, he was still there while he was here' (*Sermons* III/7: 263a).
10 One notes here Calvin's discussion on the relationship of words to things: 'things ordained by God borrow the names of those things of which they always bear a definite and not misleading signification, and have the reality joined with them. So great, therefore, is their similarity and closeness that transition from one to the other is easy' (section 21, new translation). The Latin does suggest more hesitancy with regard to the correspondence between word and thing, the tokens (*notae*) standing in for things absent *fallacem significationem semper gerunt* (always bear a distorted signification). Nevertheless he will speak, both in Latin and in French, of an affinity (*propter affinitatem/l'affinité*) between the object signifed and the sign (Calvin: 1936, 665 (1,019/370)).
11 Calvin, as it is well known, relates eucharistic presence to a trinitarian operation. The Spirit spans the distance between Christ in heaven above and the believer below. Calvin's trinitarianism, which expresses to my mind a modalism, has been well documented, as, indeed, has Calvin's doctrine of the eucharist. I have dealt with neither of them in depth here since my attention has been upon the complexities of

body, space, time and representation as Calvin figures them in his understanding of eucharistic presence. See Gerrish: 1993; Butin: 1996.

12 Calvin himself speaks of how 'we may experience (*sentiamus/sentions*) his (Christ's) power in the communication' (Calvin: 1936, 652 (1010/359)). It is the analysis of this 'experience' which is followed through in several recent accounts of the eucharist (see Sokolowski: 1993; Marion: 1991a and Chauvet: 1995).

13 Coincidence is possible only if God does not deceive, and so, by faith, subjective judgements can concur *in their interpretation* about the true meaning of things. Otherwise coincidence is arbitrary, and contractual in a world of conflicting evaluations.

14 On the relationship of time to desire see Levinas: 1987.

15 See Michael Gillespie for an account of assertion and the will with respect to Descartes' *cogito* in Gillespie: 1996.

16 His younger contemporary, Louis Marin, will term this 'spatial play' in his analyses of utopias. Marin's concern with 'utopics' bears a close relation to Certeau's concerns with 'mystics', as the cross-referencing in the work of both authors bears out. See Marin: 1984.

17 For a further examination of space in St Teresa's work see Sheila Hassell Hughes: 1997, 376–84.

18 The problem for institutions is that they acquire a logic (and inertia) of their own such that although they might begin by serving the needs of the society which establish them, their impulse towards development and the expansion of their influence can bring about a overturning of priorities so that, as Cornelius Castoriadis recognised, society is then viewed as serving them (Castoriadis: 1997, 110). This is particularly difficult for the Church when it begins to view itself as an institution akin to other economic institutions – encouraging line – management strategies, employment transparencies, feasibility studies, development plans, that it might compete more effectively in the market-place of leisure activities.

7 THE EROTICS OF REDEMPTION

1 Barthes examines the dialectic between pleasure and bliss as it pertains to the reader of texts. The dialectics of desire give rise to a 'living contradiction': a split subject who, simultaneously, enjoys, through the text, the consistency of his or her selfhood and its collapse, its fall. (Barthes: 1990, 21).

2 It does need to be added that, for Barthes, this economy of desire is libidinal. It is an economy in which the other is never to be possessed and continually teases. It is not a theological account, an analogical account of desire. Hence, in the encounter with which he is most concerned (the encounter between a reader and a text) the disruptions, shocks, disturbances and pleasures of recognition all install a sense of loss or mourning that language inflects.

3 Marriage in its widest theological application does not imply here that there is no room in the Kingdom of God for those who are single. There is such a role, but there is no room in the Kingdom of God for isolation, for atomistic individualism. Being uninvolved in a long-term partnership can nevertheless, and will nevertheless, involve 'single' people in a multitude of other relationships with varying degrees of closeness and intimacy. Single people are also erotic persons. Put briefly, because 'marriage' figures forth ecclesial communion, it figures forth also the intratrinitarian community which makes possible, and conditions, the nature of all relationality. My teaching on 'marriage' here, in its widest application beyond sexual dimorphism, would only imply a radical critique against solipsism and ideologies of self-sufficiency.

4 See Webster: 1995. He argues that with Barth 'the human person under grace remain[s] an agent' (110) and that, as such, humanity is a true covenant-partner with God. He employs the language of participation and incarnation and writes of such

agency as 'neither identical with, nor in competition with, the action of God, but in correspondence with God's activity' (167). He develops this ground for an ethics of reconciliation, theologically, by pointing out that Barth does not espouse a Christomonism that inhibits all other agency. I have much in sympathy with Webster's study. My explorations of Barth do, however, raise the question of the nature of this 'correspondence' and wonder whether it is adequately worked out by Barth. As Webster observes, 'everything hangs on a just appreciation of the dialectic of Barth's argument' (184). But dialectical method, as a Christology that is freeze-framed by paradox, does not sublate dualism, but only perpetuates it. And dualism must be sublated if we are to move beyond the impasses of univocity and equivocity and develop an analogical world-view. See Rogers 1995 and Ward 1995 for accounts of Barth's doctrine of analogy.

5 Two excellent and intriguing books have been published concerning Barth's relationship with his secretary Charlotte von Kirschbaum and his wife Nelly. See Kobler: 1989 and Sellinger: 1998. Sellinger's book has extensive discussions of the way in which Kirschbaum may have influenced Barth's 'anthropology of gender' and his construal of the *imago dei* (92–114, 135–63).

6 Barth rehearses romantic erotics – the erotics of Frederick Schlegel's *Lucinda* and Wagner's *The Flying Dutchman*. Only with Barth there is a fundamental difference. This metaphysics of heterosexuality does not have as its telos a spiritualised androgyny and a disembodiment.

7 See Kobler: 1989 and Selinger: 1998 for accounts of how Barth's enormous output was only possible because of the total dedication of the two women who composed his *ménage à trois*. Charlotte von Kirschbaum shared Barth's overwhelming conviction that much work had to be done.

8 For accounts of Barth's difficulty with the doctrine of the Holy Spirit see Williams: 1979, 147–93 and Rosato: 1981. Rosato asks, pointedly, 'Is this really a theology of the Spirit?' (188). For a reply see Hunsinger: 2000, 148–85.

8 CITIES OF ANGELS

1 Evidently it is the size of the angelic host which is significant. For angels have appeared in films before, most notable as part of the Hollywood response to the Second World War – *A Guy Named Joe* (1941) – and its aftermath – *It's a Wonderful Life* (1946) and *Stairway to Heaven* (1946). Furthermore, Serres, Wenders and Irigarary will all cite the importance of Rilke's angels in *Duino Elegies*.

2 In the director's cut, it is made more evident that Ford himself is a replicant.

3 Children are often given a redemptive role in Wenders' films. Their innocence enables them to be closer to the angelic perception of things, as the children in both *Wings of Desire* and *Far Away So Close* exemplify. '[T]he Wenders child represents the richness and immediacy of being, where connection rather than fragmentation prevails' (Kolker and Beicken: 1993, 53). Furthermore, is this lesson about words and the objects they refer to, children possess a 'prelapsian ability to enjoy unmediated language and the simple relationship of word and thing, of language and being' (ibid., 55). Los Angeles is not the name of a city, or just the name of a city; it is, for the child, immediately related to heaven and those who watch out for us. It is a significant feature of *Far Away, So Close* that the angel saves the child. This is the suggestion in *The End of Violence* – that the child alone cannot redeem the adult, a more transcendental innocence is required. The child only confirms the new position and perspective Mike Max has been forced to find for himself within the world. 'As I see children as models for seeing and thinking and feeling, perhaps I also see them as models for sustaining relationships' (Wenders: 1997, 45).

4 It is difficult not to hear in these words a reference to Walter Benjamin's angel of history.

5 Irigaray frequently draws upon the medieval idea of the three ages elaborated by Joachim of Fiore (1132–1202): The Age of the Father relating to the Old Testament, the Age of the Son relating to the New Testament and the final age being the Age of the Spirit of the Bride. See Irigaray: 1993,147–9.

6 '[Wenders] makes homelessness a virtue, an aesthetic' (Kolker and Beicken: 1993, 161). The theme of journeying into endless exile, dwelt upon by such modernists as Baudelaire and Benjamin is taken up philosophically as a major motif in the work of Levinas and Certeau (see Ward: 1996, 153–72 and 2000, 1–14; Bauerschmidt: 1996, 1–26)).

9 CITIES OF THE GOOD: THE REDEMPTION OF CYBERSPACE

1 See Dunne: 1965, 81–109. He reads Plato from the bottom up, arguing that everyday society always fails in its aspiration to fulfil its ideal form because of time and change. But we can read Plato from the top down, arguing that everyday society is made possible by and participates in its ideal form and in the Good, the form of forms. In this reading the just society becomes possible when regulated by the Good (through the philospher-king).

2 Augustine is important because, following Augustine comes the rise of the Christian *imperium*. By Gregory the Great's time Rome is no longer a symbol of paganism, but of Christian dominion. The West has lived in, through and beyond that dominion. Christian hegemony is fast disappearing beneath not only secularism and pluralism, but also critiques of colonialism, cultural politics, and Eurocentrism. We are now entering a world in which Christian practice, always diverse, bears public testimony to its truth without the authority and legitimation structures of old to socialise the people. It no longer has the cultural power to form in the same way as even fifty years ago. We are closer then to the Christian Church in the times of Augustine than to the Church of Aquinas, or Calvin, or Wesley, or William Temple.

3 '*Sic enim superbia perverse imitatur Deum*' *De civitate Dei*, XIX. 12.

4 This doctrine of representation is significant for the difference it reveals between Augustine and Hegel. We saw, in Chapter 5, how Hegel insufficiently thinks through how his own work is caught up in the production of representations. In many respects, Hegel's conception of *Sittlichkeit* in civic life has close parallels with Augustine's understanding of justice and the good in the two cities, but Augustine's healthy agnosticism and hearty self-awareness makes him aware of the provisionality of his own judgements and assertions.

5 See R.A. Markus: 1970, 120–52. Markus points out that this resistance to a Roman catholicity was in keeping with certain traditions of the African church. The Donatists emphasised the complete separation of the godly from the impious, the pure and sanctified from the impure and earthly. Augustine resisted this extreme as well. On the importance of the Donatist teachings of Tychonius, see Markus.

6 One of the famous cruxes of Augustine's work manifests itself here. How can a theologian support the forced conversion of people to the Christian faith and the persecution of 'heretics' (like the Donatists), when the Church was not to be identified with the secular powers of this world? Various answers have been posed by the scholars.

7 'The looseness of (Augustine's) conception of "nature" is too notorious to require comment' (Markus: 1970, 143). But this looseness masks difficulties, particularly when it comes to the question of analogy and the shadow of equivocity which plays about Augustine's later writing.

8 See *Confessions* 5.14.24 in which Augustine narrates how Ambrose taught him to read the Old Testament allegorically.

9 Knowledge of the *saeculum qua saeculum* is, of course, only available from the theological perspective, for Augustine. There is no *saeculum* as such where the com-mingling of the two cities in the same temporal and sociological space is not recognised: there is only the world.

10 'Augustine seems intent to validate simultaneous citizenship in a variety of communities which cross-cut institutional structures' (Scott: 1995, 161). I think we must distinguish between Augustine's acceptance, even validation, of this pluralism and modernity's liberal pluralism. I would argue that R.A. Markus is wrong to suggest that 'Augustine's theology should at least undermine Christian opposition to an open, pluralist, secular society' (Markus: 1970, 173). Augustine, as a Christian, is profoundly critical of the pluralism in the *secular*, but, for him, there is no social amelioration possible, only transfiguration (and with transfiguration transplantation, from one city to the other) He does not validate pluralism as such – in fact he judges it – rather he is simply describing what is and making the observation that certain forms of government limit the damage possible by unbridled *dominandi libido*, effecting a social peace (not a theological or even an ontological peace) which is shared by citizens of both cities.

11 Augustine is close here to Karl Barth's understanding of *analogia fidei* as an *analogia relationis* and an *analogia Christi*. For Barth too we employ words improperly when we do not understand their meaning Christologically.

12 Interesting here is Thomas More's response to Martin Luther. For More draws a comparison between Luther's spiritual apartheid and the Donatist heresy (More: 1963).

13 See Markus: 1970, but a certain Barthianism is also evident in O'Donovan.

14 Augustine does not open the way for a natural theology, a movement from the natural to the theological. Plato, of course, spoke about the Good beyond Being, and so the line analogy and the cave demonstrate a movement towards the forms, but not that which is the Form of the forms, the Good itself.

15 'Millennium Taskforce' published on the internet by Manchester Millennium Ltd, <http://www.manchester-millennium.org.uk>.

16 Ibid.

17 'New Strategy for the 21st Century', published on the internet by the Manchester City Council, <http://www.manchester.gov.uk>.

18 'Venture Capital', published on the internet by the Manchester City Council, <http://www.manchester.gov.uk>.

19 'Corporate Finance', published on the internet by the Manchester City Council, <http://www.manchester.gov.uk>.

20 'British Telecom, Norweb Communication, Cable and Wireless Communications and Energis are amongst the major investors in an area which has full Integrated Services Digital Network (ISND) and optical fibre cable networks.' 'Telecommunications', published on the internet by the Manchester City Council, <http://www.manchester.gov.uk>.

21 See Forrester: 1997.

22 It is this ability to do this which marks out Gerard Loughlin's *Telling God's Story* (1995) as a new departure in narrative theology.

23 It does this by decentralising and democratising the sites for cultural production, making each of us a contributor, a participant.

24 Cyberspace as such fulfills the old law of Aristotelian and neo-Platonic mimesis: that representation should not copy but create the world anew, produce a better more perfect world.

25 Hence the correlation observed between virtual reality, high-tech and New Age spirituality. See Ziguras: 1997, 197–211.

26 One might compare this with theological accounts of the giving of gifts, of grace, in Milbank (1995) and Webb (1996).

BIBLIOGRAPHY

Adams, Marilyn McCord (1987) *William Ockham*, vols I and II. Notre Dame: University of Notre Dame Press.

Adams, Robert McCormick (1981) *Heartland of Cities: Surveys of Ancient Settlement and Land Use*. Chicago: University of Chicago Press.

Alliez, Eric (1996) *Capital Times*. Minneapolis: University of Minnesota Press.

Altizer, Thomas T. (1966) *The Gospel of Christian Atheism*. London: Collins.

—— (1967) *Towards a New Christianity: Readings in the Death of God Theology*. New York: Harcourt, Brace and World.

Altizer, Thomas T. and William Hamilton (eds) (1968) *Radical Theology and the Death of God*. Harmondsworth: Penguin.

Anderson, Benedict (1983) *Imagined Communities: Reflections on the Origin and Spread of Nationalism*. London: Verso.

Anderson, Pamela Sue (1998) *A Feminist Philosophy of Religion: the Rationality and Myths of Religious Belief*. Oxford: Blackwell.

Aquinas, Saint Thomas (1964) *Summa theologiae*, vol. 1: *Christian Theology* (1a. 1), tr. Thomas Gil. London: Blackfriars; Eyre and Spottiswoode.

—— (1964) *Summa theologiae*, vol. 3 *Knowing and Naming God* (1a. 12–13), tr. Herbert McCabe. London: Blackfriars; Eyre and Spottiswoode.

—— (1965) *Summa theologiae*, vol. 28: *Law* (1a2ae. 90–7), tr. Thomas Gilby. London: Blackfriars; Eyre and Spottiswoode.

—— (1968) *Summa theologiae*, vol. 9: *Angels* (1a.50–64), tr. Kenelm Foster. London: Blackfriars; Eyre and Spottiswoode.

—— (1975) *Summa theologiae*, vol. 56: *The Sacraments* (3a.60–5), tr. David Bour. London: Blackfriars; Eyre and Spottiswoode.

Asad, Talal (1993) *The Genealogies of Religion: Discipline and Reasons of Power in Christianity and Islam*. Baltimore: Johns Hopkins University Press.

Augustine (1873) *Tractate de Johanno*, two vols, tr. John Gibb. Edinburgh: T.&T. Clark.

—— (1956) *On the Merits and Remission of Sins and on the Baptism of Infants*, in Philip Scaff (ed.), *St. Augustine: Anti-Pelgian Writings*. Grand Rapids: Michigan.

—— (1963) *De trinitate*, tr. Stephen McKenna. Washington: Catholic University of America Press.

—— (1968) *De magisto*, tr. Robert Russell. Washington: Catholic University of America Press.

—— (1972) *De civitate Dei*, tr. Henry Bettenson. Harmondsworth: Penguin Books.

—— (1975) *De dialectica*, tr. B.D. Jackson. Dordrecht: D. Reidel.

280

—— (1979) *Epistles in Nicene and Post-Nicene Fathers of the Christian Church*, vol. 1, Philip Schaff (ed.). Michigan: William Eerdmans.

—— (1982) *De Genesi ad litteram*, tr. John Hammond Taylor. New York: Newman Press.

—— (1991) *Confessions*, tr. Henry Chadwick. Oxford: Oxford University Press.

—— (1993) *Sermons*, III/6 and III/7, tr. Edmund Hill. New Rochelle: New City Press.

—— (1995) *De Doctrina christiana*, tr. R.P.H. Green. Oxford: Clarendon Press.

Ayer, A.J. (1959) *Philosophical Essays*. London: Macmillan.

—— (1963) *The Foundation of Empirical Knowledge*. London: Macmillan

Balthasar, Hans Urs von (1990) *Mysterium Paschale*, tr. Aidan Nichols OP. Edinburgh: T.&T. Clark.

—— (1991) *The Glory of the Lord. V. The Realm of Metaphysics in the Modern Age*, tr. Oliver Davies *et al.* Edinburgh: T.&T. Clark.

—— (1992) *Theo-Drama: Theological Dramatic Theory III: Dramatis Personae*, tr. G. Harrison. San Francisco: Ignatius Press.

Baratin, Marc (1981) 'Les Origines stoiciennes de la theorie Augustinienne du Signe', *Revue des Etudes Latines* 59.

Barth, Karl (1933) *The Epistle to the Romans*, tr. Edwyn C. Hoskyns. Oxford: Oxford University Press.

—— (1972) *Protestant Theology in the Nineteenth Century*, tr. Brian Cozens. London: SCM.

—— (1975) *Church Dogmatics*, I.1, tr. G.W. Bromiley. Edinburgh: T. & T. Clark.

—— (1958) *Church Dogmatics*, II.1, tr. T.M.L Parker *et al.* Edinburgh: T. & T. Clark.

—— (1958a) *Church Dogmatics*, III.1, tr. J.W. Edwards, *et al.* Edinburgh: T. & T. Clark.

—— (1960) *Church Dogmatics*, III.2, tr. Harold Knight *et al.* Edinburgh: T. & T. Clark.

—— (1960a) *Church Dogmatics*, III.3, trs. G.W. Bromiley and R.J. Ehrlich. Edinburgh: T.& T.Clark.

—— (1961) *Church Dogmatics*, III.4, tr. A.T.MacKay *et al.* Edinburgh: T. & T. Clark.

Barthes, Roland (1985) *The Fashion System*, tr. Matthew Ward and Richard Howard. London: Cape.

—— (1990) *The Pleasure of the Text*, tr. Richard Miller. Oxford: Blackwell.

Barzilai, Shuli (1997) 'Augustine in Contents: Lacan's Repetition of a Scene from the *Confessions*', *Literature and Theology* 11, 2 (June): 200–21.

Bataille, Georges (1987) *Eroticism*, tr. Mary Dalwood. London: Marion Boyars.

Baudrillard, Jean [1976] (1993) *Symbolic Exchange and Death*, tr. Iain Hamilton Grant. London: Sage.

—— (1995) 'The Virtual Illusion: or the Automatic Writing of the World', *Theory, Culture and Society* 12: 97–107.

Bauerschmidt, Frederick Christian (1996) 'The Abrahamic Voyage: Michel de Certeau and Theology', *Modern Theology* 21, 1: 1–26.

Bauman, Zymunt (1992) *Intimations of Postmodernity*. London: Routledge.

Beattie, Tina (1998) 'One Man and Three Women – Hans, Adrienne, Mary and Luce', *New Blackfriars* 79, 294 (February): 95–103.

Becker, Carl L. (1932) *The Heavenly City of the Eighteen Century Philosophers*. New Haven: Yale University Press.

Bell, David and Valentine, Gill (1995) *Mapping Desire: Geographies of Sexualities*. London: Routledge.

Bell, Duran (1991) 'Modes of Exchange: Gift and Commodity', *Journal of Socio-Economics* 20, 2: 155–67.

Berman, David (1988) *A History of Atheism in Britain: From Hobbes to Russell*. London

Bhabha, Homi (1994) *The Location of Culture*. London: Routledge.

Biel, Gabriel (1965) *Canonis Misse Expositio*, Lectio XLVIII, Heiko A. Oberman and William J. Courtney (eds).Wiesbaden: Franz Steiner Verlag.

Blumenberg, Hans [1966] (1983) *The Legitimacy of the Modern Age*, tr. Robert M. Wallace. Cambridge, MA: MIT Press.

—— (1993) 'Light as Metaphor for Truth: At the Preliminary Stage of Philosophical Concept Formation', tr. J. Anderson, in D.M. Levin (ed.) *Modernity and the Hegenomy of Light*. Berkeley: University of California Press.

Boas, Franz (1914) *The Handbook of American Indian Languages*. Washington, DC: Bureau of American Bulletin 40.

Bourdieu, Pierre (1991) *Language and Symbolic Power*, tr. and ed. John B. Thompson. Cambridge: Polity Press.

—— (1993) *The Field of Cultural Production: Essays on Art and Literature*, tr. and ed. Ronald Johnson. Cambridge: Polity Press.

Boyarin, Daniel (1993) *Carnal Israel: Reading Sex in Talmudic Culture*. Berkeley: University of California Press.

Boyd, Stephen B. *et. al* (eds) (1996) *Redeeming Men: Religion and Masculinity*. Louisville: Westminster John Knox Press.

Boyer, Christine (1994) *The City of Collective Memory*. Cambridge, MA: MIT Press.

Boyle, Nicholas (1998) *Who Are We Now? Christian Humanism and the Global Market from Hegel to Heaney*. Edinburgh: T. & T. Clark.

Brantley, William F. (1996) 'Thunder of New Wings: AIDS – a Journey Beyond Belief', in Stephen B. Boyd *et al*. (eds), *Redeeming Men: Religion and Masculinities*. Louisville: Westminster John Knox Press.

Bray, Alan (1982) *Homosexuality in Renaissance England*. London: Gay Men's Press.

Brito, Emilio (1979) *Hegel et la tache actuelle de la christologie*. Paris: Editions Lethielleux.

Brown, Malcolm (1999) 'Plurality and Globalisation: The Challenge of Economics to Confessionalism', unpublished seminar paper.

Brown, Peter (1995) 'St. Augustine and Political Society', in Dorothy F. Donnelly (ed.), *The City of God: A Collection of Critical Essays*. New York: Peter Lang: 17–35.

—— (1998) *The Body and Society: Men, Women, and Sexual Renunciation in Early Christianity*. London: Faber and Faber.

Buber, Martin [1922] (1958) *I and Thou*, tr. Ronald Gregor Smith. New York: Scribner's.

Buescher, Gabriel N. (1950) *The Eucharistic Teaching of William of Ockham*. Washington: The Catholic University of America Press.

Burbidge, J.W. (1992) *Hegel on Logic and Religion: The Reasonableness of Christianity*. New York: State University of New York Press.

Burgin, Victor (1988) 'Geometry and Abjection', in J. Tagg (ed.), *The Cultural Politics of Postmodernism*. Binghampton: SUNY.

Burke, Kenneth (1941) *Philosophy of Literary Form: Studies in Symbolic Action*. Berkeley: University of California Press.

—— (1950) *The Rhetoric of Motives*. Berkeley: University of California Press.

—— (1966) *Language as Symbolic Action: Essays on Life, Literature and Method*. Berkeley: University of California Press.

Burkhalter, Byron (1999) 'Reading Race Online: Discovering Racial Identity in Usenet Discussions', in Marc A. Smith and Peter Kollock (eds), *Communities in Cyberspace*. London: Routledge: 60–75.

Burleigh, John H.S. (1949) *The City of God*. London: Nisbet & Co.

Burnell, Peter (1995) 'The Problem of Service to Unjust Regimes in Augustine's *City of God*,' in Dorothy F. Donnelly (ed.), *The City of God: A Collection of Critical Essays*. New York: Peter Lang: 37–49.

Butin, Philip Walker (1996) *Revelation, Redemption and Response: Calvin's Trinitarian Understanding of the Divine/Human Relationship*. New York: Oxford University Press.

Butler, Judith (1987) *Subjects of Desire: Hegelian Reflections in Twentieth Century France*. New York: Columbia University Press.

—— (1990) *Gender Trouble: Feminism and the Subversion of Identity*. London: Routledge.

—— (1993) *Bodies that Matter: On the Discursive Limits of 'Sex'*. London: Verso.

—— (1997) *The Psychic Life of Power: Theories in Subjection*. Stanford: Stanford University Press.

Butler, Stuart M. (1981) *Enterprise Zones: Greenlining the Inner Cities*. London: Heinemann.

—— (1991) 'The Conceptual Evolution of Enterprise Zones', in Roy E. Green, *Enterprise Zones: New Directions in Economic Development*. London: Sage.

Bynum, Caroline Walker (1992) *Fragmentation and Redemption: Essays on Gender and the Human Body in Medieval Religion*. New York: Zone Books.

Cadden, Joan (1993) *The Meaning of Sex Difference in the Middle Ages: Medicine, Science and Culture*. Cambridge: Cambridge University Press.

Cajetan, Cardinal [1498] (1959) *The Analogy of Names*, tr. Edward A. Bushinski and Henry J. Koren. Pittsburgh: Duquesne University Press.

Calvin, Jean [1559] (1864) *Institutio Christianae Religionis [1559]*, in *Corpus Reformatorum vol. xxx, Joannis Calvini Opera Quae Superrunt Omnia vol. II*. Brunsvigae: CA. Schwetschke et filium.

—— (1936) *Institutes of the Christian Religion*, vols 1 and 2, tr. John Allen. Philadelphia: Presbyterian Board of Christian Education.

—— (1958) *Institution de la religion Chretiènne. Livre 4*. Geneva: Labor et Fides.

Calvino, Italo [1982] (1989) *The Literature Machine*, tr. Patrick Creagh. London: Picador.

—— [1972] (1974) *Invisible Cities*, tr. William Weaver. Orlando: Harcourt Brace & Company.

Campbell, Scott and Fainstein, Susan (1996) *Readings in Planning Theory*. Oxford: Blackwell.

Caputo, John. D. (1997) *The Prayers and Tears of Jacques Derrida: Religion Without Religion*. Bloomington: Indiana University Press.

Carrette, Jeremy (2000) *Foucault and Religion*. London: Routledge.

Carrier, James (1991).'Gifts, Commodities, and Social Relations: A Maussian View of Exchange', *Sociological Forum* 6, 1: 119–36.

Castelli, Elizabeth (1991) ' "I will make Mary Male": Pieties of the Body and Gender Transformation of Christian Women in Late Antiquity', in Julia Epstein and Kristina Straub (eds), *Body Guards: The Cultural Politics of Gender Ambiguity*. London: Routledge: 49–69.

Castells, Manuel (1983) *The City and the Grassroots: A Cross-Cultural Theory of Urban Social Movements*. London: Edward Arnold.

—— (1989) *The Informational City: Information Technology, Economic Restructuring, and the Urban-regional Process*. Oxford: Blackwell.

—— (1996) *The Rise of the Network Society*. Oxford: Blackwell.

—— (1997) *The Power of Identity*. Oxford: Blackwell.

—— (1998) *The End of the Millennium*. Oxford: Blackwell.

Castoriadis, Cornelius [1975] (1997) *The Imaginary Institution of Society*, tr. Kathleen Blamey. Cambridge: Polity Press.

Cavanaugh, William T. (1998) 'The City: Beyond Secular Parodies', in John Milbank, Catherine Pickstock and Graham Ward (eds), *Radical Orthodoxy*. London: Routledge: 182–200.

Cavarero, Adriana (1995) *In Spite of Plato: a Feminist Rewriting of Ancient Philosophy*. Cambridge: Polity Press.

Certeau, Michel de (1984) *The Practice of Everyday Life*, tr. Steven Randall. Berkeley: University of California Press.

—— (1986) 'Mystic Speech', in *Heterologies: Discourse on the Other*, tr. Brian Massumi. Minneapolis: University of Minnesota Press.

—— (1987) *La faiblesse du croire*. Paris: Seuil.

—— (1988) *The Writing of History*, tr. Tom Conley. New York: University of Columbia Press.

—— (1992) *The Mystic Fable*, tr. Michael B. Smith. Chicago: University of Chicago Press.

—— [1974, 1994] (1997) *Culture in the Plural*, tr. Tom Conley Minneapolis: Minnesota Press.

—— (1998) 'How is Christianity Thinkable Today?', in Graham Ward (ed.), *The Postmodern God*. Oxford: Blackwell: 142–55.

—— (1998a) 'White Ecstasy', tr. Frederick Christian Bauerschmidt and Catriona Hanley, in Graham Ward (ed.), *The Postmodern God*. Oxford: Blackwell: 155–58.

—— (2000) 'Walking in the City', in Graham Ward (ed.), *The Certeau Reader*. Oxford: Blackwell: 101–18.

—— (2000a) 'Believing and Making People Believe', in Graham Ward (ed.), *The Certeau Reader*. Oxford: Blackwell: 119–27.

Chandler, Tertius and Fox, Gerald (1974) *3000 Years of Urban Growth*. London: Academic Press.

Chapelle, Albert (1963–71) *Hegel et la religion, t. 1: 'La problematique'; t. 2: 'La dialectique; Dieu et la Creation', t. 3: 'La dialectique; La Théologie et l'Église': Annexes*. Paris: Editions Universitaires.

Chauvet, Louis-Marie (1995) *Symbol and Sacrament: A Sacramental Reinterpretation of Christian Existence*, Collegeville: The Liturgical Press.

Christopherson, Susan (1994) 'The Fortress City: Privatized Spaces, Consumer Citizenship', in Ash Amin (ed.), *Post-Fordism: A Reader*. Oxford: Blackwell: 409–27.

Church of England (1985) *Faith in the City*. London: Church House Publishing.

Cixous, Hélène (1975) (with Catherine Clement) *La Jeune Née*. Paris: UGE.

—— [1982–3] (1990) ' "The Egg and the Chicken"; Love Is Not Having', in *Reading with Clarice Lispector*, tr. Verene Andermatt Conley. London: Harvester Wheatsheaf: 98–122.

—— (1991) 'Tancredi Continues', in Deborah Jenson (ed.), *'Coming to Writing and Other Essays'*, tr. Sarah Cornell *et al.* Cambridge, MA: Harvard University Press: 78–103.

Connell, R.W. (1995) *Masculinities*. Cambridge: Polity Press.

Cooper, Simon (1997) 'Plenitude and Alienation: The Subject of Virtual Reality', in David Holmes (ed.), *Virtual Politics: Identity and Community in Cyberspace*. London: Sage: 93–106.

Cox, Harvey (1965) *The Secular City*. London: SCM.

—— (1984) *Religion in a Secular City: Towards a Postmodern Theology*. New York: Simon and Schuster.

Crites, Stephen (1998) *Dialectic and Gospel in the Development of Hegel's Thinking*. Pennsylvania: The Pennsylvania State University Press.

Cubitt, Sean (1998) *Digital Aesthetics*. London: Sage.

Cunningham, Conor (1998) 'Language: Wittgenstein after Theology', in John Milbank, Catherine Pickstock and Graham Ward (eds), *Radical Orthodoxy*. London: Routledge: 64–90.

—— (2000) 'Philosophies of Nothing: Reconstructing Metaphysics', Unpublished Ph.D. dissertation.

Cupitt, Don (1995) *The Last Philosophy*. London: SCM.

Davis, Mike (1990) *City of Quartz*. London: Verso.

—— (1998) 'Beyond Blade Runner' in *Ecology of Fear: Los Angeles and the Imagination of Disaster*. London: Picador: 359–422.

Deane, Herbert A. (1995) 'Augustine and The State: The Return of Order upon Disorder', in Dorothy F. Donnelly (ed.), *The City of God: A Collection of Critical Essays*. New York: Peter Lang: 51–73.

Debord, Guy [1967] (1977) *The Society of Spectacle*. Detroit: Black and Red.

Deleuze, Gilles and Guattari, Felix [1972] (1984) *Anti-Oedipus: Capitalism and Schizophrenia I*, tr. Robert Hurley *et al*. London: Athlone Press.

—— [1981] (1988) *Spinoza: Practical Philosophy*, tr. Robert Hurley. San Francisco: City Lights Books.

—— [1968] (1990) *Expressionism in Philosophy: Spinoza*, tr. Martin Joughin. New York: Zone Books.

Der Derian, James (1998) 'Introduction' in James Der Derian (ed.) *The Virilio Reader*. Oxford: Blackwell.

Derrida, Jacques [1972] (1982) *Margins of Philosophy*, tr. Alan Bass Brighton: The Harvester Press.

—— (1987) '*Comment ne pas parler: Denegations*', in *Psyché*. Paris: Galilee: 535–96.

—— [1980] (1991) 'At this Very Moment in this Work Here I am', tr. Simon Critchley, in Robert Bernasconi and Simon Critchley (eds), *Re-reading Levinas*. London: Althone Press: 3–48.

—— [1996] (1998) 'Faith and Knowledge', tr. Samuel Weber, in Jacques Derrida and Gianni Vattimo (eds), *Religion*. Cambridge: Polity Press: 1–78.

—— [1992] (1995) *The Gift of Death*, tr. David Willis. Chicago: University of Chicago Press.

Descartes, René [1637] (1984) *Discourse on Method*, in *The Philosophical Writings*, vol. II, tr. John Cottingham *et al*. Cambridge: Cambridge University Press.

—— [1641] (1984) *Meditations on First Philosophy*, in *The Philosophical Writings*, vol. II, tr. John Cottingham *et al*. Cambridge: Cambridge University Press.

—— [1644] (1985) *Principles of Philosophy*, in *The Philosophical Writings of Descartes*, vol. I, tr. John Cottingham *et al*. Cambridge: Cambridge University Press.

Dickey, Laurence (1988) *Hegel: Religion, Economics, and the Politics of the Spirit 1770–1807*. Cambridge: Cambridge University Press.

DiNoia, Joseph (1990) 'American Catholic Theology at Century's End: Postconciliar, Post-modern and Post-Thomistic', *The Thomist* 54: 499–518.

Dogan, Mattei and Kasarda, John D. (eds) (1988) *The Metropolis Era*, vol. 1: *A world of Giant Cities*; vol. 2: *Mega Cities*. Newbury Park, California: Sage Publications.

Dollimore, Jonathan (1998) *Death, Desire and Loss in Western Culture*. Harmondsworth: Penguin Books.

Donath, Judith S. (1999) 'Identity and Deception in the Virtual Community', in Marc A. Smith and Peter Kollock (eds), *Communities in Cyberspace*. London: Routledge: 29–59.

Dougherty, James (1980) *The Fivesquare City: The City in the Religious Imagination*. Notre Dame: University of Notre Dame Press.

Douglas, Mary (1966) *Purity and Danger: An Analysis of Concepts of Pollution and Taboo*. London: Routledge and Kegan Paul.

Doxiadis, Constantinos (1968) *Ekistics: Introduction of the Science of Human Settlement*. London: Hutchinson.

Driver, Tom (1965) 'Sexuality and Jesus', *Union Seminary Quarterly Review*, 20 (March): 235–46.

Drummond, Henry (1988) *The City without a Church and Other Addresses*. London: Hodder and Stoughton.

Dunn, James D.G. (1989) *Christology in the Making: An Inquiry into the Origins of the Doctrine of the Incarnation*. London: SCM.

Dunne, John S. (1965) *The City of the Gods*. London: Sheldon Press.

Duval, André (1985) *Des Sacraments au Concile de Trente*. Paris: Les Editions du Cerf.

Edwards, Tim (1990) 'Beyond Sex and Gender: Masculinity, Homosexuality and Social Theory', in Jeff Hearne and David Morgan (eds), *Men, Masculinities and Social Theory*. London: Unwin Hyman.

Ellul, Jacques (1970) *The Meaning of the City*, tr. Dennis Pardee. Grand Rapids: William Eerdmans.

Engels, Friedrich [1845] (1987) *The Condition of the Working Class in England*. Harmondsworth: Penguin Books.

Etlin, Richard E. (1994) *Frank Lloyd Wright and Le Corbusier: The Romantic Legacy*. Manchester: Manchester University Press.

Evans, Gareth (1982) *The Varieties of Reference*, John McDowell (ed.). Oxford: Oxford University Press.

Fainstein, Susan (1996) 'Planning in a Different Voice', in Scott Campbell and Susan S. Fainstein (eds), *Readings in Planning Theory*. Oxford: Blackwell: 456–60.

—— (1996a) 'Flexible Sexism', in Scott Campbell and Susan S. Fainstein (eds), *Readings in Planning Theory*. Oxford: Blackwell: 212–48.

Farrow, Douglas B. (1998) 'The Doctrine of the Ascension in Irenaeus and Origen', *ARC: The Journal of the Faculty of Religious Studies McGill University*, 26: 31–50.

Farthing, John L. (1988) *Thomas Aquinas and Gabriel Biel: Interpretations of St. Thomas Aquinas in German Nominalism in the Eve of the Reformation*. Durham: Duke University Press.

Featherstone, Mike (1994) 'City Cultures and Post-modern Lifestyles', in Ash Amin (ed.), *Post-Fordism: a Reader*. Oxford: Blackwell: 387–408.

Feckes, Carl (1927) 'Gabriel Biel, der erste grosse Dogmatiker der Universität Tübingen in seiner wissenschaftlichen Bedeutung', in *Theologische Quartalschrift* 108: 50–76.

Fernandez, James W. (1972) 'Persuasion and Performances: Of the Beast in Every Body … And Metaphors in Everyman', *Daedelus* (Winter): 39–60.

—— (1974) 'The Mission of Metaphor in Expressive Culture', *Current Anthropology* 15, 2 (June): 119–45.

Ferretter, Luke (1998) 'The Trace of the Trinity: Christ and Difference in St. Augustine's Theory of Language', *Literature and Theology*, 12, 3: 256–67.

Field, J.V. (1997) *The Invention of Infinity: Mathematics and Art in the Renaissance*. Oxford: Oxford University Press.

Figgis, J.N. (1921) *The Political Aspects of St. Augustine's 'City of God'*. London: Longman, Green and Co.

Findlay, J.N. (1970) *Ascent to the Absolute*. London: Allen and Unwin.

Fish, Stanley (1980) *Is There a Text in This Class? The Authority of Intrerpretive Communities*. Cambridge. MA: Harvard University Press.

Fishman, Robert (1977) *Urban Utopias in the C20th*. New York: Basic Books.

Fitzpatrick, P.J. (1994) *In Breaking of Bread: The Eucharist and Ritual*. Cambridge: Cambridge University Press.

Forrester, Duncan (1997) *Christian Justice and Public Policy*. Cambridge: Cambridge University Press.

Foucault, Michel [1966] (1970) *The Order of Things: an Archaeology of the Human Sciences*. London: Tavistock Publications.

—— (1979) *Michel Foucault: Power, Truth and Strategy* (eds) M. Morris and P. Patton. Sydney: Feral Publications.

—— [1971] (1984) 'Nietzsche, Genealogy, History', in Raul Rabinow (ed.), *The Foucault Reader*. Harmondsworth: Penguin: 76–100.

—— [1976] (1981) *The History of Sexuality: An Introduction*, tr. Robert Hurley. Harmondsworth: Penguin Books.

—— (1997) 'The Birth of Biopolitics', in Paul Rabinow (ed.), *Ethics, Subjectivity and Truth*, tr. Robert Hurley *et al*. Harmondsworth: Penguin: 73–9.

Freud, Sigmund [1900] (1953) *The Interpretation of Dreams*, two volumes, tr. James Strachey. London: Hogarth.

—— [1930] (1961) 'Civilization and its Discontents', in *The Complete Psychological Works of Sigmund Freud*, vol. XXI, tr. and ed. James Stratchey. London: Hogarth Press: 64–143.

—— [1905] (1961) *Three Essays in Human Sexuality*, in *The Complete Psychological Works of Sigmund Freud*, volume VII, tr. and ed. James Stratchey. London: Hogarth Press: 123–233.

—— [1913] (1961) *Totem and Taboo*, in *The Complete Psychological Works of Sigmund Freud*, volume XIII, tr. and ed. James Stratchey. London: Hogarth Press: 1–161.

—— [1914](1957) 'On Narcissism: An Introduction', in *The Complete Psychological Works of Sigmund Freud*, volume XIV, tr. and ed. James Stratchey. London: Hogarth Press: 73–102.

—— [1921] (1955) *Group Psychology and the Analysis of the Ego*, in *The Complete Psychological Works of Sigmund Freud*, volume XVIII, tr. and ed. James Stratchey. London: Hogarth Press: 69–143.

—— [1927] (1961) 'Future of an Illusion', in *The Complete Psychological Works of Sigmund Freud*, volume XXI, tr. and ed. James Stratchey. London: Hogarth Press: 5–56.

Freudenthal, Gideon (1986) *Atom and Individual in the Age of Newton: On the Genesis of the Mechanistic World View*, tr. Peter McLaughlin. Dordrecht: D. Reidel Publishing Company.

Fuchs, Emil [1921] (1968) 'The Unconditional Seriousness of Our Piety: A Reply to Friedrich Gogarten', in James Robinson (ed.), Louis De Grazia and Keith R. Crim (tr), *The Beginnings of Dialectical Theology*. Richmond: John Knox Press: 306–10.

Fukuyama, Francis (1992) *The End of History and the Last Man*. London: Hamish Hamilton.

Fulkerson, Mary McClintock (1994) *Changing the Subject: Women's Discourses and Feminist Theology*. Minneapolis: Fortress Press.

Funkenstein, Amos (1986) *Theology and the Scientific Imagination*. Princeton: Princeton University Press.

Gatens, Moira (1996) *Imaginary Bodies: Ethics, Power and Corporeality*. London: Routledge.

Geertz, Clifford (1973) *The Interpretation of Cultures*. New York: Basic Books Inc.

Gellrich, Jesse M. (1985) *The Idea of the Book in the Middle Ages: Language, Theory, Mythology, and Fiction*. Ithaca: Cornell University Press.

Gerrish, Brian (1993) *Grace and Gratitude: The Eucharistic Theology of John Calvin*. Edinburgh: T & T Clark.

Giddens, Anthony (1984) *The Constitution of Society: Outline of a Theory of Structuration*. Cambridge: Polity Press.

Gil, José (1998) *Metamorphoses of the Body*, tr. Stephen Muecke. Minneapolis: University of Minnesota Press.

Gillespie, Michael Allen (1996) *Nihilism Before Nietzsche*. Chicago: University Of Chicago Press.

Girard, René [1972] (1977) *Violence and the Sacred*, tr. Patrick Gregory. Baltimore: John Hopkins University Press.

Gogarten, Friedrich [1920] (1968) 'Between the Times', in James Robinson (ed.), Louis De Grazia and Keith R. Crim (tr.), *The Beginnings of Dialectical Theology*. Richmond: John Knox Press: 277–82.

—— [1920a] (1968) 'The Crisis of Our Culture', in James Robinson (ed.), Louis De Grazia and Keith R. Crim (tr.), *The Beginnings of Dialectical Theology*. Richmond: John Knox Press: 283–300.

Golding, Martin (2000) 'Photography, Memory and Survival', *Literature and Theology* 14, 1 (March): 52–68.

Graham, Elaine (1996) 'Theology in the City: Ten Years After *Faith in the City*', *Bulletin of the John Rylands University Library of Manchester* 78, 1, Spring: 173–91.

Greenberg, David F. (1988) *The Construction of Homosexuality*. Chicago: University of Chicago Press.

Greenblatt, Stephen (1988) *Shakespearean Negotiations: The Articulation of Social Energy in Renaissance England*. Oxford: Clarendon Press.

Griffin, David Ray (1989) *God and Religion in the Postmodern World: Essays in Postmodern Theology*. Albany: SUNY Press.

Guiton, Jacques (1981) *The Ideas of Le Corbusier*. New York: G. Braziller.

Gurevich, A. (1985) *Categories of Medieval Culture*. London: Routledge.

Gutting Gary (ed.) (1994) *The Cambridge Companion to Foucault*. Cambridge: Cambridge University Press.

Hall, Peter (1996) *Cities of Tomorrow: An Intellectual History of Urban Planning and Design in the Twentieth Century*, second edition. Oxford: Blackwell.

—— (1998) *Cities in Civilization*. London: Weidenfeld and Nicolson.

Halley, Peter (1995) 'Notes on Nostalgia', excerpt in Sophie Watson and Katherine Gibson (eds), *Postmodern Cities and Spaces*. Oxford: Blackwell: 20.

Halperin, David (1990) *One Hundred Years of Homosexuality and Other Essays on Greek Love*. London: Routledge.

Harding, Sandra (1993) 'Rethinking Standpoint Epistemology: "What is Strong Objectivity?" ', in Linda Alcoff and Elizabeth Potter (eds), *Feminist Epistemologies*. London: Routledge: 49–82.

Harloe, Michael and Fainstein, Susan (1992) 'Conclusion' to *Divided Cities: New York and London in the Contemporary World*. Oxford: Blackwell: 236–68.

Haraway, Donna (1991) *Simians, Cyborgs and Women: the Reinvention of Nature*. London: Free Association Press.

Harrison, Verna E.F. (1992) *Grace and Freedom According to St. Gregory of Nyssa*. Lampter: Edwin Mellen Press.

Harvey, Anthony (ed.) (1989) *Theology in the City*. London: SPCK.

Harvey, David (1984) *The Urbanization of Capital*. Oxford: Blackwell.

—— (1987) 'Flexible Accumulation through Urbanization: Reflections on "Post-modernism" in the American City', *Antipode* 19, 3: 260–86.

—— (1990) *The Condition of Postmodernity*. Oxford: Blackwell.

—— (1996) *Justice, Nature and the Geography of Difference*. Blackwell: Oxford.

Hawkins, Peter S. (ed.) (1986) *Civitas: Religious Interpretations of the City*. Georgia: Scholars Press.

Hayek, Friedrich (1944) *The Road to Serfdom*. Chicago: University of Chicago Press.

Hegel, Wilhelm Friedrich (1956) *Lectures on the Philosophy of History*, tr. John Sibree. New York: Dover Publications.

—— (1962) *Lectures on the Philosophy of Religion Together with a Work on the Proofs of the Existence of God*, vol. III, tr. E.B. Speirs and J. Burdon Sanderson. London: Routledge and Kegan Paul.

—— (1974) *Lectures on the History of Philosophy*, vol. 3, tr. Elizabeth S. Haldane and Frances H. Simson. London: Routledge and Kegan Paul.

—— (1974a) *Hegel: The Essential Writings*, F.G. Weiss (ed.). New York: Doubleday and Company.

—— (1977) *Phenomenology of Spirit*, tr. A.V. Miller. Oxford: Clarendon Press.

—— (1988) *Lectures on the Philosophy of Religion*, ed. Peter C. Hodgson, tr. R.F. Brown *et al*. Berkeley: University of Califonia Press.

—— (1991) *Elements of the Philosophy of Right*, ed. Allen W. Wood, tr. H.B. Nisbet. Cambridge: Cambridge University Press.

Heidegger, Martin (1972) *Time and Being*, tr. Joan Stambaugh. New York: Harper & Row.

Heim, Michael (1993) *The Metaphsyics of Virtual Reality*. Oxford: Oxford University Press.

Herdt, Gilbert (ed.) (1993) *Third Sex, Third Gender: Beyond Sexual Dimorphism in Culture and History*. New York: Zone Books.

Hillis, Ken (1999) 'Toward the Light "Within": Optical Technologies, Spatial Metaphors and Changing Subjectivities', in Mike Crang, Phil Crang and Jon May (eds), *Virtual Geographies: Bodies, Space and Relations*. London: Routledge.

Hobbes, Thomas (1968) *Leviathan*. Harmondsworth: Penguin.

—— (1888) *Elements of the Law*, ed. F. Tönnies. Oxford: Thorton.

—— (1976) *Thomas White's De Mundo Explained*, tr. Harold Whitmore Jones. London: Bradford University Press.

—— (1998) *On the Citizen*, tr. Richard Tuck and Michael Silverthorne. Cambridge: Cambridge University Press.

Hugh of St Victor (1991) *The Didascalicon of Hugh of St. Victor: A Mediaeval Guide to the Arts*, tr. Jerome Taylor. New York: Columbia University Press.

Hughes, Sheila Hassell (1997) 'A Woman's Soul is Her Castle: Place and Space in St. Teresa's *Interior Castle*', *Literature and Theology* 11, 4 (December): 376–84.

Huizinga, Johan (1996) *The Autumn of the Middle Ages*, tr. Rodney J. Payton and Ulrich Mammitzsch. Chicago: University of Chicago Press.

Hume, David (1975) *Enquiries Concerning Human Understanding and the Principles of Morals*. Oxford: Clarendon Press.

Hunsinger, George (2000) *Disruptive Grace: Studies in the Theology of Karl Barth*. Michigan: Eerdmans.

Hunt, Lynn (ed.) (1993) *The Invention of Pornography: Obscenity and the Origins of Modernity*. New York: Zone Books.

Interrogate the Internet Group (1996) 'Contradictions in Cyberspace: Collective Response', in Rob Shields (ed.), *Cultures of the Internet: Virtual Spaces, Real Histories, Living Bodies*. London: Sage.

Irenaeus (1910) *Adverses Haereses*, vols I and II, tr. Alexander Roberts and W.H. Rambaut. Edinburgh: T. & T. Clark.

Irigaray, Luce (1985) *Speculum of the Other Woman*, tr. Gillian C. Gill. New York: Cornell University Press.

—— (1991) *Marine Lover of Friedrich Nietzsche*, tr. Gillian C. Gill. New York: Columbia University Press.

—— (1992) *Elemental Passions*, tr. Joanna Collie and Judith Still. London: Athlone Press.

—— (1993) *Sexes and Genealogies*, tr. Gillian C. Gill. New York: Columbia University Press.

—— (1993a) *An Ethics of Sexual Difference*, tr. Carolyn Burke and Gillian C. Gill. Ithaca: Cornell University Press.

—— (1998) 'Equal to Whom?' tr. Robert L. Mazzola, in Graham Ward (ed.), *The Postmodern God*. Oxford: Blackwell: 198–213.

Jackson, B. Darrell (1969) 'The Theory of Signs in St. Augustine's *De Doctrina Christiana*', *Revue des Etudes Augustiniennes* XV.

Jacob, Janet (1962) *The Death and Life of Great American Cities*. London: Jonathan Cape.

Jakobson, Roman (1987) 'Two Aspects of Language and Two Types of Aphasia' and 'Marginal Notes on the Prose of the Poet Pasternak', in Krystyna Pomonska and Stephen Rudy (eds), *Language in Literature*. Cambridge, MA: Harvard University Press.

Jameson, Fredric (1991) *Postmodernism, or, The Cultural Logic of Late Capitalism*. London: Verso, 1991.

Jantzen, Grace (1998) *Becoming Divine*. Manchester: University Of Manchester Press.

Jardine, Alice and Smith, Peter (1987) *Men in Feminism*. New York: Metheun.

Jardine, Lisa (1996) *Worldly Goods*. London: Macmillan.

Jasper, Alison (1998) *The Shining Garment of the Text: Gendered Readings of John's Prologue*. Sheffield: Sheffield Academic Press.

Jencks, Charles (1984) *The Language of Postmodern Architecture*. London: Academy

—— (1991) 'Postmodern vs. Late-Modern', in Ingeborg Hoesterey (ed.), *Zeitgeist in Babel: The Post-Modernist Controversy*. Bloomington: Indiana University Press: 4–21.

—— (1992) *The Post-Modern Reader*. London: Academy.

—— (1993) *Heteropolis: Los Angeles, the riots and the strange beauty of hetero-architecture*, London: Academy Editions.

Jensen, Paul N. (1989) *Metropolis/Fritz Lang*. London: Faber.

Jordan, Tim (1999) *Cyberpower: The Culture and Politics of Cyberspace and the Internet*. London: Routledge.

Kant, Immanuel (1960) *Religion Within the Limits of Reason Alone*, tr. Theodore M. Greene and Hoyt H. Hudson. New York: Harper & Row.

—— (1983) 'Speculative Beginning of Human History', *Perpetual Peace and Other Essays: on Politics, History, and Morals*, tr. and ed. Ted Humphrey. Indianapolis: Hackett.

Kantorowicz, Ernest H. (1957) *The King's Two Bodies: A Study in Mediaeval Political Theology*. Princeton: Princeton University Press.

Kasinitz, Philip (ed.) (1995) *Metropolis: Centre and Symbol of our Time*. London: Macmillan.

Kaufman, Peter Iver (1995) 'Redeeming Politics: Augustine's *City of God*', in Dorothy F. Donnelly (ed.), *The City of God: A Collection of Critical Essays*. New York: Peter Lang: 75–91.

Kavanagh, Aidan (1984) *On Liturgical Theology*. New York: Pueblo Publishing Company.

Kellner, Douglas (1989) *Jean Baudrillard: From Marxism to Postmodernism and Beyond*. Cambridge: Polity.

King, Desmond S. (1987) 'The State, Capital and Urban Change in Britain', in Smith and Feagin.

Klotz, Heinrich (1988) *The History of Postmodern Architecture*, tr. Radka Donnell. Cambridge MA: MIT Press.

Kobler, Renate (1989) *In the Shadow of Karl Barth: Charlotte von Kirschbaum*, tr. Keith Crim. Louisville: Westminster Press.

Kolker, Robert Phillip and Beicken, Peter (1993) *The Films of Wim Wenders: Cinema as Vision and Desire*. Cambridge: Cambridge University Press.

Kollock, Peter (1999) 'The Economies of Online Cooperation: Gifts and Public Goods in Cyberspace', in Marc A. Smith and Peter Kollock (eds), *Communities in Cyberspace*. London: Routledge: 220–39.

Koyré, Alexander (1957) *From the Closed World of the Infinite Universe*, tr. Baltimore, MD: John Hopkins University Press.

Kristeva, Julia (1982) *Power of Horror: An Essay on Abjection*, tr. Leon Roudiez, New York: Columbia University Press.

—— (1986) 'Freud and Love: Treatments and its Discontents', tr. Leon S. Roudiez in *The Kristeva Reader*. Oxford: Blackwell: .

—— (1988) *In the Beginning Was Love: Psychoanalysis and Faith*, tr. Arthur Goldhammer, New York: Columbia University Press.

Labarthe, Philippe Lacoue (1989) *Typography: Mimesis, Philosophy, Politics*. Cambridge, MA: Harvard University Press.

—— (1990) *Heidegger, Art and Politics*, tr. Chris Turner. Oxford: Blackwell.

Lacan, Jacques (1975) *Le seminaire de Jacques Lacan. Livre I: Les écrits techniques de Freud 1953–4*. Paris: Editions du Seuil.

—— (1977) *Écrits: A Selection*, tr. Alan Sheridan. London: Tavistock Publications.

—— (1979) *Four Fundamental Concepts of Psycho-Analysis*, tr. Alan Sheridan. Harmondsworth: Penguin Books.

—— (1982) *Feminine Sexuality: Jacques Lacan and the École Freudienne*, eds Juliet Mitchell and Jacqueline Rose. Basingstoke: Macmillan.

—— (1992) *Seminar VII: The Ethics of Psychoanalysis*, tr. Dennis Porter. New York: Norton.

Lakeland, Paul (1984) *The Politics of Salvation The Hegelian Idea of the State*. Albany: SUNY.

Lanier, Jaron and Biocca, Frank (1992) 'An Insider's View of the Future of Virtual Reality', *Journal of Communication* 42, 4: 150–72.

Laqueur, Thomas (1990) *Making Sex: Body and Gender from the Greeks to Freud*. Cambridge, Mass: Harvard University Press.

Larkin, Philip (1955) *Less Deceived*. Hessle: Marvell Press.

Lasch, Christopher (1980) *The Culture of Narcissism*. London: Abacus.

Latour, Bruno (1993) *We Have Never Been Modern*, tr. Catherine Porter. Cambridge, MA: Harvard University Press.

—— (1995) with Michel Serres, *Conversations on Science, Cutlure and Time*, tr. Roxanne Lapidus. Michigan: University of Michigan Press.

Lauer, Quentin (1982) *Hegel's Concept of God*. Albany: SUNY.

Lauretis, Teresa de (1987) *Technologies of Gender: Essays on Theory, Film, and Fiction*. Basingstoke: Macmillan.

Le Corbusier (1965) *Towards a New Architecture*, tr. Frederick Etchells. London: The Architectural Press.

—— (1989) *Poème de l'angle droit*, Paris: Fondation Le Corbusier.

Lefebvre, Henri (1991) *The Production of Space*, tr. Donald Nicholson-Smith. Oxford: Blackwell.

—— (1996) *Writings on Cities*, tr. Eleonore Kofman and Elizabeth Lebas. Oxford: Blackwell.

LeGates, Richard T. and Stout, Frederic (eds) (1996) *The City Reader*. London: Routledge.

Levinas, Emmanuel (1987) *Time and the Other*, tr. Richard Cohen. Pittsburgh: Duquesne University Press.

Lévi-Strauss, Claude (1967) *Structural Anthropology*, tr. Claire Jacobson and Brooke Grundfest Schoept. New York: Anchor Books.

Liebeschuetz, Wolfgang (1992) 'The End of the Ancient City', in John Rich (ed.) *The City in Late Antiquity*. London: Routledge.

Liggett, Helen (1996) 'Knowing Women/Planning Theory', in Scott Campbell and Susan F. Fainstein (eds), *Readings in Planning Theory*. Oxford: Blackwell: 451–5.

Lindbeck, George A. (1984) *The Nature of Doctrine: Religion and Theology in a Postliberal Age*. Philadelphia: Westminster.

Lingis, Alphonso (1989) *Deathbound Subjectivity*. Bloomington: Indiana University Press.

Lloyd, Howell A. (1991) 'Constitutionalism', in J.H. Burns, *Cambridge History of Political Thought 1450–1700*. Cambridge: Cambridge University Press.

Lloyd, Genevieve (1993) *The Man of Reason: 'Male' and 'Female' in Western Philosophy*. London: Routledge.

—— (1994) *Part of Nature: Self-Knowledge in Spinoza's Ethics*. Ithaca: Cornell University Press.

Longino, Helen (1993) 'Subjects, Power and Knowledge', in *Feminist Epistemologies*, eds Linda Alcoff and Elizabeth Potter. London: Routledge: 101–20.

Longinus [*c.*1st century AD] (1965) *On the Sublime*, tr. T.S. Dorsch. Harmondsworth: Penguin Books.

Loughlin, Gerard (1995) *Telling God's Story : Bible, Church and Narrative Theology*. Cambridge: University of Cambridge Press.

—— (1998) 'Erotics: God's Sex', in John Milbank, Catherine Pickstock and Graham Ward (eds), *Radical Orthodoxy*. London: Routledge: 143–62.

Louth, Andrew (1989) 'Augustine on Language', *Literature and Theology* 3.2: 151–8.

de Lubac, Henri (1949) Corpus Mysticum. 2nd edition. Paris: Aubier.

Lyotard, Jean-François [1979] (1984) *The Postmodern Condition: A Report on Knowledge*, tr. Geoff Bennington and Brian Massumi Manchester: Manchester University Press.

—— (1991) *The Inhuman*, tr. Geoffrey Bennington and Rachel Bowlby. Cambridge: Polity Press.

—— (1992) *The Libidinal Economy*, tr. I.H. Grant. London: Athlone Press.

—— (1994) *Lessons in the Analytic of the Sublime*, tr. Elizabeth Rottenberg. Stanford: Stanford University Press.

McDowell, John (1994) *Mind and World*. Cambridge, MA: Harvard University Press.

Macey, David (1988) *Lacan in Contexts*. London: Verso.

—— (1994) *The Lives of Michel Foucault*. London: Vintage.

Macfarlane, A. (1978) *The Origins of English Individualism*. Oxford: Blackwell.

MacIntyre, Alasdair (1981) *After Virtue: A Study in Moral Theory*. London: Duckworth.

—— (1990) *Three Rival Versions of Moral Enquiry*. London: Duckworth.

Macpherson, C.B. (1964) *The Political Theory of Possessive Individualism. Hobbes to Locke*. Oxford: Oxford University Press.

Maffesoli, M. (1988) 'Jeux de masques: postmoderne tribalisme', in *Design Issues* 4, 1–2.

—— (1991) 'The Ethic of Aesthetics', in *Theory, Culture and Society* 8: 7–20.

Maisels, Charles Keith (1993). *The Near East: Archaeology in the 'Cradle of Civilization'*. London: Routledge.

Malcolm, Noel (1987) 'Hobbes and Spinoza', in J.H. Burns (ed.), *Cambridge History of Political Thought*. Cambridge: Cambridge University Press: 545–50.

Maloney, George A. (tr.) (1976) *Hymns of Divine Love by St Symeon the New Theologian*. New Jersey: Denville.

Mandel, Ernst (1978) *Late Capitalism*, tr. Joris de Bres. London: Verso.

Marin, Louis (1984) *Utopics: Spatial Play*, tr. Robert A. Vollrath. New Jersey: Macmillan.

—— (1989) *Food for Thought*, tr. Mette Hjort. Baltimore: John Hopkins University Press.

Marion, Jean-Luc (1991) *La Croisée de visible*. Paris: La Différence, 1991.

—— (1991a) *God Without Being: Hors Texte*, tr. T. Carleson. Chicago: University of Chicago Press.

Markus, R.A. (1970) *Saeculum: History and Society in the Theology of St. Augustine*. Cambridge: Cambridge University Press.

—— (1975) 'St. Augustine on Signs', *Phronesis* 2.

—— (1994) '*De Civitate Dei*: Pride and the Common Good', in *Sacred and Secular: Studies on Augustine and Latin Christianity by R.A .Markus*. Aldershot: Varorium.

—— (1995) 'Two Conceptions of Political Authority: Augustine's *De civitate dei* XIX 14–15 and Some C13th Interpretations', in Dorothy F. Donnelly (ed.), *The City of God: A Collection of Critical Essays*. New York: Peter Lang: 93–117.

Martin, Dale (1995) *The Corinthian Body*. New Haven: Yale University Press.

Martindale, Don (1960) 'Prefatory Remarks' to Max Weber's *The City*, tr. Don Martindale and Gertrud Neuwirth. London: Heinemann.

Martinich, A.P. (1992) *The Two Gods of Leviathan: Thomas Hobbes on Religion and Politics*. Cambridge: Cambridge University Press.

—— (1999) *Hobbes: A Biography*. Cambridge: Cambridge University Press.

Mason, Richard (1997) *The God of Spinoza*. Cambridge: Cambridge University Press.

Massey, Doreen (ed.) (1994) *Space, Place and Gender*. Cambridge: Polity.

Maurice, F.D. (1996) *Democratic Socialism in Britain: Classic Texts in Economic and Political Thought 1825–1952*, David Reisman (ed.), vol. 2 *The Christian Socialists: F. Denison Maurice, Charles Kingsley and John Malcolm Ludlow*. London: Pickering and Chatto.

McGilligan, Patrick (1997) *Fritz Lang: The Nature of the Beast*. London: Faber.

McLuhan, Marshall (1964) *Understanding Media: The Extensions of Man*. London: Macmillan.

Meeks, Wayne A. (1986) 'St. Paul and the Cities', in Hawkins.

Mele, Christopher (1999) 'Cyberspace and Disadvantaged Communities: The Internet as a Tool for Collective', in Marc A. Smith and Peter Kollock (eds), *Communities in Cyberspace*. London: Routledge: 290–310.

Merleau-Ponty, Maurice (1962) *The Phenomenology of Perception*, tr. Colin Smith. London: Routledge.

Milbank, John (1992) 'Problematizing the Secular: The Post-Postmodern Agenda', in Philippa Berry and Andrew Wernick (eds), *The Shadow of Spirit: Postmodernism and Religion*. London: Routledge: 30–44.

—— (1995) 'Can the Gift be Given?', *Modern Theology* 2, 1 (January): 119–61.

—— (1998) 'Sublimity: the Modern Transcendent', in Paul Heelas (ed.), *Religion, Modernity and Postmodernity*.Oxford: Blackwell: 258–84.

Milbrath, Lester (1985) 'Pathologies in Giant Cities'. Paper presented at the Barcelona Conference on Giant Cities, 25 February–2 March, Barcelona.

Mirandola, Pico della [1487] (1948) *Oration on the Dignity of Man*, tr. Elizabeth Livermore Forbes, in Ernst Cassirer, Paul Oskar Kristeller and John Herman Randall (eds), *The Renaissance Philosophy of Man*. Chicago: University of Chicago Press.

Mitchell, Juliet (1975) *Psychoanalysis and Feminism*. Harmondsworth: Penguin.

Mollenkorf, John and Castells, Manuel (eds) (1991) *Dual City: Restructuring New York*. New York: Russell Sage Foundation.

Montag, John (1998) 'Revelation: The False Legacy of Suarez', in John Milbank, Catherine Pickstock and Graham Ward (eds), *Radical Orthodoxy: The New Theology*. London: Routledge: 38–63.

More, Sir Thomas (1963) 'Responsio ad Lutherum', in *Collected Works*, vol. 5, ed. J.M. Headley, tr. Sister Scholastica Mandeville. New Haven: Yale University Press.

Moss, David and Gardner, Lucy (1998) 'Difference – The Immaculate Concept? The Laws of Sexual Difference in the Theology of Hans Urs von Balthasar in *Modern Theology* 14, 3 (July): 377–401.

—— (1999) 'Something Like Time; Something like the Sexes – An Essay in Reception', in *Balthasar at the End of Modernity* by Lucy Gardner, David Moss, Ben Quash and Graham Ward. Edinburgh: T. & T. Clarke: 69–137.

Mosse, George (1996) *The Image of Man: The Creation of Modern Masculinity*. Oxford: Oxford University Press.

Muers, Rachael (1999) 'A Question of Two Answers: Difference and Determination in Barth and von Balthasar', *Heythrop Journal* 40: 265–79.

Mumford, Lewis (1973) *The City in History: Its Origins, its Transformations, and its Prospects*. Harmondsworth: Penguin.

Musurillo, Herbert (ed. and tr.) (1979) *From Glory to Glory. Texts from Gregory of Nyssa*. New York: Paulist Press.

Nadler, Steven (1999) *Spinoza: A Life*. Cambridge: Cambridge University Press.

Nancy, Jean-Luc (1991) *The Inoperative Community*, tr. Peter Connor *et al*. Minneapolis: University of Minnesota Press.

—— (1993) *The Experience of Freedom*, tr. Bridget McDonald. Stanford: Stanford University Press.

—— (1994) 'Corpus', tr. Claudette Sartiliot in Juliet Flower MacCannell and Laura Zakarin (eds) *Thinking Bodies*. Stanford: Stanford University Press.

Neumann, Dietrich (ed.) (1996) *Film Architecture: Set Designs from Metropolis to Blade Runner*. Munich: Pestel Verlag.

Newman, Barbara (1995) *From Virile Woman to Woman Christ: Studies in Medieval Religion and Literature*. Philadelphia: University of Pennsylvanian Press.

Nietzsche, Friedrich (1956) *The Birth of Tragedy*, tr. Francis Gotting. New York: Doubleday.

—— (1992) *Ecce Homo*, tr. R.J. Hollingdale. Harmondsworth: Penguin.

Noonan, John T. (1957) *The Scholastic Analysis of Usury*. Cambridge, MA: Harvard University Press.

Northcott, Michael (1998) *Urban Theology: A Reader*. London: Cassell.

Nunes, Mark (1997) 'What Space is Cyberspace? The Internet and Virtuality', in David Holmes (ed.), *Virtual Politics: Identity and Community in Cyberspace*. London: Sage: 163–78.

Nygren, Anders (1953) *Agape and Eros*, tr. Philip S. Watson. London: SPCK.

Nyssa, Saint Gregory of (1978) *Life of Moses*, tr. Abraham J. Malherbe and Everett Ferguson. New York: Paulist Press.

—— (1979) 'On the Making of Man', in Philip Schaff and Henry Wace (eds) *Gregory of Nyssa, Dogmatic Treaties etc.* Michigan: Wm. B. Eerdmans.

—— (1979a) *Commentary on the Canticle of Canticles*, excerpts in Herbert Musurillo (ed.) *From Glory to Glory: Texts from Gregory of Nyssa's Mystical Writings*. Crestwood, NY: St Vladimir's Seminary Press.

O'Brien, Jodie (1999) 'Writing the Body: Gender (Re)production in Online Interaction', in Marc A. Smith and Peter Kollock (eds), *Communities in Cyberspace*. London: Routledge: 76–104.

Ockham, William of (1930) *De Sacramento Altaris*, T. Bruce Birch (ed.). Burlington: The Lutheran Literary Board.

O'Donovan, Oliver (1980) *The Problem of Self-Love in Augustine*. New Haven: Yale University Press.

—— (1995) 'Augustine's City of God XIX and Western Political Thought', in Dorothy F. Donnelly (ed.), *The City of God: A Collection of Critical Essays*. New York: Peter Lang.

Oliver, Simon (1999) 'The Eucharist Before Nature and Culture', *Modern Theology* 15, 3 (July): 331–53.

Olshan, Joseph (1995) *Night Swimmer*. London: Bloomsbury.

Olson, Alan M. (1992) *Hegel and the Spirit: Philosophy as Pneumatology*. Princeton: Princeton University Press.

On, Bat-Ami Bar (1993) 'Marginality and Epistemic Privilege', in Linda Alcoff and Elizabeth Potter (eds), *Feminist Epistemologies*. London: Routledge: 83–100.

O'Regan, Cyril (1994) *The Heterodox Hegel*. New York: State University of New York Press.

Origen (1954) *On Prayer*, tr. John J. O'Meara, in *Ancient Christian Writers* vol.19. New York: Newman Press: 15–140.

Ortner, Sherry (1973) 'Key Symbols', *American Anthropology* 75, 5: 1339.

Patton, Phil (1986) *Open Road*. New York: Simon and Schuster.

Pecora, Vincent (1989) 'The Limits of Local Knowledge', in H. Aram Veeser (ed.), *The New Historicism*. London: Routledge: 243–76.

Pickstock, Catherine (1997) *After Writing: The Liturgical Consummation of Philosophy*. Oxford: Blackwell.

—— (1999) 'Thomas Aquinas and the Quest for the Eucharist', *Modern Theology* 15, 2 (April): 159–80.

Pile, Steve (1996) *The Body and the City: Psychoanalysis, Space and Subjectivity*. London: Routledge.

Plato (1961) *The Republic*, in Edith Hamilton and Huntingdon Cairns (eds) *The Collected Dialogues of Plato*. Princeton: Princeton University Press.

Poulantzas, N. (1978) *State, Power, Socialism*. London: Verso.

Poovey, Mary (1998) *The History of the Modern Fact: Problems of Knowledge in the Sciences of Wealth and Society*. Chicago: University of Chicago Press.

Porter, Roy and Hall, Lesley (1995) *The Facts of Life: The Creation of Sexual Knowledge in Britain 1650–1950*. New Haven: Yale University Press.

Poster, Mark (1990) *The Mode of Information: Poststructuralism and Social Context*. Oxford: Polity.

—— (1994) 'A Second Media Age?' *Arena Journal* 3: 49–92.

—— (1997) 'Cyberdemocracy: The Internet and the Public Sphere', in David Holmes (ed.), *Virtual Politics: Identity and Community in Cyberspace*. London: Sage: 212–28.

Preston, Peter and Simpson-Housley, Paul (eds) (1994) *Writing the City: Eden, Babylon and the New Jerusalem*. London: Routledge.

Preston, Ronald (1981) *Exploration in Theology 9*. London: SCM.

—— (1991) *Religion and the Ambiguities of Capitalism*. London: SCM.

Proust, Marcel [1913–27] (1981) *Remembrance of Things Past*, tr. T. Kilmartin. Harmondsworth: Penguin

Pseudo-Dionysius (1987) *The Complete Works*, tr. Colm Luibheid. New York: Paulist Press.

Putnam, Hilary (1990) *Realism with a Human Face*. Cambridge, MA: Harvard University Press.

Pynchon, Thomas (1963) *V.* London: Picador Books.

—— (1966) *The Crying of Lot 49*. London: Picador Books.

Quinn, Naomi (1991) 'The Cultural Basis of Metaphor', in James W. Fernandez, *Beyond Metaphor: The Theory of Tropes in Anthropology*. Stanford: Stanford University Press.

Radin, Paul (1945), *The Road of Life and Death: A Ritual Drama of the American Indians*. New York: Pantheon Press.

Redman, C.L. (1978) *The Rise of Civilization: from Early Farmers to Urban Society in the Ancient Near East*. San Francisco: Freeman.

Regis, Ed (1990) *Great Mambo Chicken and the Transhuman Condition: Science Slightly over the Edge*. London: Viking Press.

Renfrew, Colin (1989) *Archaeology and Language: The Puzzle of Indo-European Origins*. Harmondsworth: Penguin.

Rheingold, Harold (1993) *The Virtual Community: Homesteading on the Electronic Frontier*. New York: Addison-Wesley.

—— (1991) *Virtual Reality*. London: Secker and Warburg.

Ricoeur, Paul (1965) *History and Truth*, tr. Charles A. Kelbley. Evanston: Northwestern University Press.

—— (1982) 'The Status of *Vorstellung* in Hegel's Philosophy of Religion', in Leroy S. Rouner (ed.), *Meaning, Truth, and God*. Notre Dame: Notre Dame Press.

—— (1984) *Time and Narrative*, vol. 1, tr. Kathleen McLaughlin and David Pellauer. Chicago: University of Chicago Press.

—— (1985) *Time and Narrative*, vol. 2, tr. Kathleen McLaughlin and David Pellauer. Chicago: University of Chicago Press.

—— 1988) *Time and Narrative*, vol. 3, tr. Kathleen McLaughlin and David Pellauer. Chicago: University of Chicago Press.

—— (1992) *Oneself as Another*, tr. Kathleen Blamey. Chicago: University of Chicago Press.

Ripa, Jean de (1957) *Conclusiones*, A. Combes (ed.). Paris: Vrin.

Ritzdorf, Marsha (1996) 'Feminist Thoughts on the Theory and Practice of Planning', in Scott Campbell and Susan F. Fainstein (eds), *Readings in Planning Theory*. Oxford: Blackwell: 445–50.

Robinson, John A.T. (1952) *The Body: A Study in Pauline Theology*. London: SCM.

Rogers, Eugene (1995) *Thomas Aquinas and Karl Barth: Sacred Doctrine and the Natural Knowledge of God*. Notre Dame: University of Notre Dame Press.

Rosato, Philip J. (1981) *The Spirit as Lord: The Pneumatology of Karl Barth*. Edinburgh: T. & T. Clark.

Rose, Gillian (1993) *Feminism and Geography*. Cambridge: Polity.

Rosenau, Helen (1972) *The Ideal City*, revised second edition. London: Routledge and Kegan Paul.

Roudinesco, Elizabeth (1990) *Jacques Lacan and Co., A History of Psychoanalysis in France*, tr. Jeffery Mehlman. London: Free Association Books.

Rousselle, Aline (1993) *Porneia: On Desire and the Body in Antiquity*, tr. Felicia Pheasant. Oxford. Blackwell.

Ruello, Francis (1992) *Théologie naturelle de Jean de Ripa*. Paris: Beauchesne.

Ruether, Rosemary Radford (1978) 'The Sexuality of Jesus' published, in *Christianity and Crisis*, 38 (May 29): 134–37.

—— (1983) *Sexism and God-Talk: Towards a Feminist Theology*. London: SCM.

Runciman, David (1996) The *Guardian*, 24 April.

Ruokanen, Miika (1993) *Theology of Social Life in Augustine's* De Civitate Dei. Göttingen: Vandenhoeck and Ruprecht.

Russell, Bertrand [1917] (1994) 'The Ultimate Constituents of Matter,' in *Mysticism and Logic*. London: Routledge: 121–39.

Rykwert, Joseph (1988) *The Idea of the Town: The Anthropology of Urban Form in Rome, Italy and the Ancient World*. Cambridge, MA: MIT Press.

Saatchi, Charles (1998) *Sensation: Young British Artists from the Saatchi Collection*. London; Thames and Hudson.

Sabbah, Francoise (1985) 'The New Media', in Manuel Castells (ed.), *High Technology, Space and Society*. Beverley Hills: Sage.

Sacksteder, William (1987) 'Spinoza's Attributes, Again: An Hobbesian Source', in *Studia Spinozana* 3:125–50.

Sapp, Stephen (1976) *Sexuality, the Bible, and Science*. Philadelphia.

Sassen, Saskia (1991) *The Global City: London, New York and Tokyo*. Princeton: Princeton University Press.

—— (1994) *Cities in a World Economy*. London: Pine Forge Press.

Sawday, Jonathan (1995) *The Body Emblazoned: Dissection and the Human Body in Renaissance Culture*. London: Routledge.

Schaff, Philip and Wace, Henry (eds) (1979) *Gregory of Nyssa, Dogmatic Treaties etc.* Michigan: Wm. B. Eerdmans.

Schehr, Lawrence R. (1997) *Parts of Andrology: On Representing Men's Bodies*. Stanford: Stanford University Press.

Schleiermacher, Friedrich [1799] (1958) *Speeches on Religion to its Cultured Despisers*. New York: Harper Torchbooks.

—— [1830] (1989) *The Christian Faith*. Edinburgh: T. & T. Clark.

Schreiter, Robert J. (1985) *Constructing Local Theologies*. London: SCM.

Schroeder, W.H.J. OP (1978) *Canons and Decrees of the Council of Trent*. Rockford: Tan Books.

Schweitzer, Albert (1954) *The Quest for the Historical Jesus*, tr. W. Montgomery. London: Adam and Charles Black.

Scott, A.J. and Roweis, S.T. (1977) 'Urban Planning in Theory and Practice: An Appraisal', *Environment and Planning* A, 9: 1097–1119.

Scott, Joanna V. (1995) 'Augustine's Razor: Public vs. Private Interests in *The City of God*', in Dorothy F. Donnelly (ed.), *The City of God: A Collection of Critical Essays*. New York: Peter Lang.

Scretan, Catherine (1987) '*La reception de Hobbes aux Pays-Bas au XVIIe siècle*', in *Studia Spinozana* 3: 27–46.

Seitz, Christopher R. (1997) 'The Two Cities in Christian Scripture', in Carl E. Braaten and Robert W. Jenson (eds), *The Two Cities of God: The Church's Responsibility for the Earthly City*. Grand Rapids: William Eerdmans.

Selinger, Suzanne (1998) *Charlotte von Kirschbaum and Karl Barth: A Study in Biography and the History of Theology*. University Park: Pennsylvania State University Press.

Sennett, Richard (1994) *Flesh and Stone: The Body and the City in Western Civilisation*. New York: Norton.

Serres, Michel (1980) *Le Parasite*. Paris: Bernard Grasset.

—— (1993) *Angels: A Modern Myth*, tr. Francis Cowper. Paris: Flammarion.

Shanks, Andrew (1991) *Hegel's Political Theology*. Cambridge: Cambridge University Press.

Shapin, Steven (1994) *A Social History of Truth: Civility and Science in Seventeenth Century England*. Chicago: Chicago University Press.

Shapin, Steven and Schaffer, Simon (1985) *Leviathan and the Air-Pump*. Princeton: Princeton University Press.

Shklar, Judith N. (1976) *Freedom and Independence*. Cambridge: Cambridge University Press.

Silver, Victoria (1996) 'Hobbes on Rhetoric', in *The Cambridge Companion to Hobbes*, ed. Tom Sorell. Cambridge: Cambridge University Press:

Simmel, George (1995) 'The Metropolis and Mental Life', in Kasinitz.

Skinner, Quentin (1996) *Reason and Rhetoric in the Philosophy of Thomas Hobbes*. Cambridge: Cambridge University Press.

Slevin, James (2000) *The Internet and Society*. Cambridge: Polity Press.

Smith, Bruce R. (1991) *Homosexual Desire in Shakespearean England: A Cultural Poetics*. Chicago: University of Chicago Press.

Smith, Jonathan Z. (1986) 'Jerusalem: The City as Place', in Hawkins.

Smith, Michael Peter and Feagin, Joe R. (eds) (1987) *The Capitalist City*. Oxford: Blackwell.

Soja, Edward W. (1987) 'Economic Restructuring and the Internationalization of the Los Angeles Region', in Smith and Feagin.

—— (1989) *Postmodern Geographies: The Reassertion of Space in Criticial Social Theory*. London: Verso.

—— (1995) 'Heterotopologies: A Remembrance of Other Space in the Citadel-LA', in Sophie Watson and Katherine Gibson (eds), *Postmodern Cities and Spaces*. Oxford: Blackwell: 13–34.

—— (1995a) 'Postmodern Urbanization: The Six Restructurings of Los Angeles', in Sophie Watson and Katherine Gibson (eds), *Postmodern Cities and Spaces*. Oxford: Blackwell: 125–38.

—— (1992) 'Inside Exopolis: Scenes from Orange County', in M. Sorkin (ed.), *Variations on a Theme Park: The New American City and the End of Public Space*. New York: Noonday Press.

Sokolowski, Robert (1993) *Eucharistic Presence: A Study in the Theology of Disclosure*. Washington: The Catholic University of America Press.

Soleri, Paolo (1969) *Arcology: The City in the Image of Man*. Cambridge, MA: M.I.T. Press.

—— (1970) *Visionary Cities*. New York: Praeger.

Solomon, Robert C. (1983) *In the Spirit of Hegel*. Oxford: Oxford University Press.

Sommerville, C. John (1992) *The Secularization of Early Modern England: From Religious Culture to Religious Faith*. New York: Oxford University Press.

Sorkin, Michael (1996) 'See You in Disneyland', in Susan Fainstein and Scott Campbell (eds), *Readings in Urban Theory*. Oxford: Blackwell: 392–414.

Spinoza, Baruch de (1958) *Political Works*. Oxford: Oxford University Press.

—— (1958a) *Tractatus Theologico-Politicus*, in *Political Works*.

—— (1985) *A Short Treatise*, ed. and tr. Edwin Curley, *The Collected Works of Spinoza*, vol. I. Princeton: Princeton University Press.

—— (1996) *Ethics*, tr. Edwin Curley, London: Penguin Books.

Spivak, Gayatri Chakvarorty (1994) in *Thinking Bodies*, eds Juliet Flower MacCannell and Laura Zakarin. Stanford: Stanford University Press.

Springborg, Patricia (1995) 'Thomas Hobbes and Cardinal Bellarmine: Leviathan and "The Ghost of the Roman Empire", in *History of Political Thought*, vol. XVI. No.4. Winter: 503–31.

Staten, Henry (1995) *Eros in Mourning*. Baltimore: John Hopkins University Press.

Steinberg, Leo (1996) *The Sexuality of Christ in Renaissance Art and Modern Oblivion*. Chicago: University of Chicago Press.

Stern, Robert (1994) 'MacIntrye and Historicism', in John Horten and Susan Medius (eds), *After MacIntyre: Critical Perspectives on the Work of Alasdair MacIntyre*. Cambridge: Polity Press.

Stevenson, J. (1988) 'The New Jerusalem', in L.M. Smith, *The Making of Britain: Echoes of Greatness*. London: Macmillan: 53–70.

—— Stump, Eleonore (1982) 'Theology and Physics in *De sacramento altaris:* Ockham's Theory of Indivisibles' in Naman Kretzmann (ed.) *Infinity and Continuity in Ancient and Medieval Thought*. Ithaca: Cornell University Press: 207–30.

Süskind, Patrick (1987) *Perfume*, tr. John E. Woods. Harmondsworth: Penguin.

Sutcliffe, Anthony (1981) *Towards the Planned City: Germany, Britain, the United States and France 1780–1914*. Oxford: Blackwell.

Sweet, Ronald F.G. (1997) 'Writing as a Factor in the Rise of Urbanism', in Walter E, Aufrecht, Neil A. Mirau and Steven W. Gauley (eds), *Urbanism in Antiquity: From Mesopatamia to Crete*. Sheffield: Sheffield Academic Press.

Swinburne, Richard (1977) *The Coherence of Theism*. Oxford: Clarendon Press.

Tartt, Donna (1992) *The Secret History*, London: Penguin Books, 1992.

Tawney, R.H. (1921) *The Acquisitive Society*. London: Bell.

—— [1926] (1984) *Religion and the Rise of Capitalism*. Harmondsworth: Penguin.

Taylor, Charles (1985) *Philosophy and Human Sciences: Philosophical Papers I*. Cambridge: Cambridge University Press.

Taylor, Mark C. (1984) *Erring: A Postmodern A/theology*. Chicago: Chicago University Press, 1984.

—— (1999) *About Religion: Economies of Faith in Virtual Culture*. Chicago: Chicago University Press.

Temple, William (1928) *Christianity and the State*. London: Macmillan.

—— (1942) *Christianity and the Social Order*. London: Penguin.

Teske, Roland J., SJ (1996) *The Paradoxes of Time in Saint Augustine*. Milwaukee: Marquette University Press.

Theunissen, Michael (1970) *Hegels Lehre vom absoluten Geist als theologisch-politischer Traktat*. Berlin: Walter de Gruyter.

Thiemann, Ronald F. (1985) *Revelation and Theology*. Notre Dame: University of Notre Dame Press.

Tilley, Christopher (1999) *Metaphor and Material Culture*. Oxford: Blackwell.

Tillich, Paul (1952) *Courage to Be*. New Haven: Yale University Press.

Timberlake, Michael (1987) 'World-System Theory and the Study of Comparative Urbanization', in Smith and Feagin.

Tönnies, Ferdinand (1955) *Gemeinschaft und Gesellschaft. Community and Association*, tr. Charles P. Loomis. London: Routledge and Kegan Paul.

Toulmin, Stephen (1990) *Cosmopolis: The Hidden Agenda of Modernity*. Chicago: Chicago University Press.

Trumbach (1984) 'Gender and the Homosexual Role in Modern Western Culture: the 18th and 19th Centuries Compared' in *Which Homosexuality?* ed. Alman *et al.* London: Gay Men's Press: 149–69.

—— (1991) 'The Birth of the Queen: sodomy and the emergence of gender equality in modern culture, 1660–1750' in *Hidden from History* eds M.B. Duberman *et al.* Harmondsworth: Penguin Books: 129–40.

Turner, Victor (1967) *The Forest of Symbols*. Ithaca: Cornell University Press.

—— (1974) *Drama, Fields and Metaphors*. Ithaca: Cornell University Press.

Vance, Carole S. (1995) 'Social Construction Theory and Sexuality', in Maurice Berger, Brian Wallis and Simon Watson (eds), *Constructing Masculinity*. London: Routledge: 37–48.

Van der Wee, Herman (1990) 'Structural Changes in European Long-Distance Trade, and Particularly in the Re-export Trade from South to North', in James D. Tracy (ed.), *The Rise of Merchant Empires: Long-Distance Trade in Early the Modern World 1350–1750*. Cambridge: Cambridge University Press: 14–33.

Vattimo, Gianni (1988) *The End of Modernity: Nihlism and Hermeneutics in Post-Modern Culture*, tr. Jon R. Synder. Cambridge: Polity.

—— (1997) *Beyond Interpretation: the Meaning of Hermeneutics for Philosophy*, tr. David Webb. Cambridge: Polity.

Venturi, Robert, Brown, Denise Scott and Izenour, Steven (1978) *Learning from Las Vegas*. Cambridge, MA: MIT Press.

Virilio, Paul (1991) 'Interview', *Art and Philosophy*. Milan: Giancarlo Politi Editore.

—— (1995) 'Speed and Information: Cyberspace Alarm!' tr. Patrice Riemens in *ctheory* 27 September 27th.

—— (1998) *The Virilio Reader*, James Der Derian (ed.). Oxford: Blackwell.

—— (2000) [1990] *Polar Inertia*, tr. Patrick Camiller. London: Sage.

Waggoner, Lynder S. (1996) *Fallingwater: Frank Lloyd Wright's Romance with Nature*. Fallingwater: Western Pennsylvania Conservancy.

Wakeford, Nina (1999) 'Gender and the Landscapes of Computing in an Internet Café', in Mike Chang, Phil Chang and Jon May (eds), *Virtual Geographies: Bodies, Space and Relations*. London: Routledge: 178–201.

Wallace, John (1979) 'Only in the Context of a Sentence do Words have any Meaning', in Peter A. French *et al.* (eds), *Contemporary Perspectives in the Philosophy of Language*. Minneapolis: University of Minnesota Press: .

Wallace, Ronald J (1953) *Calvin's Doctrine of Word and Sacrament*. Edinburgh: Scottish Academic Press.

Wallerstein, Immanuel (1974) *The Modern World-System: Capitalist Agriculture and The Origins of the European World-Economy in C16th*. London: Academic Press.

—— (1980) *The Modern World-System II: Mercantilise and the Consolidation of the European World-Economy 1600–1750*. London: Academic Press.

—— (1984) *The Politics of the World Economy*. Cambridge: Cambridge University Press.

Ward, Graham (1991) 'The Theology of Metonymy', *Modern Theology* 7, 4 (July): 335–49.

—— (1994) 'Mimesis and Christology', *Literature and Theology* 8, 1 (January): 1–30.

—— (1995) *Barth, Derrida and the Language of Theology*. Cambridge: Cambridge University Press.

—— (1995a) 'Theology and the Crisis of Representation', in Gregory Salyer and Robert Detweiler (eds), *Literature and Theology at the Century's End*. Atlanta: Scholars Press: 131–58.

—— (1996) *Theology and Contemporary Critical Theory*, first edition. London: Macmillan.

—— (1996a) 'Words of Life: Hosting Postmodern Plenitude', *The Way* 36, 3 (July): 225–35.

—— (1996b) 'Divinity and Sexuality: Luce Irigaray and Christology', *Modern Theology* 12, 2 (April): 231–58.

—— (1996c) 'On Time and Salvation: The Eschatology of Emmanuel Levinas', in Sean Hand (ed.), *Facing the Other: The Ethics of Emmanuel Levinas*. London: Curzon Press: 153–72.

—— (1998) *The Postmodern God*. Oxford: Blackwell.

—— (1999) 'Kenosis: Death, Discourse and Resurrection', in *Balthasar at the End of Modernity*, Edinburgh: T. & T. Clark: 15–68.

—— (1999a) '*Allegoria*: Reading as a Spiritual Exercise' *Modern Theology* 15, 3 (July): 271–95.

—— (1999b) 'Theology and Masculinity' *The Journal of Men's Studies* 7, 2 (Winter): 281–6.

—— (2000) *Theology and Contemporary Critical Theory*, second, enlarged edition. London: Macmillan.

—— (2000a) 'Karl Barth and Postmodernity', in John Webster (ed.), *The Cambridge Companion to Karl Barth*. Cambridge, Cambridge University Press: 274–95.

—— (2000b) 'Language and Silence', in Oliver Davis and Denys Turner (eds), *Apophasis*. Cambridge: Cambridge University Press.

—— (2000c) 'Towards a New Theology of the City', in *Cultural Values* 1(3): 156–89.

Watson, Sophie and Gibson, Katherine (1995) *Postmodern Cities and Spaces*. Oxford: Blackwell.

Weaver, Clive (1985) *Regional Development and the Local Community: Planning Politics and Social Context*. Chichester: Wiley Press.

Webb, Stephen H. (1996) *The Gifting God: A Trinitarian Ethics of Excess*. Oxford: Oxford University Press.

Weber, Max (1960) *The City*, tr. Don Martindale and Gertrud Neuwirth. London: Heinemann.

Webster, John (1995) *Barth and the Ethics of Reconciliation*. Cambridge: Cambridge University Press.

Weil, Simone (1952) *Gravity and Grace*, tr. A. Wills. New York: Putnam.

Weimar, David (1966) *The City as Metaphor*. New York: Random House.

Wenders, Wim (1991) *The Logic of Images: Essays and Conversations*, tr. Michael Hoffmann. London: Faber

—— (1997) *The Act of Seeing: Essays and Conversations*, tr. Michael Hoffman. London: Faber.

Williams, Rowan (1979) 'Barth and the Triune God', in Stephen Sykes (ed.), *Karl Barth: Studies in His Theological Method*. Oxford: Oxford University Press: 147–93.

—— (1989) 'Language, Reality and Desire in Augustine's *De Doctrina*', *Literature and Theology* 3.2: 138–50.

—— (1996) 'The Body's Grace' in Charles Hefling (ed.), *Our Selves, Our Souls and Bodies: Sexuality and the Household of God*. Cambridge, MA: Cowley Publications.

—— (1998) 'Logic and Spirit in Hegel', in Philip Blond (ed.), *Post-Secular Philosophy: Between Philosophy and Theology*. London: Routledge.

Wilson, Robert R. (1986) 'The City of the Old Testament', in Hawkins, Peter S. (ed.) *Civitas: Religious Interpretations of the City*. Georgia: Scholars Press.

Wise, Patrica (1997) 'Always Already Virtual: Feminist Politics in Cyberspace', in David Holmes (ed.), *Virtual Politics: Identity and Community in Cyberspace*. London: Sage: 179–96.

Wittgenstein, Ludwig (1953) *Philosophical Investigations*, G.E.M. Anscombe (ed.). Oxford: Blackwell.

—— (1974) *On Certainty*, tr. Denis Paul and G.E.M. Anscombe. Oxford: Blackwell.

—— (1979) *Wittgenstein and the Vienna Circle: Conversations recorded by F. Waismann*. Oxford: Blackwell.

Wittig, Monique (1992) *The Straight Mind and Other Essays*. Boston: Beacon Press.

Wolf, Peter (1974) *The Future of the City*. New York: Billboard Publications.

Wolfe, Tom (1987) *Bonfire of the Vanities*. London: Cape.

Wolfson, Elliot R. (1995) *Circle in the Square: Studies in the Use of Gender in Kabbalistic Mysticism*. New York: SUNY.

Wood, Allen W. (1991) 'Introduction' to *Elements of the Philosophy of Right* ed. Allen W. Wood, tr. H.B. Nisbet. Cambridge: Cambridge University Press: vii–xxxii.

Wright, Frank Lloyd (1935) 'Broadacre City: A New Community Plan', in *Architectural Record* LXXVII (April).

—— (1945) *When Democracy Builds*. Chicago: University of Chicago Press.

—— (1953) *The Future of Architecture*. New York: Horizon Press.

Wuthnow, Robert (1998) *After Heaven: Spirituality in America Since the 1950s*. Berkeley: University of Calfornia Press.

Young, Frances M. (1983) *From Nicaea to Chalcedon*. London: SCM.

Yovel, Yirmiyahu (1989) *Spinoza and Other Heretics* vol. 1: *The Marrano of Reason* and vol. 2: *Adventures in Immanence*. Princeton: Princeton University Press.

Ziguras, Christopher (1997) 'The Technologization of the Sacred: Virtual Reality and the New Age', in David Holmes (ed.), *Virtual Politics: Identity and Community in Cyberspace*. London: Sage: 197–211

Žižek, Slavoj (1994) 'How to Give a Body a Deadlock', in Juliet Flower MacCannell and Laura Zakarin (eds) *Thinking Bodies*. Stanford: Stanford University Press: 60–77.

—— (1997) *The Plague of Fantasies*. London: Verso.

Zizoulas, John D. (1985) *Being in Communion: Studies in Personhood and the Church*. London: Darton, Longman and Todd.

Zvi, Ehud Ben (1997) 'The Urban Centre of Jerusalem and the Development of the Literature of the Hebrew Bible', in Walter E. Aufrecht *et al.* (eds), *Urbanism in Antiquity: From Mesopotamia to Crete*. Sheffield: Sheffield Academic Press.

INDEX

absence 74, 127, 167, 251; *see also* lack
absolute *Geist* 139–40, 186
absolute truth 144
accountability 74
aesthetics, of absence 60, 74, 150, 218
agape 183, 185, 186, 190–1, 201
AIDS 81–2, 96
alienation 35, 180–1
allegorical reading 89
American City Beautiful Movement 39
amor 76, 174
amor dei 227–8, 230
amor sui 227–8, 230
analogia Christi 191–2, 198
analogia entis 191, 192
analogia fidei 191–2, 194, 234
analogia relationis 194
analogical world-view 70, 118, 224, 229,
    254; analogy 129–30, 157, 230;
    difference 188, 257; ecclesial–civic
    relation 236; embodiment 205;
    identification 108; reasoning 165;
    rethinking 70, 137
Anderson, Benedict 146, 150
angels: angelologies 207–8, 222–3; cities of
    205–24; flesh of 219–21; knowledge of
    72, 216–19, 237; tongues of 212–15
the Annunciation 221
annunciations 212
anthropology, Christian 117, 121
antimodernism 50
aporetics 101, 165, 253
appearance 157, 161
Aquinas, Saint Thomas 2, 117, 156–62,
    222

Aristotle 110, 127
artificial intelligence 47–8
the Ascension 97–8
ascensions 112–14
atheism 43, 45, 69, 128, 138
atheologies 43, 45, 69
atomism 170; cosmic 132; cyberspace 248,
    249; Hobbes 127–8; modernity 90;
    ontological 167; postmodern 94; reality
    86; social 28, 58, 75, 132, 167
Aufhebung 144
Augustine 6, 7, 13, 24, 257; *amor* 76;
    analogical world-view 229; City of God
    226–38; desire and the Good 134;
    infant Jesus 99; justice 234–5; love 235;
    presence 156–61; the present 158;
    representation 228–9; time 233–4
Ayer, A. J. 86

Babylon 33, 49, 227
Bacon, Francis 37
Balthasar, Hans Urs von 7, 188
Barth, Karl 8, 44, 48, 97, 131, 159, 174,
    184–5, 188–99, 211
Barthes, Roland 21, 185, 186, 231
Bataille, George 183
Baudrillard, Jean 21, 23–4, 54, 60–1, 253
Bauhaus movement 63, 231
Bauman, Zygmunt 118–19, 150, 247
Bebauugsplan 28–9
being 134, 135, 164–5, 169, 208
belief production 196
believing, politics of 71–4, 207–8
Berlin 28–32, 38
Bhabha, Homi K. 258

biblical origins of secularism 46
biblical view of the city 32–8
Biel, Gabriel 161
biological determinism 125
biological difference 193–4
biological essentialism 125, 194, 202
biopower 34
Blake, William 39
Boas, Franz 14
bodies: angelic 222–1; broken 81–2; civic
    126, 236; cyberspace 247; devaluation
    of the 169; discursive practices 83, 167;
    dissemination of 92, 93–4; ecclesial 236;
    eucharistic 102, 152–3; floating signifier
    105; forgetting of 144; forms of desire
    75; individual 126; metaphorical nature
    95; pluralised 174–81; prelapsarian 100;
    sacramental 179–80; *soma* 83;
    textualities of 93, 110, 115–16;
    theologies 182, 247
body of Christ 76, 91–3, 95, 144, 176–81,
    257; as bread 82–3, 102, 103, 163–4; the
    Church 108; crucifixion 103–8;
    displacement 97–116; extendibility 102;
    flesh of 98, 116; as gendered Jew 113–16;
    iconic status 104–5; language 110;
    mutability 102
Bourdieu, Pierre 14, 58
Boyle, Robert 127
Bray, Alan 122
bread, eucharistic 82–3, 102, 103,
    163–4
Buber, Martin 172
Buñel, Luis 29, 30
Burke, Kenneth 14
Butler, Judith 18, 82, 98, 115, 121, 137,
    145–6, 180, 195–6, 231
Bynum, Caroline Walker 110

Calvin, Jean 156, 157, 161–7, 227
Calvino, Italo 52–3
capitalism 34–6, 50–1, 53–4, 146, 211;
    symbolic 58
caritas 76
Casino 63, 65, 77
Castelli, Elizabeth 82
Castells, Manuel 54, 242, 244–7, 256–7
Cathedral, as metaphor 29, 31, 36
Catholicism 68, 69, 158, 159, 167

Certeau, Michel de 7, 14–15, 19, 21, 73–4,
    110, 112, 126, 180, 223; city as text
    230–1; *corpus mysticum* 92, 94; eucharistic
    body 162; the now 170; place and space
    154, 176–9; scriptural economy 248;
    white ecstasy 135
Chardin, Teilhard de 48, 69
Chomsky, Noam 9
Christ: Church 114; face of 101–2; as
    gendered Jew 113–16; logic of
    displacement 112–13; as Logos 110–11,
    113, 234; Risen 97; as Subject 114–15;
    transcorporeality 81–96, 97, 115; Virgin
    Mary 114, 115, 221; *see also* body of
    Christ
Christianity 143–4; anthropology 117,
    121; apartheid 49–50; Christian atheism
    43, 45; cities 27–8, 68–70, 75–7;
    communities 123–4, 258–9; desire 76–7,
    123–4, 150–1, 182; embodiment 180–1;
    gender transgression 106; imaginary
    222–1; love 259; materiality 62;
    metaphysics 117; post-Christian atheism
    69; privatisation 75–6; secular world 70;
    semiotics 236; time 192, 196
Christology 114–16, 183
Christomonism 115
Christopherson, Susan 67
Church: body of Christ and 108, 113,
    176–81; erotic community 152–81;
    Heavenly city 229; in Hegel 141–2;
    Jesus and 114; paternalism 28;
    sanctification of difference 202
cinema *see* film
cinematography 30
circumcision 98–9
cities 61; American City Beautiful
    Movement 39; biblical view of 32–8;
    capitalism 34–6, 57; Christian responses
    27–8, 68–70, 75–7; city development
    33–6; City of God 227–38; City Pride
    Initiative 239–40; cosmology 77; earthly
    227, 237; *Faith in the City* 27–8, 44, 51,
    62; fiction 4, 59–60; in film 28–32,
    243–4; futuristic 28–32; global 215,
    239; of the good 225–60; of habitation
    259–60; as language 232; myths 59;
    Old and New 51; parasitic 49;
    postmodern 53–62; radiant 40, 42, 43,

231; redemption 205–6; secularity and 32–8, 43–4; as text 230–1; theologies of 43–51, 77, 226; virtual reality 231–2; walking in 231; *see also* urban...
civic bodies 126, 236
Cixous, Hélène 168, 197, 200, 206
clones *see* cyborgs
Commission on Urban Priority Areas 1985 27–8, 44, 51, 63
commonwealths 126–7, 136–7
communication 74, 111, 164, 225; *see also* telecommunications
communitarianism 258
communities: Christian 123–4, 258–9; civil 135; *communitas* 39; of desire 117–51; embodied rationalities 132; erotic 123–5, 148, 152–81; Experimental Prototype Community of Tomorrow 59; from imagined to virtual 146–51; homosocial 124–5; ideal 148; imagined 129; inoperative 75; modernity 125; production of 242; of the spirit 137–46; virtual 150–1, 167, 244–7, 250
Competitive Industrial Capitalist City 34–5
Connell, R. W. 199–200
conservative theology 48–50, 69
constructivism *see* social constructivism
consumerism 64, 172
consumption of the present 59
Corbusier, Le 40–2, 48, 50, 63, 231
Corporate-Monopoly Capitalist City 35–6
corporeality 50, 87–91, 144, 193
corpus 81–4, 110, 170
corpus mysticum 84, 91–6
corpuscularity 84–7
cosmology: Aristotle 127; cities 77; cosmic atomism 132; cosmological order 39–40, 126; theology of the city 77, 260
Council of Trent 1551 159, 161, 167, 180
Cox, Harvey 44, 46–8, 50, 68–9
creation 89; de-creation 95; doctrines 77, 164, 256; God and 172, 189–90, 202; *Mensch* 190; out of nothing 108; the Trinity 159
crucifixion 99, 103–8
Crystal Palace 35, 50
cultural body 236–7
cultural capital 58

cultural metaphors: angels 222–4; reading of 14–17, 17–21; significant signs 21–4; signification 5–9; social semiotics 9–14
cultural studies 121–2
cultures: biological determinism 125; of death 60; re-enchantment of 207; of seduction 68, 77, 125
Cupitt, Don 69
cyberpunk buildings 67
cyberspace 42, 54, 118, 236, 247–56, 257; bodies 247; communities in 244–7; cyber cities 242–4; cybersex 149, 150, 251; danger of 149–50, 168; eroticism of 150; history 248; holistic spatiality 250–1; praxis 249; redemption of 225–60; theological investigation 247–56; time 249; virtualities 242; *see also* virtual reality
cyborgs 206, 210, 256; *see also* hybrids; vampires

Davis, Mike 67–8
de-creation 95
'the Dead Tec' design 67
death: culture of 60; of God 43, 45, 61, 223, 251, 252; instinct (*thanatos*) 125 184
deconstruction 156
Deleuze, Gilles 121, 146
demonstrative identification 84–6, 93
Derrida, Jacques 40, 145, 155, 157, 168, 169–70, 253
Descartes, René 72, 85, 125, 127, 164, 176, 254
desire: Christian 76–7, 107–8; Christ's body 104–6; cities of 53; commonwealths 126–37; communities 117–51; dialectic of 185–6; difference and 172, 201; embodiment 75; endless 52–77, 252; erotic 227; Freud 122–6; gendered 56, 101; the gift 190; God 184, 190, 198; the Good 134; for knowledge 251; lack 101, 127; ludic 119; masculinity 124–5; mimesis 103, 110; modernity 121, 125, 136–7; the mother 107; motion 127; nationalistic 146; phallic 56, 107, 169, 197, 219; phenomenology of 146; privative 127; reason 133; self-interest of 126; subjects of 118, 120–6, 251; symbolic

community and 147–8; telos of 132; a
theology of 187–94, 198; time 156;
truth and 122–3; virtual other 149
determinism 46, 54, 125
dialectic 141–2, 144, 185–6
diastasis 184, 189, 199
diastema 172
différance 110, 145, 155, 169–70
difference: in analogy 257; desire 172, 185;
difference-in-relation 184, 187, 255;
soterilogy 185–6; theology 254; *see also*
sexual difference
digitality 75, 176
Disney 39, 58–9, 66, 68
displacement 93, 97–116, 146–7, 154
dissemination, bodily 93–4, 106
divine *Geist* 186
docetism 115
Douglas, Mary 14, 109, 180
Doxiadis, Constantinos 48
doxology 215
Drummond, Henry 27
dualisms 36, 164, 165; *agape* and *eros* 183,
185, 186; Christology 114;
consciousness and the given 169;
Metropolis 31; mind–body 127, 129;
mind–world 155; state and ecclesia 126;
subversion of 252–3
dunamis, trinitarian 89
Dunne, John S. 44–6
Dynamegalopolis 48

earthly cities 227, 237
ecclesia 117–18, 125, 126, 131
ecclesial body 236–7
economic reorganisation 55–6
ecstasis 140
ecumenopolis 48
egocentric space 85
Ekistics 48
Ellis, Havelock 122, 201
Ellul, Jacques 48–50
embodiment: analogical world-view 205;
Christian 180–1; desire and 75, 185;
eucharistic 102, 152–3; gendered 195;
nature of 82, 100; rationalities 132;
social construction 115, 121–3
empiricism 169
Engels, Friedrich 35, 238

enterprise zones 57–9
epistemology 82, 252–3
equivocity 136, 155, 165, 233
eros 76, 125, 201; *agape* 183, 185, 186;
Freudian 123; New Testament and 184;
post-Enlightenment 146; sanctification
in marriage 183–4; theology of 151;
transformation of 125
erotic communities 148; alternative 77; the
Church 152–81; Freudian egos 123–4;
homosocial 124–5
erotics: crucifixion 104; cyberspace 150;
male gaze 119; of redemption 182–202;
transfiguration 100–1; trinitarian 198
eschatology 94, 154, 187; doctrines 77;
realised 37, 40, 41, 86, 177; secularised
145
eschaton 38–43, 112, 251, 257
espace 154, 176
the eternal 158, 171–2
eternal life 108
ethics, cyberspace 249
eucharist 82–4, 91, 144, 162; eucharistic
body 102, 174–81; eucharistic bread
82–3, 102–3, 163–4; eucharistic We
153–4, 181; the fraction 106, 108,
152–5, 171, 237; participation 171–4;
presence 154–5, 170–81; present tense
154–5; spatiality 164
evangelicism 69
Evans, Gareth 85
evil 38, 89, 106, 139, 215, 233
Experimental Prototype Community of
Tomorrow (Disneyland) 59

Fabianism 39, 70
faith, privatisation of 36, 75–6
Faith in the City 27–8, 44, 51, 62
the feminine 115, 210
feminist epistemology 82
Fernandez, James W. 14
fiction, city in 4, 59–60
Figgis, Mike 63–4, 64
film: cinematography 30; the city 28–32,
55, 77, 243–4; modern 35–6, 38,
43–51; post-apocalyptic 51; postmodern 63–5
Fish, Stanley 83
flesh 98, 116, 219–21

flexible accumulative capitalism 53–4
Foucault, Michel 14–18, 19, 76, 122–3, 150, 231; biopower 34; desire 146; power 145; technologies of self 115
fraction, eucharistic 106, 108, 152–5, 171, 237
Free Enterprise Zones, Los Angeles 65
free will 127
Freud, Sigmund 106–7, 190, 236; desire 101; interpretation of dreams 9–10; sexuality 122–6
Fuchs, Emil 7–8
Fukuyama, Francis 47
Fulkerson, Mary McClintock 199–200
The Full Monty 55
full presence 86, 167
fundamentalism, American 68–9

Geddes, Patrick 39
Geertz, Clifford 14, 17, 18–19, 20
Geist 137, 139–40, 143, 186, 189
Gemeinschaft 32, 35
gender: Christian transgression 106; cities 49–50, 52; construction through marriage 183; corporeality 50; crucifixion 105; desire 56; economic restructuring 55; geography 34; resurrection 110; technologies of 115, 186–7; theology and 194–5
genealogy of presence 156–70
geography 34, 56–60
Germanic folk-myth 30–1
Gesellschaft 32, 35, 131
Gibson, William 59–60, 248
the gift 190, 255
Gil, Jose 81
globalisation 28, 54, 244, 246, 255; cities 215, 239; global economy 35, 66, 241–2
gnosticism 113, 170, 209, 236
God: attributes 132; body of 113, 126, 127, 130, 132; city of 227–38; creation 172, 189–90, 202; death of 43, 45, 61, 223, 251, 252; desire 136–7, 172, 184–5, 190, 198; extermination of the name of 60; as the gap 224; Godhead 99, 170, 202; grace 226; Hobbes 127–31; materiality 127, 130; omnipresence 113; paternity 98–9; presence 109; Spinoza

131–7; as Spirit 137, 138; triune 37; truth guarantor 130
the good 133–4, 139, 225–60
Gospels 100, 111; John 98, 109, 111; Luke 98, 101, 102, 103, 104, 111, 112; Mark 83–4, 91–2, 98, 101–4, 111; Matthew 98, 101–4, 111, 222
Gotarten, Friedrich 8
graphé 156
Great Exhibition, Britain 35
Greenblatt, Stephen 14–15, 103

Hall, Peter 39, 43–4, 51, 57
Halley, Peter 58
Harding, Sandra 82
Harvey, Anthony 27
Harvey, David 50–1, 54
Hase, Carl 209
Hayek, Friedrich 57
Heavenly city 227, 229, 237
Hegel, Wilhelm Friedrich 85, 106, 137–46, 236; the absolute 250; Christian religion 143–4; Church 112–13; desire 121, 190; ethics–politics relation 135; family unit 123; incarnation 93; linear infinite 172; revision of 142–3; sexual difference 188; the subject 121; women 144–5; world history 140
Heidegger, Martin 44, 155, 170, 186
Heim, Michael 250
hermeneutic ontology 71, 74
hetero-spatiality 177–8, 179
heteropolis 33, 41–2, 44, 62–8; Christian responses 68–70, 75–7
heterosexism 182
heterosexuality 119, 177–8, 182, 201
heterotopia 52
Hick, John 44
historical determinism 46
Hobbes, Thomas 126–31, 136–7, 236
Hobrecht, James 28–9
holism, cyberspatial 250–1
hom(m)osexuality 125, 197–8, 202, 220
homosexuality 122, 124–5, 201; *see also* same-sex relations
homosociality 124–5, 131
Horsfell, Thomas 29
Howard, Ebenezer 38–9
Hugh of St Victor 7

human *Geist* 186
Humbolt, Friedrich 9
Hume, David 43, 87
hybrid spatiality 177–8
hybrids 208–12, 220–1; *see also* cyborgs;
    vampires
hyperreality 54, 60, 66, 252

the I 127, 175–6, 178, 193
I-It relation 172
I-Thou theology 46, 190
I-want 173
Idea 141, 142–3, 235
idealism 107
identification 196; demonstrative 85–6,
    93
identity politics 254
identity-thinking 247
imagined communities 129, 146–51
imago dei 188, 199, 235
imitatio Christi 77, 114
immanence 132
incarnation 70, 76, 98–9, 116
incarnational embodiment 50
incarnationalism 219–20
incest 99, 124
individualism 46, 132, 228
inequalities, production 241–2
infinite, linear 17, 172
information is power 256
Inner Urban Area Act 1978 57
inoperative community 75
intellectual love 133, 135
internet 245, 247, 253, 254
interpretation 9–10, 62, 230
intertextuality 188, 192
intratextuality 92
Irigaray, Luce 110, 125, 186, 197, 201,
    206, 219–23

Jakobson, Roman 10, 11, 12, 53
Jameson, Fredric 3, 66–7
Jantzen, Grace 210
Jencks, Charles 3, 33, 65, 66, 67, 69
Jerusalem 33, 49, 227; New 51, 237
Jesus *see* Christ
jouissance 148, 149, 170, 184, 185
judgment, suspension of 228–9, 257–9
justice 234–5, 246

Kant, Immanuel 37–8, 85, 106
kenosis 92, 108, 141
Kettelhut, Erich 29, 31
kitsch 63
Klotz, Heinrich 67
knowledge 228–9; angels 72, 216–19, 237;
    artificial intelligence 47–8; atomisation
    252–3; desire for 251; discernment and
    88–9; *poiesis* 213; total 250; true 132;
    will 143
Kracauer, Siegfried 217
Krafft-Ebing, Richard von 122
Kristeva, Julia 76, 185

Labarthe, Philippe Lacoue 91, 250–1
Lacan, Jacques 10, 12–13, 53, 106–7, 121,
    190, 236; desire 101, 146–7, 185; ideal
    community 148; law of the Father 92;
    phallus 219; the Real 157; world-view
    168–9
lack 101, 106–7, 148, 167, 169, 172–3,
    190
Lang, Fritz 28–32
language: of appearance 161; body of
    Christ 110; city as 232; of light 40–1;
    linguistic philosophy 155; print
    languages 146–7; replacement of
    religion 146–7; sacramental realism
    164–5
Lanier, Jaron 250
Laqueur, Thomas 186
Las Vegas 62–5, 68
late-capitalism 50–1, 53–4
Latour, Bruno 208, 222
Lauretis, Teresa de 115, 195
Le Corbusier 40, 41, 42, 48, 50, 63, 231
Leaving Las Vegas 63–5
Lefebvre, Henri 34, 61–2, 176–7, 208,
    223
Légende 212–14
legitimation 71–2, 166
Lévi-Strauss, Claude 12, 14, 124, 182
Leviathan 127, 129
Levinas, Emmanuel 20, 94, 155, 175, 179,
    187
liberal humanism 70
liberal individualism 228
liberal theologies 43–4, 185–6
liberalism, subject of 254

libido: Christian communities 123–4; dynamics of urban life 53; economies of desire 53–4, 76, 170, 187–94; *libido dominandi* 49, 56, 126, 251; logic 106–7; subject 122
libido dominandi 175
lieu 154, 176
light: language of 40–1; metaphysics 159; reason and 40; of revelation 40; truth 247
liminality 105
linguistic philosophy 155
literacy 4
liturgy, liturgical space 177
Locke, John 85
logic: of analogy 230, 236, 254; ascension 113; body of Jesus 113; displacement 112–13; libidinal 106–7; privation 77; secular 118; theo- 74, 113
logocentrism 155, 157, 168
Logos 110–11, 113, 234
Los Angeles 65–8
love: Augustine 235; Christian 259; God 190; intellectual 133, 135; trinitarian 174, 201–2, 237
Lubac, Henri du 7, 179
ludic desire 119
Luther, Martin 161, 226
Lyotard, Jean-François 3, 145, 168, 170, 253

MacQuarrie, John 44
male desire 198–9
male gaze 119
Manchester 238–42, 259
Mandel, Ernst 55
Manicheanism 69
Marion, Jean-Luc 172
marriage 182–3, 187; angels 220; Christian time 192; doctrine of 197; gender construction 183; sanctified eros 183–4
Marshall, F. H. A. 122
Martin, Dale 102
Martinich, A. P. 128–9
Marx, Karl 35, 39
masculinity 100
materialism 63, 84, 87, 94
materiality: Christian theology 62; Christ's body 98; construction 195; God 99,

130; resurrection 110; significance of 117; truth 137
mathematical truth 41–2
The Matrix 242–4
matter 82, 89, 99, 144
Maurice, F. D. 70
McDowell, John 86, 87
McLuhan, Marshall 72, 155
Mensch 190, 193
mercantile city 34
messianism 251
metaphorics: bodies 95; cultural 14–21, 222–3; cyberspace communities 244–7; matter 99; nature of the body 95; social semiotics 9–14
metaphysics: Christian 117; dualisms 252; heterosexuality 201; homosexuality 201; idealism 107; of light 159; modernity 47, 130
Metropolis 28–32, 38, 43, 244
Milbank, John 252
mimesis 103, 110
mind–body dualism 127, 129, 172
miracles 87, 89
Mitchell, Juliette 124
modernity: anti-modernism 50; atomism 90; city myth 59; communities of desire 125; dualisms 252–3; eucharist 162; late 211; metaphysics of 47; onto-theology 167; postmodernity relation 81–2; purity aspiration 208–9; radical critique of 94–5; real presence 167; social harmony 36–7; subject of desire 136–7, 251; synthesis aspiration 32; *thanatos* 184; theology 50; time 170
Montag, John 130
More, Thomas 37
motion, desire and 90, 127, 128
MUDs *see* Multiple User Domains
multinational corporations 55–6
Multiple User Domains (MUDs) 149, 255
Mumford, Lewis 47, 49, 51

Nacke, Paul 201
naming, act of 84–5, 101
Nancy, Jean-Luc 75, 86–7, 93, 95, 168, 169–70
nationalistic desire 146
natural law 127–30, 132

natural theology 41–3, 48, 69, 165, 197
necrophilia 45
negative ontology 168–9
neo-Nietzscheans, French 145
neo-tribalism 150
network society 244–7
New City 51
New Jerusalem 51, 237
New Testament poetics 111
Newton, Isaac 40
Nietzsche, Friedrich 14, 133–4, 185, 206, 223
nihilism 45–6, 70, 87, 92, 138, 185
nominalism 136, 162, 164, 252; equivocity 130; postmodern 60
Noosphere 48
the now 37, 170
Nygren, Anders 183, 184
Nyssa, Saint Gregory of 76, 87–91, 113, 116, 157, 184

objet petit a 101, 147
Ockham, William of 7, 130, 160, 161, 162
O'Donovan, Oliver 230, 234
Old City 51
Oliver, Simon 167
Olshan, Joseph 200
Olson, Alan M. 142
On, Bat-Ami Bar 82
ontologies: atomism 167; economies of desire 191–2, 251; foundations 72; hermeneutic 71, 74, 253; negative 168–9; onto-theology 155, 165, 167; ontological scandal 81–96, 100, 101, 103, 157; soft 223
orgasm 119–20, 150, 170, 185; *see also jouissance*
Ortner, Sherry 14, 22–3
the other 139, 149, 168
ousia 90

parasitic city 49
parler-femme 220, 223
participation 152–3, 165, 236
paternalism, Church of England 28
paternity, God 98–9
patriarchy 124
patristic theologies 99
Patton, Phil 255

Peacocke, Arthur 43
pentecost 112
Pentecostalism 69
Pepper, Stephen C. 22
perception 84–5
personhood, subjectivity 114–15
phallocentrism 197
phallus 56, 107, 169, 219; *see also* lack
phenomenology of desire 146
phonocentrism 168
photographic instantaneity 40
Pickstock, Catherine 252
Plato 4, 6, 40, 45–6, 125, 143, 199, 226, 233–5
pluralised body, eucharistic 174
pluralism 237
pluralist values 47
Poe, Edgar Allan 13
poiesis 213, 247
poiotes 90
polarisation 241
the political 103–4, 218, 230
politics of believing 71–4, 207–8, 254
Polkinghorne, John 43
the pornographic 120, 125–6
positivism 89, 92, 94
post-apocalyptic films 51
post-Christian atheism 69
post-Fordism 53–4
Poster, Mark 251, 253
postmodernity 211; broken bodies 81–2; cities 53–62, 59, 69; films 63–5; modernity relation 81–2; neo-Darwinian theism 69; nominalism 60; postmodern condition 53; sociology 247; the sublime 149; theological responses to the city 69; theologies beyond 70
poststructuralism 155, 168, 170
Poulantzas, N. 62
power 34, 103–4, 206, 251, 256
pragmatism 46, 166
prelapsarian bodies 100
presence: Aquinas 156–61; Augustine 156–61; Calvin 161–7; cyberspace 249; eucharistic 154–5, 170–81; full 86, 167; genealogy 156–70; God 109; the other 168; present 155–6, 161–7; the real

157, 159–60, 160–1, 167; sacramental 155–6; self-presence 40; truth 166
the present: Book of Common Prayer 161; consumption of 59; eucharistic tense 154–5; presence and 155–6, 161–7; as such 154–5
print-capitalism 146
print-languages 146–7
private investment 58
the Private Shop (sex shops) 118–20, 150
privativity 36, 75–6, 127
privitas 228
Pseudo-Dionysius 6–7, 211
public land-use 58
purity, production of 208–9
Putnam, Hilary 86

queer theory 116, 194

radiant city 40, 42, 43, 231
radical evil, principle 38
Radin, Paul 14
rational utopia 177, 178
Ray Griffin, David 69
re-enchantment 207, 214, 224
reading 14–21, 89, 128, 182, 188
the real 95, 148, 157, 168, 169; being real 208; re-enchantment of 214; real presence 156; redemption of 217
realised eschatology 37, 40, 41, 86, 177
realism, sacramental 157–8
reality, virtual 149, 231, 245–6, 251–2
realpolitik 35
reason 16, 40, 127, 133, 165, 166
redemption 123–4, 172, 182–202, 225–60
reference 166–7, 252
reification 35, 36, 170, 180–1
religion, as language 146–7
Renaissance 34, 126–7
representation 138, 256; allegorical reading 89; Augustinian doctrine 228–9; economy of 60; embodiment 82; nature of 134–5; of the state 143; transparent 72–3, 246
res publica 232
resurrection 70, 95, 97, 108–12
revelation 40, 130–1, 145; Book of 41, 226, 237
Rheingold, Howard 255

Ricoeur, Paul 179
riots, urban 28, 57, 60, 67–8
Robinson, John 44
Rohr, Mies Van der 63, 231
Roman Catholicism *see* Catholicism
Rousseau, Jean-Jacques 37, 147
Ruello, Francis 160
Runciman, David 120
Ruskin, John 39

sacramental economies 162–3
sacramental presence 155–6
sacramental realism 157–8
sacramental world-view 179–80
sacred sex 183–7
salvation 130–1
same-sex relationships 96, 197, 200–1
Sassen, Saskia 239–41, 247
Saussure, Horace Bénédict 10, 12, 13
Schleiermacher, Friedrich 175, 188
Scholastics 165
Schweitzer, Albert 113
science fiction 59–60
scienta sexualis 76
Scorsese, Martin 63, 65, 77
Scotus, Duns 155, 160
scriptural economy 248
scriptures, interpretation 230
secularism 126, 247, 252; Biblical origins 46; cities and 32–8; eschatology 145, 154; logic 118; space for 129–30; theological acceptance 69–70
seduction, cultures of 68, 77, 118–19, 125
self 40, 107–8, 115, 250
semiosis 90–1, 254
semiotics 9–14, 199–200, 236
sense-data privilege 85–6
Serres, Michel 19, 51, 172, 206, 210–15, 222
sex: cybersex 149, 150, 251; sacred 183–7; science of sexology 122; *scienta sexualis* 76; sex shops 118–20, 150; truth 122–3
sexual difference 186; Hegel 188; theology of 189–94, 199–202; trinitarian 202
sexuality: desire and truth 122–3; Freud 122–6; heterosexism 182; heterosexuality 119, 177–8, 201; hom(m)osexuality 197–8, 202, 220; homosexuality 122, 124–5, 201; of Jesus

113; metaphysics 201; same-sex relations 96, 197, 200–1
shopping 120
the sign: arbitrariness 146, 147; Baudrillard 60; empty 164–5; semantic drift 232; signified 163–4; *signum* and *res* 163–4, 227; which are significant 21–4
signification 5–9, 110, 155, 224
signifiers 82, 105
Simmel, George 35
simulacra 54, 59, 60–2, 74, 251
simulation 54
Smith, Michael Peter 54
the social 118, 147
social atomism 28, 58, 75, 132
social bonds 32, 35, 131
social constructivism 121–3, 133–4, 194–5
social contract 32
social existence 208
social instinct 123
social semiotics 9–14, 199–200
social technologies *see* technologies
Societas Jesu 131
sociological atomism 167
Socrates 233; *see also* Plato
soft ontology 223, 253
Soja, Edward 66, 67
Soleri, Paolo 48
soma (body) 83, 84
Song of Songs 116, 192–3
soulless materialism 93
space: aporetic 165; ascension 112; for belief 74; Christian theology of 62; *diastema* 172; economy of desire 167; egocentric 85; *en Christoi* 173, 176; eucharistic 164; of flows 245; gender relations 56; in historical systems of fact 178; institutional church 176–81; Las Vegas 64; liturgical 177, 180; movement in 231–2; perception 85; practices 230–1; redemption 116; for the sacral 105, 223; for the secular 129–30; space-time 61, 160, 257; spatial order 163; for the subjective will 137; symbolic 111–12; temporality 160; textuality 177–8; tradition and 179, 180; transformations in 54; virtual 150; *see also* cyberspace

spatiality 160, 208; eucharistic 164; hetero- 177–8, 179; holistic 250–1; hybrid 177–8; temporality 160
spectacle, society of 162
Speragmos 86
Spinoza, Baruch de 93, 126, 131–7, 236, 250
spirit: community of 137–46, 146; God as 137, 138
the spiritual 48, 108–9, 193, 230
Spivak, Gayatri Chakravorty 94
Star Trek 57–8
the State 126, 135, 137, 140–1, 143
Steinberg, Leo 98
the subject 92; commodification 124; of desire 118, 120–6, 136–9, 251; liberalism 254; libidinal 122; modernity 136–7, 251; Renaissance 126–7
subjectivity: ecstatic 139; gendered 186–7; judgment-making 166; personhood and 114–15; social technologies of 145; space 137; Spinoza 135; the will 137
the sublime 102, 149, 170
surveillance 118–19
Swinburne, Richard 43
symbolic capitalism 58
symbolic environments 245–6
synthesis 32

Tawney, R. H. 27, 70
Taylor, Charles 14, 18, 20, 62–3
technological society, critique 48–50
technologies: advanced 32; gender 115, 186–7; orgasm 119–20; self 115; spiritual relation 48; subjectivity 145
technopolis 46, 47
telecommunications 222, 239, 249; *see also* cyberspace
Temple, William 70
temporal, eternal and 158
temporality, spatiality 160
text, city as 230–1
textualities 93, 110, 115–16, 199
textuality 92, 177–8, 192
thanatos 125, 184
theism, postmodern neo-Darwinian 69
theo-logic 74, 113
theologies: atheologies 43, 45, 69; beyond postmodernism 70; of bodies 182, 247;

of the city 43–51, 69, 77, 226;
conservative 48–50, 69; creation 256;
cyberspace 247–56; death of God 45; of
desire 187–9; difference 189–94,
199–202, 254; of *eros* 151; gender
194–5; grammar of 145; I-Thou 46,
190; liberal 43–4, 185–6; materiality 62;
natural 41–2, 43–51, 69, 165, 197;
onto-theology 155, 165, 167; patristic
99; reading 128, 182; secularism 69–70;
signification 5–9; the social 118; space
62; virtual 224
Tilley, Christopher 14
time: Christian 62, 192, 196; conception of
233–4; crucifixion 108; cyberspace 249;
desire's relation to 156; determining 3–5;
Disneyland 59; God 234; Messianic
promise 101; modernity's 170; the
question of 2–3, 63; resurrection 110–11;
space-time 61, 160, 257; textualities of
199; timeless 245; *see also* presence;
present
tongues of angels 212–15
Tönnies, Ferdinand 32, 34, 35, 39
transcorporeality 81–96, 97, 115
transfiguration 99–102, 100–1
transmutation 87, 89
transparency 169, 246
transposition, eucharistic 102–3
transubstantiation 161
trinitarian difference 105, 202
trinitarian *dunamis* 89
trinitarian erotics 198
trinitarian love 174, 201–2, 237
trinitarian participation 236
Trinity 138, 159, 234
triune God 77
truth 45, 144; appearance 157; effects of
168; God as guarantor 130; light 247;
materiality 137; mathematical 41–2; as
méconnaisance 168; presence 166;
question of 45; sexual desire 122–3; *sub
species aeternatis* 132
Turner, Victor 14, 22, 105

Übermenschen 206
univocity 134–5, 155, 169, 183; of being
164–5; of desire 185
Unwin, Raymond 39

UPAs *see* Urban Priority Areas
urban geographies 56–60, 241
urban life, libidinal dynamics 53
urban planning 28, 29, 38–43, 53–4, 58
Urban Priority Areas (UPAs) Britain 27, 44
urban riots 28, 57, 60, 67–8
urban studies 29
utopias 37, 38, 176–8, 179, 226

vampires 49, 206; *see also* cyborgs; hybrids
Vattimo, Gianni 3, 20
Virgin Mary 109–10, 114, 115, 221
Virilio, Paul 249
virtual cities 42–3
virtual communities 146–51, 167, 244–7,
250
virtual economies 224
virtual other 149
virtual reality 149, 242, 251–2; cities 231;
culture of 245; the eucharist 167;
subject of desire 251; *see also* cyberspace
virtual space 150
virtual theologies 224
the visible 160, 162, 163
the Void 169

Wachowski brothers 242–4
Wagner, Richard 30, 250
walking the city 231–2
Walt Disney Concert Hall 66
Ward, Keith 44
the We 153–4, 179, 180–1
Weber, Max 39, 51, 214
Weil, Simone 95
Wenders, Wim 29–30, 216–19, 222, 224
Westin Bonaventura Hotel 66–7, 69
Wiles, Maurice 44
will: confluence of 140–1; determinative of
form 133–4; evil 139; free 127; for the
good 139; independence of 132;
knowledge 143; subjective 137; to power
206
Wittgenstein, Ludwig 71, 86, 212, 232
women 124–5, 144–5
world history 140
world-view, analogical *see* analogical world
view
Wright, Frank Lloyd 39–40, 41, 48, 231
writing and urbanism 4

Wuthnow, Robert 207

Zion 33
Žižek, Slavoj 11, 13, 21, 94, 95, 147–50, 156, 168–70